To Exist as a Problem

ALSO AVAILABLE FROM BLOOMSBURY

To Exist as a Problem

Being Black, Being Palestinian

Zahi Zalloua

BLOOMSBURY ACADEMIC
LONDON • NEW YORK • OXFORD • NEW DELHI • SYDNEY

BLOOMSBURY ACADEMIC
Bloomsbury Publishing Plc, 50 Bedford Square, London, WC1B 3DP, UK
Bloomsbury Publishing Inc, 1359 Broadway, New York, NY 10018, USA
Bloomsbury Publishing Ireland, 29 Earlsfort Terrace, Dublin 2, D02 AY28, Ireland

BLOOMSBURY, BLOOMSBURY ACADEMIC and the Diana logo are trademarks of
Bloomsbury Publishing Plc

First published in Great Britain 2026

A catalogue record for this book is available from the British Library.

A catalog record for this book is available from the Library of Congress.

ISBN: HB: 978-1-3505-5901-1
PB: 978-1-3505-5902-8
ePDF: 978-1-3505-5903-5
eBook: 978-1-3505-5904-2

Typeset by Newgen KnowledgeWorks Pvt. Ltd., Chennai, India
Printed and bound in Great Britain

For product safety related questions contact productsafety@bloomsbury.com.

To find out more about our authors and books visit www.bloomsbury.com
and sign up for our newsletters.

To the Defenders of the Dead

Contents

Acknowledgments

Palestine is on fire. And the world's leaders allow it to burn. But so long as Israel's impunity fails to register as a problem, we stand as problems ourselves. "We" refers here, naively, to anyone horrified by the current state of reality, which, I should add, has been rotten for longer than most imagine. The truth of this rottenness has never been a mystery for the world's wretched, but the rest of us are now coming to a similar realization. Writing during America's war on terror and illegal invasion of Iraq, Edward Said could still find comfort in (the promise of) the university. "For all its often noted defects and problems," Said maintained, "the American university—and mine, Columbia, in particular—is still one of the few remaining places in the United States where reflection and study can take place in an almost-utopian fashion." Things have changed. Columbia's grave capitulation to the unprincipled demands of power touches all of us. The American university—any university for that matter—will not survive in its idealized form (as a place where we cultivate the tools of understanding and harness a passion for justice) if we do not reckon with the world's tolerance of genocide, if we do not mount an effort to squash what June Jordan described as the "laughter of evil" resounding across the globe, emanating from all the genocidaires and supremacists committed to a hierarchical vision of the world.

This is the painful backdrop behind *To Exist as a Problem: Being Black, Being Palestinian*. The title was born during an exchange with Daniel Schultz, a friend and colleague at Whitman College. We were both present at the Whitman student encampment for Palestine. It was the end of the Spring 2024 term, and student organizers held space at the camp for curious parents and family members, in town for graduation, wanting to know more about the maligned solidarity movement. Daniel and I were brainstorming about a joint roundtable for the upcoming fall term, exchanging ideas and relating W. E. B. Du Bois's musings on being a problem to philosophical debates over the Jewish problem, the Palestinian problem, and the afterlives of slavery and coloniality. The fact that these generative ideas took root in a place of political resistance, in a refusal to acquiesce to the dominant anti-Palestinian narrative, is not lost on me. If, in late Spring 2024, the university could still be seen and felt as a site of insurgency (though the crackdown clearly had already begun), at the time I write these words campuses are yielding to the forces of a full counterinsurgency, to a vicious backlash against the university as imagined and cherished by Said and many of us. Hopelessness sets in. Anti-anti-utopianism is what we're fighting for.

Calling for (more) solidarity is my response to these fascist times. Solidarity for Palestine makes clear that the murderous status quo cannot—must not—go on. Such solidarity compels us to question our ontology and libidinal attachments, to question who counts and who doesn't. Palestine is bigger than Palestine. I deeply believe that the national and worldwide protests over Gaza are spurred on by the systemic problems that gave rise to the outpouring of support for the movement for Black lives and point to a lingering deep anger and *ressentiment* at America's political class and its Western counterparts for the abysmal failures of reform as an answer to the violence of racialized policing and the supremacist order it underpins and supports. For Blacks and Palestinians, the world system does not need fine-tuning—it needs an overhaul. *To Exist as a Problem* points to the continued need for a vibrant anti-racist, anti-colonial Left, to the urgency of a reignited Black-Palestinian solidarity movement. It is my sincere belief that problems love company.

Writing is an outlet, a copy strategy, a way to translate and channel my rage, but also quite frankly physically exhausting and mentally depleting, marked by moments of doubt and tribulation. Fortunately, I have been able to draw on the love of my brother Mounir for strength and motivation in these often-trying times. For the many encounters and exchanges at conferences and symposia that significantly contributed to the writing of this book, I thank Linda Martín Alcoff, Dina Al-Kassim, Azad Ashim Sharma, Jake Blevins, Chris Breu, Clint Burnham, Chad Cordova, Nuraan Davids, Ben Davis, Jeffrey R. Di Leo, Valérie Dionne, Jennifer Kwon Dobbs, Christian Haines, Morteza Hajizadeh, John Harfouch, Peter Hudis, Agon Hamza, Peter Hitchcock, Derek Hook, Janine Jones, Ilan Kapoor, Randy LeBlanc, Michael Marder, Sophia McClennen, Paul Allen Miller, Brian O'Keeffe, Nitzan Lebovic, Nelson Maldonado-Torres, Jodi Melamed, Noelle McAfee, Dirk Moses, Oded Nir, Maple Razsa, Chandan Reddy, Julian Rios Acuña, Avital Ronell, Arnab Roy, Frank Ruda, Khalil Saucier, Russ Sbriglia, Ben Schreier, Mitchell Smith, Rob Tally, Alberto Toscano, Sjoerd van Tuinen, Daniel Tutt, George Yancy, and Slavoj Žižek. Special thanks go out to Rafat Asad for allowing me to use another of his amazing artworks in this book. I am very grateful to Liza Thompson and Miraya McCoy at Bloomsbury for their meticulous attentiveness to this project.

At Whitman, students continue to be an inspiration, reminding me of the stakes of teaching. My courses, especially "Contemporary Literary Theory" and "The Palestinian Question," proved immensely generative for my thinking. I've benefited greatly from my colleagues at Whitman as well. I'm particularly thankful to M. Acuff, Susanne Beechey, Shampa Biswas, Matt Bost, Chetna Chopra, Tarik Elseewi, Denise Fernandes, Giramata, Camilo Lund-Montaño, Gaurav

Majumdar, Lydia McDermott, Libby Miller, Lauren Osborne, Kaitlyn Patia, Daniel Schultz, Andrea Sempértegui, Ozge Serin, Daniel Smith, Lisa Uddin, and Xiaobo Yuan. I also want to thank student research assistant Faith Crossman for her invaluable collaboration on this project. And, as always, my greatest appreciation goes to Nicole for her indelible mark on my life and writing.

Portions of the "introduction" appeared in "The Palestinian Problem as a Problem of Being," *Philosophical Salon* (October 7, 2024) and "Fascism from the Standpoint of Its Racialized Victims," *Philosophical Salon* (March 24, 2025). Portions of Chapter 1 appeared in "The Irreproachable Victim and the Cruel Grammar of Zionist Capitalism," *Philosophical Salon* (December 9, 2024) and in "Anatomy of the Human: Fanon and Žižek," *Crisis and Critique* 12, no. 1 (2025): 342–64. Portions of Chapter 2 appear in "On Being a Problem," in *South Atlantic Quarterly* 116, no. 2 (forthcoming). Portions of Chapter 3 appear in "Becoming Black, Becoming Palestinian," in *symplokē* 33, no. 1–2 (forthcoming). This project was supported in part by a Louis B. Perry Summer Research Grant.

Introduction: A Problem of Being

In the first pages of *The Souls of Black Folk*, W. E. B. Du Bois famously meditates on the question, "How does it feel to be a problem?"[1] This is the question white liberals think or want to ask Black people but never pose directly. Rather, they dance around it. They make sure to express their admiration for Black achievements and equally register their outrage at anti-Blackness. *Obama was a courageous president. Isn't Trump just awful?* George Yancy rightly draws attention to the ontological underpinnings of the question. What is thematized as a problem is *being* itself. The question is not "How does it feel to *have* problems?" but "How does it feel *to be* a problem?"[2] In *To Exist as a Problem*, I want to think through the ontological dimensions of the problem of racialized and racializing beings, by considering anti-colonial theorist Frantz Fanon's dark and yet generative notion of the "zone of nonbeing"[3] alongside the Black and Palestinian questions, framed together as a problem of and for ontology.

Fanon acknowledges, with some disquietude, the overdetermination of Blackness; there is no neutral ontology to draw from, no neutral arbitrator that would settle the Black question fairly or favorably, that would allow him to resist the aggressive white/colonial gaze determining his being as nonbeing, his lived experience as immaterial and unworthy of humanist concern and meditation:

> Ontology does not allow us to understand the being of the black man, since it ignores the lived experience. ... The black man has no ontological resistance in the eyes of the white man. From one day to the next, the Blacks have had to deal with two systems of reference. Their metaphysics, or less pretentiously their customs and the agencies to which they refer, were abolished because they were in contradiction with a new civilization that imposed its own.[4]

Black problemhood is always in the white eyes of the beholder.[5] Without a metaphysics, or a symbolic order of his own, the unsovereign Black man stands exposed. The "white man" falsifies Fanon's facticity, inscribing him in a past phantasmatically constructed "out of a thousand details, anecdotes, and stories."[6] An "ontological explanation"[7] of Black being is wanting; the white racist gaze not only distorts the being of Blacks, it also compromises how Blacks perceive themselves since the grammar of ontology is white, inhospitable to racialized non-Europeans. Whiteness engulfs Fanon's very being: "The white man is all around me; up above the sky is tearing at its navel; the earth crunches under my feet and sings white, white. All this whiteness burns me to a cinder."[8] White ontology excises Black people from the human family, driving them further and further into the zone of nonbeing, a state indistinguishable from social death. Black being embodies the figure of the antihuman, its being is *sous rature*, under erasure, and better described and visualized as Black ~~being~~ (I return to the significance of this barring below). In the "afterlife of slavery,"[9] as Saidiya Hartman importantly terms it, the "atmosphere"[10] of anti-Blackness permeates white civil society, residing in its collective unconscious. Nothing crystalizes anti-Blackness's enduring quality more clearly and paradoxically than the "freedom" of the freed slave. Formal emancipation turned freedom into a source of cruel irony for those who were no longer legally objects of possession but still lacked the material equality and socioeconomic opportunities needed to perform the liberal and capitalist modes of self-possession now required of them by the law. Or as Keeanga-Yamahtta Taylor puts it, glossing Hartman, "freedom from bondage" came to be lived excruciatingly as "freedom to starve."[11]

Today's anti-Black racism is not a remnant of a regrettable past that only occasionally manifests its ugly head in hate crimes and police brutality—as the stubborn "bad apples" thesis would have it, thereby tossing the (anti-Black) status quo a lifeline. No, anti-Blackness is a central and systemic problem, intrinsic to white civil society, its tentacles rooted deep in our collective unconscious. Blackness conjures and designates barbarism, baseness, and sexual violence.

In *Citizen: An American Lyric*, Claudia Rankine recounts anti-Blackness's many eruptions in everydayness. In one of her vignettes, the narrator, who is presumably going to see a trauma counselor to help her cope with her exposure to anti-Black racism, confronts a white therapist who initially treats her with same racism from which she is seeking refuge:

> The new therapist specializes in trauma counseling. You have only ever spoken on the phone. Her house has a side gate that leads to a back entrance she uses for patients. You walk down a path bordered on both sides with deer grass and rosemary to the gate, which turns out to be locked.
>
> At the front door the bell is a small round disc that you press firmly. When the door finally opens, the woman standing there yells, at the top of her lungs, Get away from my house! What are you doing in my yard?
>
> It's as if a wounded Doberman pinscher or a German shepherd has gained the power of speech. And though you back up a few steps, you manage to tell her you have an appointment. You have an appointment? she spits back.

Then she pauses. Everything pauses. Oh, she says, followed by, oh, yes, that's right. I am sorry.

I am so sorry, so, so sorry.[12]

In making the appointment, the therapist must have imagined the narrator white—a case of "the epidermalization of sound," as Yancy calls it.[13] And here no matter your class distinction (as a Black academic), your body—your flesh— poses a threat. The individuality of her Black body is evacuated in the white psyche. The "racial epidermal schema" turns her into a "phobogenic object."[14] Her skin—reduced to a disfigured and disfiguring image, to a surface ontology, if you will—triggers white anxiety.

Incidentally, the narrator represents for whiteness the exception that proves the rule: Blacks are unacademic. To sound Black is to sound vulgar, uneducated, primitive, and, of course, dangerous. In the white supremacist imaginary, your fantasized voice must match your fantasized body! The narrator (because she is Black) is an ontological outsider, always already a trespasser, who doesn't belong to the therapist's world of care. The narrator seeks help, entry into the human world, but she is thematized instead, objectified, and nullified by the therapist's negrophobia.

As with Rankine, Fanon laments such ontological setbacks: "Yet this reconsideration of myself, this thematization, was not my idea."[15] If you're (thematized as) Black, the world rarely acquiesces to your rhythm and bodily orientation. The space you're in has already been colonized by whiteness. You're caught in an anti-Black *huis clos*; giving Sartre's play a racial twist: *hell is white people*. Basic assumptions about what the workings of the world are met with agonizing disappointments. Consider the full implication of Rankine's demoralizing example: if a trauma counselor—who, ironically, is a seemingly ideal interlocutor, as an "expert" in identifying and caring for the pain of others— is so deeply caught up in the anti-Black libidinal economy, what are the chances that a non-expert—someone less self-reflective and thoughtful about others— will do any better to manage her white gaze? And even the apology raises further questions: Is the therapist apologizing because she got caught? How sincere is she really? Is the apology sufficient enough to undo her ingrained anti-Blackness? Is the therapist unconsciously blaming you for trying to fake your cursed ontology by sounding white? Drenched in criminality, the Black imago of white America aligns Blackness with savagery, nonhumanity, worldlessness, and nonbeing in perpetuity.

Palestinian being does not fare any better. If Black being denotes irrationality, slaveness, and fungibility, Palestinian being suffers the marks of Orientalism and Zionism, with the latter harnessing the epistemic powers of the former to legitimize Israel's settler-colonial regime. Under Western/white/settler eyes, Palestinians exist as a problem for a multiplicity of reasons. The fact of Palestinian embodiment represents both a demographic threat, an existential menace to Zionist space, to an Israel which masquerades for the Western world as a democratic state, and a psychic hazard, as Palestinians' refusal to disappear continually thwarts Israel's sense of its own moral and military superiority—its colonial right to carve up the region as it pleases. Here it is crucial to make a distinction between Judaism and Zionism. The Palestinian is a problem not for Judaism (for Jews) but for Zionism (for Zionists as settler supremacists).

My critique of Zionism has never been about Jewish attachment to the land but rather Zionists' chauvinistic and racist claim to exclusive sovereignty over its "national homeland"—to a superior sovereignty that negates an inferior sovereignty—which is part and parcel of Israeli colonization. The vision of Palestine as a home of refuge for Jews fleeing persecution has a powerful appeal. But the problem is that Palestine was never the empty land—the *terra nullius* and barren desert awaiting cultivation, the phantasmatic idea of "making the desert bloom"—promised by Zionists. And this point in the argument marks the moment when critics contesting the use of settler colonialism as an analytic typically assert a series of interrelated claims: *Yes, but Zionism is dynamic, complicated, and multifaceted; settler colonialism and white supremacy do not do justice to the richness of Zionist movement of liberation; remember that Zionists like Martin Buber envisaged the possibility of coexistence with the Indigenous population, and so forth*. But evoking complexity typically functions today as pure ideology; it does not work to advance debate but rather to obfuscate actually existing Zionism and conceal a prevailing settler narrative about Palestinian domination (the obverse side of Jewish liberation)—that can, of course, be contested but not simply discarded or treated *a priori* as unimportant and anti-Semitic without a shred of evidence.

In the current Zionist-biased public discourse, there is strong pressure from Western governments and pro-Israel groups to equate anti-Zionism with anti-Semitism (and Israel with Jews). Everything in this book pushes in the other direction. There is no fair hearing of the Palestinian question under this troubling and mendacious conflation of Judaism and Zionism. When we willfully ignore the words of Theodor Herzl, the founder of political Zionism, who wrote, "If I wish to substitute a new building for an old one, I must demolish before I construct,"[16] we fail to observe and address the genocidal manifestation of Herlz's observation: *If I wish to substitute a new people for an old one, I must exterminate before I can live*. It is clear that Herzl envisaged the land of Palestine in colonial terms.

To Zionism's apologists, we say Israel's colonial practices never ended; its settler sovereignty has only expanded.[17] A Zionist Israel is committing *ethnic cleansing* with the backing of most Jewish Israelis.[18] Decoupling Zionism from Israel's racial and colonial war machine would be an act of interpretive malpractice, a disingenuous attempt to obfuscate Zionism's rationalization of Israel's serial criminality. Steve Salaita crystallizes the stakes: "If Zionism survives, we die."[19]

Zionist survival is a zero-sum game. Even the words "Palestinian" and "Palestine" offend Zionist sensibilities. They are a scandal—pointing to an antecedent Indigeneity, to another people's relation to the land—an intolerable idea for today's "sober" mainstream Zionists. The legitimacy of reclaiming the land of Israel (Palestine as "Eretz Israel")—the Zionist solution to the Jewish problem—is at play. For Zionism to realize its ambitions of a Greater Israel, complete control over the whole of historic Palestine, Indigenous Palestinians must be derealized and denationalized, made to disappear physically, discursively, and ontologically.

Zionists cannot tolerate the presence of Palestinians on their ancestral land. A "burning hatred" for all things Palestinian, as Andreas Malm argues, "inflamed the Zionist project from its beginning."[20] And for this reason, a Zionist Israel is, or must become, a killing machine, turning Gaza into "a killing field,"[21] compelled to butcher Palestinians day in and day out, during times of war, times of "truce," and times of "peace," these latter two ever only manifesting as ideological versions of the first. Violence against Palestinians subtends all three. Truce or peace with the Israeli government without a reckoning with settler colonialism— insofar as it represents "the all-important context"[22]—returns us to a war that is guaranteed *not* to end, to an oppressive situation, and cannot register as anything but murderous obfuscation. The Palestinian problem—a problem because Palestinians refuse to acquiesce to unconditional surrender or auto-genocide—persists in all three times: war, truce, and peace.

The violence visited on Palestinians does not represent a response to some wrongdoing on their part (though Israel would like to make the world believe that Palestinians deserve their fate, that its disproportionate actions are a just consequence of Hamas's Operation Al-Aqsa Flood on October 7, 2023).[23] Israel is not interested in disciplining or assimilating Palestinians; it wants them gone (by any means necessary). From the standpoint of Zionists, Palestinians are culpable for being Palestinian, for being Indigenous to the land, for standing in the way of a Greater Israel. As Mohammed El-Kurd observes, "it is almost simplistic to say that we are guilty by birth. Our existence is purely mechanistic; we are reminded, through policy and procedure, that we are unfortunately born to die."[24] Zionism decrees a cruel future for Palestinians: *We are born to perish not flourish*. The drive to erase Palestine (from the map) and Palestinians (from the land) is constitutive of Zionist settler-colonial ideology and has underpinned the Israeli state's eliminationist politics from its earliest days to the present. The call to eradicate Hamas, turning the largest open-air prison into the largest "open-air graveyard,"[25] is but the latest military and ideological manifestation of the colonial project to conquer and annihilate the Palestinian people.

Israel's obsession with "permanent security,"[26] spills beyond Occupied Palestine. The state displays an unrelenting pathological desire to bomb Arab and Muslim-majority nations. This is why I and an increasing number of scholars and activists reject the name "Israeli Defense Forces" or IDF, the Israeli army's mystifying official appellation. The army's modus operandi is not defensive or protective but offensive and destructive. It violates the sovereignty of neighboring states (especially Lebanon and Syria) at will, utterly disregards the law of occupation, and continually tramples on international legal guardrails designed to protect civilian and human rights. Haim Bresheeth-Zabner has carefully documented the ideological metamorphosis of the IDF over the last decades, observing that "changes in the nature, size, and character of the IDF were driven by the shifting challenges since 1967, when the IDF started functioning as an army of occupation. The last time the IDF faced a foreign army in major combat was in 1973."[27] Israel's peace treaties with Egypt and Jordan, and its neutralization of Lebanon and Syria, enabled the Israeli government to focus on its fundamental task: "fighting a Palestinian population of (then) over two million civilians, without an organized or functional leadership, army, or any other civic or national government." This is how, as Bresheeth-Zabner writes, "the IDF became the Israel Occupation Forces."[28] Indeed, it is far more honest to understand and designate Israel's war machine as the IOF, or Israeli Occupation Forces. IOF reminds us of the inconvenient truth that occupiers or colonizers don't have a right to self-defense under international law—but the occupied or colonized do. This does not give the oppressed party *carte blanche* to resist in any manner they choose; international laws prohibiting the targeting of civilians still remain in force, for instance. Yet rather than apply the law (upholding the right to self-defense while condemning and imposing consequences for the killing of civilians and other breaches of law wherever they occur), Israeli and other Western powers cite civilian deaths as a pretext to pathologize, delegitimize, and foreclose *all* Palestinian resistance, armed or otherwise (giving righteous lip service to international law all the while repeatedly transgressing it themselves). Seeing the IDF as the IOF moves us away from an Orientalist representation of Israel as a vulnerable democracy besieged by a horde of illiberal Arabs, and positions us to better understand the ethos of wanton Zionist violence—a violence aimed at punishing the *being* of Palestinians and not their *doing*. Existence is resistance, and that's an existential problem for Zionists.

Analytically speaking, the term IOF indexes Palestinian insecurity, the originary violence and ongoing state terrorism that Israel, with the help of Western allies and corporate media, tries to conceal. Israel purports to be safeguarding its Jewish nationals while it is primarily stealing and occupying the land of another people. In the Zionist cultural imaginary, Palestinians are *in* but not *of* the world;[29] they are construed and imagined by Zionism as immanent problems. And is it at all surprising that US police forces frequently go to Israel for training in "worst practices"?[30] Israel turbocharges desires for invulnerability and irreproachability, providing models for subjugating Black bodies who fundamentally don't belong, whose existence is lived under constant suspicion. George Yancy captures the dread of being Black in an anti-Black world: "I know in my gut that the murder of another Black person by the state is not a question of *if*, but of *when*."[31] Training with Israelis is a recipe for (more) disaster and mayhem. Israel's necropolitical practices install and perfect in American police officers a will to dominate the killable, a will to "Palestinize" already racialized or blackened bodies back home. From the supremacist standpoint, being Black, being Palestinian are problems in need of carceral or deadly solutions. *Repression or extermination?*

In *To Exist as a Problem*, I trace the mechanisms by which Blacks and Palestinians are made into problems of ontology, ignored and belittled, damned to incarceration or early termination, while also pursuing another understanding of the term problem, an understanding that explores Blacks and Palestinians as problems in a sense other than the one bluntly dictated by the petrifying white and settler gazes. Problematizing the Black and Palestinian questions turns them anew into genuine problems, true questions.[32] This critical reformulation of being Black and being Palestinian insists on the problems' symptomatic qualities, staging the problems as an invitation, a call to reckon, at once, with the settler order of things and an anti-Black world, where a critique of one system of devastation and oppression necessarily opens to the other.

We may cast ontology as the villain. Hitherto the Western study of beings has been anti-Black and anti-Palestinian, colonial and Orientalist to its core. But the ontology we have inherited is not the end of story. *Black Skin, White Masks* constitutes Fanon's gift, a gift that renders visible the wickedness of Western ontology, understood as a field of domination and mastery, while simultaneously dislocating and decolonizing ontology in his writings by contextualizing and demystifying its various operations. To exist as a problem is, in part, to be caught between two ontologies, an existing ontology that treats you as a lingering problem, an acute problem, or a problem to exterminate, and an ontology to come that casts problems as symptomal sites ripe for critique and invention, turning the notion of problemhood back on the accuser: *Why do you say I'm a problem? Who are you to tell us we are a problem?* The shift from the "I" to the "We" is intentional. Thinking (with) problems requires a relational orientation. Avoiding treating problems in isolation can guard against the impulse to fetishize, to elevate some problems over others, or to downgrade the relevance of some in relation to others. My guiding principle is Saidian, "never solidarity before criticism."[33] Taking up the cause of Blacks and Palestinians should never come at the cost of critical engagement. Paternalism is a plague formatted by white liberalism that must be avoided whenever perceived or detected.

While my focus is on Black and Palestinian problems, the Jewish problem will necessarily form a significant part of this study. The Jewish problem/question sets the stage for thinking critically the relation between problemhood, race, and racism. Anti-Semitism refers to the hatred of Jews, to the enjoyment of Jewish pain and death, to the dehumanization, demonization, and abstraction of Jews (of the sort: all Jews are x or let's do x to all the Jews). It ranges from discrimination to an eliminationist attitude toward Jews, that is, the Third Reich's "Final Solution." I follow Raz Segal and others in troubling the International Holocaust Remembrance Alliance (IHRA) definition of anti-Semitism, which Israeli politicians and their Western enablers weaponize to shield Israel, to immunize it from criticism for its many crimes, including ethnic cleansing and genocide.[34] Birthed in no small part by what John Harfouch and Heike Schotten insightfully describe as a Zionist "antisemitism Industrial Complex," the IHRA definition criminalizes Israel's critics, especially anti-Zionists and scholars of settler colonialism, who are unfairly and maliciously smeared, accused of normalizing Jewish hate, and made to stand for the face of a manufactured "new anti-Semitism."[35]

Segal thoughtfully shifts the terrain from definitions of anti-Semitism that consider the concept in isolation (typically in the goal of highlighting its absolutism or "eternal"[36] quality, its singularity and uniqueness, so as to stress the concept's exemplary status, "the master key to hate,"[37] when it comes to understanding racism) to one that puts it in dialogue with Islamophobia, demonstrating the degree to which problems are often entangled. Against hierarchical forms of ranking, Segal's approach fosters "cooperation and solidarity," ideals and commitments "that are crucial in the struggle against racism in all its forms."[38] An eye for entanglement will guide my engagement with the problems of being Black and being Palestinian (and, by extension, with anti-Blackness and anti-Palestinianness). To echo Fanon, *When you hear someone insulting Jews, pay attention; he is talking about us.*[39] Anti-Semites are Palestinophobes and Islamophobes; they are no friends or allies of Blacks and Palestinians. For that matter, they are an obstacle to any anti-racist emancipatory movement.

The subtitle of my study, *Being Black, Being Palestinian*, both draws on my positionality as a diasporic Palestinian and unabashedly expresses my commitment to Black liberation. My teaching, scholarship, and activism bear the mark of these dual and inseparable concerns. Critical Black Studies has been an immensely formative and generative space for me. But I do not pretend to speak for Black people. My goal is to think with Critical Black Studies, through/from the field's challenges and iconoclastic stances. My Left is anti-colonial, anti-racist, and anti-capitalist. To agitate for Blacks and Palestinians is to agitate for a better world, a just world, a world no longer saturated by an economic system's obscene greed and voracious appetite for destruction and profit. Blacks and Palestinians know very well the deathly taste of necropolitics. During the 2014 Ferguson protests for Black lives, Palestinians shared on social media tactics for dealing with police tear gas, since both Palestinians in the Occupied Territories and the Ferguson protestors were being hit with the same American-made tear-gas canisters. Black and Palestinian problems are the world's problems. Today's Gazafication logic is giving Western leaders goosebumps, recalling for them the colonial ways of old when the "superior" Europeans disposed of "inferior" non-Europeans and stole their land and goods. Is Israel the new normal (the normal of colonial days) without scruple? Blacks, Palestinians, and those committed to global justice are emphatically saying *No!* We cannot, must not, allow Israel to get away with genocide! A Black agenda and a Palestinian agenda thus meet in their refusal to let oppressors of any shade proceed with impunity, subjugate and exploit at will, and callously divide the world into those who are worthy of care and those who are expellable and genocidable.

We cannot afford to forget about the lessons of the Black Lives Matter (BLM) movement: "Who matters and who doesn't?" "Who is free and who is cageable?" Such questions affect how we conceive of problems and craft their solutions. Slavoj Žižek puts the matter clearly: "I think that the task of philosophy is not to provide answers, but to show how the way we perceive a problem can be itself part of a problem."[40] And I would add that if a problem is badly formulated, solutions always risk compounding the problem. Take, for example, the ways major human rights organizations have accused the Israeli state of apartheid.[41] Seeing Israel as an apartheid regime is a significant turning point for us in the pursuit of justice for Palestinians. At the same time, there is a risk of compounding the Palestinian problem if the charge of apartheid stands on its own, absent a settler-colonial framework. For liberals, the remedy to apartheid is *inclusion*, more cultural rights for Palestinians from the Israeli government. This internal or domestic solution fails, however, to account for the colonial theft of Palestinian land and displacement of the land's Indigenous population. The Palestinian problem is never truly addressed if we do not critically engage the racial ideology of Zionism and its guiding presence in Israel's settler-colonial project—its colonial conquest of historic Palestine.[42] For anti-colonial theorists, the remedy to colonial apartheid is *decolonization*, "an agenda for total disorder," as Fanon imagined it.[43] This anti-colonial remedy doesn't stop at formal equality as in the move from Jim Crow to New Jim Crow, where anti-Black racism persists in both, less explicitly in the latter than the former, but no less deadly: recall the extrajudicial murders of Michael Brown, Tamir Rice, and Eric Garner, Breonna Taylor, Tyre Nichols, George Floyd, and so many others. Unlike its liberal counterpart, anti-colonial reason calls into question the very social coordinates of the settler-colonial system—what the liberal program of *inclusion* remains stubbornly obliviously to. I will return to Israeli apartheid throughout the book, but my discussion will always be framed through the prism of settler colonialism and its Zionist racial ideology.

My own diasporic experience has undoubtedly made me susceptible to problems, especially of being seen as a problem (an exilic stranger), and shaped the stances I have come to take on entangled struggle and solidarity. I was born in Beirut, Lebanon in 1971 to Palestinian parents who had fled Palestine, as did hundreds of thousands, as a result of the Nakba, the catastrophe brought about by the Zionist invasion of historic Palestine. The trauma of dispossession and displacement followed my family. The civil war in Lebanon drove us to flee to Paris, France, in 1976. Then in 1983, my father decided to reunite the family, joining my oldest brother, who had come directly to the United States upon leaving Beirut. I consider myself part of the Palestinian diaspora. Our exile was not willed but forced on us. Yet exile is also a gift (the lesson of Edward Said), a gift of sight, in the vein of Du Bois's notion of "double-consciousness";[44] it enabled me to cultivate a skepticism about identity, about its appeal and violence (Lebanon for the Lebanese; France for the French; America for Americans— or in the current idiom, "Make America Great Again (MAGA)," meaning "Make America More White Again," "Make the West Great Again," a formulation used by Italian Prime Minister Giorgia Meloni).[45] Foreigners and outsiders are often *ab initio* problems for the zealot and/as nationalist. France has its "Arab/Muslim problem"; Germany decries the "imported" anti-Semitism allegedly brought to the homeland by Muslims (Turks, Syrians, and other non-Europeans);[46] and America, at the dawn of Donald Trump's first presidency, will always be marked by the chant in Charlottesville, Virginia, "Jews will not replace us"—which is itself a mosaic of entangled racisms and racial anxieties, drawing on old anti-Jewish conspiracy theories supplemented with fantasies of threats from within and without, against lazy Black people who unjustly benefited from the Civil Rights movement and BLM movement, and the processes of globalization, opening the borders to illegal aliens. The racializing chant "Jews will not replace us" formally can accommodate a variety of racist versions: such as Blacks and "illegals/ invaders" will not take "our" (white) jobs, and "Sharia law will not replace the US constitution." Or by extension: "Muslims will not replace us," as in the Great Replacement Theory, according to which Jewish elite are overwhelming the West with Muslim migrants in order to remove or displace its white and Christian population.[47] In his second term Trump has continued to stoke Islamophobia, warning against the threat of Sharia law overtaking the West, while Republican lawmakers, following his lead, introduced the "Preserving a Sharia-Free America Act" to Congress in October 2025.[48]

To exist as a problem during times of fascist backlash makes life even more unbearable. In the United States, Trump is also waging a war against "wokeism," cruelly targeting and policing trans people and gender theory (or what he fantasizes the field to be), turning "Palestinian" into a slur, abolishing existing mechanisms meant to attenuate racial inequity (however limited they are politically), and negating and ridiculing the hardship of society's vulnerable bodies, in order to reestablish a heteronormative, patriarchal, Christian, white world.[49] Being Black, being Palestinian puts you in the eye of the fascist storm, the target of a merciless counterinsurgency. Trump casts himself as the "Law and Order" president—the Racist-In-Chief, if you will. Agitating for Black lives and racial justice, being-with Blacks and being-with Palestinians, teaching Critical Race Theory (CRT), promoting racial awareness and ways to combat anti-Black racism, along with Diversity, Equity, and Inclusivity (DEI) initiatives are all deemed irrationally anti-American, charged with weakening the nation's core principles. A new McCarthyism takes aim at Palestinians and pro-Palestinian supporters agitating against genocide in Gaza and for the liberation of Palestine. Principled stances are met with unrelenting cruelty and defamation. And let's be clear from the start. Trump and the right-wing takeover of the US government would have never happened without the moral bankruptcy of the Democratic Party, without the Biden–Harris administration's abysmal responses to the ubiquity of anti-Blackness (in Joe Biden's failure to address the structural racism in policing and incarceration, taking the young Black vote for granted; and let's not forget Kamala Harris's delusional and disastrous chase for the "Dick Cheney unicorn vote" late in the presidential race) and America's (more than) complicity with Israel's genocidal campaign in Gaza (in its unconscionable upending of national and international laws by continuously supplying Israel with weapons for annihilating Palestinians, opting instead to demonize, with rabid Republicans, the student Palestinian solidarity movement).

Having said that, being Black and being Palestinian under Trump's fascist regime creates new challenges, where the pretense of operating within the parameters of a hegemonic liberal order has been all but scrapped. The status quo was bad enough. This new autocratic regime wants to break the back of the liberal order. As a belligerent sovereignty, Trump's America operates as it wishes, outside the law, and it weaponizes the law whenever it serves its draconian objectives, as with the provision of the 1952 Immigration and Nationality Act used to detain green card holder and Palestinian student activist Mahmoud Khalil, turning him into a foreign policy concern, making him a problem for US/Israeli interests.[50] With Trump and his henchmen in power, the world's zone of care shrinks by the minute. A cowardly and unprincipled opposition party finds itself incapable of standing for the most disposable and dispensable—the most killable—at home and abroad.

The Becoming Palestinian of the World

The signifier Palestinian has come to mean many things to many people. For the distorted mind of Trump, it signifies a racial slur, something that puts the other on the defensive. Trump accused then-President Biden of being a "weak Palestinian."[51] We can imagine his rebuttal: *Don't you know that I'm a Zionist who greenlighted and funded Israel's genocide*? Trump also leveled the charge (of being Palestinian) against senator minority leader Chuck Schumer: "Schumer is a Palestinian, as far as I'm concerned. He's become a Palestinian." Trump continues: "He used to be Jewish. He's not Jewish anymore. He's a Palestinian."[52] We can hear Schumer complaining: *No, I'm not a Palestinian; I'm not the problem; I'm still Jewish*. Liberals worry. Schumer's Zionist pedigree is at stake. Trump is violating the shared consensus of anti-Palestinianness. Trump is unfair and wrong. Schumer is *not* a Palestinian. In fact, we could easily qualify Schumer as an expansionist Zionist. After all, Schumer was the first Democrat to "applaud" Trump's controversial (i.e., illegal) decision to move the US embassy to Jerusalem, during his first presidency, breaking with American policy and further normalizing the violation of international law.[53]

Trump and the Right love to pathologize all supporters of Palestine, from those calling for an end to the suffering and slaughter of Gazans to those demanding an end to Israeli coloniality and the liberation of Palestine. Republican leadership understand the becoming Palestinian of the world through the prism of college and university campuses. During congressional hearings in 2024 concerning an "uptake" in reported cases of anti-Semitism on college campuses, an enraged Rep. Elise Stefanik (R-NY) captured best this moment of counterinsurgency, acting as the big Other, channeling the authority of society's rules and laws, demands accountability from university presidents. Zealously dictating the Zionist terms of academic freedom and salivating at the chance to crack down on any Palestinian activism, Stefanik willfully distorts, among many things, the Palestinians' internationally enshrined right to resist Israel's illegal Occupation— as in the cry "Intifada" (literally meaning uprising)—and aspirational chants like "From the river to the sea, Palestine will be free," which are securitized and maliciously turned into unequivocally anti-Semitic genocidal calls, with virtually no pushback from Western mainstream media.[54] In a similar vein, Secretary of State Marco Rubio describes international students who protested against Israel's genocidal campaign "lunatics,"[55] champing at the bit to revoke even more US visas and expelling conscientious objectors to the Gaza War. Made ugly and immoral, Palestinian activism warrants condemnation across party lines.

Trump's executive order, "Restoring Truth and Sanity to American History," casts activists and scholars calling for a reckoning with America's anti-Blackness as insane for wanting to strip America of all of its significant accomplishments. The order directs Vice President Vance to eliminate "divisive race-centered ideology" from Smithsonian museums, educational and research centers, and the National Zoo.[56] "Improper" race-focused cultural production is too divisive and will not be tolerated. Cultural work that doesn't align with whiteness and nationalism will be on the chopping block. MAGA means make America less ashamed of its racism again. Being Black in an anti-Black world and wanting to change that world at a discursive and material level makes Black people a problem, lunatics and "thugs" (this is the language that Trump used to talk about the BLM activists after the murder of George Floyd),[57] in the same category as pro-Palestinian supporters. Trump, unlike Democrats, effortlessly collapses the struggles for Black and Palestinian liberation.[58] Thinking these movements together is a move that I strongly agree with but for obviously infinitely different reasons. For the Trump administration, becoming Palestinian is yet another example of becoming "woke." It goes against sanity and normalcy insofar as a sane and normal person would recognize American greatness. The message of those in power is clearly: *There will be no solidarity with Palestinians* here—and definitely no revisiting the event of BLM and the fact of anti-Blackness.

In the hands of the Right, we might say that "the becoming Palestinian of the world" is figured disparagingly as the becoming terrorist of college and university campuses, as an indicator that a "new anti-Semitism"—tying together neo-Nazis, Muslims, and the global Left—is spreading across the world, leaving Israel vulnerable and all alone.[59] On this baseless charge, becoming Palestinian comes at the expense of being Jewish (which magically ignores the high number of Jewish students involved in the movement for Palestine). Needless to say, this is not what I have in mind by the concept. My formulation, "the becoming Palestinian of the world" (to which I'll return in Chapter 3), riffs on Achille Mbembe's own important articulation of "the becoming Black of the world" in *Critique of Black Reason*.[60] In Mbembe's lexicon, "Black" represents the brutal dissolution of Africans into "things, objects, and merchandise"[61] for colonial and capitalist gain. At the same time, Mbembe insists that he doesn't see this logic as aimed exclusively at Black bodies. He puts emphasis not so much on the "afterlife of slavery," a recurring concern for the Afropessimists (to which I will turn shortly), as on the generalizability of slavery as a condition today. Global capitalism is itself no longer obeying the distinction between the human and the Black/slave, the West and the rest:

> Now, for the first time in human history, the term "Black" has been generalized. This new fungibility, this solubility, institutionalized as a new norm of existence and expanded to the entire planet, is what I call the *Becoming Black of the world*. ... The systematic risks experienced specifically by Black slaves during early capitalism have now become the norm for, or at least the lot of, all of subaltern humanity.[62]

Under early capitalism, it was the African human body itself that is commodified, not his capacity to work (the worker's labor-power): Black being enters the marketplace. Now, a tyrannical global capitalism is transforming human beings into violable and disposable objects as this system did at its outset when it converted African bodies into Black flesh for maximum profit. In our contemporary situation, only the obscenely well-off are truly immune from blackening, from instrumentalization and animalization. Starting with people residing in the Global South, but making its way to the Global North, a ravenous capitalist logic that imparts fortune to some and doles out misery to most is generating a boundless stock of new captives, new blackened objects. Becoming Black attests to the self's subjugation to the dominating system. From chattel slavery to the New Jim Crow, "to be a slave," writes Hartman, "is to be under the brutal power and authority of another."[63] "Slave life, in many ways, is a form of death-in-life," writes Mbembe.[64] In 1951, the Civil Rights Congress in the United States attested to this enduring brutal reality when it submitted to the United Nations a petition titled, *We Charge Genocide*: "The genocide of which we complain is as much fact as gravity. The whole world knows of it."[65] The Civil Rights movement changed the facade but not the reality of gratuitous violence and economic disempowerment of Blacks. The "nonevent of emancipation" persists.[66] Ontological coercion continues to underwrite the conditions of Black labor and existence. A cruel capitalism has honed its disciplinary and necropolitical ways by renewing its enslavement practice of turning humanity into subaltern humanity. Another metaphysical mutation is thus taking place under an increasingly predatory and racial capitalism. Mbembe warns of a form of capitalism that has effectively parted ways with democratic principles that, in the past (at the least for Western nations), kept it in check as it expanded across the globe.

It is not difficult to see the ways in which an unchained capitalism undergirds Palestine/Israel, where a military-industrial complex greases the wheels of Israel's war machine, transforming Gaza—the site of a "racialized surplus population" and battle-tested weapons[67]—into a profitable apocalyptic death-world.[68] In its necropolitical imaginary, Israel is sovereignly exercising its "capacity to define who matters and who does not, who is disposable and who is not."[69] In the well-documented Gaza carnage, we witness how mattering is a bodily quality differentially allocated. Who is afforded the privileges of the humanity is an effect of power or political ontology. To speak of the world as becoming Palestinian is to speak of the un-mattering of the world. Gaza crystalizes the ways in which a colonial mentality and a fascist orientation work hand in hand. A Zionist narrative bestows moral value and grievability to Jewish lives while it deprives Palestinians (and those who support them) of dignity and worth, turning them into surplus humanity, rendering the Indigenous population killable with impunity. *We charge Israel and the United States with genocide*. To signal the becoming Palestinian of the world is to issue a dire warning.

Being and ~~Being~~

Anti-colonial critique prods us to consider what it means to say that Palestinian *being* is a problem. It alerts us to its genocidal possibilities, intimating an unfixable situation; the problem is not what Palestinians *do* but what Palestinians *are*—whence the prevalence of gratuitous violence (the violence visited on Palestinians is not the result of a transgression—their guilt lies in their being). Doing is a mere expression of being. There is something wrong at an ontological level. Their being is lacking, fraught, not fully that of a *human* being; they fall outside the parameters defining humanity. On this racist account, Palestinians are ontologically degraded, depleted of what makes a human human. When I say "Palestinian being" it really means "Palestinian ~~being~~." I'm drawing here on the work of Afropessimists who visualize Black negation by barring key concepts such as ~~subjectivity~~ and ~~being~~. For example, Frank Wilderson writes: "What is a Black? A subject? An object? A former slave? A slave? The relational status, or lack thereof, of Black ~~subjectivity~~ (subjectivity under erasure) haunts Black studies as a field just at it haunts the socius";[70] and Calvin Warren muses: "Black ~~being~~ is the evidence of an ontological murder, or onticide."[71]

Who is responsible for Palestinian negation, for "Palestinocide"? For the racist, as in Du Bois's example, the fact of being a problem is intrinsic to Palestinianness. Edward Said points in a different direction. The origins of the ontological demotion lie elsewhere; they are not found in nature or a ready-made ontology but in knowledge production, in the discursive production of otherness. Orientalism, a discipline invested in producing knowledge about the Orient, has played a significant role in the construction of Palestinian being as backward, undesirable, dangerous, and irrational. Inhospitality characterizes the Western world's attitude toward Palestinians. "To the West," Said writes, "to be a Palestinian is in political terms to be an outlaw of sorts, or at any rate very much an outsider."[72] Outlaws and outsiders are by definitions problems. And I should note that Orientalism after 9/11 (which then–Israeli Prime Minister Ariel Sharon masterfully exploited, hitching Israel's unrelenting war on Palestinians to America's endless war on terror) has only intensified the demonization of Palestinians, turning Palestinians into a bigger or nastier problem, reducing them, in the Western cultural imaginary, to religious fanatics and bloodthirsty terrorists.[73] The sanctioned response to Palestinian being is revulsion and suspicion.

Against the backdrop of a masterful Orientalist discourse, Said's critique is far-reaching. It invites us to revisit the question of the human. Rather than asking abstract and timeless questions about the human—what constitutes a human being? what is proper to the human? and so on—a Saidian approach politicizes and historizes the question of the human. *Who* is asking the question? And *how* is the answer produced? Said was quite attentive to the fact that identities are never forged or produced in isolation, in a historical vacuum. The formation of personal or collective identities is always a relational matter; for the West, it necessarily implicates the creation of racialized others. Under an Orientalist framework, Western subjects invent themselves through their invention of the Orient—through their determination of the *being* of the Orient. As Said puts it, Orientalism "has less to do with the Orient than it does with 'our' world."[74] Orientalism can here be reconceptualized as a kind of libidinal disposition; it is really about "us," about the desiring Western world, about our own culturally approved desires, wishes, fears, anxieties, insecurities, and vulnerabilities.

As a style of thinking, Orientalism is about the West's *construction* of the Orient as an object of knowledge and mastery, and, in this respect, always tells us more about the knower than the known. Orientalism is not so much about knowledge of the Orient, of its culture and history, but is rather, in Said's words, "a kind of Western projection."[75] In making sense of the world, the West *invents* the East so as to better define itself, its identity, in opposition to its antagonistic Oriental other, to what *it is not*. Orientalism, then, describes this ideological process in which European identity is defined and elevated at the expense of non-European others—who are both defined and devalorized. The Orientalist subject *narrates* while the Oriental other is *narrated*.

To say that the Orient is an Orientalist invention is not only to question Orientalism's epistemological accuracy, to ask, for instance, Do its knowledge claims match up with reality, the reality of Palestinian lives in Gaza? To say that Orientalism invents is also to challenge its ontological production of others. Against Orientalism's will to power, Said insists that the notions of the Orient and the West lack "any ontological stability."[76] A ruthless critique of Orientalism exposes how ontology is put in the service of racialization, turning the colonized into things that can be subjugated, tortured, or killed with impunity. This is as true for the West Bank as it is for Gaza. Consider Israeli Foreign Minister Israel Katz's call for the ethnic cleansing of the West Bank. Writing on social media, Katz feels empowered to air his criminal and apocalyptic vision without any fear of accountability: "We need to deal with the threat exactly as we deal with terror infrastructure in Gaza, including the temporary evacuation of Palestinian civilians and any other step needed. This is a war for everything and we must win it."[77] In this "war for everything," displacement and dispossession, *ontocide* and *econocide*, take front stage.[78] Israel's genocidal war aims at the destruction of Palestinian being and all of the socioeconomic structures that sustain Palestinian life.

Orientalism greases the wheels of Israel's racist system, hardening the will of its nationals. It helps to normalize Katz's aspiration of a "war for everything"—*who are these Arabs wanting equality and freedom, self-determination on the land of Greater Israel? Hamas is guilty of another "breach of civilization";*[79] *they are the new Nazis and, we know, there are no innocent people in Gaza.*[80] *Palestinians are a problem for the world, for humanity. It is not genocide when you're dealing with evil.* Palestinian resistance must lack any legitimacy in order to legitimize the criminal military campaign in Gaza, and the most effective way to green-light the genocide is to represent all Palestinian fighters as callous terrorists, who behead children and engage in *systematic* rape as a weapon of war.[81] As with the colonial myth of the predatory and hypersexualized Black male, the most vile of lies about Palestinians appear credible because a Zionist/white supremacist horizon has already deemed them guilty, beyond the pale; they are "guilty until proven otherwise and otherwise is often impossible."[82] Their guilt possesses an ontological weight—difficult to shake or overcome. When Palestinians are made to stand for evil incarnated, then genocide or what Fayez Sayegh called *"racial elimination"*[83] is obviously what they deserve.

Orientalism paves the way for Israeli society's indifference to Palestinian devastation (the large protests against Prime Minister Benjamin Netanyahu are mostly about his failures to free the hostages and prevent October 7—the Occupation and the genocide are *not* what's motivating Israel's resistance from within), for its prideful state and "moral abyss."[84] Israeli politicians writ large mobilized fear and hatred of Palestinians—sentiments ingrained in Zionist culture *ab initio*: Indigenous Palestinian bodies jeopardize the enjoyment of the holy land and settler Zionists' way of life. Orientalism in its Zionist permutation, distilled to its racist core, creates and sustains an imperialist ontology, a necropolitical world where Palestinian lives and Jewish lives are not, and can never be, equally grievable. Or to put it slightly differently, and more polemically, the grievability of Israeli Jews is predicated on the ungrievability of Palestinians. A Zionist Israel follows a colonial script. *For me to count, you must not. My selection depends on your "dysselection."*[85]

To exist as a problem is thus to have been rendered a problem, rendered ungrievable, rendered disposable. It is to have your humanity suspended, erased, or barred. I want to linger a bit on the relation between problematization and the human. Sylvia Wynter captures well the ways in which a problem becomes racialized once the other's humanity in put in doubt at a libidinal and cultural level. The psychological "wage of whiteness," as Du Bois defined it, is the psychological wage of humanity:

> The white group of laborers, while they received a low wage, were compensated for by *a sort of public and psychological wage*. They were given public deference and titles of courtesy because they were white. They were admitted freely with all classes of white people to public functions, public parks, and public schools. The police were drawn from their ranks and the courts, dependent on their votes, treated them with leniency as to encourage lawlessness. Their vote selected public officials, and while this had small effect upon the economic situation, it had great affect upon their personal treatment and the deference shown them.[86]

There is a white libidinal enjoyment in *not* being a problem. To illustrate her point, Wynter meditates on the acronym, "N.H.I.," or "No Humans Involved," a shorthand used mainly to designate young Black men. Following the 1992 acquittal of the police officers charged with beating Rodney King, a report on the LA Police Department's practices observed that the police and "public officials of the judicial system of Los Angeles routinely used the acronym N.H.I. to refer to any case involving a breach of the rights of young, jobless, black males living in the inner city ghetto."[87] "N.H.I." is a symptom of an anti-Black world, a world whose "classificatory schema"[88] normalizes and naturalizes the violence visited upon the surplus humanity of white America. NHI absolves and comforts; in declaring NHI, in affirming anti-Blackness, you earn libidinal rewards, partake in whiteness's reward structure, and get to enjoy both the phantasmatic plenitude of your being, because it is not barred, and the fact that ~~being~~ is someone else's problem.

For Wynter, our current world operates according to the "present conception of the human being" overrepresented as "Man" (white, male, able-bodied).[89] Strictly speaking, under the colonial tyranny of Man, you are not born human but become one, and some never do. "*Being human*," Wynter explains, "can therefore not pre-exist the cultural systems and institutional mechanisms, including the institution of knowledge, by means of which we are socialized *to be* human."[90] Humanity is ontologically written out of Black ~~being~~. Overdetermined from the outside, Blackness is thingified, repelled, maligned, and made worldless. NHI conveys the currency of anti-Blackness, the normalization and self-evidentness of Black nonbeing.

I want to argue that the appalling label NHI reflects a similar dehumanizing logic at work in the disfiguration of Palestinians as well. The Israeli government gives its police and military *carte blanche* to deal "in any way they please" with those who fall under that world-canceling classification.[91] In the words of Basel Adra—codirector of the Oscar-winning documentary *No Other Land*[92]—it is "as if no humans live here," as if NHI in the state-sanctioned terrorizing of West Bank community of Masafer Yatta. Settler violence harassments are a crushing daily feature of Palestinian social life. NHI, we might say, bonds Zionist communities— they feel messianically and apocalyptically committed to the ontological liquidation of Palestinian existence.

Still, Palestinians practice what they call *sumud*, a resilient steadfastness, at once individual and collective. It is a spirited way of life that enables them to tirelessly resist Israel's necropolitics, the Zionist regime's invisibilization of Palestinian life and its vilification of their struggle for land and resources. Some enacts their daily resistance by relentlessly documenting the malicious deeds committed by settlers and soldiers. What Palestinians share in common is an axiomatic refusal to disappear and cede their homes to the Zionist usurpers. NHI is met with *sumud*: We're a stubborn problem that will not go away!

Not surprisingly, America offers its own version of a Palestinian NHI. We can hear an echo of this disregard for Indigenous life closer to home when corporate media report that Palestinians "are killed" or "are dead," but Israelis are "slaughtered" or "massacred," overrepresented as liveable/mournable and would-be victims.[93] We hear it as well when coverage of Israeli bombings in Gaza focuses on numbers over names and stories, disputes the numbers themselves (questioning the depth and reality of the decimation inflicted on Palestinians), and omits the cause of death through an agent-less, passive voice. Consider the headline of a CNN report, "About 1 in 100 people in Gaza has been killed since October 7."[94] As Žižek notes, "There is a consistent effort [on the part of mainstream media] to shape and manipulate our perception of what is going on [in Gaza], so as to limit the emotional impact. ... These forms of 'soft' censorship pervade public discourse."[95] The passive structures are no accident. They engage in what Omar El Akkad describes as the "unmaking of meaning";[96] it is a form of language that misdirects our affective and cognitive attention, indexing the nonhumanity of the Palestinians who are made into victims without a victimizer. They are killed but never murdered; they are dead, but no perpetrator is in sight. Their demise needs no further inquiry; there are red lines (genocide, ethnic cleansing), but they don't apply to Israel. Why the Israelis are committing this genocide, how they are allowed to commit the "crime of crimes," whether there is an end to the Israelis' "bloodlust,"[97] falls away in this absolving grammar.

NHI casts Blacks and Palestinians as a particular kind of problem, a problem to which "human" solutions, strictly speaking, don't apply. An ideology of NHI pushes Palestinians and Blacks further and further into the Fanonian zone of nonbeing:[98]

There is a zone of nonbeing, an extraordinarily sterile and arid region, an incline stripped bare of every essential, from which a genuine new departure can emerge. In most cases, the black man cannot take advantage of this descent into a veritable hell.[99]

This is quite a complex passage that I keep returning to in my classes and writings. The zone of nonbeing describes an "ego collapse,"[100] the ontological dissolution of identity. *Who you are* is unsettled at the core level. People find themselves in the zone of nonbeing for a variety of reasons. You might find yourself in an existential crisis. What am I doing with my life? Is this who I want to be? Am I going to have my life dictated by family, society, or peer pressure? Presumably, you emerge from the zone of nonbeing once you forge a new project, posit a new identity—this is the person that I want to be, this is this image that I project of my self in the future. Though the zone of nonbeing clearly disables, it also enables. As Fanon tells us, you can take advantage of this descent into a veritable hell. However, he also immediately draws attention to the fact that in most cases Black people are unable to transcend their situation. Why? They live in an anti-Black world that enjoys what Du Bois called the "problem of the color-line,"[101] ontological partitions and hierarchical divisions, that finds gratification in racial classification, in distinguishing between those who stand for the human, those deemed nonhuman, and those who inhabit the category of the not-quite-human.[102] The difference between nonhuman and not-quite-human can be enormous. For the Afropessimist, the nonhuman designates exclusively Black being. "Human life" (that of whites and non-Black people of color) is premised on "Black death for its existence and for its conceptual coherence. There is no world without Blacks, yet there are no Blacks who are in the World."[103] The nonhuman that guarantees all human life is and can only be Black.

To illustrate his point, Wilderson is fond of decoupling Black and Palestinian struggles, claiming that we're dealing with qualitatively different forms of antagonisms. In October 2014, during the anti-police protests happening in Ferguson, Missouri, Wilderson, in an interview, flatly rejects any rapprochement between the Palestinian struggle and the Black struggle for justice:

> So right now, pro-Palestinian people are saying, "Ferguson is an example of what is happening in Palestine, and y'all are getting what we're getting." That's just bullshit. First, there's no time period in which black police and slave domination have ever ended. Second, the Arabs and the Jews are as much a part of the black slave trade—the creation of blackness as social death—as anyone else. As I told a friend of mine, "yeah we're going to help you get rid of Israel, but the moment that you set up your shit we're going to be right there to jack you up, because anti-blackness is as important and necessary to the formation of *Arab psychic life* as it is to the formation of Jewish psychic life."[104]

Wilderson insists on the need to "radically differentiate between Blacks and all others,"[105] and not succumb to what he dubs the "ruse of analogy."[106] Ferguson is *not* Palestine; being Black is *not* being Palestinian. Yes, but who is claiming this crude equivalence? Moreover, the connection being made between Black and Palestinian struggles is not unidirectional ("so right now, pro-Palestinian people are saying ..."), coming exclusively from Palestinians, imagined cynically by Wilderson as usurpers and manipulators of Black rage.[107] The banner "From Ferguson to Palestine, occupation is a crime" speaks to a shared experience of subjugation and to a collective and universalist desire for liberation.[108]

In any case, the least we can say is that Wilderson simplifies, distorts, and obfuscates. The language of "Arab psychic life" reeks of Orientalism; it flattens Arab heterogeneity; his words homogenize the Palestinian population, assuming all Palestinian Arabs and all "Arabs" share the same mind, without any distinctions of power, culture, and positionality among them. And the hierarchy of human, not-quite-human, and nonhuman is useful insofar as it allows you to describe an individual or group's positionality in the zone of nonbeing. But Wilderson and other Afropessimists reify these categories; whites are human, non-Black people of color are not-quite-human, and Blacks are nonhuman. So for Wilderson if you're not-quite-human, if your humanity is only degraded, you (the Palestinian in this case) are still considered derogatorily as belonging to the "junior partners of civil society,"[109] and thus necessarily "antagonistic to Blacks."[110] Can a being which is genocidable by default belong the "human family"? Can a being—who lacks personhood in the eyes of Western leaders—qualify as a "junior partner"? For the Afropessimist, the Black question is infinitely different, or of a different order, than the Palestinian/Indigenous question. Palestinians want inclusion into the world (be fully recognized by the United Nations, for instance), Blacks want to destroy it (to release Blackness from slaveness; the human and its existential perks must dissolve).[111] Worlding is an ontological privilege or right for humans that is not afforded or extended to Blacks: "Native peoples are told that their world is incompatible with the European world. But *we're* told we have no right to make or inhabit worlds at all (whether Native or European)."[112] The Palestinian aspiration is to become human (realize her human potentiality), which makes her complicit with the reproduction of anti-Blackness. Ruling out *a priori* that Palestinians could be fully invested in ending anti-Black racial thinking, in dismantling the racial-colonial matrix of the human (and thus actively contribute to the destruction of an anti-Black world) lacks political imagination. Like Wynter, I find it more generative to think of the "human other" as wretched, the damned (*les damnés*) in Fanon's sense of the term.

Fanon and Wynter do not hierarchize the racialized victims of fascist colonial violence nor do they treat them as simply interchangeable and devoid of historical specificity. They are more ambivalent and capacious on human others than the Afropessimists. The difference between not-quite-human and nonhuman arguably lies in the degree to which the wretched are situated in the zone of nonbeing—and this requires relating anti-Blackness to other systems of oppression, such as capitalism, patriarchy, and settler colonialism. Relating doesn't have to mean flattening. In doing so, we can account for the ways "Black faces in high places"[113]—members of the Black political class—are shielded from *some* anti-Blackness (tied to socioeconomic status, for example), but never fully immunized from white supremacy and patriarchal capitalism, especially if you're a Black woman. It is hard to see how Black faces in high places are not obstacles to Black and universal liberation, and still less reducible to nonbeing or being, locked or ontologized in their slaveness. This is by no means to minimize anti-Blackness, which can trigger at any time, turning the socioeconomic privilege of a Black individual into a deadly problem, with ontocide catching up with Black being. At the same time, the fact of a Black elite troubles the "not-quite-human" and "nonhuman" opposition. As I read them, these categories are not absolutes but possess a heuristic value, pointing to the historical dynamic relation between being and being: how becoming being, realizing the fullness of being, has everything to do with becoming white and bourgeois.[114] Blacks are not immune to the seductions of capital and normativity, to wanting to be/becoming white and bourgeois. As Cornel West notes, "We've had Black faces in high places for the last 50 years. They've become very much beholden to the same police power, the same Wall Street power, the same Pentagon power, the same presidential power."[115] A politics of representation finds its political limits. Having sanctioned power posits you on, or in proximity to, the side of the human, *not the enslaved*.

My wager is that the not-quite-human and nonhuman are on the other side of the human. They are cut off from the sanctioned ontology and caught up in the zone of nonbeing in a quasi-permanent way. The not-quite-human believes, or rather is made to believe, that they can be saved, that they are eligible for some ontological upgrade in the future if they play their identity cards right (you can join the Black or Brown elite). In contrast, the nonhuman is the un-integratable other par excellence, and must remain nonhuman insofar as this hollowed-out other is needed to secure the meaning and coherence of the human. There can be no "human" without this contrasting other. A change in the ontological status of the nonhuman would entail a seismic shift in the social order itself. But whereas the Afropessimists insists that the destruction of the world must pass through the Black/slave, I argue that the space of the nonhuman can never be rigidly ontologized as Black; there are no pure or absolute states of nonbeing or ~~being~~, no transhistorical wretched, that would occupy the position of the timeless victim/problem.[116] To exist as a problem is a worldly matter, a meditation on *historical* ontology.

The Problem of ~~Being~~ in Fascist Times

Wynter and Fanon help us connect the act of becoming a problem with the erasure of one's humanity. Those designated by the acronym NHI are *in* but not *of* this world—*they are objects, never subjects* (I return to the logic of objects/ subjects in Chapter 3). They are seen as *"justly* shut out" from a world of being and care.[117] A Fanonian formulation of Du Bois's "How does it feel to be a problem?" might be, "How does it feel to be relegated to the zone of nonbeing?" How do you exit from such a hellish zone? How do you become unproblematic? And what would it all entail?

One response, which we might describe as liberalism's go-to solution, is empathy. For the liberal subject, the Black problem, the Palestinian problem, is often framed as a problem of empathy deficit. Blacks and Palestinians suffer from a lack of empathy, we're told. Unlike the Right, which promotes a hateful fantasy of post-raciality, the "progressive" liberal Left recognizes the crushing presence of anti-Blackness in the United States (although the Democratic politicians that they elect are not ready to do anything about it, beyond taking a knee in solidarity with BLM).[118] On anti-Palestinianness, this Left is on the fence—the phenomenon of Progressive Except for Palestine (PEP).[119] The liberal elite see a younger generation committed to the Palestinian cause, but their consciousness of the Palestinian problem has been mediated for decades by an aggressively Orientalist and Zionist vision of Palestinians; their collective unconscious has been shaped by the Zionist ideology holding that any critique of Israel puts Jewish life at risk. Still, some liberals-cum-progressive, despite the backlash that they are likely to receive, are moved by Palestinian suffering, by the horrors of Israel's unrelenting punitive campaign in Gaza. They want to put an end to it: Ceasefire now!

But here we need to proceed carefully. The fact that empathy is so "selective" and unevenly extended should give us pause.[120] Empathy is a double-edged sword: it can humanize the marginalized, the abandoned of the world (they don't deserve their suffering), and yet it can also eclipse the political situation, the colonial condition of Palestinians in Gaza. We must keep the libidinal dimensions of anti-Blackness and Palestinophobia at the center of the analysis but do so by insisting on the historical, political, and cultural production of these libidinal economies, which are through and through colonial—and, today, once again inflected by a resurgent fascism. Here, considering the parallels between Zionism and fascism, I want to probe the ways in which fascism functions not only as an ethnonationalist ideology but also as a kind of libidinal disposition to see, narrate, and desire the world, your world, in a particular way.[121] I'm interested in the libidinal logic of fascism, its psychic and affective operations: how fascism traffics in phantasmatic images of rebirth, organic wholeness, unity, rooted in a stable ontological order; how it locates the inevitable instability that threatens these images not in ontology itself, in the inconsistency of the symbolic order, but in disturbing figures of otherness—the enemies of the people. In the fascist playbook, such calcified figures are often racialized, dehumanized, and animalized agents of disorder, spiritual decadence, and corruption (as in Hitler's genocidal image of the Jew as "vermin"), so that a natural harmonious system—a fully enjoyable order absent injustice and imbalance—is, in principle, always retrievable, once the source of the excess or discord has been located and neutralized or exterminated. Being Black, being Palestinian serves that function in the fascist imaginary, fueling a rhetoric of lost/restored wholeness and *jouissance*. Imagine a world without Blacks (a safe world where Law and Order would no longer be needed in the same way) and a world without Palestinians and their supporters (a Jewish-friendly world where Zionism would have eradicated the moral rot that fosters anti-Semitism).

But to shift gears and delve further into the intricacies of fascism, we might ask, what does fascism look like from the standpoint of its racialized victims, from the standpoint of those taken as problems to eliminate? My question here is inspired by Edward Said's key 1979 essay, "Zionism from the Standpoint of Its Victims," and Ella Shohat's own important adaptation in 1988, "Zionism from the Standpoint of Its Jewish Victims."[122] Taking up this perspective allows us to ask and see how fascism becomes operative in political regimes not readily understood as fascist. It allows us to interrogate the liberal position in the United States in relation to its complicity with and enabling of fascist politics. And it allows us to offer new answers to the question, *How might we imagine anti-fascist resistance?*

Fascist states craft their nation's birth as a moment of jubilation, and work to repress any signs of dissent, anything that might challenge established values and induce a crisis of legitimacy. Israel's illiberal 2011 Nakba Law attempts to do just that.[123] The Nakba Law withholds state funds from cultural and educational institutions that mark the horrors visited on the Palestinian people in 1948.[124] A Zionist Israel, which claims to be Jewish and democratic, displays its fascism primarily in its mistreatment of its minoritized Palestinian citizens (over 20 percent of the Israeli population) and, far more flagrantly, in its occupation of Palestinian territory. Palestinian identity is repeatedly denied; Israeli politicians frequently claim that there is no such thing as a "Palestinian people."[125] The West Bank is Judea and Samaria. Metaphysical Indigeneity surpasses historical Indigeneity.[126] The biblical idea of chosenness is weaponized; it now means being chosen to annihilate and subjugate within impunity, to crowd out and displace Palestinians, who present themselves as "a people like any other people."[127] The Israeli government refers to the Palestinian citizens of Israel, the Nakba survivors of 1948 and their descendants, as its *Arab* citizens. Moreover, these de-Palestinized *citizens* do not enjoy the full rights afforded to Israeli *nationals*, since Israel, through its 2018 Basic Law, defines itself explicitly as "the Nation-State of the Jewish People,"[128] effectively codifying its apartheid character. *Israel must be defended*. Anything that draws attention to its Zionist settler-colonial beginnings must be thwarted. If you're a Palestinian citizen of Israel, for example, you do not learn about your Indigenous culture and history in school. The state denies Palestinian students this right of cultural empowerment; it divorces Palestinians from their past. In Gaza, this approach is taken to a grotesque level. The Israeli state is erasing the children of Gaza by killing them (about 70 percent of the dead in Gaza are women and children),[129] by destroying their environment (ecocide, medicide, domicide, making the Strip uninhabitable and unhealable, making all life as such unlivable),[130] and by intentionally and systematically obliterating homes and the education system, arresting, imprisoning, and killing teachers, students, and staff, and demolishing the very infrastructure that sustains such a system, from school buildings to library and museum collections to cultural heritage sites: scholasticide.[131]

Fanon deciphers settler colonizers' malefic agenda: "Colonialism is not satisfied with snaring the people in its net or of draining the colonized brain of any form or substance. With a kind of perverted logic, it turns its attention to the past of the colonized people and distorts it, disfigures it, and destroys it."[132] One of scholasticide's serious effects is that it expunges memory and civilization, making it an instance of what Christian Noakes describes as "dispossession through amnesia."[133] Scholasticide is one key manifestation of cultural genocide;[134] it doesn't simply delegitimize Palestinian knowledge-production, but disrupts the generational transfer of knowledge, which fits perfectly the fascist settler-colonial state's logic of elimination: an erasure of Palestinian past is part and parcel of an erasure of Palestinian being.

There is an ease with which Israeli fascism resonates with America, and not only with the Islamophobic, warmongering, or populist Right but also, and more disturbingly, with its liberal center. Compared with the sympathy they expressed for the BLM movement, for example, liberal elites have been far less understanding and generous in their reaction to the Palestinian solidarity movement sparked by Israel's genocidal campaign in Gaza after the Hamas raid on October 7, 2023. The anti-Zionism of the pro-Palestine activists didn't sit well with the liberal center. America's liberal political class and mainstream media outlets have adopted an "Israelocentric perspective,"[135] embracing the Israeli state's talking points and illustrating once again the veracity of the phenomenon, *PEP*: agitating for a "Free Palestine" is anti-Semitic, endangering the lives of Jews all around the world; there is no genocide, only civilizational defense; no ethnic cleansing, only the legal elimination of terrorists and "human animals";[136] there are no innocent Gazans (and the same applies to West Bankers and Jerusalemites); Israel is not violating American law or international law—it is acting in self-defense; Israel is not a colonial apartheid regime; it is not engaged in an illegal occupation; Prime Minister Benjamin Netanyahu is not a war criminal, and, that's right, America will not comply with the International Criminal Court's anti-Semitic warrant for his arrest.

In such a context, securing empathy for Palestinians seems like a moral victory, especially if we consider what happened, or rather didn't happen, at the Democratic National Convention this August. After the DNC put on display the usual suspects—the Clintons and the Obamas—along with anti-Trump Republicans and the parents of an American-Israeli hostage taken by Hamas on October 7, the DNC was confronted with a request from the Uncommitted movement to allow a Palestinian to speak at the Convention.[137] One of the names floated was that of Palestinian-American Ruwa Romman, a Georgia state representative and Democrat; Uncommitted members proposed that her speech be edited and vetted by the Harris campaign. After days of negotiations the request was declined. No Palestinian voices were heard on the DNC stage. Romman shared her speech with the media, describing it herself as "sanitized," that is, as stripped down to a basic plea to preserve human life, and purged of any broader political policy claims that might prompt disagreement.[138] Her goal was clear: humanizing the Palestinian people so that their slaughter in Gaza may come to an end. There was no reference to Palestinian genocide, no references to Israel's settler colonialism and apartheid regime. No, Romman personalized her story, speaking instead of her close relationship with her grandfather, who had experienced firsthand the hardship of displacement in 1948. Now that he is no longer with her, she wondered what he would have said about the displaced

Gazans today, about a suffering that he knew too well. Ruwa Romman's speech ended with a call for solidarity, praising a *Democratic Party. … that fights for an America that belongs to all of us—Black, Brown, and white, Jews and Palestinians, all of us, like my grandfather taught me, together.*

One can speculate that this speech could have been quite popular with the progressive liberal Left, the kind of Left that candidate Harris needed to win back. If you're part of the liberal elite, this was an incredible opportunity not only to bridge the empathy deficit when it came to Palestinians but also to co-opt the message that Palestinian lives matter,[139] to affirm that yes, Palestinian lives matter *so long as they fit our terms*. We can feel for the innocent victims, the children and kindly grandfathers, and understand the need to provide them aid without altering in any fundamental way our commitment to the political status quo: the defense of Israel as a Jewish and settler state, and by extension, its eliminationist politics. So what could explain this refusal of Palestinian voices, of a Palestinian voice, a *tamed* Palestinian voice? A crude calculus must have won over Harris's camp. It is less harmful to Harris's political success if the DNC displays blatant anti-Palestinianness (and you could score points with the Islamophobes—though Trump seems to have this market cornered) than to appear in any way anti-Semitic, or insufficiently pro-Israel. If there is a 1 percent chance that a Palestinian seen and heard might unsettle their "narratively condemned status,"[140] and thus change the coordinates of the Palestinian-Israeli "conflict" (by introducing, for instance, the idea of Palestine; the idea that Israelis are colonial invaders and occupiers of Palestinian land; the idea of Palestinian liberation), then establishment Democrats would have no choice but to nip the threat in the bud and thoroughly de-Palestinianize the DNC. The Democratic Party's Zionist credentials cannot be subject to debate.[141] The DNC must be purified of anti-colonialism and Palestine. The liberal elite support IHRA's definition of anti-Semitism: anti-Zionism is anti-Semitism! If Biden was a "weak Palestinian," as Trump had defined, was the fear now that Harris, if she entertained any action that could curtail Israeli military action, would be labeled a "strong Palestinian," a figurative Palestinian that courageously enabled an actual Palestinian to narrate the heart-wrenching plight of her people?[142]

We are at a political impasse. The Democratic Party is clearly not interested in reckoning with the Palestinian problem. They are quite willing to live with the hypocrisy. On the seventy-fifth anniversary of the Geneva Conventions of 1949,[143] then–Secretary of State Antony Blinken could, on the one hand, commemorate the occasion with a plea to respect international humanitarian law (we're not Russia), and, on the other, be a cheerleader for Israel's genocidal campaign (we're worse than Russia), which makes a mockery of human rights and the international laws that institute and protect them.[144] The dishonest but affable Blinken has been replaced by the petulant and warmongering Marco Rubio—but the unconditional military support of a genocidal Israel remains basically the same (now we have a demeanor and a rhetoric that matches the full brutality of American foreign policies). American hypocrisy is, of course, assisted by mainstream media.[145] Shamelessly compliant with state power, mass media don't dwell on the fractures and violence of American democracy, especially when no "humans" are involved. They are more eager to manufacture problems, like the global Left's supposedly rampant anti-Semitism, its Jewish problem, than to discuss how the Biden–Harris administration created a Palestinian problem of its own making.

Academic institutions, liberal media, and the Democratic Party, have thus all played a sinister part in manufacturing public consent for genocide, suppressing and minimizing Palestinian perspectives, hampering the Palestinian right to narrate their colonial/racial situation (by naming their oppressors and determining their futures), and operating according to the ingrained and naturalized Zionist colonial belief that Israeli lives count enormously more than Palestinian ones. Call it racial superiority. Whose oppression matters and whose doesn't? And, if not immediately, at least retrospectively? The Democratic Party hasn't hindered or attenuated fascism's explosion in the United States (Trump's supercharged MAGA agenda) but facilitated it. The Biden–Harris Administration's disregard for Palestinian life in Gaza came back to haunt the Democratic Party domestically. As Noura Erakat correctly emphasizes, to combat fascism we must "fight it on two fronts of U.S. state violence: at home and abroad."[146] The Democratic Party is failing on both fronts; it disappoints at the most basic level. "If pro-Palestine activists, trans and immigrant communities are being demonized by the Right," Miles Kampf-Lassin sensibly notes, "it's the job of an opposition party—which claims to represent the working class—to stand with them, not kick them out of the tent."[147] A principled Democratic Party wouldn't—and that's the problem. We're dealing with a political party unwilling to question, let alone sever, its affective and material support for Israel's war machine.

Calls for ending the genocide, for example—a subject matter that would have galvanized the core base of the Democratic Party—were not issued, undoubtedly discarded by higher-ups and consultants for being too divisive (even now pundits are criticizing the Democratic leadership for spending too much time on trans issues and reproductive rights—in other words, too much "wokeness" and/as identity politics). We must demand that the Democratic Party rein in unchecked support for the state of Israel. What kind of world this world will be cannot be allowed to be dictated by the American Israel Public Affairs Committee (AIPAC), and still less by opportunistic right-wing groups posing as allies to Jewish people. *Sorry, but this is not anti-Semitic no matter how many times you say it is.* We're not trafficking in anti-Semitic tropes when we back up our political interventions with specific, concrete observations, when we point, for example, to the "historic sums, donated by corporate tycoons, to unseat progressive Squad Reps. Cori Bush (D-Mo.) and Jamaal Bowman (D-N.Y.)."[148] What is more valuable to the longevity and ideals of the Democratic Party? Is it siding with AIPAC, a lobby whose mission is to immunize a necropolitical Israel, a criminal Israeli state, a colonial state of older days, that posits itself brazenly outside of international law, on account of "its messianic origin and destination"?[149] Or is it progressive voices who fight for economic and racial justice for all, that is, domestically and internationally?

Not only did the Democratic Party refuse to put an end to the genocide of Palestinians and push back against America's imperialist character and its military-industrial complex from within, the Democratic leadership scapegoated Palestinians and their supporters. Trump was handed a gift. Right-wing fascism simply perfected the liberal center's anti-Palestinian ethos, shifting the emphasis from marginalization of Palestinian voices (we don't want to hear from/about them) to their criminalization (we want to put the "Hamas sympathizers" behind bars). We should also mention that a kind of Palestinization of trans bodies is also thrown into the mix. If the Democratic party and liberal elite were all too compliant in discrediting, demonizing, and punishing Palestinians and their allies, Trump took this fascist logic of punching down, mercilessly going after society's least privileged members, and applied to the trans and migrant communities. Palestine is a crash course in Western militarism, imperialism, and fascism.

America, in its actions and policies, stands on the side of genocide, on the wrong side of history. Blaming every problem on Hamas has not convinced the Global South (which is all too familiar with the ravages of Western imperial violence), and the Global North, starting with its own internally colonized communities, is growing skeptical about the United States' talking points. Proponents of the Israeli state have convinced the Western elite that the Palestinian problem is contagious (though, given the West's general penchant for Orientalism and racialized Islamophobia, it didn't need much convincing). Not only are Palestinians a problem, but so too are their supporters. Protests and encampments against the genocide turn Palestinian activists into a sanctionable problem, stripping them of their privileges (if they had them to begin with—speaking here primarily of the many people of color who have stood with Palestine), rendering them *persona non grata* to be punished by doxing, termination, arrest, deportation, suspension, or expulsion, as in the case of Mahmoud Khalil. Being Palestinian or standing with/for Palestine and Palestinians, as many international activists do, puts you in a state of perpetual insecurity, in the crossfire of power and violence. *Who has the right to have rights?*

The convergence of liberal Democrats, conservative Republicans, and fascist authoritarians on the question of the Palestinian problem points to the limits of empathy as a political program as well as the "latent monstrosity of being-human"[150] with which any emancipatory politics must effectively confront. Generating empathy is, of course, critical for getting bodies out on the streets protesting the suffering of society's marginalized. We've witnessed the effects of this appeal in the 2020 protests against anti-Blackness sparked by the murder of George Floyd, and we're witnessing it again with the Gaza solidarity movement. But we cannot forget that empathy operates within the limits of humanitarian reason. It works to put an end to the immediate suffering of Palestinians. At the same time, it is ill-equipped to reckon with Zionist settler colonialism, and falls well short of answering the "call for a rewriting of our present now globally institutionalized order of knowledge."[151] Yes, empathy humanizes the wretched of the world, but its pitfalls are significant.[152] It is prone to sentimentalism and narcissistic projections, admittedly unreliable, and all too cruel when it fails to manifest. Moreover, empathy in the hands of humanitarian reason cannot address structural antagonisms or adequately respond to a brutal colonial regime that dehumanizes Palestinians and de-civilizes Israelis day in and day out.[153]

Mohammed El-Kurd takes great care to disclose the cost of a liberal humanizing of the Palestinian: "The problem is, if you want to humanize the Palestinian, you have to *defang* the Palestinian."[154] Generating the image of the good or innocent Palestinian comes with significant drawbacks: first, it seals us in our suffering, and thus limiting the ways the West can imagine Palestinians; second, it makes us complicit in our own partial (or unequal) humanization; we must appeal to the liberal standard for recognition: "We are not human, automatically, by virtue of being human—we are to be *humanized* by virtue of our proximity to innocence: whiteness, civility, wealth, compromise, collaboration, nonalignment, nonviolence, helplessness, futurelessness."[155] The becoming human of Palestinians involves multiple operations, meant to grant us humanity only when we adhere to a set of ideals that are anathema to Palestinian resistance. As a result, the Palestinian as "perfect victim" is a defanged or decaffeinated Palestinian. The liberal's perfect Palestinian equals a peaceful, or rather docile and unproblematic, Palestinian, removed from the political struggle for liberation.

I cannot see how more empathy alone can put an end to Zionism's normalization of Israel's utter disregard for international law. The affectivity of empathy can easily coexist with the coloniality of Man, the existing and overrepresented "genre of the human."[156] White subjects, caught in liberal ideology, come to enjoy their outrage; with liberal *jouissance*, they can feel virtuous about their affective response to the victimized Palestinians without having to interrogate or change in any meaningful way the ontological difference and division that separates them from Palestinians. The same can be said about white liberal support for the movement for Black lives. White liberals support the Black struggle against white supremacy as long as it exempts their white innocence, as long as their guilt translates into surplus-enjoyment (I'm touched by Black suffering so I'm better than the supremacists). *Change without real change* characterizes the liberal motto.

A liberal standpoint or agenda (incremental change such as more empathetic imaginings with society's excluded) does little to challenge the public political discourse about Palestine/Israel. Moreover, appeals to affect can readily be channeled toward life-destroying ends, tapping into that "latent monstrosity of being-human" that remains an immanent possibility for all of us. A fascist Zionist libidinal economy does just that; its eliminationist desires are not so much engineered or manufactured by Israel's fascist regime as they are brutally unleashed. This "diabolical dimension"[157] of being human has erupted in Gaza for the world to see. Ziofascists succeeded in channeling our most destructive energies toward the annihilation of Palestinians, disavowing their cruelty (a manifestation of the inhuman core of being human) and projecting it onto *all* Palestinians (I return to the avowal and disavowal of cruelty in Chapter 1). When you turn Palestinians into pure creatures of evil, you ideologically prep the judgment of eradication, that a defective people, marked by civilizational lack, deserve genocide; only a permanent erasure can prevent future harm to the Jewish people. A fascist Zionist libidinal economy routes the desires and fears of Jews, teaching Israel's nationals what and who to desire, hate, and identify with. Zionism serves a structuring concept for Israel/Jewish identity. As a collective unconscious, it encourages vigilantism, naked violence, and colonial domination of Palestinians. Xenophobic attitudes are fully naturalized, as in the settlers' reflexive chant, "Death to Arabs." In their full-blown hatred, settlers do not see Palestinians, only Arabs, a homogenized, mystified, and Orientalized enemy that must be eliminated. Anti-Palestinianness is a Zionist mode of identity, a *Weltanschauung*, a way of being and hating in the world, of understanding one's place and righteous destiny in this world.[158] Fascism/Zionism from the standpoint of its racialized Palestinians is an endless source of terror. And let's not overlook the murderous *jouissance* that fascist Zionism produces and mobilizes in its zealots. There is material and affective enjoyment in the spoils of the Occupation (in fulfilling the Zionist imperative to settle and colonize the entire land of Israel), in becoming a pariah on the geo-political scene, in thwarting the will of the United Nations; an institution that Ziofascists decry as anti-Semitic, another figure of the global enemy.[159] Without a fascist Israel, there is no possibility of a mythified and mythifying Greater Israel, of a completely harmonious Israel—meaning an Israel free of Palestinians and its pro-Palestine detractors. The Zionist injunction, "Make Israel Greater Again," requires the most vile of racisms coupled with an ethnic politics and a feeling of racial superiority. Fascism is up to the task. As the "villa in the jungle,"[160] Israel can just go ahead and exterminate the brutes.

As a collective fantasy of racial and cultural superiority, fascist Zionism provides its Jewish nationals a "cognitive mapping"[161] of the world, which works hegemonically, often, unconsciously to organize the Zionist attitude, suppress the colonial situation (the need for socio-diagnosis: why do Palestinian resist?), and orient them to a life where the Occupation is not the problem, but anti-Semitism is. Zionist thinking is a kind of conspiratorial thinking.[162] Anyone who dares to object to Israeli policies (including leading human rights organizations [e.g.,

Amnesty International, Human Rights Watch, B'Tselem], the International Court of Justice, the International Criminal Court, Jewish organizations [e.g., Jewish Voice for Peace, IfNotNow], BLM chapters, Médecins Sans Frontières, the Red Nation, non-Jewish students protesting in solidarity with Palestinians) is branded hateful and treated as part of a global anti-Semitic scheme to delegitimize and harm Jews/Zionists. We are ironically witnessing here the anti-Semitic notion of the "Jewish plot" in reverse; it is the Zionist Anti-Defamation League (ADL) and the fascist Zionists who are seeing "Hamas sympathizers" everywhere, allegedly dominating the world of public opinion and intentionally misrepresenting Israeli actions and policies in order to usurp the moral authority of Israeli leaders and endanger Jewish lives. By this logic, the world as a totality hates Israel (meaning Jews). Israel's genocide is not the cause but the disclosure of this truth. In their daily existence, many Israeli Jews see what they are conditioned to see and discard, for the most part, what doesn't fit the sanctioned Zionist narrative. The phantasmatic image of "Hamas sympathizers" plays a pivotal part in sustaining Zionist desire/identity: they are the ultimate obstacle now to the full enjoyment of Zionism, to (maintaining) its respectable standing among liberal Western nations[163] (with the ironic twist that the same "Hamas sympathizer" label also supplies a libidinal kick to Zionists, a sense of pride in defending the Jewish people—fighting the "good fight"—against an overwhelming enemy, retelling, if you will, the David and Goliath story in a distorted form). What is a Zionist Israel without its "Hamas sympathizers"?

As a political ideology, fascist Zionism imposes and enforces a fixed ontology; under its horizon, Zionism's identitarian claims about Jews and Arabs have an ineluctable force, seemingly unimpeachable, because they are theologically sanctioned. Fascist Zionism at once exploits and fuels what we may call, after Jacqueline Rose, a "passion for Zion,"[164] amplifying both the psychic attachment to the contested land and the lustful hatred of "Arabs": those bodies who must be subjugated, whose presence, or rather unsanctioned Indigeneity, represents a scandal. Unhappy with any check on their righteous power, Ziofascist politicians not only defy international law but also yearn for more authoritarian control over the law at home—whence Netanyahu's "judicial coup," his right-wing coalition's bid for more dictatorial governance. Fascism from the standpoint of its liberal Zionist victims stops here, in the right-wing government's assault on Israel's judicial authority and independence. On Palestinian matters, Israel's Supreme Court has green-lighted the illegal settlements and has never mounted anything resembling a check on executive power.

In these fascist times, even the word "Nakba" is no longer a taboo term. Right-wing politicians shamelessly embrace it. Journalist David Sheen captures well the normalization of this ugly sentiment in a tweet: "A decade ago this Israeli fascist group's slogan was 'Nakba is bullshit.' Now it's 'No victory without Nakba.'"[165] If the liberal Zionists of the proverbial "peace camp" may feel guilt or even shame for the unjust treatment of Palestinians, the Ziofascists of the "genocide camp" derive a perverse gratification from Palestinian abjection and subjugation, sadistically calling for a repetition of the Nakba,[166] for its full realization in Gaza and the West Bank (we're witnessing "the Gazafication of the West Bank"[167] by Israeli soldiers and settlers collaborating in the dispossession, home demolition, and displacement of Palestinians). Zionist liberal guilt or shame, on its own, does little to advance the Palestinian cause. As Audre Lorde avers,

> [Guilt] is a response to one's own actions or lack of action. If it leads to change then it can be useful, since it becomes no longer guilt but the beginning of knowledge. Yet all too often, guilt is just another name for impotence, for defensiveness destructive of communication; it becomes a device to protect ignorance and the continuation of things the way they are, the ultimate protection for changelessness.[168]

For shame to gain an emancipatory force, and not just index another form of impotence, the shame felt for Israel would need both to alter one's consciousness (a psychic divestment from a Zionist settler-colonial state, an apartheid Israel; a refusal to let a Ziofascist Israel define/distort the legacy of Judaism as conquest and dispossession) and translate into action, into a ceaseless commitment to the liberation of the Palestinian people: to be Jewish is to prevent the genocide of others—"Never Again for Everyone." Wanting to belong to (a just/decolonized) Israel does away with all tribalistic rhetoric of "unconditional patriotism," which can only lead to majority support for the Gaza genocide. Simply put, a shameless Israel is likely to be a fascist Israel.

Anti-Colonial Critique and/as Unlearning Desire

Fascism's racial matrix of the human predates its genocidal eruption in Europe. Attending to what Alberto Toscano names "fascisms before fascism" deepens our understanding of fascism's political maneuvers and libidinal appeals.[169] The "*longue durée*" of fascism, a more expansive understanding of the concept, returns us to Black enslavement and colonialism, and their crushing afterlives.[170] Taking up the perspective of the enslaved/colonized boldly recasts fascism as a fact of coloniality. For the racialized bodies (the internally colonized) living in liberal democracy, who, again, are *in* but not *of* this world, whose rights are never guaranteed, social existence, Black embodiment, is lived habitually under duress. State violence sniffs out Black problems. A militarized police presence in Black communities was never meant to protect and serve their citizens. As James Baldwin put it in 1966, to live in America as a Black man is "to live in occupied territory."[171] In Harlem, Black presence itself, not action, is the problem—the solution to the problem thus defined is state-sanctioned or naturalized violence in the form of incarceration or liquidation.[172] Here, I think, a different approach to fascism opens up. Reading fascism from below, from the perspective of the colonized and internally colonized, as some of us are beginning to do, allows for a different image of fascism to emerge. In *The Colonizer and the Colonized*, Albert Memmi writes, "Every colonial nation carries the seeds of fascist temptation in its bosom. What is fascism, if not a regime of oppression for the benefit of a few? ... There is no doubt in the minds of those who have lived through it that colonialism is one variety of fascism."[173] Fascism as a regime of oppression, with a long history of violence, has a simplistic clarity about it. And yet, here, we should resist the quick impulse to abstract from Memmi's observation its racial dimension, not because we lose the particularity of the fascism experienced by the colonized, but because we overlook its concrete universality, an account of fascism in its pure brutality, fascism minus what remains of the liberal order, meant to protect "us." Fascism without its non-European racialized victims is miserably insufficient. Racial fascism discloses how far human depravity can go. In Gaza, in the world's first livestreamed genocide, we witness the true nature of oppression and dispossession of being; in today's concrete historical situation, Gaza is not just another example of a war-torn region, of mass civilian death and suffering. Rather, Gaza, like Auschwitz, has become a "concept-name."[174]

But this is not to elevate the injustice of Palestinians above the injustices of others. We hear this cynical form of reasoning from people who want to derail the discussion about genocide by asking why we are so fixated on Palestinians. What about Sudan? Aren't we ignoring the injustices and sufferings of others, those who are truly voiceless? This impoverished form of thinking can only reason in terms of a zero-sum game—*if you state your care for X you must not care about Y*. Gaza matters not because Sudan doesn't. Gaza matters because it crystalizes racial injustice and exposes an egregious racial matrix of the human. Gaza matters because it calls on us to question what stands for the human. Shifting the tectonic plates of colonial humanism creates the possibility of another kind of struggle, where Palestinian liberation would not make Sudanese and other raced others un-matter. Palestinians would avoid the path of Ashkenazi, or European-descended, Jews who ceased to be a problem once that they were admitted among the ranks of Europe's white supremacists (and turned the Indigenous people of Palestine into a problem). Commenting on Israel's welcomed reception among Western nations, Franco Berardi points to the ontological upgrade of Jews, the *no longer* exterminable, no longer a problem. In the past Jews were treated as antagonistic enemies, part of the wretched, others with whom no coexistence is morally and politically possible, but now "they are no longer the enemy of our superior race, but a part of it. Therefore they have been granted the privilege that we already have: the privilege of the colonizers, of the exploiters, of the exterminators."[175] Gaza matters because it exemplifies the devastating effects of a fascist logic when it is fully unleashed on racialized people whose humanity has been permanently suspended and ontologically barred, and whose ecological environment (basic access to food and clean water, safety and shelter) has been deliberately turned to ruins.[176] This is why, as Yanis Varoufakis notes, we need to "fixate" on Gaza.[177] Our response to Gaza tells us something about who we are, and what we're willing to live with. It scrambles "our" pragmatic and reasonable priorities. The fact of Gaza pierces the order of our default ideals. It denotes disaster, a terrifying place where you are—where you have been historically rendered—genocidable in advance. To be Gazan is to be on "death row";[178] it is to await your annihilation.

We may, then, critically ask: Is fascism only truly considered fascism—and repulsive to the West—when white or European bodies are oppressed, when fascism misfires and turns on its own? In *Discourse on Colonialism*, Aimé Césaire weighs in and offers an anti-colonial rebuke to the Western outrage over the Holocaust, incisively reframing and exposing the subject of the outrage as "the very distinguished, the very humanistic, the very Christian bourgeois."[179] The will to brutalize (non-whites) is constitutive of the European subject, an irrevocable facet of bourgeois hegemony. According to Césaire, each subject "has a Hitler inside him, that Hitler *inhabits* him, that Hitler is his *demon*."[180] This "inner Hitler" however is only allowed to express itself, be itself, in foreign lands. Nazi Germany morally erred by turning Hitler's vicious will at fellow Europeans, at fellow humans:

> What [the European subject] cannot forgive Hitler for is not the *crime* in itself, *the crime against man*, it is not *the humiliation of man as such*, it is the crime against the white man, the humiliation of the white man, and the fact that he applied to Europe colonialist procedures which until then had been reserved exclusively for the Arabs of Algeria, the coolies of India, and the blacks of Africa.[181]

In the white cultural and libidinal imaginary, it is not a true crime to rob, exploit, and dominate an inferior race. Arabs, unskilled native laborers, and Blacks were/are *a priori* oppressable identities. Even oppression is rehabilitated or rehabilitatable if the enslaved is imagined as constitutively devoid of possibilities. As Christina Sharpe recounts, a pernicious whiteness severely constricts the imagination of her students who are unable to envision another life or world for the enslaved: "'Well, they were given food and clothing; there was a kind of care there. And what would the enslaved have done otherwise?' The 'otherwise' here means: What lives would Black people have had outside of slavery? How would they have survived independent of those who enslaved them?"[182] Slavery saves the savages. Slavery means survival, and survival excuses social death. And Nelson Maldonado-Torres also notes: "Colonization equals civilization, and civilization justifies annihilation (ethnic cleansing and genocide) as well as dispossession."[183] In 1967, Fayez Sayegh translates Zionism's racial ideology, its expansionist/eliminationist logic, in ontological terms: "Every Israeli who is in Israel today is there because an Arab has been ousted. Israel is, because Palestine has been made not to be. The being of Israel is the non-being of Palestine."[184] Under a Zionist horizon, Jewish being destroys Palestinian being, and Israel devours Palestine. Racial superiority characterizes the European/settler/Zionist gaze. Consider Winston Churchill's degrading discourse, his racist assessment of Indigenous populations to the Palestine Royal Commission in 1937: "I do not admit ... that a great wrong has been done to the Red Indians of America, or the black people of Australia ... by the fact that a stronger race, a higher grade race ... has come in and taken its place."[185] *Might makes right. Make Might Right Again. Usurpers, welcome.*

Today Western leaders may not be saying this publicly, but they are in practice enacting the core supremacist belief of all colonial powers, justifying then and now the Zionists' dispossession and displacement of Palestinians. Europeans reaped the benefits of Hitlerism abroad (colonialism or the legitimized violence of a superior race), but Hitlerism at home—the Shoah as "boomerang effect"[186]—was a betrayal (treating Europeans as non-Europeans, whites as non-whites) and deemed intolerable. Césaire's mode of address—*Hey Europe, you have a fascist problem dating from colonial times*—finds a receptive ear in Fanon who is appalled and enraged by the West's staggering historical crimes and murderous deeds. He writes in *The Wretched of the Earth*: "When I look for man in European lifestyles and technology I see a constant denial of man, an avalanche of murders."[187] This passage from Fanon echoes Walter Benjamin's staggering observation that "there is no document of culture which is not at the same time a document of barbarism."[188] Every iteration of the human face is also an iteration of its racial fascist defacement. Western civilization, from the standpoint of the colonized, manifests as Western cruelty. Jean-Michel Aphatie, a well-known French journalist, made what is essentially a Césairean point in a television interview, when he gestured to the "Hitlerisms before Hitlerism," opening a justified comparison between France's disavowed colonial brutality of Algeria (1830–1962) and Nazi Germany's 1944 decimation of Oradour-sur-Glane, a village in west central France. Unsettled by Aphatie's comment, the anchor accusatively asked, "We [the French] behaved like the Nazis"; Aphatie's response is sublime: "The Nazis behaved like us."[189]

Césaire's reflections on Hitlerism/colonial racism reverberate for Fanon. Remembering hearing a political speech by his fellow Martinican; Fanon cites him from memory:

When I switch on my radio and hear that black men are being lynched in America, I say that they have lied to us: Hitler isn't dead. When I switch on my radio and hear that Jews are being insulted, persecuted, and massacred, I say that they have lied to us: Hitler isn't dead. And finally when I switch on my radio and hear that in Africa forced labor has been introduced and legalized, I say that truly they have lied to us: Hitler isn't dead.[190]

Today, we might say, *When I turn on the news and hear that undocumented Brown children are being targeted in their schools by Immigration and Customs Enforcement (ICE), I say they have lied to us: Hitler isn't dead. When I see that a disproportionate number of Blacks are being incarcerated and murdered by the US police, I say that they have lied to us: Hitler isn't dead. When I turn on the news and hear that the Greek coastguard threw migrants overboard to their deaths, I say that they have lied to us: Hitler isn't dead. And finally when I see that Gazans are being starved and bombed in hospitals, I say truly that they have lied to us: Hitler isn't dead.* The Greek coastguard abuses indexes not only a violation of the migrant's rights under international law; it points to the *longue durée* of colonial abuse of Africans and slaves.[191] While right-wing fascists celebrate the defense of America and Europe, liberal defenders of the European Union and internationalism prefer to contain the damage, arguing for more humane treatment of the non-white, non-Europeans.

Liberal opinion notwithstanding, we still dwell in, and are affected by, the afterlives of Hitler. Hitlerism reimagined survives. Hitler stands for a colonial racial matrix that legitimizes and authorizes the will to subordinate and exterminate, and that generates beings who count and nonbeings who are exterminable. Western powers approve the complete destruction of Gaza; they authorize Israeli Jews' inner Hitler to brutalize the Palestinian people. To evoke Fanon, *What is the status of Palestine? A systematic dehumanization.*[192] Europe's colonial adventures continue vicariously via Israel's genocidal campaign on the Palestinian people. Fascism and settler colonialism work in tandem: the face of this inner Hitler is the inner settler not only in Occupied Palestine (where racialized state terrorism—dished out by the Israeli military and the unhinged settler movement—thrives) but also in Israel proper (where every national is hailed and called on to surveil the enemy within). In this respect, Black Lives Matter chants and Palestinian Lives Matter chants are fundamentally anti-fascist, intended to jam the colonial West's "*ontological* fascism,"[193] its racial privilege to incarcerate, police, deworld, demonize, racialize, colonize, exploit, starve, maim, and exterminate (unsettlingly, the list could go on). We cannot, must not, allow Israel to get away with genocide. Blacks and Palestinians express a collective *No!* to a fascist agenda, a generalized and generalizable necropolitics; *No!* to "the good old times," murderous utopias, and nostalgic visions of harmonious communities minus their hated Palestinian and Black others (and their willful comrades in resistance); and a collective *Yes!* to equality and freedom for all; a *Yes!* to a principled rage that opens to other wretched—that is in solidarity with the world's surplus humanity—never enamored with or exhausted by the intensity of their own suffering.

Following Césaire and Fanon, colonialism and anti-Blackness need a hearing in the West. But this is no endorsement of a zero-sum game, an "Oppression Olympics"[194] that crowns the essential victim, which ultimately only satisfies the liberal center: *Talk as much as you want about race but change nothing at the structural level.* Reading fascism from below, from the standpoint of its racialized victims, can help us forge an anti-colonial and anti-fascist response that effectively breaks with the liberal center, the white bourgeoisie, resisting the lure of identity politics (and all forms of tribal politics) and an easy "Diversity, Equity, and Inclusion" (DEI) in favor of an emancipatory universal politics.[195] Understanding the Shoah as a form of colonialism challenges its ideological claims of "uniqueness," but doesn't relativize or minimize the unbearable force of Auschwitz and the "Never Again for Everyone" that it generated.[196] On the contrary, it enables and builds on what Michael Rothberg dubs a "multidirectional" approach to trauma studies, making analogical analysis of fascist states and scenes potentially far more dynamic and generative.[197] Foregrounding a colonial racial matrix, that produced Jews as "vermin" and Palestinians as "human animals," sends us back to the West's earlier forgotten or repressed colonial crimes—its brutal commodification of non-European lives—to read *otherwise* the colonial horrors of the past (and thus refuse the liberal impulse to rank them by perpetuating a "hierarchy of suffering")[198] so as to better confront our present and future horrors. Against a futurology that forecasts more and more catastrophes, more and more genocides and ecocides, an anti-colonial Left bucks "the present trends in society"[199] and insists on the belief that the generation of new anti-fascist desires remains both possible and indispensable. A hegemonic liberal order is not enough. Hitlers are multiplying. Fascists are emboldened. The world is burning. We need to ask for more. De-Nazification must undergo anti-colonial critique, and so must our resistance to fascism.

Education is a crucial generator of such resistance and critique—and thereby a key site of struggle for all colonial and fascist regimes.[200] Toscano rightly stresses "the extreme importance of the nexus of education and fascism today."[201] In this "battleground,"[202] right-wing governments decry the ways students are subjected to leftist indoctrination. They purport to intervene in the name of students. In Israel, this is where you root out anti-Zionists, leftist brainwashers who corrupt the young by making them hate their nation. Disharmony lies exclusively in Israel's detractors not in Israel's settler-colonial system. University students pick up on this fascist vibe. Some (along with faculty) resist any encroachment on academic freedom; others agitate for the stronger side. The National Union of Israeli Students, for instance, is pushing a law, with the backing of the Israeli education minister, that would effectively criminalize dissent and fire faculty for "supporting terror" (the act of speaking up against Israel's Occupation and genocide of Palestinians is not considered an act of free speech but willfully misconstrued as an "incitement to terrorism," aiding the enemy, which thus publicly disqualifies the speaker as a rational and credible interlocutor and opens her to prosecution).[203]

We clearly see parallels in America. From the start of his second term, Trump went to work implementing his fascist agenda, issuing executive orders, and setting his sights on all those deemed to be infecting or weakening America: DEI programs, woke gender ideology, illegal immigrant invaders, and haters of America. "Operating within a fascist logic,"[204] as Judith Butler describes Trump's playbook, enables him and his accomplices to target vulnerable minorities, who are unjustly blamed for America's ills: from trans people to Haitians whose "Temporary Protected Status" is being revoked. Unsurprisingly, Trump also seized on the awful lie of equating anti-Zionism with anti-Semitism, calling pro-Palestinian supporters "Hamas sympathizers," labeling them terrorists, or terror supporters, subjecting international students and noncitizens to further and needless scrutiny, visa cancellation, and potential "ideological deportation."[205] Trump wants to make Palestine radioactive.

The war on pro-Palestinian campus activists does not end with international students. Green card holders are not spared either, as the government's abusive overreach in Mahmoud Khalil's case clearly demonstrates.[206] A Task Force to Combat Antisemitism, led by the US Department of Justice, is criminalizing pro-Palestinian support in schools and on college campuses. Leo Terrell, senior counsel to the assistant US attorney general for civil rights, warned conscientious protesters: "You see all these disorderly demonstrations, supporting Hamas and trying to intimidate Jews? We are going to put these people in jail—not for 24 hours, but for years."[207] Free speech alchemically becomes hate speech. The world-canceling accusation of anti-Semitism creates a legal opportunity for the government to strip you of rights. Khalil, in a letter he dictated over the phone from an ICE detention in Louisiana, asks, "Who has the right to have rights?"[208] This Arendtian question is quite apt.[209] In its lawfare, the Trump administration has turned Khalil into a problem, exempting him from protection, denying him the right to have rights. To be sure, a "defense of rights" is mainstream, even a "liberal platitude," but when the rights in question are attached to a Palestinian body, a problematic body, securing rights for Khalil casts the endeavor in different light, with the significant potential of upending America's "hegemonic ideology."[210] In the eyes of this unscrupulous government, Khalil is not a moral person: he is really a terrorist. If having rights is a privilege, and not a right (a "universal right to politics," as Étienne Balibar puts it),[211] then the government is permitted to suspend the privilege and remove you from the realm of (protected) humanity, relegating you to a zone of injustice or ~~justice~~ (a justice crossed out, indexing the constitutive unjustness of our neocolonial world), where stateless and rightless beings are made to dwell in ontological and legal limbo. Without the right to have rights, Khalil would join the rank of those reduced to "their bare status as members of the human species."[212] And as we painfully know, unprotected humans, left to the whims of the state's authority, are subject to abduction, abuse, torture, and deportation with impunity.

There is a crushing irony here. The extreme damage that the weaponization of the accusation can inflict on the wrongly accused is more often than not leveled with no evidence and plenty of distortion. Instrumentalizing the charge of anti-Semitism—from the liberal Left to the fascist Right, and thus consolidating America's anti-Palestinianness—is a counterinsurgent tactic, and "the weapon of choice for people who have no argument," as Rashid Khalidi eloquently put it.[213] And when white supremacist fascists viciously deploy the label of anti-Semitism (playing their own game of cancel culture), in the name of preserving a harmonious Jewish life, we're in deep trouble. Similarly, when Trump "thinks outside the box," as his admirers like to say, and proposes to take ownership of the Gaza Strip, turned into rubble by bombs mostly supplied by the United States, in the name of Palestinians' own well-being, we are in deep trouble again. But who is really pushing back? Democratic establishment, mainstream media, campus administrators? None of the above!

Jennifer Ruth seizes well what many of us are feeling and thinking:

> Between the Trump team's attacks and higher education's appeasement, we must reclaim our universities for ourselves. Academic freedom is not Trump's to take or boards' to give away. Our commitment to truth-telling will not be compromised by lobbying groups, donors and politicians, and the governance of our institutions will not be outsourced to boards for whom we are appendages to investment portfolios. Our universities will be by and for the people who work and study at them, not by and for finance capitalists, "broligarchs" and fascists.[214]

Even when presidents of colleges and universities genuinely want to protect their students, they often go about it the wrong way. They reason that students and faculty should not bring too much attention to their campuses. Their message: we will respect your academic freedom, but please do not make visible, collective demands (such as divest from Israel and/or the military-industrial complex) that could trigger a retaliation from the Trump administration and hurt our most vulnerable student in danger. We say the opposite: What is putting all of us in danger is the failure to collectively stand up and thwart Trump's fascist overreach. Stop gaslighting us. There is no "golden mean" position here. Trump is neither a rational nor a moral interlocutor. We (faculty and students across colleges and universities) can begin by affirming that pro-Palestinian speech (about Israeli genocide, colonial apartheid, and the Occupation) is *not* hate speech, that anti-Zionism is *not* anti-Semitism, followed by divestment motions targeting industries that obscenely profit from the death of civilians and the destruction of environments.

Fault lines are crystalizing. Campus administrators are facing a massive attack on academic freedom and the mission of public higher education.[215] New York City is ground zero for the anti-Palestinian backlash. Witness the new McCarthyism impacting universities. In February 2025, New York Governor Kathy Hochul ordered Hunter College, which is part of the City University of New York system, to remove a job ad for a "cluster hire" in Palestinian studies (one in the humanities and the other in the social sciences). This is the "controversial" job listing: "We seek a historically grounded scholar who takes a critical lens to issues pertaining to Palestine including but not limited to: settler colonialism, genocide, human rights, apartheid, migration, climate and infrastructure devastation, health, race, gender and sexuality. We are open to diverse theoretical and methodological approaches."[216] A Democratic governor in a blue state displayed no hesitation in accepting the baseless accusation, made by pro-Israel groups, that critically studying Palestine—and any attempt to examine Israel's participation in settler colonialism and apartheid—constitutes an anti-Semitic act, a contemporary manifestation of "blood libel." As expected, Hochul's office performed outrage, calling for "a thorough review of the position to ensure that antisemitic theories are not promoted in the classroom."[217]

The Trump administration is already punishing universities for allegedly failing to protect Jewish students and faculty. In an act of extortion that would make the most seasoned mobster blush, Trump has leveraged the suspension of $400 million in federal funding from Columbia University to force it to crack down on campus anti-Semitism.[218] After this first fascist strike, Columbia capitulated almost immediately, fully, and unambiguously. There was no doubt an irony here, since Columbia had been quite hostile to its pro-Palestine activists. One might have expected that Columbia would be the university to emulate, noting how its former, disgraced president, Minouche Shafik, threw her students and faculty under the bus during the shameful 2024 congressional hearings. In response to the university's surrender, US Education Secretary Linda McMahon stated that Columbia is not where it should be, but "on the right track."[219] The government's demands will not be satisfied because they aren't meant to be satisfied. Anti-Semitism has never been the problem for the fascist Right; the problem has always been higher education itself.[220]

This vulgar practice of (threatening universities for not) silencing Palestinian voices is a desperate attempt at holding on to a discredited pro-Israel, American status quo. It is a fear that college education will not operate as an "ideological state apparatus," and simply aid in the reproduction of social reality (in which Israel is part of the "good guys" narrative), a fear that education might result in unlearning, in questioning a Zionist narrative that puts all the blame on Palestinians in the guise of a war on Hamas. When "full solidarity with Israel" is asserted as the given, as an apolitical situation and condition, Palestinians become the problem for—or a menace to—humanity, banned from the realm of intersubjectivity, no relationality is afforded to them. This is ideology in its most violent form; you are *a priori* removed from recognition. As Žižek keenly observes, "to impose one's own political stance as apolitical is the most brutal ideological operation one can imagine because it disqualifies in advance any critique."[221] Unlearning the public discourse about Palestine/Israel begins with the *re*politicization of the Palestinian problem.

Students for Justice in Palestine (SJP)—including many Jewish students—are unlearning the script endorsed by the political class defining what constitutes anti-Semitism. Ziofascists and their Western enablers know that unlearning can undetermine futures, can be more painful and disorienting than learning something new, because it profoundly undoes and denaturalizes your existing racist interpretive frameworks. In their call to halt this unlearning, we are bullied into believing in the absurd: Becoming less Orientalist causes you to be more anti-Semitic (by becoming less racist, you become more racist—and never in this framework might the fights against Islamophobia and anti-Semitism be in any way generatively related to one another). And if universities provide a place to think critically about Orientalism and colonial modes of knowing, then universities become a festering petri dish for anti-Semitism. Discredited Harvard law professor Alan Dershowitz says as much in a tweet: "Elite universities are highly financed incubators of anti-Semitism and anti-Americanism."[222] As Muhammad Ali Khalidi notes, Zionism and its disseminators in the United States "attempt to reestablish and enforce ignorance."[223] Zionism yearns for prior times when there was no need for lawfare, when college students were blissfully ignorant of Israel's killing machine (because, in no small part, Palestinian voices and perspectives were, and still are, almost always excluded from mainstream news).

College students however are indeed unlearning; they refuse to be disciplined, to accept without question Israeli state propaganda (*hasbara*); they refuse to comply with their own authoritarian regime's attempts to reeducate them into viewing Israel as a liberal and democratic beacon. This shifting reality is producing Zionist anxiety. Younger people are redefining the protocols of critical engagement: Israel's global stock is on the decline. The challenge now is who will stand with Palestinians and their supporters. The student protests staged for the world *what speaking truth to power and about power looks like*. Their passion for justice exposes its noticeable absence among many intellectuals in these new McCarthyite times. Edward Said's words are more relevant than ever:

Nothing in my view is more reprehensible than those habits of mind in the intellectual that induce avoidance, that characteristic turning away from a difficult and principled position, which you know to be the right one, but which you decide not to take. You do not want to appear too political; you are afraid of seeming controversial; you want to keep a reputation for being balanced, objective, moderate; your hope is to be asked back, to consult, to be on a board or prestigious committee, and so to remain within the responsible mainstream; someday you hope to get an honorary degree, a big prize, perhaps even an ambassadorship. For an intellectual these habits of mind are corrupting *par excellence*. If anything can denature, neutralize, and finally kill a passionate intellectual life it is the internalization of such habits. Personally I have encountered them in one of the toughest of all contemporary issues, Palestine, where fear of speaking out about one of the greatest injustices in modern history has hobbled, blinkered, muzzled many who know the truth and are in a position to serve it. For despite the abuse and vilification that any outspoken supporter of Palestinian rights and self-determination earns for him or herself, the truth deserves to be spoken, represented by an unafraid and compassionate intellectual.[224]

Arundhati Roy wryly offers some tips for not becoming a problem in academia. Avoid Palestine, but if you're drawn into a conversation on that controversial topic, be careful and stick to the liberal script, look out for your self-interest, and adopt its suggested indifference to the slaughter of Palestinians: "In the U.S., to speak of intifada—uprising, resistance, in this case against genocide, against your own erasure—is considered to be a call for the genocide of Jews. The only moral thing Palestinian civilians can do, apparently, is to die. The only legal thing the rest of us can do is to watch them die. And be silent. If not, we risk our scholarships, grants, lecture fees, and livelihoods."[225] Academia is a minefield. Palestine is a taboo problem. As with the Red Scare, Palestinian sympathies attract trouble and scrutiny.[226] Proceed with care.

But the genie is out of the bottle. For a younger generation of student-activists there is no going back to a liberal Israel, absent an ontological reckoning with Zionist-Israeli identity. The pro-Palestine students adopt a skeptical and "hysterical" pose toward the authority of the master/settler/colonizer. As Žižek notes, following Lacan, "the hysterical subject who incessantly probes the Master's knowledge is the very model of the emergence of new knowledge."[227] New knowledge about Palestine/Israel is in dire need. Palestine hystericizes. The students are not satisfied with the official public discourse; they dispute the predominant Zionist/Orientalist regime of truth: *Why are we what you are telling us that we are (misguided, supporters of terrorism, self-hating Jews, etc.)? Why are you telling us that NHI in Gaza and the West Bank?*

We cannot, must not, allow Israel to get away with genocide. The student protests and encampments for Gaza have been an ethically courageous and bold attempt to do just that.[228] They objected to Israeli warfare and were met with American lawfare. There can be no return to October 6, to business as usual, with the Occupation on the back burner. The annihilation of Gaza discloses what Didier Fassin names "an enormous gulf in the global moral order,"[229] an unsuturable gash in the global social fabric, an antagonism that can no longer be contained, denied, or pushed to the side. Only anti-colonial reason, in its unabashed universalist aspirations, offers a transformative political response to the Palestinian question. It returns us to the material socioeconomic conditions of Israel's settler colony, to the conditions underpinning Palestinian abjection. It jams the Zionist/Western gaze. It rebukes the racist settler state along with its imperialist Western enablers.

Black and Palestinian problems are a problem of being. The West has damned their being, banishing Blacks and Palestinians to the dreadful—and ambivalent—zone of nonbeing. We know that the white racist solution to the Black problem is disenfranchisement and abandonment, the incarceration of Blacks—*forget about the Black question, NHI*. We know that the Zionist solution to the Palestinian problem is ethnic cleansing and genocide, the destruction of Palestinians—*forget about the Palestinian question, NHI*. For the anti-colonial Left, the problem sends us back to settler colonialism and its racial matrix of the human, and the solution to it lies in abolishing Man and reinventing the human. Under Zionist coloniality, Palestinians are "made into the physical referent of the idea of the irrational/subrational Human Other."[230] There is no unsettling of the Zionist paradigm "without a redescription of the human."[231] Exiting the zone of nonbeing, and thus daring to think the unthinkable (humans *are* involved), means scrambling the building blocks of an anti-Black world and upending the settler order of things or it means nothing at all.

The chapters that follow stage the entanglement of being Black and being Palestinian in a world where white and Zionist gazes construct us as less than human, rendering us problems to be summarily subdued or eliminated by whatever means necessary. To exist as Black and Palestinian is to exist as a problem: we refuse to go away; we refuse to sacrifice our comrades in struggle for the liberal promise of inclusion in a rotten global system whose moral bankruptcy has only made its defenders and beneficiaries all the more ferocious and predatory.

In Chapter 1, "Anatomy of the Human," I take up the challenges of thinking anew and otherwise the "human" of humanism. My inspiration comes from Fanon, who sets up the two concepts in the opening pages of *Black Skin, White Masks*. Fanon claims that his book aims for a "New Humanism," but he also ascertains that the Black subject is *not* a human being (and thus not truly a subject), that the racialized object of Western modernity dwells in or rather is relegated to the zone of nonbeing. And, understandably, this is a moment dear to the Afropessimists: a disclosure of the fundamental racial matrix of the human. Fanon's vision of a new humanism seems to lose all credibility when Black being is revealed to be irremediably outside the family of human beings. What kind of resistance follows from this insight? Can any resistance follow? For the Afropessimists, the future for Blacks is bleak. I take this skeptical pessimism for the human in a different direction. Like the Afropessimists, I reject optimism, understood as a liberal orientation invested in reform and/as progress. I contend that the opposite of pessimism is not optimism but a critical pessimism. It is a pessimism that operates within and beyond the Afropessimist analytic. The pessimism that I'm envisioning here opposes anti-Blackness and settler coloniality in the same breath. It strikes at humanist grammar, foregrounding what Žižek names the "inhuman core of being-human," and the racial matrix of the human that underpins it. And for this reason, it is a universalist pessimism, devoid of separatist ambitions and *open to all*, that interrogates the paradigm of the Human, that demands justice for the living and the dead. The latter is intrinsic to the reconfiguring of the former: the living Human. As activists and scholars, we are interpellated "to defend the dead," a saying Christina Sharpe borrows from NourbeSe Philip's poem "Zong #15" in her bold articulation of Black Studies. Lingering on the dead—the problems of the past and recent past—is indissociable from the labor of *ressentimental* pessimism, a refusal to move on and comply with the dictates of the powerful; it entails an ontological mood, an orientation, a care, a refusal to accept that Black and Palestinian lives were never meant to appear as lives.

In Chapter 2, "The Gift of ~~Being~~ (a Problem)," I consider the pharmacotic character of the zone of nonbeing: how it functions both as a curse and a gift. Born in this hellish zone, Black and Palestinian bodies struggle to live; they tirelessly push back against the world's life-denying technologies. But, perhaps more importantly, *what disables enables*. And yet some thinkers like Fred Moten are not eager to exit the zone of nonbeing, if by exiting we mean embracing a ready-made identity, an identitarian logic that restores a phantasmatic model of being/the Human. Whiten yourself and you will become less of a problem. Lingering in the zone of nonbeing involves resisting your ontological dispossession without yearning for a murderous self-possession, without substituting sovereignty for dispossession. Against the false and forced choice between dispossession or sovereignty, between nothingness and identity, Moten implores us to entertain a different orientation toward being, preferring instead to adopt Édouard Glissant's defamiliarizing formulation, "consent not to be a single being." By consenting not be a single being, my exit from the zone of nonbeing is not premised on my election to the zone of *single* beings. Consenting not to be a single being is, in effect, consenting to be a problem. Unruly bodies do not so much question their status as a problem (why do you say that I'm problem?) as subversively identify with the world-canceling label. Motenist fugitivity meets Saidian exile. Such fugitive and exilic bodies relish the opportunity to add their name to the tradition of feminist killjoys, to make those cozy with power uneasy, to make those who dominate and silence squirm in their seat of privilege.

In Chapter 3, "Becoming Object," I explore the ineluctable demands of solidarity. Wilderson, who is generally hostile to the idea of Black-Palestinian solidarity, introduces the idea of becoming object as the (only) way to relate to, or be in relation with, Black people. As in Chapter 1, becoming object tarries with pessimism. My wager is that Black-Palestinian solidarity is a powerful antidote to a depoliticized pessimism, a pessimism consumed by one's suffering. It is a dialecticized pessimism that short-circuits its identitarian pull (the libidinal attachment to one's woundedness, functioning as a psychic compensation for being a problem insofar as the symbolic order interpellates you as a problem and yet bribes you, directs you to enjoy your identity/identity politics within the limits of liberal reason alone, within the confines of a life-draining racial system in which you are pushed to hold on to your shrinking civil rights and ignore the genocide abroad). This dialecticized pessimism opens to solidarity, shifting from "I" to "We," from "I am suspicious of you and the world" to "I am skeptical of this world and what it wants for/from us." The standard Afropessimist position—my suffering/problem is incommensurable to yours; I remain a problem so that you can work out your own problems with the state and improve your lot in society, at the expense of Blacks—does not hold. Our wretchedness binds us. Inclusivity here lacks the toothlessness of the liberal model. To act in solidarity with Blacks and Palestinians expands worlds at a time when fascist global forces rally to shrink them.

Chapter 1

Anatomy of the Human

The purchase of humanism lingers. Its grammar still finds a receptive audience; indeed, the "human" of humanism is what many on the outskirts of society yearn for. In the Western world, if you want to be included in the ranks of society's protected and privileged, your humanity must be made recognizable; you must conform or submit to the authoritative and normative white gaze. The grammar of humanism purports to be universalist, but it is racialized *ab initio*. This grammar—how humanism frames and interprets the world—is enveloped in whiteness, yet leaves this racial/colonial matrix unacknowledged. Humanism seduces the wretched of the earth—you, too, it says, can come to enjoy (your) humanity. It promises ontological plenitude, a humanity prior to the fall into history and raciality; humanism is in the business of ontological upgrades, allowing those who lack humanity, the excluded, to achieve the fullness of being human, to become included. To be fully human is to have, in Arendtian terms, "the right to have rights"; to be fully human is not to have problemhood be constitutive of your being. You never ask a full-fledged human being, *How does it feel to be a problem?* Again, human subjects may *have* problems but, in principle, they *aren't* problems. And to separate further the human from its others, human subjects are often problem detectors. We might say that there is an "inner cop" in every white human subject, policing the language, behavior, and being of blackened others, and thus policing the borders of the human.[1] So what does it mean to be included under the umbrella of humanism/whiteness/universalism? What is a racialized being to do?

On one hand, the wretched look at humanism with envy and anger. They want to be protected by its authority, but they resent humanism's unconscionable neglect of their being. On the other hand, they are pessimistic and skeptical of humanism's claim of/to the universal, the same way Edward Said objected to Europe's "blithe universalism."[2] The wretched see humanism's appeal as manipulative; they don't believe that humanism can shed its inhospitable Eurocentrism, its libidinal attachment to whiteness. In this light, we might ask, Is humanism for the non-European/colonized desirable but, because of its racial matrix, unreachable? Or is humanism itself an obstacle to liberation? Should it be seen as a pernicious paradigm that, regardless of what its apologists say, necessarily draws a line between the human and the other, divesting from some bodies in order to invest in others? Who is human to me and who is not? Which others must be ignored or sacrificed to better my humanist situation? It is safe to say that humanism comes with ideological baggage. But can we simply jettison the grammar of the human, including human rights discourse, without exponentially increasing the vulnerability of the wretched?

In this chapter, I want first to think these urgent and disquieting questions through the meditations on humanism that Frantz Fanon opens up. On the first page of *Black Skin, White Masks*, Fanon claims that his book aims for a "New Humanism," but on the next he also notes that the Black subject is *not* a human being, that the racialized subject of Western modernity is consigned to the zone of nonbeing. Fanon's vision of a new humanism sets the stage for a dialectical critique informed by a relentless pessimism. It involves a radical dislocation and a libidinal rewriting of the category of the human itself: a new humanism that grapples with the racial matrix of the human. This new vision questions a European humanism that posits the bourgeois, white, male subject as the measure of all things. Or to put it slightly differently, Fanon's new humanism—this humanism *à venir*—radically breaks with a humanist tradition that both disavows the role of race in imagining the human and makes racialized others constitutive of its definition of the *white* human. What comes after the white human? Is it the human minus whiteness, a human truly purified of its ontical qualifications and markers (genre, race, etc.)? Answering yes to this last question might be tempting (it would reflect a commitment to Black humanism and the quest to reform humanism's legacy), yet to do so would be to miss the ambivalence and depth of Fanon's critique. Whiteness and humanity are inextricably tied. Black humanism and other versions of humanism do not register fully the ontological impact of whiteness on our idea of the "human." That the human subject of humanism might very well be unsalvageable is something that we have to seriously consider. But this pessimistic assessment may not be a setback in our moral aggrandizement; rather, it could serve as an opportunity for invention. As Fanon taught us, an invention worthy of its name introduces something that deroutinizes our quotidian lives. Invention, the "real leap," emerges only via a full reckoning with humanism and its racial grammar/matrix.[3]

Needless to say, this reckoning begins with the zone of nonbeing. Who or what dwells in this site where ontological deprivation and upheavals (can) happen? Being can be read in at least two ways: a barred being stands for a human being whose humanity has been suspended or metaphysically destroyed; this is how Frank Wilderson describes the becoming Black of Africans when he asserts, "Africans went into the ships and came out as Blacks."[4] From the standpoint of humanism, ~~Africans~~ (Blacks) are no longer classifiable as human. Contrarily, a barred being can gesture to an otherwise of the human, to a human no longer explainable or rescuable by the existing humanist grammar. It is this otherwise than human, the ~~being~~ of the zone of nonbeing, that I have in mind in speaking of the posthuman. When I use "post," I also want to complicate but not necessarily reject the idea that "*post-*" means "after" in the sense that what comes after has moved beyond what came before, intimating a jagged break with the metaphysical Human of humanism. Musing on the postmodern, Jean-François Lyotard famously warns against thinking of the "*post-*" exclusively in terms of an unsullied progression of events, or conversely as a reiteration of the same phenomenon in a new facade.[5] A posthuman Fanon, if there is such a thing, emerges through a critical undoing of the ontological divide between the human and the not-quite-human/nonhuman. For me, the idea of a posthuman Fanon recalls Slavoj Žižek's notion of the "inhuman core of being-human"[6]; both, we might say, are disclosed in and produced by the zone of nonbeing. Not unlike Fanon, Žižek is invested in a universalist philosophy that comes to terms with the human subject, abandoning the glorious humanist vision of a mega-actant for an unsettling, divided subject. The posthuman names the subject's monstrous core, the human after its radical degentrification—after its exposure to the Real, after its banishment into to the zone of nonbeing.

Putting these thinkers in dialogue brings into focus the politics that emerge from a critical scrutiny of the human and humanism. Fanon and Žižek, in my reading, come to their similar assessment from two radically different positions— *by different means we arrive at the same end*. And yet the different steps they take tell us something important about how to combat a humanism that continues to function as an oppressive paradigm, fostering a "cruel optimism"[7] for those wretched beings—Blacks, Palestinians, among numerous others—who think a recognition of their humanity can rescue them, or at least protect them, from danger and annihilation. Humanism and humanity operate as if they were interchangeable. A recognition of the other's humanity becomes the precondition for a civil relation, an end to hostility. We are the same. We can remember one of the signs by BLM activists stating in plain language, "We are human too." Similar formulations also proliferated in the many pro-Palestinian protests against Israel's war on Gaza.

It is hard to object to any protester's desire to be recognized as human amid a new Jim Crow and Israel's normalization of genocide. I fully sympathize with the impulse to counter an anti-Blackness and anti-Palestinian racism that insidiously infiltrates much of our public discourse about Blacks and Palestinians. Yet I think the appeal to the human—to the transcendental subject—cannot stand on its own. The human has a checkered history, traversed by chattel slavery and settler colonialism, forged in its murderous encounters with who or what it deemed outside its zone of interest or being. The (white, male, Christian, able-bodied) human, in its evocation and deployment, has not existed without the denigrated others—*others as problems*—through which it is defined: the not-quite-human, the nonhuman, the animal, the non-European, the Oriental, the enslaved, the Native, the feminine, the Jew, the Muslim, and so on. We must attend carefully to this past if we are to elaborate a new humanism, or posthumanism, capable of making the inventive leap required for justice.

Humanism's Liberal Politics

Humanism promotes the human, and by extension human rights. It casts dehumanization as the problem, and humanization as the cure. Humanization purports to return you to humanity, to your given nature as human. Fanon and Žižek are not completely hostile to the effort to defend the ostracized and demonized by recognizing their humanity when such recognition entails an acknowledgment of the others' complexity, which, in turn, means that their being cannot be abstracted or reduced to their race, religion, or countries' actions, for instance. Žižek signed his name, for example, to a letter calling for restraint and vigilance in the ways we talk about others/enemies in the context of Israel's genocidal retaliation to Hamas's unprecedented attack. The signatories describe themselves as "proponents of human rights," as belonging to the "Pro-Human Camp."[8] They reasonably state: "The dehumanization of Israelis and Jews, as well as Palestinians and Muslims, is unacceptable. A person is not merely a representation of a collective identity, history, events, or political orientation. A consistent humanistic approach must address all these unacceptable developments." Fanon equally has no patience with abstraction, be it to demonize or idealize others: "We shall show no pity for the former colonial governors or missionaries. In our view, an individual who loves Blacks is as 'sick' as someone who abhors them. Conversely, the black man who strives to whiten his race is as wretched as the one who preaches hatred of the white man. The black man is no more inherently amiable than the Czech; the truth is that we must unleash the man [*lâcher l'homme*]."[9] "Unleash the human" is arguably Fanon's *cri de guerre*. Žižek puts his own universalist spin on the feminist slogan, "Women's rights are human rights": "The greatness of modern feminism [is] not just we women want more. It's we women want to redefine the very universality of what it means to be human. This is for me this modern notion of political struggle."[10] At the end of *The Wretched of the Earth*, Fanon again evokes the idea of a "new human."[11]

And yet both Fanon and Žižek reject identitarian projects, which tame or disavow the most unsettling aspects of being-human, in favor of universalist projects that harness the paradoxes of nonbeing in being, of an inhuman constitutive of the human, *what is in the human more than human*. Some of Fanon's readers may object that I'm underestimating his investment in humanism, as manifested in his concern for the ways we ought to treat each other. In Fanon's words: "I find myself one day in the world, and I acknowledge one right for myself: the right to demand human behavior from the other [*exiger de l'autre un comportement humain*]."[12] The right to be treated humanly and humanely by the other is Fanon's assertion and defense of his humanity, his insistence that he is not to be instrumentalized, abstracted as an object, or reduced to the function of a tool. Or in Kantian terms, he asks to be treated as an end and not merely as a means. A "consistent humanistic approach" precisely requires treating every human as a human being. The scandal of course is that we don't. The letter from the Pro-Human Camp calls on us to do so, but it is unmistakably tinged with bothsidesism. It is as if both sides are demonizing or racializing the other in the same way and to the same effect, as if the humanity of Israelis and the humanity of Palestinians are equally in danger. To be a Jewish Israeli today and remain silent when your government is slaughtering Palestinians next door is *not* beyond reproach. You're not being reduced to your nation's will but judged on your (in)actions. The charge of complicity with genocide and ethnic cleansing is *not* about the dehumanization of Jewish Israelis, it is a call for their moral responsibility—for a reckoning with Zionism, Israel's dominant racist ideology. An uncritical humanistic approach risks collapsing anti-Zionism into anti-Semitism. To put it bluntly, the letter removes the Western racial matrix from the equation, ignoring that Palestinians begin from a place of exclusion and negation, that they are always already subjugated to a racializing colonial/Zionist/white gaze that not only silences them but casts and frames them as dangerous, violent, and deceitful: *Palestinians, and their supporters, claim that they're anti-Zionists, fighting against Palestinian racism, but, in reality, they're anti-Semitic (yet more evidence of our vile nature).*

There is no doubt that anti-Semitism has wreaked havoc on the Jewish people from the blood libels of medieval times to our contemporary period. The racialization of the Jews reached its most severe form and expression in Auschwitz, and the creation of Israel was, in large part, a measure to assuage Western guilt. Israeli Jews became white (again), secured "whiteness by permission,"[13] once the Western world accepted Israel's geopolitical position (and endorsed its self-description as the "villa in the jungle."[14] A Zionist Israel, a "European pawn," as James Baldwin described it, spoke the racist language of European colonialism, mirroring a familiar image to the West.[15] The redemptive force of Israel's birth (Jews got their humanity/whiteness back after it was brutally suspended by the Third Reich) covered over Israel's settler-colonial DNA. "Exterminate the brutes,"[16] the colonizer's racist imperative to dispossess and quash unruly Natives (i.e., any Native who refuses to surrender or disappear), is as operative in Israel's genocidal campaign in Gaza as it was in Israel's founding in 1948 and even in the Zionist colonization of Palestine in the late nineteenth century.[17] In this light, I ask, can the Pro-Human Camp truly accommodate

Palestinian being without wrestling with the West's oppressive racial matrix of the human?

Under a humanistic horizon, the currency of the human remains quite high; to be human is to have one's life constitutively matter. But this humanity has been systematically denied to the wretched, or the blackened beings of modernity— whence the indefatigable cry "Black Lives Matter." Its racist counter, "All Lives Matters," rings hollow. Why? Its humanistic credential lacks credibility. You say universalism; I see in your actions only particularism. In principle, all lives do in fact matter, but the problem is that all things are precisely not equal; the historical configuration of power regimes impacts the allocation of value, which some possess, and others don't.[18] Racism is at the heart of the imbalance of social justice. The chant names a structural problem, or rather an *ontological* problem that inhibits Black humanity from being acknowledged. We're seeing a similar struggle at play in the genocidal Gaza war. Talks of Palestinian humanity disconcert a large swath of Zionists and pro-Israel supporters. With humanity comes rights—let's keep in mind Mahmoud Khalil's pointed question, "Who has the right to have rights?" Adi Callai's observation hits the mark: "The most radical position comes directly from the simplest question: are Palestinians human beings? If your answer is emphatically yes, unambiguously and without reservations, then you are a lost cause to Zionism. Because if Palestinians are human beings, then their self-defense is legitimate, and the defense of their continued existence is necessary."[19] Whenever self-defense is evoked when talking about Palestine/Israel it is always Israel's self-defense that is touted as self-evident.[20] For the West, Israeli humanity is indubitable while Palestinian humanity lingers as a problem, as a question—*How human is that other?*

But what kind of problem/question are the Palestinians? Recognition of Palestinian humanity/suffering does not necessarily open to supporting their self-defense, their anti-colonial resistance, that is, their revolutionary armed struggle. Humanitarian reason, compounded by the liberal fetish of nonviolence, blocks and crowds out anti-colonial reason. The liberal subject can be "woke" but he does not want to endorse any form of violence or upheaval to the established order of things—this goes for the Boycott, Divestment, and Sanction (BDS) movement as well, insofar as it moves to delegitimize Israel, disclosing its operations as that of a murderous, illiberal state. The liberal big Other tolerates a degree of dissidence but carves out an exception for Palestine. The expression of pro-Palestine camp cannot make people uncomfortable; and, of course, it is the pro-Israel crowd who gets to decide the boundaries of the comfortable, to declare pro-Palestinian supporters anti-Semitic: *Zionist identity must be protected.* Free speech is universal except when agitating for Palestinian liberation. Whereas the Palestine exception is meant to halt pro-Palestinian support, "the Israel exception"[21] shields the genocidal state, accelerating Palestinian annihilation. Only against this gloomy background can the liberal subject "support" Palestinians (believing that Palestinian children shouldn't be starved or bombed) while leaving settler-colonial realities and their ontological partitions of Palestine/Israel unquestioned.

At one level, recognizing Palestinian suffering is not a negligible gain, for to consider Palestinians as victims is better than invisibilizing them through indifference or epistemic violence, of the kind effortlessly generated by a post-9/11, Orientalist vision of their being as religiously fundamentalist, irrational, violent, and intrinsically anti-Semitic. If indifference might translate as an affective divestment from Palestinian being/humanity, willful misrepresentation certainly condemns Palestinians to social death, to the zone of nonbeing, where they await their biological death. Zionist discourse about Palestinians is first and foremost a racist one. And here, following Toni Morrison, we should understand that racist discourse's full ontological impact:

> Oppressive language does more than represent violence; it is violence; does more than represent the limits of knowledge; it limits knowledge. Whether it is obscuring state language or the faux-language of mindless media; whether it is the proud but calcified language of the academy or the commodity driven language of science; whether it is the malign language of law-without-ethics, or language designed for the estrangement of minorities, hiding its racist plunder in its literary cheek—it must be rejected, altered and exposed. It is the language that drinks blood, laps vulnerabilities, tucks its fascist boots under crinolines of respectability and patriotism as it moves relentlessly toward the bottom line and the bottomed-out mind. Sexist language, racist language, theistic language—all are typical of the policing languages of mastery, and cannot, do not permit new knowledge or encourage the mutual exchange of ideas.[22]

Echoing Žižek's hysterical demand for "new knowledge," Morrison locates the challenge to its arrival or realization in a fascist rhetoric of control and domination, a description of oppressive language that naturalizes and mystifies, closely resembling the operations of Zionist discourse. Morrison's "faux-language of mindless media" meets Omar El Akkad's "unmaking of meaning." The objective of such language is to actively hinder or undo knowledge of Palestinians (they don't exist, and if they do exist, they're terrorists) stems from an expansionist and eliminationist logic. Since October 7, after Hamas's attack in Southern Israel, a clear "philosemitic McCarthyism,"[23] underwritten by a Zionist hermeneutic, is enjoying policing activists, students, faculty, or any conscientious person (and, again, many of them Jews) invested in justice and a desire to understand the plight of the Palestinian people. Zionist discourse, along with the amplification of its message via Western news outlets (the perfect example of "the faux-language of mindless media"), has irresponsibly generated a consent for genocide, enabled by the systematic dehumanization and animalization of Palestinians.

Recall what former Israeli defense minister Yoav Gallant infamously said: "I have ordered a complete siege on the Gaza Strip. There will be no electricity, no food, no fuel, everything will be closed. We are fighting human animals and we act accordingly."[24] In case you're tempted to say that Gallant was talking only about Hamas fighters, recall that nearly 70 percent of the dead in Gaza are women and children. Gallant stands as one the architects of the Palestinian genocide. Israel's war is not a war against Hamas, but primarily a war against the Palestinian people, because for Zionists there is really no difference between the two—they're all terrorists by virtue of their failure to cede their homeland, submit to Zionist reason, and accept their own displacement and erasure. The criminality of Zionist discourse is of course matched by Israel's military brutality, its sadistic hunger for collective punishment. "No Hamastan," Netanyahu's language, means no Palestinians in Gaza.[25]

Acknowledging Palestinian victimhood is anathema to Zionist discourse. Victimhood names a Palestinian suffering and also implies an injustice—which *might* spark a desire to see beyond the haze of Zionist *hasbara* (propaganda). Victimhood is better than problemhood, right? The liberal center, of course, tries to differentiate its position from that of Ziofascists[26] like Israeli cabinet members Itamar Ben-Gvir and Bezalel Smotrich who sadistically celebrate Palestinian destruction and constantly call for more annexation of Palestinian land. White liberals worry about the rise of anti-Semitism, so they are careful to cast their support of Palestinians only along the lines of humanitarian needs. Palestinian babies should not die from hypothermia,[27] but Hamas must be condemned, cannot be defended; the more "radical" will also say that Netanyahu must go. But if liberals may consider Palestinians as victims, they are also quick to point the finger at Palestinians (Hamas) for the misery of Gazans. For the more "radical" liberals, who want to separate themselves from the abysmal American administrations, both Palestinian and Israeli leadership are to blame—*a curse on both your houses* type of reasoning. Indeed, they are proud of their nuanced and measured reasoning. However, the liberal position, in whatever shade you prefer, disappoints. Recognition of Palestinian being becomes contingent on the likelihood of liberal empathy. As I mentioned in the introduction, this human emotion remains a double-edged sword for Palestinians and their supporters. On the one hand, empathetic liberals acknowledge Palestinian suffering. The call for empathy—Palestinians saying, "We are human too"; their supporters saying, "They are human too"—has clearly made headway in public opinion (despite an aggressive anti-Palestinian corporate media). On the other hand, empathy feeds a cruel optimism. I believe that it has reached a plateau. People across the world did march in protest of Israel's Gaza genocide, and many of them were moved by empathy. Still, we cannot forget that empathy by itself doesn't open to a confrontation with Israel's settler-colonial apartheid. It acquiesces too quickly to the demands of humanitarian reason. Worse, it depoliticizes the struggle of the Palestinians, failing to grasp the racial antagonism at the heart of Israel's genocidal enterprise. Being horrified by the suffering of Palestinians at the hands of a vicious Israeli military doesn't make you, in and of itself, committed to the Palestinian struggle for liberation. And this is what Palestinians need; this is the only thing capable of altering the coordinates of the debate. *I should say that this not a far-fetched ask; the West does it effortlessly in its support of Ukrainian resistance to another bullying nuclear power.*

The alternative to both Ziofascists and the liberal center lies in liberating Palestinian existence from the prison house of both Zionist reason and humanitarian reason so that "the mutual exchange of ideas" can take place, to recall Toni Morrison's words. And so, adapting Freud's formulation, we ask, *What does a Palestinian want?* Elias Sanbar's 1982 interview with Gilles Deleuze, pointedly titled "The Indians of Palestine," is a good place to start. Sanbar, editor of the then new journal *La Revue d'Études Palestiniennes*, expresses the Palestinian dilemma of being determined from without, abstracted by an oppressive Zionist-Western-white gaze that demonizes all forms of Palestinian resistance, and by a debilitating humanitarian gaze that can only detect Palestinian passivity and abjection. The Western script was and continues to be incapable of translating the plight of Palestinians as a problem of dispossession and liberation. Palestinian "humanity" is still only decipherable in the limited and limiting language of refugees. Western powers display a stubborn unwillingness to see Palestinians as "a dispossessed people in need of a political solution."[28] If Palestinians dare to challenge their interpellation as passive victims, and exercise agential control over their situation as would any people protecting their land from invaders, they are automatically tagged as terrorists, illegitimate interlocutors, subjected to extrajudicial murder. Against the images of refugees or militarists, Sanbar pushes "the image of the Palestinian combatant"[29] who struggles to gain visibility, and who participates in a political project. As he clarifies, "before we imposed the reality of our presence, we were thought of only as refugees. When our resistance movement made clear that our struggle could not be ignored, we were again reduced to a cliched image: we were seen as pure and simple militarists. This image was isolated and reproduced ad infinitum. We were perceived as standing for nothing else. It is to rid ourselves of the militarist image in the strict sense, that we prefer this other image of the combatant."[30] In a psychoanalytic register, George Yancy explains that "the imago of the 'Dirty Arab' or the 'Palestinian terrorist' is what takes visual precedence over the Arab/Palestinian as human, as possessing dignity and infinite value."[31] More a projection than a representation, the imago of the menacing Palestinian, or its debilitated counterpart, infiltrates the white collective psyche. The abject Gazan and the Hamas terrorist, images that tirelessly circulate in our contemporary collective unconscious and libidinal economy, continue to constrain, stifle, and distort our knowledge of Palestinians, obscuring their state and struggle for liberation.

What does a Palestinian want? Calling for and securing a ceasefire are initial steps. But let's not forget that the liberation of the Palestinian people is the fundamental goal of the resistance, not bare life. Our long-term struggle is against Israel's colonial apartheid regime and its powerful imperialist enablers. How many liberals will follow Palestinians toward that end? Who will push back against Israel's expansionist logic? Who will demand accountability for Israel's crimes? Not unlike the weaponization of the charge of anti-Semitism, that of terrorism effectively distracts and silences pro-Palestinian voices. As Pranay Somayajula elaborates:

> To invoke the word "terrorism," within the conventional bounds of liberal discourse, is to bring the debate to a screeching halt—we can argue back and forth as much as we like over the question of whether this or that military operation was carried out in the right manner, adhering to the proper rules and protocols of legitimate warfare, but when terrorism enters the discussion, there can be no equivocation. There is no spectrum of acceptable opinions, no room for reasonable disagreement when it comes to terrorism. There are only two sides—those who are with the terrorists, and those who are against them.[32]

"Israel cannot negotiate with terrorists" is a familiar refrain. Evoking terrorism shuts down any critical engagement with the Palestinian question and delegitimizes in advance our defense of the Palestinian cause—turning the cause into a problem to be judged with absolute prejudice. To appear legible and decriminalized under a liberal Western gaze, we must perform worthiness by distancing ourselves not only from Hamas, but from any form of resistance (such as BDS). Our Palestinianness (terrorism) must be drained out of our being. Success in this liberal (Zionist-sanctioned) framework means that the perfect victim is ultimately the perfect dead victim—our life is potentially grievable only when we die and our innocence can be retroactively assured. A living Palestinian stands for a Palestinian terrorist in waiting.[33]

Conversely, there is no space afforded to Israeli state terrorism. Not unlike American state-sanctioned violence, this phrase is never uttered in public discourse; it is not permitted under the hegemonic liberal order (and even less so in the echo chambers of the far Right—where Israel's militarized law and order ethos is aspirational, an object of envy for the alt-Right in the United States). *Liberal states don't terrorize, and do not lock people up without just cause,* goes the story; *they maintain order.* What remains unsaid but understood is the corollary that flows from this: *liberal states enforce the racial (and racist) status quo. Keep this in mind and stay in line if you do not want to be considered a problem.*

In the white political imaginary, the two images of victim and terrorist seemingly exhaust what being Palestinian *is and can be.* For this reason, the countervailing notion of a combatant holds promise for contesting and thinking anew and otherwise the question of Palestinian humanity, or the question of humanity as such, not because Palestinians hold some special place in the order of beings; unlike the Zionist claim to Jewish exceptionality (we are unlike other people, we are the Chosen People, etc.), Palestinian combatants earnestly present Palestinians as "a people like any other people."[34] I want to linger on the universality of this Palestinian observation, and on the ways this humanity is itself ontologically impacted by settler colonialism. In other words, what does "humanity" look like from the standpoint of the inhabitants of the zone of nonbeing, from the perspective of the wretched? What kind of people are the Palestinians?

Read through a Fanonian lens, "a people like any other people" could be rewritten as "a wretched people like any other wretched people." Here a contrast with Emmanuel Levinas might be illustrative. Levinas, too, ties humanity to wretchedness, to the traumatic experience of Jewish enslavement: "The traumatic experience of my slavery in Egypt constitutes my very humanity, a fact that immediately allies me to the workers, the wretched, and the persecuted people of the world."[35] He also couples Jewish exceptionalism with the evils of the Shoah, registered in his dedication of *Otherwise than Being* "to the memory of those who were closest among the six million assassinated by the National Socialists, and of the millions on millions of all confessions and all nations, victims of the same hatred of the other man, the same anti-Semitism."[36] Anti-Semitism emerges as the master-code, covering all hatred and racist violence. In their rarity and singularity, the Jewish people come to stand for pure human vulnerability: they are (rendered) the timeless Victim. No one can match, let alone exceed, the imago of the Jewish victim. Under this Zionist horizon, everyone else is an imperfect copy of the ontologized form of (Jewish) wretchedness, never having fully experienced the uniqueness of their suffering: "We are *not* a wretched people like any other people." "Never Again" applies exclusively to Jews. Adding "for Everyone" to "Never Again" relativizes the trauma of the Shoah—and thus merits the charge of anti-Semitism.

The example of Palestinian wretchedness follows a different logic; it displays what Žižek calls a materialist use of examples, a form of exemplarity that contrasts with an idealist use, which I take Levinas's Jewish example to illustrate. According to the idealist approach, "examples are always imperfect, they never perfectly render what they are supposed to exemplify, so that we should take care not to take them too literally"; but "for a materialist," by contrast, "there is always more in the example than in what it exemplifies: that is, an example always threatens to undermine what it is supposed to exemplify since it gives body to what the exemplified notion itself represses, is unable to cope with."[37] To return to the relation between humanity, wretchedness, and peoplehood, my reformulation of Sanbar's observation, "a wretched people like any other wretched people," can be reread as exerting pressure on the notion of humanity that it is supposedly meant to exemplify ("we are a people like any other people"); in the process of exemplifying wretched peoplehood it exposes humanity to its metaphysical other (~~being~~), to what humanists repress or disavow, to what the paradigm of the human is unable or unwilling to confront (that the human needs its constitutive other to exist). There is thus always more in the exemplarity of Palestinian humanity or peoplehood; their wretchedness unsettles our understanding of the positive, self-contained human.

Wretchedness names the state and condition of the historically damned, subjects expelled from the zone of interest, or subjects that simply never belonged to the zone of being. Their affliction transforms their being (human), deforms their relation to themselves, others, and the world; their dignity turns to humiliation, and their aspirations to dead-ends. An ontological abyss separates the wretched from the human. Here a liberal humanist would work to close the gap dividing the wretched from the human: what the wretched of the world need is more empathy, more humanization. But what if the problem wasn't so much with being wretched as with being human? I want to ask, *What does it take to be or become human? What logic or matrix guarantees and produces the human? And, finally, what are the costs of this human-making to racialized beings, deemed not-quite-human or nonhuman?*

Humanism's Others

When Fanon speaks about Blackness and humanity, he is not meditating on what it means to be a Black human, as if he were merely translating existentialism for an anti-racist struggle, forging a Black existentialism to fight against anti-Blackness. We should keep front and center that for Fanon, the Black human is a barred Black ~~human~~ (barred *because* Black). As per the Afropessimist account of Fanon, the emergence of the "Human" can only be secured at the expense of Black people—"the Human Other is Black."[38] Legally or formally speaking, you might be ontically free, but ontologically you remain a slave. Blackness denotes slaveness. This is the insidious logic underwriting the "afterlife of slavery," which turns anti-Blackness into the naturalized background of everyday human existence. Anti-Blackness is part and parcel of America's founding violence. The policing of Black bodies—the law's preserving violence in its everydayness— prolongs America's racist core.

The human and the Black are caught up in a non-dialectical logic. For Blacks to live, the human must die. That is to say, the reign of the white human must come to an end. But the classical posthumanist move of abandoning the human by recentering the presence of nonhuman actants affecting our lives and the world will not do. Talks of flat ontology move too quickly from the demise of the human to nonhumans, and obscure rather than elucidate the problem of being Black.[39] And in this respect, I share the Afropessimist reticence or suspicion of posthumanism, though I depart from the Afropessimist reading by de-ontologizing and re-historicizing the zone of nonbeing and making it speak more expansively to Fanon's wretched of the earth—to those on the receiving end of colonial or supremacist violence and erasure. I want to think through the historico-ontological dimensions of the problem of wretchedness by considering Fanon's notion of the zone of nonbeing alongside the colonized figure of the Palestinian. With the Gaza War, we're witnessing a "return" to colonial cruelty, to the ideology of *might makes right*. The racial matrix of the human gives Israel and other Western nations cover: *we're the humans and they are the brutes. And brutes must be exterminated*. With Operation Iron Swords, we're also witnessing an ontological definition and enactment of genocide: the IOF is starving, maiming, and massacring Palestinians and driving that collective body into the Fanonian zone of nonbeing. In short, we're dealing with what can be described as "Palestinocide."

What facilitates Palestinocide is an ideological narrative and logic that aggressively defaces Palestinians, that removes the face of the Palestinians to clear the path for a full necropolitics. A Levinasian-inspired humanism here would plead for an undoing of the racist relation of comprehension and a return to the face of the Palestinians (something that Levinas himself avoided in his infamous interview after the 1982 Sabra and Shatila massacres in West Beirut, Lebanon—the Palestinian ~~autrui~~ never manages to disarm Levinas, to trouble his Zionism). Philosophically speaking, the irreducible face is what is proper to the human. It passively labors against the economy of the Same. But for the wretched, the face is suspended; there is no face to trigger infinite responsibility nor unconditional hospitality. Facelessness is constitutive of being wretched. In this vertical partition, they are effectively inferior to the human. We can map the wretched onto the human/nonhuman, or the human/posthuman, divide. One thing is clear: the wretched are cast outside the humanist order of things. They are historical creatures, and yet the wretched's relation to the zone of nonbeing is marked by a quasi-permanence. In principle, the zone of nonbeing is an ontological reset; *it enables as it disables*. The destruction of your social ego liberates you by opening up the possibility of a radical refashioning of the symbolic self. The way down is the way up. To this life-affirming existentialist insight, Fanon adds a substantial caveat. There are systemic social forces—the white/settler gaze, a racist symbolic order—holding the wretched back/down. You are a wretched being if you cannot take advantage of this descent into a veritable hell. That is to say, wretchedness gains ontological rigidity when human consciousness stalls after the dissolution of the ego, when transcendence fails to surge. Social death, the zombification of life, characterizes the condition of the wretched. The wretched are never seen or treated as humans. Their disposability becomes a predicate of their being. The zone of nonbeing all but guarantees their damnation and termination. And it is hard to imagine today a starker image of this unlivable zone of nonbeing than the Gaza Strip.

Though this is the first livestreamed genocide, Western leaders have systematically failed to put an end to Israel's far-ranging criminality, have failed to treat Palestinians as fellow humans of a planetary order, as possessing livable and grievable lives. Within the ideological paradigm of humanism, Palestinians are either treated as nonhumans targeted by the Israeli killing machine for early elimination, or envisaged by a segment of the liberal West as not-quite-humans, degraded humans, colonized victims, in desperate need of humanitarian aid. After nearly two years of slaughter, countries across the Global North (including Australia, Canada, France, and the UK) are bestirring themselves and beginning to situate themselves *rhetorically* against genocide. EU Foreign Policy Chief Kaja Kallas articulates this "shifting" attitude: "All options remain on the table if Israel doesn't deliver on its pledges [of increase humanitarian aid]."[40] But what are we really witnessing here? Whereas there is a consensus among genocide studies scholars that Israel is committing genocide in Gaza, the consensus Western leaders are coming to is that there is a need to *contemplate* change. Palestinian starvation and the sadistic practices of the IOF are in plain sight. The response: the "bold" statement that "all options remain on the table" if Israel doesn't abide by international law. Western nations are embarrassed. They have backed a genocidal campaign whose executioner is acting too brutishly, making it difficult to remain silent. Of course, the EU and others are too shy about using the word "genocide" since it would open them up to the charge of anti-Semitism and make them "junior partners" in this crime of crimes. In this light, the claim "all options remain on the table" can only appear as pure ideology; it is as credible as Joe Biden's disastrous "Rafah redline"—which Israel gleefully crossed without any consequences. What needs to be done is *not* a mystery. Options are crystal clear: seize the wanted war criminal Netanyahu whenever the occasion presents itself (close air space to all genocidaires), stop arming the genocidal state, and impose suffocating sanctions on Israel so that it conforms with international law. Actions have consequences.

A more critical reframing of Palestinians and the colonial situation reorients us back to the zone of nonbeing and to the ontological upheavals that it is both capable and incapable of producing. For Fanon, a metaphysical architecture divides the (neo)colonial world: "Looking at the immediacies of the colonial context, it is clear that what divides this world is first and foremost what species, what race one belongs to."[41] Zionist settlers are one kind of species who dwell comfortably in the zone of *being* whereas the Indigenous Palestinians are another, banished to the zone of *nonbeing*. Zionism's "fascist ontology,"[42] to borrow Nicole Simek's apt formulation, sets the stage for Palestinocide. It erects a hierarchical order and segregates the humans from the human animals, those who matter from those who don't. Gabriel Winant underscores the ways in which Zionism translates grief for Jewish life into Zionist power.[43] Under a Zionist horizon of law and order, the Jewish Israelis who died are, according to Winant, "pre-grieved," the meaning of their deaths overdetermined and weaponized, conscripted into justifications for Palestinocide: *mourn our dead and exterminate the brutes.*

Zionism rehumanizes and whitens Jews by dehumanizing and blackening Arabs. Zionist discourse uses the Hamas attack to remind Israeli citizens and the world at large of Jewish vulnerability, reinscribing the figure of the Jew as the timeless and irreproachable Victim and, obscenely, turns the incessant work of mourning into a righteous genocidal campaign. Against the "human animals" next door, Zionists define themselves as full-fledged humans, the gatekeepers of civilization. The US political class acquiesces with Israel's assessment. In keeping with this distorted and distorting Orientalist/racist narrative, Israel's sympathizers describe the Hamas attack of October 7 not as anti-colonial armed resistance to a brutal occupation (justified or not) but more metaphysically as a "breach of civilization"[44] (this is also how European academics in Holocaust Studies typically describe the Shoah, but not chattel slavery or colonialism). This reading green-lights, as it were, the colonizers' response: genocide as a form of ethico-ontological repair. Israel's "right to self-defense" means a defense of civilization and by extension a defense of humanity and its grammar.

Fanon, not unlike Césaire, has no truck with such a European humanism that elevates Jewish victimization but ignores the suffering of the wretched. He puts the matters starkly: "[Jews] have been hunted, exterminated, and cremated, but these are just minor episodes in the family history. The Jew is not liked as soon as he has been detected. But with me things take on a *new* face."[45] This passage crystalizes the Afropessimist position. Though horrifying, this series of "minor episodes in the family history" does not mark an ontological rupture with the human (humanism as the metaphysical family of humans) but chattel slavery does.

What follows from Fanon's ruthless critique? Where does his critique lead and leave us? In denouncing the fakeness of humanist ideology is Fanon jettisoning altogether the categories of the human and humanism? Calvin Warren thinks so. The zone of nonbeing introduces a new type of nonbeing being: "This zone is a spatiotemporality without a recognizable name or grammar within the philosophical tradition. The problem of black ~~being~~ is precisely the inhabitation of an execrated condition. This is the new ontology that modernity brings into the world—a being that is not one (available equipment in the guise of human form)."[46] The metaphysical mutation of Africans into Blacks, of humans into sentient tools, speaking objects, for the purposes of fueling humanity's modernity, bears all the marks of humanism. How could this murderous tradition ever help Black folks?

Still, Fanon never stops here. He does not concede the "human" to Western humanism and other axiological frameworks. Fanon remains invested in the human, attached to the image of a "new human." Fanon's desire for "the founding of another humanity" and his laboring for "the flourishing of man and for the enrichment of humanity"[47] aligns with a *universalist* project. There is neither the Afropessimist apocalyptic sting of "let it all burn down" nor the decolonial delinking from the West and retreat into particularity. There isn't any nostalgia for a lost harmonious state prior to the dreadful colonial encounter, and Fanon's desire to "the end of the world," a passage that he quotes from Césaire's *Notebook of a Return to the Native Land*, Wilderson is also fond of praising.[48] But for Fanon, there is a politics (the unmitigated politics of decolonization) that drives this desire for ending the world. It is never a question of *destruction for destruction's sake*.

Fanon constantly returns to the "human" with the problematization of its relation to a "new humanism." This relation is trained and the human in question/crisis may have more in common with the uncanny figure of the posthuman than the all-too-familiar human of Western civilization. In Fanon's hands, the "human" of colonial humanism undergoes radical dislocation. The "humanism" that follows this invention of the new human will be *unrecognizable* because the currency of the human will no longer be supported by the racial matrix of the human. To get to this "new human," the human after its anti-colonial dislocation, we must pass through the zone of nonbeing, the zero point of subjectivity, and reorient ourselves to the inhuman perspective of objects.

In the opening page of Fanon's chapter 5 of *Black Skin, White Masks*, we witness the author's traumatic encounter with the white gaze in the first line " 'Sale nègre!' ou simplement: 'Tiens, un nègre!,' " which translates as "Dirty Nigger!" or simply, "Look, a Black!"[49] The racial slur immobilizes Fanon, arresting his status as a subject of desire. He becomes "an object among other objects" and experiences his ontological degradation as a "suffocating reification" (*objectivité écrasante*).[50] Living in the zone of nonbeing means living the life of an object.

Contrary to the Afropessimists, I argue that this description applies to the wretched more generally and to occupied Palestinians in particular. As objects that can be treated as disposable without any ramifications, Palestinian lives are violable with impunity. The erasure of Palestinian humanity is baked into the settler-colonial logic. But how should we understand the negation of Palestinian humanity? There are two ways to negate the statement "the Palestinian is human." Drawing on Žižek's reading of Immanuel Kant's distinction between negative and infinite judgments, we can say, "the Palestinian is not human" and "the Palestinian is inhuman." As Žižek insists, the two are not the same:

"He is not human" means simply that he is external to humanity, animal or divine, while "he is inhuman" means something thoroughly different, namely that he is neither human nor not human, but marked by a terrifying excess which, although negating what we understand as "humanity," is inherent to being human.[51]

The Palestinian is not an animal but a "human animal," as Gallant put it. This observation is confusing at multiple levels. Haven't you read your Darwin lately? Of course, we are human *animals*, to be distinguished from the multiplicity of nonhuman animals. Aside from his speciesist arrogance, Gallant marries humanist ontology and fascist ontology: the (Western) human is unchanging and superior to those (non-Westerns) who masquerade as humans. Gallant paints Palestinian difference as an unsettling and monstrous hybridity, an inhumanity that must be disclosed and named in order to be annihilated. The inhuman Palestinian fits perfectly well within the Zionist order of values. While the Israeli Jew enjoys all the privileges that come with cultural and metaphysical superiority, the Palestinian is a shadowy creature: *Don't be fooled by the humanoid features of the Palestinians, they are not like us.* The figure of the Palestinian is not simply outside humanity's orbit, awaiting her inclusion among liberals of all shades. Palestinians are an uncanny species. Human rights cannot be in practice fully extended to Palestinians as they can be to nonhuman animals. Standing in front of a herd of goats, a smirking IOF soldier says to another filming the joking scene for social media, "these are the only uninvolved civilians in Gaza."[52] Only the humanized "civilian" goats and other nonhuman animals are truly innocent here. Palestinians are inhuman animals, monstrous chimeras in a Gaza under the reign of a modified *NHI*: *no humans or humane animals involved.*

Legally, Palestinians are of course guaranteed rights by international law. But when the world is witnessing a genocide in plain view and Western political leaders do not call for an immediate stop to the Palestinocide, it should make you wonder if human rights actually apply to them. International law confers abstract rights but is unable to protect Palestinians from the murderous thug of the region. Akin to anti-Blackness, anti-Palestinianness is a problem of ontology. There is no humane treatment of the abominable inhuman. The Black imago terrifies whites. "Whoever says rape says black man,"[53] Fanon writes. The Palestinian imago terrorizes Zionists. Whoever says terrorism says Palestinian, I write. The "terrifying excess" of Palestinians is read by Zionists and pro-Israel supporters as evidence of their hatred and cruelty. Evoking a "Clash of Civilizations" framework is too good for Palestinians, concedes too much (the idea of Palestinian civilization/humanity). As Netanyahu put it to a sycophantic US Congress: "This is not a clash of civilizations. It's a clash between barbarism and civilization. It's a clash between those who glorify death and those who sanctify life. For the forces of civilization to triumph, America and Israel must stand together. Because when we stand together, something very simple happens. We win. They lose."[54] A "Clash of Civilizations" rhetoric does not meet the needs of the situation, to which the only satisfactory solution is revengeful genocide. Rather, vilifying Palestinians even further, Zionists frame the conflict as a clash between civilization and barbarism. In this Manichean world, Israeli Jews stand for humanity and goodness; they are "the children of light" caught up in struggle against the evil and inhuman Palestinians—"the children of darkness."[55] In the region, everything that is the opposite of this Palestinian behavior is Jewish.[56] We see here the workings of displacement. Zionists blame Palestinians for their anti-Semitism, fanaticism, and brutal violence—they see only their neighbor's faults or darkness—while being oblivious to their own disproportionate cruelty. The Occupation and the Gaza Wars serve as a tragic reminder that cruelty or inhumanity is constitutive of the human. To say something is constitutive of one's being does not mean endorsing that thing—crudely naturalizing it and immunizing oneself in advance from its potential horrors—but it does mean maintaining vigilance over our worst tendencies. Cruel acts cannot be allowed to endlessly repeat themselves: "Both [colonized and colonizer] have to move away from the inhuman voices of their respective ancestors so that a genuine communication can be born."[57] There is no "new knowledge" of Palestinians, to evoke Morrison's and Žižek's words, without forging a genuine communication between the settler and the Native.

Defending the Dead

The Afropessimists rule out communication between master and slave. New knowledge is also dismissed insofar as humanist knowledge is premised on anti-Blackness. There is no reprieve from alienation and suffering. As Jared Sexton puts it, "I am speaking here of suffering in its fullest sense: not only as pain, which everyone experiences—say, the pain of alienation and exploitation—but also as that which blacks must *bear*, uniquely and singularly, that which we must *stand* and stand alone."[58] Terror afflicting Blacks is constitutive of social existence as such. "It is never the case that this terror is *not* present. It saturates the field of encounter," adds Sexton.[59] Working within an Afropessimist horizon, while also moving to expand it, Christina Sharpe characterizes Black Studies as "the intellectual work of a continued reckoning [with] the longue durée of Atlantic chattel slavery, with black fungibility, antiblackness, and the gratuitous violence that structures black being, of accounting for the narrative, historical, structural, and other positions black people are forced to occupy."[60] Inflected by Saidiya Hartman's preoccupation with "the position of the unthought," Black Studies hungers for racial justice and otherness; its force lies in the "continued imagining of the unimaginable."[61] "New knowledge" and "genuine communication" will have to pass through this inventive interrogation of the unimaginable. Scholars and activists are interpellated "to defend the dead," a formulation Sharpe borrows from M. NourbeSe Philip.

Philip's *Zong!* addresses the eighteenth-century massacre on the slave ship Zong, during which the captain ordered more than 130 enslaved captives to be thrown overboard when the ship ran low on drinking water during the Middle Passage. The owners of the boat sought to collect on the insurance due following the loss of their "cargo"—the enslaved Africans. When the insurance company refused to pay, the case went to court, which ruled in favor of the owners of the slave ship. The case was appealed, and the verdict was reversed in favor of the insurers; it was determined that it was Zong's captain who erred in failing to maintain a sufficient stock of drinking water. Reduced to pure "cargo," the fungible enslaved bodies who died have no story to tell; their murder is never recorded as murder but as a mere insurance dispute over commodities, nothing more. The enslaved only counted as property, as things; "it wasn't possible to kill cargo or to murder a thing already denied life"[62]—*the original model for NHI.* Sharpe tarries with the injunction, "Defend the Dead." She carefully unpacks the force of these words: "What does it mean to defend the dead? To tend to the Black dead and dying: to tend to the Black person, to Black people, always living in the push toward our death? It means work. It is work: hard emotional, physical, and intellectual work that demands vigilant attendance to the needs of the dying, to ease their way, and also to the needs of the living."[63] The injunction "to defend the dead" entails an ontological mood, an orientation, a care and labor for the unsanctioned others.

Defending the dead makes Black death—and the ways we relate to it—an essential part of what it means to be Black or in solidarity with Black people, in a seemingly uninterrupted anti-Black temporality under the auspice of white supremacy. The enslaved and the colonized who did not survive their encounters with colonizers cannot be made or allowed to disappear. Defending the dead also taps into a form of *ressentiment* championed by Holocaust survivor Jean Améry. It is an un-Nietzschean manifestation of *ressentiment*, a *ressentiment* fueled by the desire not to forgive and forget the horrors of the Holocaust absent a reckoning with the Third Reich.[64] Améry affirms his "right to *ressentiment*,"[65] as W. G. Sebald put it, or what I have described elsewhere as his "public use of *ressentiment*" (supplementing Nietzsche with Kant).[66] Whereas Améry betrayed the unsettling force of his *ressentiment* when he committed to an identitarian Zionism, students' anti-genocide protests and encampments point in the opposite direction. They have expressed their collective *ressentiment* toward a supremacist Zionist regime, and boldly practiced *parrhēsia*, speaking truth to their university administrators and governments. They have denounced the complicity of companies[67] and Western powers with Israel's genocidal logics. They have enacted their version of defending the dead, resisted the derealization of Palestinian casualties wrought by an imperialist West that cannot trust the reporting coming out of "Hamas-run" Gaza, unflinchingly critiqued Israel's killing machine, and continually pointed to the unremitting injustices visited on the Palestinian people. Defending the dead is both a call for reflection and a call to action. It is not satisfied in only communicating knowledge (about Palestinian deaths and suffering) that will be neutralized by the operations of fetishist disavowal.

This is the challenge: how can knowledge (about Palestinian suffering, Palestinian struggle for liberation) emancipate? How can pro-Palestinian narratives clarify the colonial situation and change Western minds? Edward Said comments positively on the ways the horrors of the Shoah have forever impacted our collective psyche. We have made "Never Again," "Never Again for Everyone" a universal injunction. Scholars and activists, faculty and students, people of conscience throughout the world are saying that Israel's genocide of Gaza cannot be allowed to leave "the consciousness of our time" unaffected.[68] Are we going to let Israel get away with genocide? Have we become miserably habituated to the crime of crimes? "Defend the dead" is a command not to forget, not to forgive; it's a command to pierce through the atmosphere of fascism, and reckon with America's and Israel's regimes of oppression. So how do we go about rethinking the affective force of knowledge production? First, let's linger a bit on the logic of fetishist disavowal—*I know very but all the same* ... The liberal response to Gaza goes something like this: *I know very well that Palestinians are suffering, but all the same I believe that Israel has a right to defend itself* (or *I believe in the two-state solution, peace after Hamas and Netanyahu*, etc.). All the documentation of Israel's genocide, its massive aggression and devastation is neutralized, absorbed by a collective psyche; a Zionist cognitive mapping is holding in Israel, continuing to structure the perception that the nation-state is Jewish and democratic, not colonial.[69] The belief in Israel's right to self-defense, in its democratic core (Israel apart from Netanyahu and his band of crazies), blocks the possibility of permanently altering our perception of Palestine/Israel. Under Zionist eyes, "new knowledge" about Palestine and Palestinians is thwarted, either by the weaponization of the charge of anti-Semitism or the workings of fetishist disavowal. An incapacitating pessimism risks setting in: knowledge will not set Palestinians free. I ask with Mohammed El-Kurd, how do we "invent a new future" in order "to break out of the hamster wheel"?[70] How do we break out of the prison house of Western liberalism?

And yet we may want to approach the question of knowledge differently, and take the fight to Zionism at the level of the cultural imaginary—the realm of collective fantasies. I'm thinking here of Elias Sanbar's notion of "combatant"— the image of the Palestinian that exceeds its capture by the images of the abject and militarist Palestinians—and of expanding it to the realm of fiction, so that we may talk about a "combatant of the imaginary," a "disturber of libidinal economies," if you will. How do you contest a reality where the Zionist framing has more or less determined the Palestinian imago? Žižek intimates a possibility, a thinking *otherwise* the relation of fantasy to reality:

> Even if reality is "more real" than fantasy, it still needs fantasy to retain its consistency: if we subtract fantasy, the fantasmatic frame, from reality, reality itself loses its consistency and disintegrates. The lesson is thus that the very

alternative of "either accept reality or choose fantasy" is a false one: what Lacan calls *la traverse du fantasme* has nothing to do with dispelling illusions and accepting reality the way it is. This is why, precisely when we are shown someone doing just that—renouncing all illusions and embracing miserable reality—we should focus on identifying the minimal fantasmatic contours of this reality. If we really want to change or escape from our social reality, the first thing to do is to change the fantasies tailored to make us fit this reality.[71]

Lyd, a "sci-fi documentary" directed by Rami Younis and Sarah Ema Friedland, invites us precisely to change the fantasies tailored to make us fit the current Palestine/Israel reality. It does so by breaking "the continuum of history,"[72] dislodging the hold of Zionist fantasy on the ways in which we can imagine Palestinian Indigeneity and Palestine today. In its speculative world-building, *Lyd* jolts the audience. Its provocation: What if the Nakba never happened? What if Pan-Arab solidarity in the "Great Anti-Colonial War" succeeded in securing a Palestine liberated from British colonialism? What if the anti-colonial movement in Palestine also came with a decolonization of the Palestinian mind—and thus worked to avoid the pitfalls of national consciousness that Fanon warned about? What if the Jews who migrated from Europe, escaping the ravages of anti-Semitism, found a welcoming home in Palestine? Younis and Friedland explore this alternative possibility or retroactivity through the Palestinian city of Lyd or Lydda—which serves as a synecdoche for Palestine, the Nakba, and settler colonialism. *Lyd* is "an exercise in political imagination,"[73] of poetically thinking an undetermined future. In the film, we witness what a "total revolutionary change" might look like, intimating "not only a new government, but also a change in education, society and culture."[74] A Lyd without the Nakba is not simply a Lyd without the 1948 event of the Nakba. The alternate Lyd is also without the Nakba as a structure of dispossession, fragmentation, and decimation. It is Lyd without Zionist teleology, without Zionism's ideological claims to progress and civilizational embellishments. It is an unlearned and relearned Lyd, a free Lyd severed from colonial history and construction, and liberated from its relation to the catastrophic past and suffocating present, imagined beyond the debilitating horizon of the two-state solution and its "sovereignty trap"[75]—the liberal solution to the Palestinian problem—which, cruelly, can only promise Palestinian statehood (if statehood is promised at all) in the form an archipelago of Bantustans. Partial sovereignty, partial coloniality? Call it Swiss-cheese sovereignty.

Younis and Friedland take up what didn't happen in Palestine's past to animate their utopian vision of another Lyd. For me, the film defends the dead poetically, tapping into its missed realities, foreclosed possibilities, countering Zionist erasure with a kind of "Palestino-futurism," influenced by Afrofuturist techniques, with an alternate reality, another temporality, an anti-Zionist temporality, that displays Palestinians as thriving in multicultural and multireligious communities.[76]

The film casts the city of Lyd, voiced by Maisa Abd Elhadi, as the narrator of its own histories. She stresses Lyd's rich and heterogenous past, the many peoples and cultures that have lived on this contested land. No one owns the city of Lyd. Edward Said stresses the importance of recalling this history as we interpret the present and project a future for the land and its peoples:

> Palestine is and has always been a land of many histories; it is a radical simplification to think of it as principally or exclusively Jewish or Arab. While the Jewish presence is longstanding, it is by no means the main one. Other tenants have included Canaanites, Moabites, Jebusites and Philistines in ancient times, and Romans, Ottomans, Byzantines and Crusaders in the modern ages. Palestine is multicultural, multiethnic, multireligious. There is as little historical justification for homogeneity as there is for notions of national or ethnic and religious purity today.[77]

The narrator's sympathies clearly lie with the displaced and dispossessed Palestinian people who have suffered an eliminationist Zionist regime, which sought to eradicate their physical and cultural presence in Lyd. The city's name is Israelized as Lod, the linguistic erasure complementing the ontological erasure of Palestinians—Palestinocide. In Lod, Palestinian residents continue to be pushed out of many city spaces, all while Israeli officials continue to describe it as a "mixed city"—this is how Israel refers to its own cities with a significant Palestinian population—and symbol of Israeli "tolerance."

The documentary relates the current reality of Lyd/Lod, neglected by its government and known as the "drug capital"[78] of Israel, in filmed footage, speaking to witnesses and Nakba survivors along with their descendants. It interweaves this narrative with fictional animated sequences depicting an alternative past and present, in which winning the fight against British colonialism has allowed the city to develop civic structures built on its historical heterogeneity and multi-faith traditions. This Lyd infuses the moniker "mixed city" with a radically different meaning. A "new knowledge" of Palestinians is produced and communicated. This other Lyd, which stands as unfathomable or unintelligible to Zionist lenses, is flourishing, as it was prior to the British and Zionist invasions; this metropolis connected Palestine to the world, and now does so again. Its university and festivals attract students from around the world, and its residents are free to travel abroad, connect with other peoples and knowledges, and return home. It is hard not to think of the contrast with Gaza, which is "cut off from the world," as the Israeli Human Rights organization B'Tselem starkly put it.[79] And this new knowledge introduced by *Lyd* disturbs Zionists in power. As Younis notes, the scandal lies in the imagination of a Jewish American and a Palestinian citizen of Israel "to dream of a world in which everyone is free from the river to the sea."[80]

Still, the directors also temper jubilation over the city; it is not a place absent of antagonisms or problems: "We do not envision this alternate reality as a perfect utopia. The sci-fi writer Ursula Le Guin uses the term ambiguous utopia, that is what this is. Yes, many things are better, but there are subtle hints in the script that there is still racism and class divides. This is important, because we did not want to essentialise the alternate reality."[81] The ambiguous utopia is crystallized for me in the film's self-critical liberal evocation of "Palestinian privilege" in a scene imagining a primary school classroom discussion of civic duties. Hearing "Palestinian privilege" might sound absurd, comical, and even a bit cruel. But in this alternate reality, being Palestinian not only indicates that you're *not* a problem, but it also cuts through ethnoreligious identities; Muslims, Christians, Druze, and Jews as well are all Palestinian. In such a conjuncture, Palestinian privilege emerges as a problem in relation to new asylum seekers from the African nations of Eritrea and Sudan—who are lagging economically and not fully integrated into Palestinian society. Schools are the place where privileged Palestinian students are invited to question their entitlement. Palestinian privilege returns us to the question of race and class. The fact that Lyd's struggling citizens are Black would not be missed by Afropessimists. Even in this utopia, anti-Blackness rears its ugly head! Is Palestinian privilege an anti-Black problem? Is anti-Blackness not functioning as a unifying principle of all non-Blacks, what Frank Wilderson would call "anti-Black solidarity"?[82]

Palestinian privilege may be a misnomer. Overcoming Palestinian privilege is not simply about checking your privilege, of the sort: I should recognize my privilege and be more attentive to cultural difference and the needs of the economically and socially less fortunate. We see the inadequacies of this approach in America's hegemonic liberal center: woke liberalism is not so much a remedy as a distraction. You talk about inclusion and white privilege, but you're not invested in reckoning with America's structural racial and economic inequalities. Removed from any class-conscious anti-racism, and its pernicious libidinal underpinnings, combatting privilege can slip too easily into solipsistic if not narcissistic meditations about self-improvement. Checking my privilege, my fantasies, and my desires can never be solely an individual affair. As Žižek puts it, "the problem with human desire is that ... it is always 'desire for the Other' in all the senses of the term: desire for the Other, desire to be desired by the Other, and especially desire for what the Other desires."[83] Checking your Palestinian privilege, if the concept is to unsettle harmonious utopias, would require Lydians to trouble their libidinal investment in Palestinianness or Palestinian rootedness (grounded in a sense of racial and cultural superiority), and to face their bourgeois and (latent) anti-Black desires. Palestinians enjoy more than an ethnic privilege—a racial matrix of the human still underpins Palestinian polity. In *Lyd*'s Palestino-futurist reality, new desires—emancipatory desires—are not prescribed in advance (progress-as-integration into the global economy) but will need to be forged through and after the dismantling of Palestinian ethnic/racial privilege, the Black migrant problem that it generates,[84] registering another chapter in the ongoing Palestinian struggle for freedom and equality *for all*.

Lyd can be seen a critical rejoinder to liberal Zionist Ari Shavit's observation in *My Promised Land: The Triumph and Tragedy of Israel* that "if Zionism was to be, Lydda could not be. If Lydda was to be, Zionism could not be."[85] *Lyd* was a "tragedy";[86] Zionism lapsed into sin in massacring its inhabitants—but its fall had to happen. "Either reject Zionism because of Lydda, or accept Zionism along with Lydda," is the choice for fellow Israelis as Shavit formulates it.[87] He opts for the latter. Shavit "stand[s] by the damned," and he tells us why: "Because I know that if it wasn't for them, the State of Israel would not have been born. If it wasn't for them, I would not have been born. They did the dirty, filthy work that enables my people, myself, my daughter, and my sons to live."[88] Shavit condemns the liberal elite of Tel Aviv who are allegedly "blinded by political correctness," relentlessly scrutinizing "Israel's wrongdoings" to the point of fracturing Israeli unity.[89] Unlike these "bleeding-heart Israeli liberals of later years who condemn what they did in Lydda but enjoy the fruits of their deed,"[90] Shavit mixes his liberal Zionism with a dose of realpolitik. His so-called honesty avoids the bad faith of his fellow liberals, but the utter absence of accountability both aligns him with the position of Israeli far Right[91] and licenses his virtue signaling and "settler move to innocence":[92] I'm different from other Zionists, I know about Lyd and I'm disseminating that knowledge. *I know very well about the horrors of Lyd, I recorded them with sadness and pain, but, all the same, I believe in a Zionist Israel, so I "stop there"*[93] *and relieve myself of feelings of responsibility*. Shavit returns to the past but is unwilling to reimagine it in order to change or resist the contours of the present; no, this return is performed to better secure Zionist futurology—a future that excises any consideration of justice for Palestinians.[94] In contradistinction, *Lyd* challenges the anti-Palestinian temporality at work in Zionist futurology. As Lauren Collee insightfully notes, "linear time is an important weapon to genocidal regimes, which attempt to stamp out resistance by invoking a looming and inevitable end that cannot be reversed."[95]

Whereas Shavit is libidinally invested in the Israel that emerged through its violent birth, this Zionism had to be, Younis and Friedland embrace the idea of an anti-colonial/postcolonial Palestine that sets the stage for a more meaningful and generative coexistence between Palestinians and Jews. Shavit's pathos for Israel—the Zionist Jewish state—overlooks the possibility that something else could have been brought into existence, or what *is* can be imagined differently, something that escapes a zero-sum game, the genocidal view that "for me to flourish, you must die." *Lyd* dares to envisage Palestine otherwise, other than an ethnonationalist state premised on a hierarchical order of beings (the example of

Israel), and yet this Palestine remains an "ambiguous utopia," a utopia insofar as the fate of the Palestinians is not to be genocided but an imperfect or incomplete ideal, bound to produce its own outsiders, the "parts of no-part"[96] of Lyd's culture, and new problems.

The Posthuman, the Neighbor, the Inhuman

If *Lyd* invites us to reimagine Palestinians beyond abject victims or bloodthirsty terrorists, as no longer problematic but normative beings—beings in and of this world—there is always a risk of reintroducing the paradigm of the human. Undoing "Palestinian privilege" would have everything to do with undoing the racial matrix of the human. The push for tolerance and inclusivity in a vibrant Palestine might be preferable to Israel's ethnonationalist fascist state, but we cannot stop here. The hegemonic liberal order of the alternate Lyd (minus a reckoning with Palestinian privilege) is unlikely to be more successful than that of the liberal multicultural states of our timeline.

If not the Human, then what? Perhaps, we are better off starting with the ~~human~~ or posthuman. Staying with the posthuman, without crudely opposing it to being human, denotes a shift in perspective, a degentrification of the human. If systematic racism and dispossession work to dissolve the imaginary-symbolic human (a destitution, let's stress, that is imposed on the wretched), the posthuman indexes the Real, the displacement of the humanist human; the faceless wretched discloses the *real* human. The real human is a posthuman. Against Levinas and his aspirations for a pure heterology, Žižek turns to Primo Levi's figure of the *Muselmann* as an account of the "real" human, the faceless neighbor beyond recognition and accommodation, "a human being reduced to inhumanity."[97] The Levinasian face, despite its radical otherness and irreducibility to relations of comprehension, presupposes a minimum amount of gentrification. The *Muselmann* doesn't. This *Muselmann*, the Muslim man, stands for the most abject of Jews, racialized or doubly racialized or de-Judaized, and thus subalternized even further.

I take the *Muselmann* to be a posthuman creature, historically born of the camps. Having lost his ontological ties to the imaginary-symbolic world, the *Muselmann*'s being or otherness stands for everything that threatens the grammar of the Human, starting with nothingness, the desert of the Real. In this context, empathetic identifications miss their target, looking for something that is not there. The *Muselmann* is *not* someone like us, someone whom we can readily understand. To be sure, the humanist response would, again, be to try to empathize, to restore the humanity of the *Muselmann*, to rehumanize or de-posthumanize him, to undo the devastating violence done to him by the crushing reality of Auschwitz. My wager is that we need to overcome the cruel optimism that plagues humanist/humanizing projects. But this is not a call to forgo ethics and abide by the reality principle. There is a posthuman ethics that emerges from the zone of nonbeing, that critically responds to the white cruelty that drives blackened others—Blacks, Palestinians, and *Muselmänner*—into this infernal zone that responds to the unacknowledged inhumanity of the colonizer, settler, and white supremacist that hollows out and reduces others to their inhuman core. It is an ethics, but a paradoxical ethics, a kind of anti-ethics ethics, stemming from the legacy of "anti-humanism."[98] Žižek credits Lacan's "practical anti-humanism":

> In contrast to Althusser, Lacan accomplishes the passage from theoretical to practical anti-humanism, that is, to an ethics that goes beyond the dimension of what Nietzsche called the "human, all too human," and confronts the inhuman core of humanity. This does not only mean an ethics which no longer denies, but fearlessly takes into account the latent monstrosity of being-human, the diabolical dimension which exploded in phenomena usually covered by the concept-name "Auschwitz"—an ethics that would be still possible after Auschwitz, to paraphrase Adorno. This inhuman dimension is for Lacan, at the same time, the ultimate bedrock of ethics.[99]

If one can muster enough intellectual courage and acknowledge that Nazism is an immanent possibility for all of us humans—whence the ethical relevance of "Never Again" and its pertinence to Gaza, which is becoming another concept-name as a site where fascist lawmaking violence is happening—it is another matter to cast the inhuman core as "the ultimate bedrock of ethics."

This counterintuitive claim, I would argue, opens to the posthuman, to a being human that avows its own void, opacity, and monstrosity. What is proper to the human is precisely her impropriety. Žižek's twist here is that he brings his understanding of the neighbor to bear on the subject itself, on "what is in a human being more than human."[100] The real neighbor does not refer exclusively to some external other; it denotes the uncanny otherness that resides in the subject as well. Seeing yourself as neighbor happens whenever you experience a "gap" between what you are as a determinate being and the inscrutable X in yourself. In Lacanian parlance, our social ego is *not-all*. The inhuman is "absolutely immanent, the very core of subjectivity itself."[101] The subject as neighbor—as a stranger to itself—can only appear as a paradox and scandal from the standpoint of whiteness and humanism. It deprives the white humanist self of all its historical privileges: such as self-transparency, self-mastery, and autonomy. But we must keep in mind that the inhuman core of the human is as generative as it is annihilative. To paraphrase Jacques Derrida on the "strange illogical logic"[102] of autoimmunity: without inhumanity, with absolute humanity, the neighbor, reduced to its imaginary-symbolic character, would only be experienced not as disruptive event but as an extension of my socially sanctioned humanity.[103] My use of the "inhuman in the human" here finds kinship with George Yancy's idea of "being un-sutured,"[104] where my dispossession by this uncanny otherness (in the other and/or in me) is not something only to acknowledge or accept, but to cultivate, tarry with, and harness. Without the inhuman core of the subject, we would be forever sutured, engulfed in our genocidal "self-preservation,"[105] caught in ideology and in white humanism's insidious and totalizing grammar.

Being human in the zone of nonbeing casts humanity in all its nakedness — exposed, ungentrified, and devoid of its contingent and phantasmatic features. The inhumanity of the subject unmasks the pretenses of humanity. As Žižek puts it, "'Humanity' is a notion at the same level as personality, the 'inner wealth' of our soul, etc. — it is ultimately a phenomenal form, a mask, which fills in the void that 'is' subject."[106] What the humanist seeks to excise from being and transfer to nonbeing — racialized Blacks and Palestinians — is in fact constitutive of the human. We might say that cruelty is "extimate" to the subject, external but irreducibly intimate to it. This avowed cruelty demystifies and repoliticizes the human, robs the human of its purported innocence, purity, and most importantly of its whiteness and fascist scapegoating strategies.

The Politics of Trauma and the (Un) Making of the Irreproachable Victim

I want to dwell on cruelty for a bit, on this concept's phantasmatic and ideological deployment by Western politicians and corporate media outlets. Cruelty and humanity are irremediably interconnected. Essayist Michel de Montaigne decries how early modern Europeans rationalized the genocide of the Indigenous population by denying their humanity. This scene is too painfully visible in Israel's genocidal campaign in Gaza, where Palestinians are treated as barbaric, "human animals" — really meaning "inhuman animals" — marking a return to the rhetoric and practice of early colonialism. A Zionist settler-colonial Israel stands for a universal (Western) humanity — a villa in the jungle, as the racist trope goes.

Cruelty also often follows trauma, and the traumatized hold particular sway in a humanist cultural imaginary. The category is almost interchangeable with that of the victim, though we also can entertain how the victimizer/oppressor/ occupier can be traumatized as well. Ari Folman's 2008 highly acclaimed *Waltz with Bashir* is exemplary in this regard. In this animated docu-film, Folman takes up the trauma of the 1982 Sabra and Shatila massacres, exemplifying the "shoot and weep" Israeli film genre. An Israeli's personal trauma at having abetted the collective trauma visited on the Palestinian refugees massacred in the Sabra and Shatila camps is alchemically transformed into a meditation on Jewish moral depth and complexity, muddying the distinction between victim and victimizer, announcing a Zionist move to innocence while affirming the moral turpitude of the Israeli military.[107] Reinforcing humanist desires to sustain a vision of the self as humane, the "shoot and weep" narrative enables and sustains liberal Zionists' fetishist disavowal: *I know very well that Israel's right-winger prime ministers (Menachem Begin, Ariel Sharon, Benjamin Netanyahu, among others) are horrible to Palestinians, but all the same I believe that our soldiers (who come from the most moral army in the world, after all) can redeem the state of Israel. Sabra and Shatila is not who we are. We were in the streets in Tel Aviv three hundred thousand strong, condemning our government's moral failure. Israelis are complex beings; give us a chance to explain ourselves; our trauma begins in Auschwitz …*

Israel can continue to attack Lebanon, Syria, Yemen, Iran, and Qatar, while still intensifying its carnage in Gaza and increasing its deadly raids in the West Bank. And Israel continues to present itself as victim—always already under existential threat, acting in self-defense—to its nationals and Western leaders, but with a perverse twist, for now "shoot" is replaced with "commit genocide," and "weep" with "enjoy." In the original dynamic, an Israeli soldier shoots, but his self-consciousness enables him to scrutinize his actions, triggering his weeping for the harm done to abject Palestinians. Now, in genocidal Israel, there is virtually no public weeping for the Palestinians, but there is a great deal of sorrow for the victims of the Hamas attack and public displays of sadistic vengeance. Naomi Klein has documented the cultification of trauma in Israel following the horror of October 7.[108] Dark tourism, with the full support of the Zionist state, enables or rather manufactures empathic identifications with the Jewish victims. Visitors plunging into immersive installations and film dramatizations vicariously become figural victims themselves, thereby immunizing themselves, consciously or unconsciously, from any complicity in Israel's war crimes—its crimes against humanity and the crime of crimes, genocide. *I know very well that the world is lamenting Palestinian suffering, but all the same I believe that we are defending ourselves against global anti-Semitism.* From Gaza to South Africa, in the streets of the Global South and the hallways of the United Nations, on college campus across the world, anti-Semitism is presumed to be the new normal, an existential threat against which any and all means of resistance must be justified.

But liberal Zionists are not dupes. *They know very well that Netanyahu is a self-serving, megalomaniac politician, but all the same they believe that Israel must be defended.* A Manichean logic quickly sets in, as Klein describes it:

> It's a simple fable of good and evil, in which Israel is unblemished in its innocence, deserving unquestioning support, while its enemies are all monsters, deserving of violence unbounded by laws or borders, whether in Gaza, Jenin, Beirut, Damascus or Tehran. It's a story in which Israel's very

identity as a nation is forever fused with the terror it suffered on 7 October, an event that, in Netanyahu's telling, will be seamlessly merged both with the Nazi Holocaust and a battle for the soul of western civilization.[109]

We are no longer dealing with a "clash of civilizations." Ontological demotion hits rock bottom. Palestinians are now construed as a different species; it is about civilization versus animal barbarism.

In making his case, Netanyahu manufactures a storyline in which two opposing logics—traumatophilia and traumatophobia—are strangely entangled. The desire to be traumatized, to repeat the experiences of those who died or were injured and/or taken hostage on October 7, is matched with the phobic desire to stave off any future traumatic experiences, to interpret and enforce the motto "Never Again" in the most myopic and hermeneutically ungenerous way (it's only about the protection of Jewish life, regardless of the consequences). Traumatophobia propagates uncaring for your racialized enemy, of the sort witnessed in what Shannon Sullivan describes as the "white habit of untrauma," a practice fostering "white ignorance and white affective numbness towards people of color."[110] Zionist untrauma preaches a muscular vision of Jewishness (we will never march again to our slaughter—the Zionist rallying cry for the creation of a "new Jew" in the land of Israel), actively promoting both ignorance of the Palestinian people's history and struggle and a generalized hostility or indifference toward Palestinian bodies and desires.

The ideal and appeal of Zionist untrauma gains more traction in light of Israeli disappointment with the so-called peace process. Israelis gave peace a chance, and they got the Second Intifada, so goes the story. They must resign themselves to the fact that Palestinians are dangerous and unwilling to make peace with them. They lack a Palestinian Gandhi or Mandela.[111] Still, before October 7, 2023, one could still find liberal Zionists who differentiated between a "good Israel" versus a "bad Israel."[112] They wished that the state's treatment of Palestinians were more humane, that Palestinian citizens of Israel (who are classified as Arab Israelis or Arab citizens of Israel) were better integrated in society. Not all the Arabs want to harm us, they would tell themselves. Yes, there are some Palestinians who just want to coexist with us. Getting serious with Palestinian problem, they would say, Israel must deal with its 1967 problem; the illegal settlements are a global embarrassment. We need to end apartheid (but without giving land back or legally acquiescing to the right of return). Liberals would also get angry at their government when they "mowed the lawn" in Gaza every few years. *This is not who we are; Netanyahu must go.* Nostalgia imbues the liberal Zionist mindset. We're not the problem, *Netanyahu* is. "Apocalypse now, and there's nothing more natural than to glamorize the past, to miss what used to be, to glorify what never was. Israel the beautiful and the just, before the scoundrel [Netanyahu] came to power."[113] But, let's be honest, their world was never turned upside down by Palestinian suffering, by the blockade on Gaza and house demolitions in the West Bank. The good Israel versus bad Israel distinction is an ideological difference, that is, a difference without substance. The ontological core of liberal Zionists remained intact, and their sense of time was not subject to any profound disruption. The fact that Jewish-Israeliness could still take priority over Palestinianness was unchallenged.

Israel's liberal reputation is dropping. After October 7, many liberal Zionists, we're repeatedly told, "sobered up."[114] Matters intensified drastically, and the two attitudes toward trauma began to converge in disastrous ways, laying the ideological grounds for Israel's genocidal campaign in the Gaza Strip. Dark tourism—which can be explained as a form of survivor guilt, a desire to experience the horror of those you lost—finds its obscene counterpart in Israeli society's delegitimation of Palestinian tragedy. Witness the ways Israeli children and soldiers, in conformity to the Zionist superego, mock Palestinian civilians with "Arab face," which "involves veils, monobrows and even a blacked-out tooth to represent the lack of dental hygiene among the Gazan population."[115] These are not private, forbidden thrills to share with a creepy few; no, they are eagerly uploaded to TikTok and other social media platforms, as "a badge of honor,"[116] for instantaneous validation.

The "weep" in the narrative "shoot and weep" becomes "enjoy," completing the transformation to "commit genocide and enjoy." This is a continuation of Zionist delight or *jouissance* in Palestinian erasure, in casting Gazans as "human animals" and in sadistically ridiculing Palestinian pain and enjoying untrauma when consuming "atrocity porn," stripping Palestinians of their right to have rights, the rights to dignity and safety.[117] Zionism's traumatophobia (which dictates that no relationality with the Palestinian/enemy can be extended) and traumatophilia (through which empathetic identification with my kin becomes constitutive of my own victimized/victimizing identity) work hand in hand in projecting the Israeli Jew as an irreproachable victim. Zionist authority can discredit Palestinian pain because it posits itself as the highest court over matters of Jewish trauma and victimhood; it credits Jewish pain as the basis for a righteous revenge, and discredits the pain of Palestinians as fabricated and self-generated (they voted for Hamas; you cannot trust the Ministry of Health in Gaza; no one is innocent in Gaza). This is the cruel grammar of Zionism: for Jews to matter, Palestinians must un-matter.[118]

The problem however is not merely that the Israeli government is shamelessly monopolizing trauma (which it is), but that Palestinians are structurally prevented from working through their trauma. Post-traumatic stress disorder (PTSD), bizarre as it might sound, entails a kind of privilege, in that it requires post-ness, a basic temporal separation between the traumatic event and your present. The work of mourning may very well be interminable, but it cannot even begin until you are temporally positioned to wrestle with the traces as traces, as recurring effects of a past on your present life. Palestinians in Gaza, especially the children, have no such luxury. As Žižek avers:

> Children in Gaza, who are continuously exposed to brutal events, very rarely show signs of post-traumatic stress. Why? Because they live in a permanent traumatic situation: they don't have time to experience a traumatic event as a horror that occurred to them. In order to survive, they have to just go on with their lives, paying attention to dangers. Post-traumatic stress is already a form of relaxation.[119]

Engulfed in a Fanonian zone of nonbeing, Palestinians need to partially exit this hellish zone before coping with their PTSD[120] ("safe zones" are, in fact, bombable zones) and collectively reckoning with the reality of having been ethnically cleansed, de-worlded or "cut off from the world." Some Israeli soldiers do suffer from PTSD—caused either by their witnessing or direct involvement in the carnage in Gaza. The brutal mass murders of Palestinians affect them, and they experience "ruptures" in their everyday existence,[121] even pushing some to commit suicide. How the Israeli military deals with the problem of PTSD is also telling. Counseling from military psychologists reorients the debilitated, traumatized soldiers back to the paradigm of October 7, upholding the right context, reminding them of the true evil of Hamas, in an effort to restore the habit or programmatic experience of Zionist untrauma, counterbalancing the trauma of war (their position as perpetrators) with the trauma of their kin (positioning them as victims who are defending themselves/Israel).[122] The latter serves to nullify the unsettling potential of the former, to stave off any disruption of the sanctioned "affective numbness" toward Palestinians: remember that your military mission is noble. As with Ari Folman, the individual trauma of the Israeli soldiers, once again, sidelines the trauma of Palestinians. Consequently, prosthetic or vicarious victimhood *normalizes* the commission of genocide, the abnormal par excellence.[123]

Montaigne's anti-colonial meditations on the genocide of the Indigenous people of the "New World" can tell us much about the mechanisms of this normalization, which we are observing in Western reactions to the livestreamed carnage in Gaza. In "Of Cannibals," Montaigne reads the conquest of the Americas through the lens of the wars of religion taking place at home in France, tackling, along the way, questions of cruelty, anger, and revenge, among other unsettling passions. Whereas Europeans imagine the Indigenous as intrinsically barbaric, Montaigne is quick to point out that cultured Europeans "surpass them in every kind of barbarity."[124] Montaigne's *j'accuse* moment: "I think there is more barbarity in *eating a man alive* than in eating him dead; and in tearing by tortures and the rack a body still full of feeling, in roasting a man bit by bit, in having them bitten and mangled by dogs and swine ... than *roasting and eating him* after he is dead."[125] To be sure, Montaigne deploys the accusation of cannibalism metaphorically, for rhetorical effect, since we discover at the end of the sentence that his fellow Frenchmen don't actually eat the flesh of others but give it to dogs and pigs. Yet he remains unwavering in his indictment; the force of his claim that there is *more* barbarity in torturing and burning living human beings—"on the pretext of piety and religion"[126]—than in the cannibalism of the Indigenous people who eat them *after* they are dead, after their ritual murder, retains its bite. This critical assessment is repeated elsewhere in the *Essays*: "Savages do not shock me as much by roasting and eating the bodies of the dead as those who torment them and persecute them living."[127]

A generous decolonial interpretation of Montaigne's essay would credit the pre/anti-Cartesian essayist for pushing back against an emerging modern European colonizing *cogito*, whose proto-form is already visible in 1492 with the "*ego conquiro*" ("I conquer, therefore I am") of the conquistadors.[128] Montaigne's reflections on the nature of the self and the human cannot be extracted from the colonial matrix of the human. While it is common to see Montaigne's respect for cultural difference as marking an alternative to a colonizing European, paving the way for a decolonial reckoning with the West and its classificatory schema, it is Montaigne's skepticism, along with his reflections on cruelty, that represents his more disturbing and significant contribution to our understanding of "being human." In his essay "Of Cruelty," Montaigne voices his unconditional objection to cruelty with his self-reflexive and ironic comment: "Among other vices, I *cruelly* hate *cruelty*, both by *nature* and by *judgment*, as the extreme of all vices."[129] Montaigne criticizes "cruelty" (it is unconditionally deemed the greatest vice) while signaling or better yet gesturing to its insurmountability with the paradoxical adverb "cruelly." Even when passionately rejecting it, Montaigne evokes the register of cruelty—cruelly—to denounce it. "Cruelly" names here Montaigne's cognitive and affective ("both by nature and by judgment") commitment to "putting cruelty *first*"[130] in his ethical orientation.

Judith Shklar reads Montaigne as announcing liberalism, but I would argue that liberalism actually gentrifies Montaigne's unsettling psychoanalytic insight into the inhuman core of humanity. It is always easier and far more convenient to see cruelty as the other's problem, as a problem in the racial other. This ineradicable vice, deemed improper to the (Western) human, this unshakable otherness, is reminiscent of the monstrosity that a subterranean Montaigne "discovers" within his own being: "The more I frequent myself and know myself, the more my deformity *astonishes me, and the less I understand myself*."[131] Self-study *gives* Montaigne a precarious and monstrous presence: "I have seen no more evident monstrosity and miracle in the world than myself."[132] Montaigne's humanity unravels as it becomes unknowable and unrecognizable, as he avows the "inhuman core" of his humanity. He "accomplishes the passage from theoretical to practical anti-humanism," boldly registering "the latent monstrosity of being-human" in his attentiveness to the circulation of cruelty at home and abroad. Before Auschwitz, the diabolical dimension of cruelty exploded in the Americas, in the conquest of the New World—another racial fascism before the fascism on European soil—a site of inhumanity, of Indigenous genocide and dispossession. For Lacan and Žižek, this inhuman dimension is not to be repressed or disavowed. It points to what is in us that is more than us. The inhuman in being human marks the Real, ontology's malleability and incompleteness, what cannot be "gentrified-domesticated" by philosophical meditations and representations. Without it there is no ethics—whence its designation as "the ultimate bedrock of ethics."

Performing this "practical anti-humanism" leads to the destitution of the self: a Montaigne who ceases *to be* human (in its imaginary-symbolic form) and becomes more posthuman (a more real human). Astonishment (at his lacking, deformed being) derails the march of humanist philosophy toward self-mastery (and the mastery of the outside world). The improper is monstrous; the posthuman/inhuman of the human is monstrous. *Je est un monstre*. Being a problem is being monstrous. Disavowing or repressing the subject's inhumanity, the price of admission to ontology, is the prelude to projecting it unto others, the wretched of the world.

It is always more convenient to see others as problems than to face the subject's own monstrosity, and Israel has done just that in following this colonial playbook and developing a "settler conquistador" ego. The conquering, colonialist ego is invested in marking the boundaries of the human and its racialized Native. What is proper to the human, the certainty of its values, is embodied by European culture, while the improper is figured as racialized difference to be driven out of the humanist framework of legibility. Colonial discourse characterizes all Indigenous existence as improper, making Natives "the colonized sub-others."[133] The conquering ego, which is more primary than the Cartesian knowing *cogito*, expresses skepticism of the very humanity of the conquered Natives, a form of skepticism Maldonado-Torres characterizes as both Manichean and misanthropic:

> Unlike Descartes's methodical doubt, Manichean misanthropic skepticism is not skeptical about the existence of the world or the normative status of logics and mathematics. It is rather a form of questioning the very humanity of colonized peoples. The Cartesian idea about the division between *res cogitans* and *res extensa* (consciousness and matter) which translates itself into a divide between the mind and the body or between the human and nature is preceded and even, one has the temptation to say, to some extent built upon an anthropological colonial difference between the *ego conquistador* and the *ego conquistado*.[134]

At one level, this colonial scene describes well the settler-colonial realities of Palestine/Israel. Palestinians occupy the position of "the colonized sub-others" whereas Israelis are the incarnation of the certainty of white European values, with a Greater Israel in waiting, in need of more conquerors/settlers. What complicates this framing of Palestine/Israel is Zionism's ideological narrative that foregrounds the history of Jewish suffering, of Jewish people being rendered "sub-others" before fighting through unimaginable suffering to achieve self-determination, to transform their status from a "problem" for Europe to a friend of Europe in the form of a peer (the state of Israel).

The colonial difference persists, but it continues to be covered over. The badge of suffering gives the state of Israel unique leeway, as we've seen in its carnage in Gaza, almost a *carte blanche* to behave however it likes. If it is attacked for whatever reason (for committing war crimes, crimes against humanity, or the crime of crimes—genocide), a reflexive logic of support among Western allies kicks in. We move effortlessly from timeless victimhood to military righteousness. Indeed, the IOF never tires of describing itself as "the most moral army,"[135] of pairing the army's military power with a matching ethical might. The army is never conceived as the problem. The truth of Israel's cruelty is repeatedly repressed in Israel's self-image, and anything allegedly cruel that Israelis may have committed is blamed on Palestinians for corrupting an original Israeli innocence. Witness the self-congratulatory observation attributed to former Israeli Prime Minister Golda Meir that forgiveness from the Israeli side will be tested, will reach its limits, not when Palestinians have killed too many Israelis but rather when Israel is asked to forgive the unforgivable, which, in her narcissistic moral vision, means to forgive the Palestinians "for having forced [Israelis] to kill [Arab] sons."[136] From the self-designated position of moral superiority, Meir muses about what it will take to put an end to the conflict between Israel and its Arab neighbors: "Peace will come when the Arabs love their children more than they hate us."[137] Israelis are proper in their love; Palestinians are improper in their hate. To paraphrase Fanon, *wickedness is Palestinian as generosity is Israeli.*[138]

From the masterful assessment of the situation, the message is clear: Arabs need to reform their savagery and keep in check their innate anti-Semitism. The monstrous Arabs need to prioritize life over death, love over hate. They need some optimism. Israel's humanity is already here. Palestinians and the rest of the Arabs need to catch up. Weaponizing the card of self-defense evacuates, as Jacqueline Rose points out, "all responsibility for Israeli state violence by lodging it inside the hearts and minds of the enemy ('You made me do it')," and it is this, she says, "that I find most chilling."[139] I agree. By discarding any sense of responsibility and immunizing itself from judgment, Israel can undertake a genocide in plain view with the support of a majority of its nationals. The Gaza genocide—the conquest of Gaza by another name[140]—is ripe for a similar vexatious interpretation of the Palestinian struggle. More than a year into Isreal's criminal operation in Gaza, Nathan Lopes Cardozo, in an op-ed in *The Jerusalem Post*, recycles the same morally repulsive logic:

One of the great tragedies of the State of Israel is that it must constantly defend itself against ongoing attacks on its citizens. When its enemies claim Israel will be wiped out, "from the river to the sea," there is no option but to defend itself with all its might. Israeli Jews are forced to rely on military power to survive. But this is a reliance that they abhor. It was Golda Meir who said, "Perhaps we will be able to forgive the Arabs for killing our sons, but it will be harder for us to forgive them for having forced us to kill their sons." It is this paradox that makes these wars so intolerable. Those who are forced to fight are those who hate it the most.[141]

Conquest as survival, or being proud of genocide, is a new low. Putting an end to Palestinian desires for unity, equality, and freedom (what the chant "From the river to see, Palestine will be free" actually entails) is a cause for national celebration. This is sadism masquerading as righteousness. All of this stems from Israel's irreproachable victim complex, as if "history has only one primary victim."[142] Being Palestinian—struggling for our liberation, resisting territorial expansion— victimized Israel, made Israel less pure, less innocent. Causes and effects are ideologically reversed. Palestinians (not the Occupation, dispossession, ethnic cleansing, or the slow genocide) are responsible for Israeli aggression, for their criminal endeavors. Killing Palestinians is "unnatural" to Israeli humanity, to Israel's "most moral army." Oded Na'aman teases out the implications of a military that sees itself as always reacting to violence, as being defensive since time immemorial: "It is not that the Israel Defense Forces is so named because it is only used defensively; rather, for Israelis, every use of the Israel Defense Forces is by definition a defensive act."[143] The IOF remains the "sacred cow" of Israeli society; its generals are/must be exempt from the allegation of any criminality.[144]

In the cultural imaginary, Israel can never occupy the position of the aggressor or victimizer.[145] Israeli hasbara sells its people and the West a simplistic but efficient narrative where the Israeli soldier is a synecdoche of "humanity" while the Palestinian people are governed by "the law of the jungle."[146] As Palestinian terror is constitutive of Palestinian being, Jewish innocence is constitutive of Jewish being. For the Zionist, Palestinian being cannot be aligned with purity or innocence—whence the animalization of all Palestinians, young and old. In the defense of Israel, everything is allowed. Palestinian mothers and children are no different from Hamas fighters. The ultranationalist Ayelet Shaked displays this line of thought in characterizing Palestinians as an infestation in need of extermination in a 2014 Facebook post quoting the late Uri Elitzur, a speechwriter and adviser to Netanyahu: "They are all enemy combatants, and their blood shall be on all their heads. Now this also includes the mothers of the martyrs, who send them to hell with flowers and kisses. They should follow their sons, nothing would be more just. They should go, as should the physical homes in which they raised the snakes. Otherwise, more little snakes will be raised there."[147] Occupied Palestine is a jungle, filled by human animals and deadly snakes from all ages; under this sinister logic the already troubling notion of collateral damage—of undesired and unfortunate killings—ceases to exist, for all, including non-combatants and children, are rightful targets. *What is a Zionist to do, other than genocide?*

Each time we utter the word "IDF" we reinforce this Orwellian designation. The Israeli military force is first and foremost an offensive rogue force, an occupation force, a conquering war machine, that brazenly violates international humanitarian laws and principles. Again, "IOF" is a far more honest description of what Israel does to its Palestinian neighbors, but not only to Palestinians; its mayhem has touched many Arab- and Muslim-majority countries. Israel appears willing to say anything to maintain the moral higher ground: *you made me do it* logic casts the victim as the instigator, exculpating, in turn, the true aggressor. Why would it stop when Western nations line up to legitimize its criminal deeds?[148] A Golda Meir for contemporary times: *No one can be forgiven for having forced the IOF to kill their mothers and children.*

Israel is not an exception in its practice and disavowal of cruelty. The West, to which Israel faithfully belongs, has a long history of projecting its own unwanted colonial cruelties onto distant racialized others. The Orient is a case in point; the Orient after 9/11 crushingly so. Israel willingly inscribes itself in this Western imperialist tradition of Arabophobia. Palestinians are barbarians, an innately terrorist people, new Nazis, pure evil or inhumanity incarnated. It didn't take long for this interpretive framework to reassert itself after the October 7 attack. Israeli historian Dina Porat indicted Hamas as the new Nazis, highlighting the nature of their cruelty: "Hamas' savage cruelty is rooted not merely in a desire for conquest and destruction but rather in the dehumanization of Jews and Israelis, deeply ingrained after years of indoctrination. We have been portrayed as subhuman creatures, much as Nazi ideology did before and during the Holocaust era."[149] Palestinian anti-colonialism is cast as anti-Semitism and the result of indoctrination—cruelty has become constitutive of the Palestinian habitus, their second nature. Palestinians are cruel creatures, and their cruelty marks Palestinian civil society. At no point does Israeli cruelty enter the picture. Porat never bothers to contextualize the Hamas attack beyond her reference of the Holocaust, which firmly anchors her Zionist horizon of intelligibility; she sidelines the Occupation and settler colonialism as contextual markers worthy of consideration in an honest assessment of Hamas's violence.

When Israel's unacknowledged cruelty is the problem of/in others, when Israel and the white West believe in their unquestioned good and innocence, sutured themselves to "racial self-preservation"[150] and apartheid logics, having projected their own repressed ugly fantasies onto the non-European others, the rest of the world suffers and burns. To adapt Max Horkheimer's saying, *Whoever is not willing to talk about the cruelty of Israel should also keep quiet about the cruelty of Hamas.*[151]

On Recentering the Wretched

Against the cruelty of the settler's Manichean logic, a Fanonian politics recenters the wretched, rejecting the all-consuming Western/Zionist horizon: no, white Europeans are not the measure of all things. While Fanon does announce a new humanism, his writings index the Herculean effort needed for the violent dislocation, psychic divestment in the predominant Western image, and reinvention of the human. Importantly, the zone of nonbeing is itself framed around two key observations about the human and its relation to whiteness and Blackness. The first comes right before—"Running the risk of angering my black brothers, I shall say that a Black is not a man [*le Noir n'est pas un homme*]"—while the second follows a page later—"The black man wants to be white. The white man is desperately trying to achieve the rank of man" [*Le Noir veut être Blanc. Le Blanc s'acharne à réaliser une condition d'homme*]."[152] David Marriott and other Afropessimists elevate the "is not" of Fanon's first statement ("the Black is not a man"), disclosing the unbridgeable abyss that separates the Black from the human.[153] In the racialized zone of nonbeing all there is is Blackness (as) nothingness. For Black people, the dissolution of the ego (social death) fails to inaugurate the formation of a new self—humanist or otherwise. Unlike the Sartrean idyllic version, Fanonian nothingness does not translate into the affirmation of freedom and transformative existence.[154] Libidinal and material constraints lock Blacks in their nonbeing. Cast in this light, the experience of the Real is itself bizarrely a kind of white/human privilege. To experience the Real as something traumatic is already to assume the reality of a gentrified self capable of being unsettled. Fanon further troubles the existentialist ideal of transcendence by formulating the exit (for Blacks) from this hellish zone as difficult and rare.

On the Afropessimist account, Black being is a position of negation ("Blackness is incapacity in its most pure and unadulterated form"),[155] a kind of pure antihuman, with Blackness giving coherence to the white human. Fanon thus qualifies his new humanism to come with the crushing actuality of a latent antihumanism, at least when it comes to the most wretched of beings. If Blackness signifies nothingness, whiteness purports to represent humanity as such. But Fanon complicates the relation between whiteness and humanity in his later statement by disclosing the vicissitudes of fantasy in his uncompromising assessment of Black and white desires: "The black man wants to be white. The white man is desperately trying to achieve the rank of man" [*Le Noir veut être Blanc. Le Blanc s'acharne à réaliser une condition d'homme*]."[156] Black being envies whiteness, but the white self is equally touched or plagued by his phantasm of humanity insofar as he knows that the being of his whiteness does not coincide with (his) humanity. So in a significant way the white self is *not* a man either. Strictly speaking, no one is a "Man" (a being absent of history)—whence white/Zionist anxiety, belligerence, and scapegoating. The human is a fetish, always a fleeting phantasm that must be ruthlessly and constantly critiqued. In an act of bad faith or willful ignorance, whites and Zionists claim the "human" as theirs, but this is propaganda for the status quo, a gross ideological lie used to enforce and legitimize the colonial hierarchical order that is, a metaphysical apartheid and an ontological partition of the world.

Against Afropessimist futurology, pessimism as critique holds a purchase on the world. My pessimism, it should also be clear, does not prioritize one wretched group over others, one problem over others. It is not a question of substituting Palestinian rage for Black rage, Palestino-pessimism for Afropessimism. Likewise, when we reclaim the humanity of Blacks and Palestinians, which is again an irresistible claim (something that you *cannot not claim*, as Gayatri Spivak might say),[157] inseparable from the claim that their lives do matter, we risk prolonging this nasty humanist lie. In adopting the default humanist framework, in defending the dead via their quasi-sanctioned rehumanization (yes, we allow you to see Blacks and Palestinians as "victims," but nothing more), we, in effect, suspend or postpone a reckoning with the racial matrix of the human, with what turns me or my Black neighbor into a problem. A posthuman horizon opens up our discussion the moment pessimism becomes dialectical, critical, the moment we hesitate and linger on this double bind, when we step back and ponder the paucity of humanism and the anti-Black and anti-Palestinian worlds that it underpins. A "new humanism," if there will be such a thing, will ironically resonate far less with the humanism of old and far more with a posthumanism that avows the neighbor within and without, and takes seriously its inhuman core.

Chapter 2

The Gift of ~~Being~~ (a Problem)

The Fanonian zone of nonbeing is a curse and a gift. Those thrown into this hellish zone are *ab initio* problems, considered suspicious, policed by a state that awaits their inevitable transgression, occasioning punishment in the form of gratuitous violence: your fault is your *being*, not so much your *doing*. The damned in/of this zone endure perpetual social death. Still, Black and Palestinian bodies—exemplars of the wretched of the earth—tirelessly push back against the world's life-stultifying technologies. They struggle to live in a settler and racist world that deems them inferior, dangerous, and unwanted. They endure and persist, practicing their *sumud* in the face of tyrannical occupiers and suffocating realities. Moreover, and perhaps more importantly, we should always keep in mind that Fanon alerts us to the emancipatory potential of this life-denying zone, from which, he tells us paradoxically, a "genuine new departure can emerge."[1] The dissolution of one's social ego creates the conditions for radical transformation or ontological upheaval. The zone functions both as damnation and salvation, punishment and hope; what renders me inoperative can also liberate me. According to the humanist/white script, the formerly wretched returns from banishment to the fold of a phantasmatic model of the Human. And yet some thinkers like Fred Moten are not so eager to exit the zone of nonbeing—if by exiting we mean embracing a ready-made identity, accepting an identitarian logic that promises ontological upgrades, a potential reintegration to the zone of being (through, for instance, the liberal politics of recognition).

Are exiting or not exiting the zone of nonbeing, then, the only options? If you exit the hellish zone, do you cease being a problem? And if you don't, are you condemned to the zone in perpetuity? What if problemhood and the zone of nothingness didn't align so neatly? What if we imagine the human as an unruly body that does not so much question her status as a problem (Why do you say that I'm problem? Why have you condemned me to this space of social death?) as subversively identify with the denigrating label of problem (as a problem for ontology), thus declining the bribes of humanism, the promise of access to the zone of being? These fugitive, and, in the Saidian sense, exilic bodies would paradoxically affirm the gift of dispossession and revel in the opportunity to add their names to the tradition of feminist killjoys, to make those cozy with power uneasy, to make those who dominate and silence squirm in their seat of ontological and sovereign privilege. Might doesn't make right. Defend the dead. The last shall be first.[2]

The Politics of Radical Dispossession

Forged by historical traumas, Blacks and Palestinians move in this world with a particular kind of awareness. The terrible gifts of the Maafa and the Nakba (a Swahili term meaning great disaster, and the Arab word for catastrophe, respectively) introduce a sense of "radical dispossession"[3] into the lives and beings of Blacks and Palestinians, the former indelibly marked by "natal alienation"[4] and the latter by the exilic. From within this wretched zone of nonbeing, Blacks and Palestinians contemplating exit first confront the gaze of their oppressors, who offer one way out, via a deadly choice: "Whiten or disappear [se blanchir ou disparaître]."[5] Put on our mask and you'll become less of a problem; if you refuse, then you'd better get out of my sight, out of my neighborhood, out of my schools, out of my homeland, and out of my mind. Yet because the mask remains for the oppressor a mask, your problemhood never falls away. As Black people living in America know well, no educational credentials, accumulation of wealth, or accommodating habits and mannerisms can fully protect one from white suspicion and aggression.

Within the Green Line, the Zionist state's insistence that Palestinians be called Arab Israelis (not Palestinian citizens of Israel) exchanges one mask—that of the terrorist—for another, that of the "Arab," whose difference from Jewish Israelis remains linguistically marked. And if you wish to continue to pass as a "good Arab,"[6] do not ever speak of the Nakba (or the Occupation, settler colonialism, apartheid, ethnic cleansing, genocide, international law, etc.). Remember: Israel is a nation of and for the Jews—Arab citizens are tolerated out of the goodwill of the Israeli state. In Occupied Palestine, there can be no passing at all—if you want to live an uncaged life, a life without state terror (from military raids to a full-blown genocide), you must disappear, by evacuating, migrating, or dying. Yet even in the diaspora, where Palestinians may have additional rights (especially if you hold citizenship in the nation where you land, as I do myself), you remain a problem for the polity, marked as suspect, your Palestinianness provokes unease for your fellow "true" citizens: Is he going to bring up Gaza and genocide? Isn't he too anti-American? If he doesn't like America, why doesn't he leave? What kind of confidence or peace of mind can we really have from Western nations that have bankrolled and justified genocide, with parties across the political spectrum united in their material and ideological support for this slaughter or, at best, their failure to call it out?

Ontologically speaking, Black and Palestinian lives do NOT matter. They don't belong to what Édouard Glissant calls "the world of likes," a harmonious world free of difference and friction in which you recognize the other as a *semblable*, an image of yourself. Black and Palestinian "difference" never registers in the anti-Black and colonial world of likes, condemning them to "a world of nonbeing," which is, strictly speaking, a "nonworld."[7] Nonworlds are *a priori* genocidable insofar as those within them were never meant to live. Palestinians were never meant to exist and survive their occupation—*leave or die*. Black people were never meant to live free—*stay quiet, stay caged, or die*.

Because of settlerism, fascism, white supremacy, and the oppressor's brutish brutality (the IOF, the militarized police in Israel and America, the West Bank settlers, vigilante community watch groups, ICE—*take your pick from this unsavory lot*), we must rethink our relation to the world and others. But against a humanist/humanitarian angle that would aim to pull the wretched out from their nonworld and integrate them into the world of likes, Fred Moten takes the opposite path, deftly tapping into the paradoxes of the zone of nonbeing, expanding and rechanneling the force of its negativity by ironically even going as far as tempering the zone's announced liberatory potential—*from where a genuine new departure can emerge*. Moten refuses to exit from the zone of nonbeing.

Rejecting the false and forced choice between dispossession or sovereignty, between nothingness and identity, between rootedness and exile, Moten points to a different orientation toward being, moving away from the murderous grammar of possession (not only self-possession but also possession of others and of land and its minerals), adopting Glissant's deroutinizing formulation, "consent not to be a single being."[8] Consenting not to be a single being is, by extension, consenting to be a problem, a thing that cannot be integrated within the counters of the human—the West's overrepresented Man as Sylvia Wynter would say—without triggering a "crisis of the human" and "the human as crisis,"[9] and I would add "crisis of worlding" and "worlding as crisis." The human—especially when conceived as a being-in-the-world—is a concept to reckon with and not simply to "theorize away."[10]

Consenting not to be a single being means consenting not to be only a single human—you can be A and not-A.[11] When the symbolic order hails you as this thing or that thing (as an ethnonationalist, for example) and you consent to your interpellation (as a privileged white), your being, humanity, and worldhood ontologically shrinks. You lock yourself in your white identity, and surrender "attempts to be many beings at the same time."[12] The world of being doesn't admit multiplicity; it actively discourages this way of being. Consenting not to be a single being throws a wrench in the Western world's classificatory schema.

It compels us to rethink our understanding of the human. But Glissant does this by playing or rusing with the liberal language of consent. He doesn't begin with a frontal refusal "no consent to …"; rather, he begins with consent and then manages to short-circuit its liberal identitarian logic by revealing what he is consenting to is *not* to be a single being. As James Martel argues, Glissant/Moten deploys "consent" as "a weapon against its own ideology."[13] Refusal returns in a delayed form as a refusal of ontological containment and classification, and even self-mastery, to be pinned down once and for all: of the sort I am X. If consenting to be a single being conforms to "the metaphysics of individuation,"[14] that puts the human in a straitjacket, producing the human as a reified, knowable, and fetishized identity, deeply embroiled in the racial matrix of the human, consenting not to be a single being declines "the proper and the proposed,"[15] and affirms the monstrous (akin to the monstrous in Montaigne's self-essaying), an improper, multiple, anarchic, and open ontology, that indexes a state of flux, entanglement, and incompleteness.

Born of trauma, suffering, and homelessness, Blacks and Palestinians have become "more and less than one"[16]—whence the appositeness of their refusals to be a single being and exit the zone of nonbeing in an unproblematic manner. Reminiscent of Luce Irigaray's *This Sex Which Is Not One*, Moten plays on the blackened self's lack, her nothingness.[17] She is *less* than her white, masculinist, and humanist counterpart; her barred sovereignty and autonomy indexes not only that she does not possess herself but that she is also *more*. The dispossessed's plurality and excess—cultivated despite, or rather because of, the zone of nonbeing, in and against habitual scenes of subjugation and dispossession—threaten the rigidity of the ontological order. Black ontology, if there is such a thing, is open, incomplete, contagious, "fugitive,"[18] and not the least interested in the humanist legacy of *hominis perfectio*, human perfection, from the Latin *perfectio*, meaning completion. In fact, as scholars within Critical Black Studies have shown, the human is not aspirational (one day I can be seen as human) but the conceptual obstacle that needs overcoming. Again, for Blacks to live, the human must dissolve. Refusing the human, libidinally divesting from the human, is not some capricious instance of misanthropy but a principled stance and a question of survival! Humans have a checkered history to say the least. Though we understandably associate our oppression with the denigration or demonization of our humanity, we have to remember that, as Moten stresses, "human beings are the agents of that denial, which ought to give us pause about claiming the status of the human. Because if humans can be slave traders, if humans can destroy the environment, if humans can do all the bad things that humans do, then maybe we ought not jump so quickly, right?"[19] Inhabiting the zone of nonbeing allows us to tarry with this question.

Ever since Western modernity, the human has taken the form of a possessor, beginning with the possession of himself. Self-knowledge is self-possession and self-mastery, which then become the preconditions for becoming a Cartesian/colonial subject, these "masters and knowers of nature,"[20] as Descartes envisioned them, who are experienced by the rest of the world, however, as masters and enslavers, genocidaires and colonizers of Indigenous lands.[21]

The dispossessed, the "more and less than one," makes for an infinitely more desirable model than the human, or rather "Human," with a capital H— that category that underwrites the subject that consents to be a single being is identitarian, a "blood and soil" kind of a subject, and is anti-gender theory, mad about woke culture, and is often nostalgic for earlier harmonious (white, imperialist, and heteropatriarchal) days. Dispossessed of that capital, the "human" that underwrites the subject that consents not to be a single being doesn't flaunt her humanity; she is not interested in enjoying the full privileges of the zone of being; rather, she enjoys "wrestl[ing]"[22] with the Human, scrambling his grammar and puncturing his narcissistic arrogance.

To wrestle is to linger in the zone of nonbeing, keeping one foot in the Lacanian Real, means that you willfully discard the liberal path of redress and submit instead to the demands of a double bind, two competing and conflicting injunctions. The first is to challenge your ontological dispossession—social death is not destiny; another existence and world are possible. The second, however, is to reject the almost irresistible temptation to affirm self-possession, a synecdoche of the Human, turn down the lure of reaping the benefits of being fully human, of mattering. We are dealing with a double *No!* You fight against your reduction to nothingness (coterminous with bare life) without conceding that identity/being is the antidote to your otherness, nothingness, or exclusion. In lingering in the zone of nonbeing, you resist your ontological dispossession, refracting the big Other's supremacist gaze, but still resist differently. You're fighting on two fronts: you're struggling against a racist system that banishes you to the zone of nonbeing, and you are, at the same time, exercising your "right to refuse what has been refused to you"[23]—access to the coveted zone of being or zone of likes. You are refusing the proposed, the liberal proper way to be (a single being), transmogrifying from ~~being~~ to being, exiting from the zone of nonbeing into the liberal realm of identity politics.

Claiming the human against the Human paints the human as a "bloody battleground, a terrible obligation, and a set of hard-won chances."[24] The (post) human enacts her humanity by questioning the proper of the human.[25] Being human is, in part, realizing that you don't coincide with yourself or with what the symbolic order dictates you to be (you're a being or ~~being~~). Moten powerfully asks: "What if all the human ever has been is just this beautiful capacity and imperative to be other than itself against the grain of coloniality's carceral reduction of earth to man's dominion and its constant relegation of whatever it loves to hate and whatever it hates to desire to the zone of the inhuman?"[26] This "beautiful capacity" can only emerge from the zone of nothingness/inhuman. Being human is ~~being human~~ *and more*.

To exist as a problem in a life-affirming way also means to wrestle with human *rights*. I ask, How does the desire "to be other than itself" relate to two seemingly agonistic rights: the Arendtian demand "the right to have rights" (recall Mahmoud Khalil's question, "Who has the right to have rights?") and Moten's "the right to refuse what has been refused to you" (a formulation inspired by Gayatri Spivak's observation that "at the bottom, the first right is the right to refuse")?[27] "The right to have rights" expresses a desire to survive, a commitment to improve human rights discourse, trying to anchor this right in the human itself and *not* make it reliant on the whims of the state. In contrast, "the right to refuse what has been refused to you" divests from that same paradigm by paradoxically using its language against a paradigm overtly attached to identity. Rights are unmistakably the tools of the master; you can use tools differently and inventively, but you are still relying on the paradigm of the human. Refusing "what has been refused to you" translates what wrestling with the Human looks like; if, at one time, I was denied certain rights because I didn't conform to sanctioned model of the human, but now I am eligible—call it my de-wretchedification—what happens to all the others who continue to be banished to the "zone of subhumanity"?[28] What happens to the other wretched, to my comrades? My new rights come with a catch; for me, to enjoy them, others must not—whence the dilemma, the excruciating double bind. I must survive in this unjust world—and rights clearly help mitigate my situation; they allow me to breathe. *And* I refuse to be conscripted into a regime that grants me the privilege of breath while others asphyxiate (I breath *because* others don't). I refuse the choices as offered: I fight for Khalil's right to have rights *and* argue for the dismantling of a paradigm that perpetuates the ontological partition of the world into zones in which some flourish and many sub-others are caught up in "endless war."[29]

Wrestling with the human casts the cry "defend the dead," discussed in Chapter 1, in a new light. It can be thought as well as, "defend the human." Here the human is freed, or at least loosen, from its coloniality, obsession for containment, and its devotion to sovereignty, the figure of the Human, but also may be, will be, incarcerated for being a problem. It is a human "unfit for subjection,"[30] for whom relationality is not an add-on but a fact of existence. This human consents not to be a single being. She stands for abolition (i.e., the true event of emancipation) and in opposition to a cruel coloniality that cages and incarcerate nonbeings, ~~beings~~, that has instrumentalized, and continues to instrumentalize, humans and the earth without accountability. Defend the human means agitating with/for those marked as wretched in their struggle to sabotage their assigned miserable fate. The injunction also guides you (back) to the zone of nonbeing and from this position of the excluded (post)human, of flesh, a degentrified human, you can reframe your/our emancipatory exit from the zone as a refusal; your/our liberation is not premised on your/our election to the zone of *single* beings. The zone of nonbeing violently "desedimentized" but it also opens the possibility of an alternative relation to being, which continues to resist its *"resedimentation"*[31] and capture in the world of likes.

In refusing the Human for the human, you decline the liberal anti-racist playbook, your interpellation into a reformist liberal system that purports to reclaim your humanity, to restore or modestly upgrade your place in the humanist order of things, governed by the hegemonic and phantasmatic model of being/ the Human. The liberation that opens up in this shift from Human to human is marked by another violence: if the first violence of racial interpellation limited your being-in-the-world, the second violence of liberation involves the undoing of your identity (a kind of un-being, *désêtre*), the very identity that a naturalized violence has cruelly made possible. As Baldwin notes, "The possibility of liberation which is always real is also always painful, since it involves such an overhauling of all that gave us our identity."[32] True equality between Blacks and whites will hurt. In an anti-Black world, liberation is not so much about unleashing who you are as it is about radically destabilizing (the affective attachment to) who you are, and with this comes a necessary level of self-violence, spurred by a political transformation, a collective upheaval against our sanctioned identity. In the refusal, you're saying *No!* to the racial logic of humanism, to the paradigm of the human, which the liberal symbolic order presents as my only lifeline, my only way out of this zone of absolute dereliction: *Aren't you tired of being a problem? You want to be better off, right? Then follow our script.*

Tarrying with/as Trouble

Consenting not to be a single being recasts the zone of nonbeing and its political and emancipatory potential. Our *exit non exit* from the zone of nonbeing is no longer premised on our election to the normative zone of *single* beings, an upgrade in/toward whiteness, the world of being and its identity politics of grace. Consenting not to be a single being means dwelling in the zone of nonbeing and staying with trouble, as Donna Haraway might say, living differently and inventively in the life-draining and flesh-making trauma of the zone of indistinction, where you might astonishingly discover the reality of multiplicity, that it is "possible to be one and multiple at the same time; that you can be yourself and the other; that you can be the same and the different."[33] Consenting not to be a single being calls for nothing short of a hysterical revaluation or transvaluation of dispossession, heeding the lessons of Black Studies: reckoning with the reverberation of being dispossessed, with "what it is to own one's dispossession, to mine what is held in having been possessed," so that it "makes it more possible to embrace the underprivilege of being sentenced to the gift of constant escape."[34] Tarrying with

Blackness produces a different set of problems; the dispossessed, as unruly problem-makers, are eager to disturb the underground of the big Other's anti-Black world of likes and its colonial zone of being. Such bodies, questioning and fugitive, "relish being a problem."[35]

Tarrying with Blackness obliges us to face the Western tradition that gave us murderous sovereignties, the commodification of everything, Indigenous genocides, and chattel slavery. But while Moten lauds the Afropessimists for pursuing this world-sundering reckoning, he does not share Afropessimism's "critical obsession with bare life."[36] On Moten's account, Blackness does not stand for a state of utter dilapidation, nor is it to be "associated with a certain sense of decay."[37] Rather, he infuses Blackness with a "dispossessive force,"[38] an untranslatability that unsettles all hermeneutic attempts at mastery and containment.[39] What Blackness *is* remains quite mysterious and elusive. Why? Because Blackness precedes ontology—whence the paradox.

Moten turns to Nahum Chandler's notion of paraontological difference to help him disimbricate Blackness from slavery's ontological ravages in order to unpack the incommensurable difference between Blackness and Black being. Chandler's paraontology relies on an innovative interpretation of W. E. B. Du Bois's notion of "double consciousness," where he stresses that the white gaze that the Black individual violently encounters never exhausts the being of Black people. Chandler develops this insight, casting Blackness as "the general possibility of the otherwise."[40] The second sight denotes a paraontological distinction, an irreducible Blackness that the white world madly intolerates. Moten generalizes Chandler's insight. The paraontological distinction enables Moten to separate between "blackness or the thinking of blackness" and "black people."[41] Moten proceeds to illustrate the paraontological distinction in his critical reading of Fanon, in which he decouples Blackness from Black being, treating the former as that which is prior to ontology, which, unlike the latter, is irreducible to its capture, to Black being ("already given ontologies"[42] fail to elucidate Blackness). With this intervention, Moten refutes a foundational premise of the Afropessimist position; he argues that Blackness is not the violent by-product of political ontology, the result of a metaphysical mutation, a "metaphysical holocaust,"[43] that transformed Africans into Blacks, brought about by chattel slavery.

But Moten here unnecessarily collapses Fanon with his Afropessimists readers. He laments that Fanon's pathological/ontological account of Blackness misses an opportunity to claim "an irremediable homelessness common to the colonized, the enslaved, and the enclosed," to bear witness to a Blackness that names "a disorder that has always been there, that is retrospectively and retroactively located there, that is embraced by the ones who stay there while living somewhere else."[44] Though Fanon paints a stark condition that there is no available ontology to counter the nullifying gaze of whiteness, Fanon does not stop here with an account of his petrification, as if it constituted his banishment to the zone of nonbeing, a one-way ticket to a living hell. Rather, Fanon does offer us something akin to Du Bois's double consciousness, which he grounds in his resistance to Western ontology through its dislocation.

In the beginning of chapter 5 of *Black Skin, White Masks*, Fanon delineates the brutality of the white gaze and his own utter failure to block its devastating impact. Indeed, Fanon opens the chapter with a visceral account of his asymmetrical encounter with the white gaze: " 'Dirty Nigger!' Or simply, 'Look, a Black!' "[45] These words traumatize Fanon, dispossessing him of his subjectivity, even of his assumed Frenchness/whiteness. Immobilized by the racial slur, Fanon painstakingly recounts his ordeal:

> Locked in this suffocating reification, I appealed to the Other so that his liberating gaze, gliding over my body suddenly smoothed of rough edges, would give me back the lightness of being I thought I had lost, and taking me out of the world put me back in the world. But just as I get to the other slope I stumble, and the Other fixes me with his gaze, his gestures and attitude, the same way you fix a preparation with a dye. *I lose my temper, demand an explanation. ... Nothing doing. I explode. Here are the fragments put together by another me.*[46]

It is important to note that in this passage we encounter two Fanons: the "I" who has exploded (either because of his anger at the white gaze or because the overwhelming gaze itself shatters him) is assisted by another Fanon, presumably the narrator of *Black Skin, White Masks*. If the first "I" finds himself in bits and pieces, radically dispossessed, the narrator, presumably working through his trauma by revisiting and in some respect reliving his pain, reassembles another self with the former's shattered pieces. The actual writing of the book is Fanon's response to ontology's failure and disappointment, to its capture of Fanon as a problem. Remember, Fanon tells us in the introduction to it is "in most cases" not "in all cases" that "the Black man cannot take advantage of this descent into a veritable hell." Having said that, we should not see Fanon as an exception to the law of anti-Blackness, as someone untouched by the ills of anti-Blackness. Far from it. He gives an account of his self, of a self caught in a colonial situation (in the French metropole!): "The black man has no ontological resistance in the eyes of the white man. From one day to the next, the Blacks have had to deal with two systems of reference. Their metaphysics, or less pretentiously their customs and the agencies to which they refer, were abolished because they were in contradiction with a new civilization that imposed its own."[47] In Lacanian parlance, anti-Blackness is everywhere, no one is immune from its reach, but it is "non-all," never complete or total. Fanon proceeds to denaturalize ontology, exposing its fake universalism and unmarked whiteness, demythifying its authority, especially in matters of race and Blackness. Fanon's first book is nothing short of a counter-ontology, not a Black ontology, but an insurgent ontology that creates as it exposes the predominant ontology's racist cultural underpinnings, its interminable disavowal and failure to reckon with its imperialist origins and practices. Isn't there something "extraontological"[48] in Fanon's dreams of ontological upheavals, the ways his text compel us to think and imagine our (non)exit from the zone of nonbeing?

Moreover, enjoying being a problem is not foreign to Fanon. On one occasion Fanon describes his interaction with a white woman. It is set within an overwhelming presence of whiteness: "The white man is all around me; up above the sky is tearing at its navel; the earth crunches under my feet and sings white, white. All this whiteness burns me to a cinder."[49] The ubiquity of whiteness triggers a meditation on his own appearance: "I sit down next to the fire and discover my livery for the first time. It is in fact ugly. I won't go on because who can tell me what beauty is?" Self-reflection builds to anger: "Where should I put myself from now on? I can feel that familiar rush of blood surge up from the numerous dispersions of my being. I am about to lose my temper. The fire had died a long time ago, and once again the Negro is trembling."[50] Fanon trembles with rage against the white world and his allocated nonplace in it. Then comes a liberal white woman who compliments Fanon on his looks:

"Look how handsome that Negro is."
"The handsome Negro says, 'Fuck you,' madame."
"Her face colored with shame. At last I was freed from my rumination. I realized two things at once: I had identified the enemy and created a scandal. Overjoyed. We could now have some fun."[51]

This is double consciousness at work. We might say that Fanon experienced a crash course in double consciousness. As a Martinican (and not an African), Fanon arrives in the French metropole (Martinique had become a French department in 1946) simply assuming that his consciousness would coincide with the standard consciousness of white French people. But he quickly and painfully learns that this isn't the case. Fanon's lived experience became irredeemably marked as other, other than French, worse than French, by virtue of the color of his skin. Fanon clearly felt he was looking at himself "through the eyes of others."[52] "Respectable" white French saw him as unsightly because Blackness was unconsciously aligned with ugliness. Fanon understood the "twoness" of his being: a French, a Black man, "two souls, two thoughts, two unreconciled strivings; two warring ideals in one dark body."[53] For both Du Bois and Fanon, Black consciousness stands miles apart from white consciousness. The latter navigates social life effortlessly whereas the former is banished, and reminded of his banishment, and he is somatically marked, bearing the full pathological weight of social death. Fanon's double consciousness provokes an identity crisis, propelling him further and further into the zone of nonbeing: "Without a black past, without a black future, it was impossible for me to live my blackness. Not yet white, no longer completely black, I was damned."[54]

And yet Fanon saw through the woman's racist language. By giving Fanon a compliment about his appearance, she was exceptionalizing him; Fanon is the exception that proves the rule: Blackness is ugly. And his response unsettles the terms of her address by refusing the "proper" (i.e., racist) civic demeanor: "the handsome Negro says, 'Fuck you,' madame." Fanon surely relished being a problem, at the very least in that interaction. Invention and ontological upheavals happen, creative acts can miraculously happen, unsettling our quotidian habits and/or derailing our state-sanctioned futures (more of the same, the reproduction of an anti-Black world).

So even in the background of an all-consuming anti-Blackness, Black agency persists. This is Moten's bold and crucial refrain to the Afropessimists. But should we also consider, with Moten, Fanon to have prematurely exited the zone of nonbeing, to have failed to tarry with Blackness? Fanon's twists and turns complicate the matter. Aside from the examples above, the new human(ism) à venir that Fanon gestures to on the first page of Black Skin, White Masks, as I intimated in Chapter 1, is unlikely to correspond to anyone or anything belonging to the normative zone of single beings. "The history of blackness," writes Moten, "is testament to the fact that objects can and do resist."[55] Fanon would concur. It is this kind of rebellion that sparks Fanon's insurgent feeling of/ for solidarity: "Every time a man has brought victory to the dignity of the spirit, every time a man has said no to an attempt to enslave his fellow man, I have felt a sense of solidarity with his act."[56] The history of Blackness is the history of resilience and resistant objects (I return to the politics of objecthood in Chapter 3). Time and time again, the dispossessed say No! to their white oppressors, and for that reason Fanon would have championed that history. This is a tradition of Blackness, or the "Black Radical Tradition," as Moten puts it after Cedric Robinson, that Fanon would have surely endorsed insofar as it refused to seal people in their race or ethnicity, and didn't artificially separate race from class concerns. As per the paraontological difference, Moten's Blackness never limits itself to a well-demarcated racial group; though Black people clearly occupy a special relation to Blackness, they have a "non-coterminous and nonexclusive relation"[57] to Blackness. If Blackness is irreducible to Black people, it makes itself present wherever a struggle for justice, against racist ontology, is taking place; this is why Moten considers his solidarity with Palestinians, his support for the BDS movement, an enactment of/in the Black Radical Tradition: "I am speaking for the boycott, in solidarity with the Palestinians, because I am committed to the insurgent alternative, whose refreshment is (in) the antinational international. The terms of that commitment are nothing other than the terms of my commitment to the black radical tradition."[58] Palestinians are confronting a cruel Zionist ontology, a colonial apartheid regime that props up fascist politicians, invests and reaps the economic and liberal rewards of a racial matrix of the human, and that partitions their world into the saved and the damned, in those who matter and those who don't. *How can Blackness and Black people not be directly implicated in the struggle for Palestinian liberation?*

Blackness is a limit on any (supremacist) ontology. It operates, as it were, in power's shadows. The lived experience of Blackness—an experience particularly available to the wretched of the earth—elicits and provokes a desire for "an ontology of disorder, an ontology of dehiscence."[59] It tirelessly labors to expose and undo humanism's ontology (the racial cult of the single being), jamming its logic and schematization—at times via withdrawals *à la* Melville's character Bartleby: "To refuse what has been refused is a combination of disavowing, of not wanting, of withholding consent to be a subject and also of refusing the work, of withholding consent to do the work, that is supposed to bring the would-be subject online. It is to prefer not to, in stuttered, melismatic, gestural withdrawal."[60] Other times, Moten stages Blackness as "pathogenic"[61] as opposed to "pathological." Blackness as a pathology submits to political ontology's *framing* of Blackness (both in the way you set up the framework of interpretation and the way a crooked police officer frames an innocent person) as a sign of criminality, an illness and threat to civil society's well-being, and thus a problem to be summarily segregated to zones of abandonment and indifference. Blackness as pathogenic operates differently; it infects the enemy, breaching the supremacist's fortress, society's white immune system.[62] Indeed, it "bears or is the potential to end the world."[63] Blackness as pathogenic doesn't so much solicit a "phenomenology of anti-blackness" as provoke an appreciation for the "wonder of blackness."[64]

If the former marks the incapacitating effects of living in an anti-Black world (what the Afropessimists have unstintingly documented in the lives of Black folks), the latter affirms its problemhood, holding an emancipatory potential for Blacks and the other dispossessed of the world. Blackness lacks and exceeds being, never coinciding with itself; it baffles white ontology which is unable to counter or tame its sabotaging queer logic. An affront to the normative regime of the proper, the dispossessed's paraontological ways introduce a generative disorder in the world. *This dispossessed that is not one* points to another way of being and belonging.

Blackness's fugitivity announces its defiant unruliness and irreducible becoming. To embrace Blackness as fugitivity is to want to derail the obedient subject, to take him offline, to steal life from the master/slaveholder/settler, to reinvest in a life previously marked for destruction, a naked life, a life (un) lived in the desert of the Real. It is to develop an eye or orientation for the paraontological, and a taste for the improper and the unsanctioned, "a desire for and a spirit of escape and transgression of the proper and the proposed."[65]

Moten's grammar of Blackness introduces possible moves that can only appear as impossible from with the racial matrix of the human. At the same time, Moten's account of Blackness can become too enigmatic even for generous readers like Calvin Warren, who zeroes in on the unthematizability of Blackness. Reading it psychoanalytically, Warren considers Blackness as an instantiation of the elusive *objet petit a*: "Our desire to move beyond 'ontological Blackness' ... becomes something similar to the psychoanalytic notion of *objet (a)*. Blackness is the imaginary wholeness or origin that we are in constant pursuit of, but never can quite approach."[66] Viewing "Blackness" as akin to the cause-object of desire of (Moten's vision of) Black Studies strikes me as right. Black Studies hungers for Blackness, but Blackness does not abide and always disappoints. No movement or theory is able to explain, contain, or satisfy Blackness's infinite demands. Blackness upends "ontological thinking,"[67] the desire for Black identity/~~identity~~, any scenario where Blackness and Black being/~~being~~ would coincide and fold into each other. Blackness always means more, or less, than is ontologically proclaimed in its name (from Black humanists to Afropessimists). Dissatisfaction pervades (or at least ought to pervade) the field of Black Studies. Blackness is always at risk of losing its destabilizing edge, subduing its paraontological resistance, and making it, in turn, just another ideological fantasy that covers over or obfuscates the primordial gap or void. On Warren's Lacanian reading, Moten's Blackness is through and through phantasmatic, located beyond the reach of the symbolic order, indexing a pre-Lapsarian state of being: a pristine Blackness untouched by Western modernity, its ontology, along with its racial matrix of the human.

Still, I wonder whether Warren's warning over the dangers of Blackness as or like *objet petit a* distorts a bit Moten's position.[68] What Warren misconstrues is the *objet petit a*'s role in fantasy: the fantasy of a primordial wholeness that sustains the desire for Blackness, that alchemically transforms the Blackness of the pathologized Black, Black ~~being~~, "into the utopian promise of the impossible fullness of *jouissance*,"[69] the plenitude and fullness of Blackness. The riposte to (Warren's reading of) Moten is not to jettison the phantasmatic *objet petit a* and accept a more responsible, and less fetishized, enjoyment of, and engagement with, Blackness—but to envision Blackness as a disorienting object, as an excessive and enigmatic object that decompletes and unsettles the subject's *Lebenswelt*. Slavoj Žižek provides an insight into the next move: the need to shift the Lacanian lens from desire to drive, from the object-cause of desire to object-loss of drive:

> While, as Lacan emphasizes, the *objet a* is also the object of the drive, the relationship is here thoroughly different: although, in both cases, the link between object and loss is crucial, in the case of the *objet a* as the object-cause of *desire*, we have an object which is originally lost, which coincides

with its own loss, which emerges as lost, while, in the case of the *objet a* as the object of the drive, the "object" is *directly the loss itself* —in the shift from desire to drive, we pass from the *lost object* to *loss itself as an object.*[70]

Once you shift from desire to drive, Blackness as *objet petit a* takes a different form; it is no longer in pursuit of "the 'impossible' quest for the lost object"[71] —the object of a desire that must be demythified and returned to a non-phantasmatic reality. Blackness thwarts all searches for impossible fullness (*à la* Négritude movement). Its political *jouissance* lies in lack itself. Relishing being a problem for/of ontology, Blackness, as a reminder and remainder of political ontology, reveals a world that is non-all, where social death is *not* destiny, where a lawless Blackness unapologetically and inventively persists.

Making Good Problems

"Consenting to be a single being" is your entry into the privileges of white civil society. It is to be comfortable at home in a time of genocide, if you will. It is to be on board with doxa, and not to stray too far from the beliefs and tastes of the ruling class. For the rest of us, it is a capitulation, a deadly concession to the supremacist logic of possession; it surrenders the gift of dispossession, neutralizing its pharmacotic effects as a gift. The dispossessed-cum-human substitutes sovereignty for dispossession in an effort to gain legitimacy and legibility, in an effort to join the privileged zones of interest and being. Relishing being a problem runs in a different direction. It embraces problemhood as a life-affirming gesture, delighting in being a problem for others, a problem for the powerful and the privileged.

The feminist killjoy occupies this position of disturbance and refusal. Shortly after October 7, Sara Ahmed expressed her solidarity with Palestine as an unqualified disturbance to the colonial order of things: "To express solidarity with Palestine is to be a killjoy, wherever we are. We get in the way because of how we mourn, or who we mourn, becoming a problem because of what we point to or because of the violence we refuse to pass over, the violence of colonial occupation, the violence enacted right now against people in Gaza by the Israeli state."[72] Decidedly pro-Palestinian and pro-Black, she calls out the gatekeepers of the zone of being, asking them, *What must take place for them, to them, to enjoy their luxuries? Who have they driven into the zone of the living dead for economic profit and affective pleasures? Are you enjoying your stock portfolios engrossed by companies with strong military ties? Are Gaza, Ukraine, and Iran good for your bottom line?* The feminist killjoy has no patience with liberals who bemoan Trump as if he alone is responsible for the massacres in Gaza and the anti-Black reality that is contemporary America.

The killjoy relishes being a problem and never capitulates in advance. She is not shy nor a team player (especially when the team is genocidal), and does not give up on lost causes. When it comes to just causes, she is all in. But her battle is always collective. The killjoy exercises her public use of *ressentiment*; in un-Nietzschean fashion, she insists on *ressentiment's* generative negativity, its own rationality, triggering a shift from *ressentiment* as a personal expression of frustration (the stuff of identity politics and anger management programs) to *ressentiment* as a collective *No!* to an unjust world; *No!* to walls that segregate our existence; *No!* to tech bro oligarchs and girl bosses; *No!* to vertical ontologies of all kinds. She is not at all interested in leveraging her pain in order to expand her privileges. She demands that change actually mean change.

The guardians of the hegemonic liberal center infuriate. Their pompous arguments about what needs to be done—their pretention to be the adults in the room, bringing wisdom and calm where student protestors for justice in Palestine bring immaturity and chaos—obfuscate the stakes of the moment. M. Gessen put a finger on the obscenity of this dynamic and the "political cynicism" of the liberal Left in August 2024, when, at a campaign rally in the Detroit area, Kamala Harris famously responded to protestors shouting their discontent about her position on Gaza with the assertion, "I am speaking now." A Black woman asserting that she is speaking can indeed unsettle the white order of things. But here Harris was not speaking to power, nor acting as a feminist killjoy relishing being a problem, but rather serving as an instrument of power by making others into problems for political gain. Simply put, Harris was punching down. Let's name Harris's "I am speaking now" for what it is: a chilling "call to order." Remember, "to be recognizable, you have to answer the call to order."[73] In other words, Harris's words messaged, stay in your lane, listen, keep your concerns domestic, and drop your distracting and meritless demands ("You know what? If you want Donald Trump to win, then say that. Otherwise, I'm speaking"). Gessen stresses Harris's inability to relate to the protesters at a profoundly existential level, to understand what a vote for Harris means for them, what it means to vote for a genocide enabler and a genocide denier:

Most Democratic voters ... can probably see themselves voting for Harris, knowing that her administration will not bring immediate relief to the Palestinian people, because they also know that on this and other issues, a Harris administration will be better than a Trump one. But some voters ... cannot stand to live in a world in which Joe Biden's vice president, who has not voiced any disagreement with the administration's Middle East policies, wins the presidency. It's not that they want Trump to win; it's that the level of political cynicism they are being asked to adopt feels unbearable.

These voters are not choosing between Harris and Trump. They are choosing between their sense of themselves as moral beings if they vote for Harris and their sense of themselves if they vote for a third-party candidate or for no one at all. ... If they vote for Harris in November, what will that say to the people of Gaza—that they'd held their noses while people died? What will they tell their children—that politics is the game of the possible, and sometimes it's just not possible to stop a genocide? What will they tell themselves to be able to sleep at night?

For these voters, the psychic price of voting for Harris—of voting at all—is extremely high. It is possible that they could be convinced to pay this price, because, of course, they know, just as I do, that a Harris Middle East policy would be infinitely preferable to a Trump one. But they have to be convinced, not dismissed. Harris has to acknowledge their existential pain, the unbearable burden of living, in some cases, with the daily fear for loved ones, their sense of alienation from a world that seems indifferent to 2,000-pound bombs and to the infliction of starvation. For a campaign that has started positioning itself as caring, humanistic and kind, the failure to acknowledge this pain and this fear is especially jarring.

That Trump is worse is not the question. The question is how a party in power during an unfolding genocide, one that has abetted that genocide and denied it was occurring, can demand unconditional support, as if it is common sense, as if stopping this slaughter and pursuing a more just domestic agenda are mutually exclusive. The killjoy in me cannot stop insisting on the inadequacies of the liberal reading. The way liberals see or misrecognize the Palestinian problem is effectively part of the problem. And by pointing it out we, of course, become the problem.

To the chagrin of white (neo)liberals in the United States and abroad, the feminist killjoy will not stay quiet about the genocide. She is divisive; she wants to be divisive. The feminist killjoy has *ressentiment* to spare; she doesn't forget and forgive the Biden–Harris administration for its colossal moral failure by not reining in Netanyahu's Zionist killing machine, and putting an end to the genocide in Gaza.[74] She challenges those in the pragmatic Left/liberal center who complain that the radical or anti-colonial Left is the problem, with its obsession with Gaza, its constant agitations and criticisms, its refusal to let anxious Democrats celebrate Kamala Harris's nomination or enjoy their "brat summer" without being questioned over their tacit endorsement of genocide.[75] The feminist killjoy "ruin[s] the atmosphere,"[76] disturbs public peace (when peace equals the repression of others, the exclusion of society's outcasts). She troubles the liberal's right to happiness, not out of spiteful envy, but, as Sara Ahmed aptly notes, out of principles: "if happiness requires turning away from violence, happiness is violence."[77] The happiness of the liberal center is self-absorbed and callous, predicated on the violence being visited daily on Palestinians. Your happiness is murderous.

In contradistinction to the liberal internationalism proffered by the Democratic Party, the feminist killjoy's *parti pris* lies with the wretched of the earth. Inspired by Black and Third World feminists, the killjoy reads up the ladder of privilege[78] and sharpens her critical tools. The "lesser of two evils" rhetoric is politically cowardly and morally bankrupt. This rhetoric, favored by liberals of all shades, as Omar El Akkad points out, diminishes us ethically and interpretively: "It … establishes the lowest of benchmarks: *Want my vote? Be less monstrous than the monsters.*"[79] The Democratic Party's sales pitch is *yes, we facilitate genocide, but we don't enjoy doing it; we're not sadist Republicans after all*. The Democratic Party's moral and hermeneutic failures is matched by the Republican Party's spirit of viciousness. As Noam Chomsky observed in 2017, the Republican Party is the "most dangerous organization on earth."[80] The lawless party of Law and Order under Trump displays its true and full obscenity. Might makes right. Between Israel and the United States, we are dealing with "the world of likes." *Genocidaires recognize Genocidaires*. Netanyahu and Trump dream of a Gaza (and West Bank) without Palestinians. In this time of Trump, in this time of fascism, the feminist killjoy calls for renewed investment in what Ahmed names "a world-making project."[81] If the far Right is libidinally invested in the phantasmatic purity of a bygone era (one that is free of gender-bending, free of talk of racism, free of Palestinians, free of migrants, etc.), the anti-colonial, anti-racist Left needs to invest affectively in life-affirming and revolutionary ideals, equality and freedom *for all*—ideals that those devoted to the world of likes (including the atrocious Democrats) will undoubtedly find off-putting. We need an "opposition party for/ of the wretched" regardless of which official party is in office. Ta-Nehisi Coates, responding to an astonished electorate, points out the degree to which the Democratic Party's unprincipled position on Palestine sets the stage for its inability to mount a genuine defense of core democratic principles: "We are at a moment right now where people are asking themselves why can't the Democratic Party defend this assault on democracy … and I would submit to you that if you can't draw the line at genocide, you probably can't draw the line at democracy."[82] If the BLM movement compelled people across continents to think, even if for a minute, about the anti-Black logic that segregates the human from its negated or racialized other, the solidarity movement for Palestine is asking us to collectively dismantle the kind of world that allows a livestreamed genocide to take place and that demonizes any individual or group that opposes its maddening perpetuation. This solidarity movement asks us to embrace being a problem for injustice, to devote ourselves to making good problems.

No Single Problems

Problems here, not unlike individuals, are *more and less than one*. Afropessimists such as Frank Wilderson would, of course, raise objections: some problems cannot structurally speak to one another: how can they if they don't share the same grammar of suffering? For the Afropessimist, there is, for example, a fundamental incommensurability between the Black problem and the Palestinian problem. Palestinians can still draw on the paradigm of the human for help in articulating their plight for justice whereas Blacks are silenced by that same paradigm that lifts up the voices of non-Black dispossessed like those of Indigenous Palestinians. At the level of paradigm, Blacks, regardless of their position in society, are slaves. For the Afropessimist, comparing problems invites confusion or falls prey to the "ruse of analogy."[83] The certitude of the betrayal anticipated by Wilderson's paranoid hermeneutic is unhelpful for dealing with problems. Problems are not to be expectionalized (this problem is *not* like any other), nor hoarded or monopolized (only *this* problem counts; to exist as *the* problem), but shared, put into critical and multidirectional dialogue with other problems. Skepticism—in the vein of Montaigne's motto "What do I know?" and Fanon's prayer, from the last line of *Black Skin, White Masks*, "My final prayer: O my body, always make me a man who questions!"[84]—rather than suspicion and its assured futurology, a continuous future extrapolated from the past, ought to guide our inquiry. We must oppose and move beyond the logic of pitting one problem (for one people) against another as if one's value and dignity were primarily dictated by egotistical reason—the sanctioned approach by liberals who always prefer local problems over global ones, identity politics over transnational ones—caught up in an interminable zero-sum game: for me to matter, you must matter less or not even matter at all—you must un-matter. Enjoying being a Palestinian problem, for instance, does *not* compel me to displace or circumvent other problems, such as the Jewish problem. No, quite the opposite. I would say that problem-envy is anathema to any form of emancipatory politics.

Analytically speaking, each genuine problem is a world. Problems are rarely self-enclosed; they overlap, mix, and spill over one another. They don't lend themselves to hierarchical ranking unless your findings and solutions are secured in advance. Problems that are decontextualized—lifted from the messiness of history, the site of struggle over meaning—are ripe for fetishization, ideological manipulation, and weaponization (for the Nazis, the Jewish problem meant the "Final Solution," i.e., a healthy Germany and Europe free of Jews; for Ziofascists, the Palestinian problem means a "Greater Israel," i.e., a Zionist Israel free of Indigenous Palestinians). The boundaries of problems are often porous. Is there an adequate response to the Palestinian problem without a serious consideration of the Jewish problem? Similarly, the Palestinian problem and the Black problem are not to be envisioned in isolation, lest we distort their meaning, weaken their force, and underappreciate their co-constitutiveness, their co-commitment to imagine and model another world. Existing as a problem with others creates the conditions "to be many beings at the same time," as Glissant might put it.[85] Is this wishful thinking or, worse, another anti-Black operation that displaces the singularity of the Black problem to which only a Black agenda can adequately and fully respond? These questions haunt me.

To begin to propose (the beginning of) an answer, I want to turn to a primal scene in Afropessimist theory, one that Frank Wilderson returns to on numerous occasions, always to make the same point that anti-Blackness is without analog and that it tacitly unifies even enemies in their shared anti-Blackness, in their "anti-black solidarity," as Wilderson slyly puts it.[86] The enemies here are Palestinians and white Ashkenazi Jews. The context is a pre-Afropessimist Wilderson who awakens from his anti-colonial leftist slumber by a story recounted by his Palestinian friend and coworker, named Sameer Bishara,[87] which, as Wilderson argues, puts on full display his friend's unconscious hatred of Blacks, crystallized in the figure of the Ethiopian Israeli soldier. The Afropessimist reading allegorizes the story as a tale of incommensurability between Palestinian suffering and Black suffering. What is apparently staged is an antagonism of problems: Black problem versus Palestinian problem. I will first outline Wilderson's interpretation of the significance of his friend's story before critically analyzing it, putting it in apposition to Moten's musings on Blackness, dispossession and the dispossessed, paraontology, and the politics of refusal.

Wilderson tells a familiar story about commitment and disappointment. A pair of young rebels, leftists invested in revolutionary anti-colonial struggles, are conversing in friendship. Outsiders in white Minneapolis, Wilderson and Sameer naturally bonded. Wilderson had just told a story about Sameer's rumble with a few Kuwaitis over their arrogance (in thinking that they could seduce away the women who Sameer and his friend were talking to, and far more importantly, in calling Sameer "stateless," which triggered his friend's rage). At this point, Wilderson stood completely with his friend, as he says: "I thought I had the same loss too; because I thought my suffering was analogous to his. I was not an Afropessimist then."[88] What follows is the transformative scene/event of betrayal. I will quote the main passage in full in order to convey Wilderson framing of his friend and his story:

My friend spoke openly [about the death of his cousin in Ramallah] as we watched the world below us rush by without even looking up to pay its respects. At one point Sameer spoke of being stopped and searched at Israeli checkpoints. He spoke in a manner that seemed not to require my presence. I hadn't seen this level of concentration and detachment in him before. That was fine. He was grieving.

"The shameful and humiliating way the soldiers run their hands up and down your body," he said. Then he added, "But the shame and humiliation runs even deeper if the Israeli soldier is an Ethiopian Jew."

The earth gave way. The thought that my place in the unconscious of Palestinians fighting for their freedom was the same *dishonorable* place I occupied in the minds of Whites in America and Israel chilled me. I gathered enough wits about me to tell him that his feelings were odd, seeing how

Palestinians were at war with Israelis, and White Israelis at that. How was it that the people who stole his land and slaughtered his relatives were somehow *less* of a threat in his imagination than Black Jews, often implements of Israeli madness, who sometimes do their dirty work? What, I wondered silently, was it about Black people (about *me*) that made us so fungible we could be tossed like a salad in the minds of oppressors and the oppressed?[89]

I must confess that each time I teach, talk about, or write on this passage I almost always notice or discover something significantly new; my readings of Wilderson's Afropessimism have ranged from paranoid to reparative readings, and everything in between. So looking at it anew is at once familiar and nearly impossible. As an antagonism of problems, Wilderson's primal scene stages not only two competing visions of suffering (Palestinian vs. Black), but the ways in which some problems, no matter how tragic (the ethnic cleansing and ongoing Nakba of Palestinians), are in principle solvable whereas another problem, *the* other problem, the Black problem is both structurally untouchable and necessary for the resolution of all other problems, including the Palestinian problem.[90]

The passage opens with a possibility for strengthening further Wilderson and Sameer's solidarity. The earlier Kuwaitis incident only gestured toward their shared condition. Palestinians are colonized by the Israeli settler state while Blacks are America's internally colonized. Now, the IOF are involved; we have institutional humiliation as a form of necropolitical discipline. Controlling the movement of Palestinian bodies at Israeli checkpoints recalls the stop-and-frisk reality of so many Black Americans (we can also recall James Baldwin's 1966 piece "A Report from Occupied Territory," which is already making explicit the shared realities of the occupied and colonized around the world, one "hideous state of affairs" resembles another).[91] This opportunity for bonding through pain (about not belonging, homelessness, being a problem) vanishes in a flash when Wilderson hears the disparaging comment about the Ethiopian Israel soldier. Sameer's shame and humiliation was at its worst when the oppressor was an Ethiopian Jew. How could this be, pondered Wilderson? Is the Ethiopian Jew really the worst that Zionist Israel has to offer? Here these words devastated Wilderson ("the earth gave way"); they ruined his proximity to and fondness for Sameer. That moment was an epiphany of sorts: anti-Blackness is the common denominator, the universal currency of humanity. Sameer, non-Black Israelis, and white Americans, all fully participate in an anti-Black libidinal economy; their collective unconscious hates Blacks. A bewildered Wilderson asks Sameer, How is it possible that Ethiopian Jews (who are economically exploited and racially stigmatized in Israel)[92] are worse than the state's Ashkenazi Jews, the European Jews who were actually responsible for the ethnic cleansing of his people? Even more frustrating, How could a Black Jew occupy the same ontological space as a normative white Jew? Wilderson's painful lesson—how a positive resolution to the Palestinian problem necessarily involves the prolongation of the Black problem—that anti-Blackness permeates the unconscious of those closest to him clearly contributed to the formation of his Afropessimism.

Sameer never responded to Wilderson, or if he did, Wilderson leaves out Sameer's reaction in his accounts of the primal scene. What could have Sameer said? Could he have attenuated his anti-Blackness? Doubled down on it? Denied it altogether? Was the scene *only* about anti-Blackness? Can a recognition of anti-Blackness obfuscate another framework equally if not more significantly relevant to the episode at hand? Having already evoked Sameer's scuffle with the Kuwaitis sets the scene for a critique of his friend's blinders, that the stateless Sameer, the dispossessed par excellence, only cares about his land, and when he wants to express his hatred of Israelis his mind conjures up the image of the Black Jew. Wilderson is by no means oblivious to the colonial situation in Palestine/Israel, but he treats it as a secondary concern. The fact that the Ethiopian Jew is holding a weapon doesn't tilt the ontological relation between humans and would-be-humans on one side and nonhumans on the other. Blacks are still slaves in the United States, Israel, and beyond whereas Palestinians are still able to fight for recognition and earn their ontological upgrade (via their sovereignty over their land). In the encounter between Sameer and the Ethiopian soldier, the former is the master, the latter the slave, paradigmatically speaking. What Wilderson doesn't factor or ignores in his account of the power relation is that according to Israel's racial matrix of the human, Palestinians are ontologically *less* than Black Jews (not to mention that he also ignores the reality of Black Palestinians in this account).[93]

A corrective to Wilderson's Afropessimist reading would argue for a settler-colonial framework that thematizes the binary relation between Native and settler. The Ethiopian Jew is a settler and Sameer is the Native. The fact of anti-Blackness does not override or displace the colonial situation, the fact of Zionist coloniality, where the Palestinian, and not the Ethiopian, is the primary target of domination. Wilderson's "ontological absolutism" about Black abjection exaggerates at best, distorts at worst.[94] In the context of Israel, Black freedom exists. Black Jews perform their agency each time a Palestinian passes through their checkpoint.[95] Jewish supremacy, Zionism, and the power relations that they entail play no role in Wilderson's reading. We can further nuance the settler's position by saying that some settlers are better understood as "migrants," since they didn't come fully out of their free will.[96] Blacks were originally forced to come to America via chattel slavery. Ethiopian Jews were subjected to harsh living conditions at home, including "religious persecution, famine and civil wars," before migrating to Israel for refuge.[97] Yes, we may want to qualify the settler/Native binary, but we shouldn't qualify it out of existence. The task is to center the settler-colonial framework without making it an exhaustive condition in our discussion of the Palestinian/Israeli antagonism along with its entanglement with race and historical ontology. Along those lines, I want to stretch the Indigenous perspective by bringing in a Motenist sensibility to the antagonism of problems. Moten's *consent not to be single being* is nowhere to be found in the competing frameworks. What would it do to this staging of the antagonism if problems were not so affectively and materially tied to racial identity as determined by one's positionality? Sameer experiences his description as stateless as a kind of ontological insult: it is intended to racialize and denigrate Palestinian being, depicting him as less than human, existentially impoverished in the world. Sameer and Wilderson would be in agreement that the solution to the Palestinian problem is land back for Palestinians, meaning a return of one's identity—to a liberated Palestinian society, to a peaceful and harmonious *"time before the settler"* as Wilderson quips.[98] Wilderson is no less invested in identity, albeit a barred ~~identity~~.[99] I am not simply saying that Wilderson and Sameer can only see the situation through their respective subject position. Rather, I am asking, how is the paraontological distinction at work here?

Both the Palestinian and the Ethiopian are racialized and consigned to the zone of nonbeing. Still, the Ethiopian soldier differs from his Palestinian counterpart insofar as he is authorized by the Israeli state to discipline and kill Palestinian bodies. With compulsory military service, subjugation of Palestinians is part and parcel of the Israeli state's DNA and formation of its nationals. To belong to and identify with Israel is to actively support Palestinian domination. The social and psychic wage of Jewishness (to adapt Du Bois's formulation, "public and psychological wage" of whiteness")[100] elevates this Black solider above all Palestinians. If Ethiopian Jews are nothing in an anti-Black Israel, Palestinians are rendered *less* than nothing by Israel's settler-apartheid regime. A Motenist reading would not stop here, however.

At a basic level, the consent to be a single being is what the dispossessed Palestinian is yearning for in this scene: he wants to exit the zone of nonbeing and become a being, a free Palestinian living in a sovereign state. The consent to be a single being is also seemingly at work in the Ethiopian Jew. He wants to belong to Israel, even though a Zionist Israel racializes him as an inferior Jew, or some in Israel deny Ethiopians their Jewishness altogether. A commitment to identitarianism ties Sameer and the Ethiopian solider together. But what if both affectively divested from a rooted sense of belonging? Paying attention to the paraontological distinction between Blackness and Black ~~being~~ allows us to bring up a host of additional issues: the Ethiopian solider obviously didn't choose the path of the *refuseniks* (conscientious Israeli soldiers who refuse to serve in the Occupied Territories and willing to accept their social ostracization that comes with their rebuke of a racist Israel); he becomes an instrument of power in the Zionist project of eliminating Palestinians. His Blackness/Black being aren't differentiated. He is the wretched within Israeli society but "magically" becomes intelligible, at home, the sovereign subject once he puts on his military gear and proceeds to control and traumatize Palestinian bodies. Anti-Palestinian racism affords him more power, more recognition, more enjoyment, more humanity: if Palestinians are human animals, *all* Israeli soldiers are humans. The Black problem for the Ethiopian is a matter of bringing this humanity back with him to Israel proper. The standard Afropessimist reading is that this attempt to smuggle humanity back into one's anti-Black civil society is a futile pursuit. But what if the logic went the other way around? What if the enduring racial stigmatization and exploitation makes dispossession the basis for his solidarity with Palestinians in the project to dismantle Israel's racial matrix of the human? This insurgency would effectively go further than the refusal of the *refuseniks*, or at least it would make race and racism in Israel central to the Zionist agenda of a perpetual war on the Palestinian people. "Ethiopian Lives Matter" would open to "Palestinian Lives Matter" and vice versa. Ethiopian subjects would engage in an act of self-violence, a symbolic suicide of sorts: they would refuse what they have been refused: equality and freedom (in Israel proper, Ethiopian Jews are still struggling for equality and freedom). Ethiopian dispossession (the Black problem in Israel) will not be assuaged by a vicious Occupation, a narcissistic attempt to reassert one subjectivity by humiliating and subjugating Palestinians. On the Palestinian side, a paraontological difference would reconfigure the Palestinian struggle. In the Zionist imaginary, Palestinian dispossession creates a Palestinian destined to disappear either by ethnic cleansing or genocide. Exiting the zone of nonbeing is a primordial desire for Palestinians. Statelessness is a horrific condition where refugees are afforded limited rights if any. Sameer's anti-Blackness is surely mediated by the idea that a newcomer to historic Palestine has far more rights than him. What remains undetermined is what are Palestinians exiting the zone of nonbeing into? Is there a way to sustain an exilic Palestinianness that yearns for self-determination without simultaneously erasing the rewards or gift of exile, a Palestinianness that labors against a Zionist violence that wants to erase it while consenting not to be single being, vying to be an exilic being?

For me, Edward Said's contrapuntal hermeneutics resonate with Moten's paraontological modality. I see an analogous logic at play in Said's view of exile, which serves as a double consciousness of sorts. As with Indigeneity, exile defines Palestinian identity; it is "the fundamental condition of Palestinian life,"[101] a condition that unites all Palestinians—from Gaza and the West Bank, from Palestinian citizens of Israel to those in refugee camps and the rest of the diaspora. To embrace exile is not to diminish in any way the material conditions that prompted the exile and dispersal (the Nakba, the Naksa, the multiple Gaza Wars, etc.). Nor can we lose sight of the truth that exile was/is part and parcel of the Zionist eliminationist plan. What an affective and cognitive attachment to exile does however is to decline to be a single being. As Glissant notes, "every diaspora is the passage from unity to multiplicity."[102] The exilic Palestinian embraces this multiplicity as the gift of diaspora. Consenting not to be a single being blocks the irresistible temptation of decoloniality, the call for rootedness prompted by the desire to return to "*a time before the settler,*"[103] a pristine time of harmony and plenitude. Exile is inseparable from dispossession, relegating the Palestinian people to the zone of nonbeing, to ontological erasure, *but it is also more.* As Moten talks of the gift of dispossession, of not having Blackness coincide with Black ~~being~~ (social death), exile is also a gift, an indicator of an alternative modality of being and relationality, a call to imagine both Palestinian sociality and the Palestinian problem differently. My point is that exile and Indigeneity are not to be crudely opposed; rather, they should be read contrapuntally and paraontologically, freed from identitarian capture and reclaimed for an emancipatory end. The encounter between Sameer and the Ethiopian soldier was a failed one. An anti-colonial and anti-racist agenda cannot afford reproducing this impasse. Moving forward, perhaps we should begin by considering what it would mean to *consent not to be a single problem.*

Chapter 3
Becoming Object

Objecthood, being an object, is a condition that most philosophers have reasonably sought to overcome or at least lessen. Simone de Beauvoir, for instance, laments the reduction of women to that of the "second sex," the inferior gender, a being whose transcendence and freedom are compromised. Under a patriarchal regime, women are reduced to the status of an object, an in-itself, lacking the for-itself of the (male) human subject. Echoing and radicalizing Beauvoir's insights, Fanon discloses Black being's inert state as an object. The white gaze is the culprit responsible for the destruction of Black being. Basically, Fanon charges the West/philosophy with *ontocide*, and the zone of nonbeing, as I've been arguing, names this ambivalent site of socio-ontological death. On the one hand, becoming object is clearly a result of historical and necropolitical processes, technologies of control and subjugation. Objecthood is mediated and produced by language, power, and culture. You are not "born" object, you become one. On the other hand, what is historically contingent, in an anti-Black world, can quickly come to have the force of ontology, a seemingly unalterable status: I *am* an object, I *am* ontologically dead. To be Black takes the form of a death sentence, a living without living; it is to be on death row, if you will. Social death announces the grim destiny of Blacks. For Blacks, emancipation never meant nor was it experienced as ontological liberation. It was ontical through and through. Among Fanon's many avid and committed readers, it is the Afropessimist camp that has harnessed Fanon's sobering reflections on the Black condition in a blistering indictment of philosophy's paradigm of the human.

Politics does not fare any better. For Afropessimists, politics not only ignores the primacy of anti-Blackness, it unconsciously thrives on it, unifying non-Black folks in their struggles for justice. Cross-racial solidarity is, in some respect, the first casualty of Afropessimism. Indeed, Afropessimists return us to anti-Blackness, not white supremacy, as the source of the racial antagonism. And yet Wilderson's hostility to cross-racial solidarity was not always that absolute and unshakeable as we discussed in Chapter 2.[1] Wilderson hints at its possibility in a 2003 conversation with Saidiya Hartman (in which, incidentally, the term "Afropessimism" was coined). Wilderson notes a "structural antagonism," a "structural prohibition"[2] that exists between Blacks and whites, or, more generally, between Blacks and non-Blacks. Drawing on Fanon, Wilderson argues that we are dealing here with two different species of being: one involves subjecthood (readily enjoyed by the colonizer and the master) and the other objecthood (mercilessly imposed on the colonized and the slave). Wilderson laments that academic discourse on racial matters obscures the singularity of anti-Blackness underpinning this antagonism. In their works, Black and white academics cover up or disavow the incommensurability of the two positions:

> Black academics assume that there is enough of a structural commonality between the black and the white (working class) position—their mantra being: "We are both exploited subjects"—for one to embark upon a political pedagogy that will somehow help whites become aware of this "commonality." White writers posit the presence of something they call "white skin privilege," and the possibility of "giving that up," as their gesture of being in solidarity with blacks. But what both gestures disavow is that *subjects just can't make common cause with objects*. They *can only become objects*, say in the case of John Brown or Marilyn Buck, or further instantiate their subjectivity through modalities of violence (lynching and the prison-industrial complex), or through modalities of empathy. In other words, the essential essence of the white/black relation is that of the master/slave—regardless of its historical or geographic specificity. And masters and slaves, even today, are never allies.[3]

Liberal America treats chattel slavery along with Indigenous genocide as relics of the past, chapters in the nation's tumultuous past. Liberals regret parts of American history, but focus on its racial progress, on the goal of integration, and the nation's redemptive aspiration to "a more perfect union," a formulation from the Preamble of the US Constitution that Senator Barack Obama famously exploited in his 2008 speech on race at the National Constitution Center.[4]

Privilege theory fails to grasp the uniqueness of anti-Blackness. Don't be fooled by all the ontical upgrades granted to Blacks; they are *still* not protected. Ontologically speaking, everything remains the same. Objecthood follows and characterizes Blackness. In Heideggerian terms, Blacks were and remain "poor in world,"[5] closer to nonhuman animals than to "world forming" humans. They are not, strictly speaking, "beings-in-the-world." Being Black is to have had your world de/unformed (the ontological process by which African turns into Black). Put slightly differently, there is a straight line from the plantation to the school-to-prison pipeline. The Afropessimist account of civil society resonates well with Michelle Alexander's disquieting conclusion in *The New Jim Crow* that the United States claims to be colorblind when it is in fact a "racial caste system." Mass incarceration has transformed an obscene number of Blacks into permanent second-class citizens.[6] Again, ontical upgrades never amount to a lifeline; in the long run, they are more cruel than helpful. They are precarious things and can be circumvented when/since their beneficiaries are interminably overdetermined from without, always already at the threshold of the zone of nonbeing. It does not take much to put Blacks back in their place, to return them to the zone of sub-humanity.

But this is not the whole picture. Wilderson briefly evokes John Brown and Marilyn Buck as examples that do not fit the master and slave relation, gesturing to another, and more radical, way of being antiwhite than privilege theory offers. Brown and Buck were revolutionary *subjects* precisely because they defected from their race and arguably underwent a quasi-ontological mutation—they become *object*—ceasing to be what they were, subjects/humans/whites, drastically changing the social coordinates of their being. They were insurrectionists: a militant abolitionist and an anti-imperialist activist, respectively. Later in *Red, White & Black*, Wilderson briefly returns to the question of becoming object as one of "becoming Black" for whites. On the ways Buck and David Gilbert, another white revolutionary, were recast *as* Blacks for their involvement in the efforts at Black liberation, Wilderson observes: "Comrades like David Gilbert and Marilyn Buck were so sincere and forthright in their active commitment to the Black Liberation Army that the state recast them as Black and threw them in prison and threw away the key."[7] Does becoming Black equal becoming object? Is objecthood synonymous with a hollowed-out Black (non)personhood? Becoming Black names the result of a political ontology, a devastating metaphysical mutation, that erects the Human at the expense of the Black. Losing your human coordinates is a symbolic death sentence; you are condemned to a social death, which increases the prospect of biological death. The white state can treat, and has treated, whites *as if* they were Black, *like* they were Black. Still, it is more correct to say that Gilbert and Buck became improper, self-corrupted, and self-compromised whites, not Blacks.[8] They sided with objects/Blacks (committed to Black liberation) and they were treated as objects/Blacks (punished for their race treason). Or conversely, if "becoming Black" for white insurrectionists means loathing and willfully gnawing at their whiteness, sabotaging it as the norm for being human, then becoming object might approximate becoming Black, becoming Black adjacent, if you will.[9]

We can contrast Wilderson's "becoming Black" with Achille Mbembe's "becoming Black of the world" from his *Critique of Black Reason*.[10] To recall, "Black" in Mbembe's lexicon denotes the unprecedented transformation of Africans into "things, objects, and merchandise"[11] for colonial and capitalist profit. But unlike the Afropessimists, Mbembe uses "becoming Black" to describe another metaphysical mutation that is taking hold under a rapacious racial capitalism. We have then two different modalities of "becoming Black."

Mbembe's warns of a form of capitalism that has effectively parted ways with democratic principles that, in the past (at the least for Western nations), kept it in check as it spread its tentacles across the globe, whereas Wilderson's remains almost a thought experiment, an exploration of what it would take to destroy the world and dismantle the armature of the Human: becoming Black/object. He envisages the possibility of revolutionary whites, those who become, in some sense, ex-whites. And in becoming ex-whites, they choose bare life in solidarity with Blacks over the social gratification of being white, over the material and libidinal luxuries of whiteness.

Ex-Whites and Comrades

In Wilderson's account becoming Black/object is not necessarily a problem but the beginning of a revolutionary intervention/invention. For Wilderson, "becoming Black" is an exploration of what it would take to destroy the world and dismantle the armature of the Human. He conceives of the possibility of revolutionary whites, those who become, in some sense, ex-whites. In becoming ex-whites, they opted for bare life in solidarity with Blacks over the material and libidinal luxuries of whiteness. Here becoming Black/object is not a problem for the being undergoing the change, but the beginning of an insurrection, a revolutionary invention and intervention. For an insurrectionist anti-racist Left, becoming object designates a full commitment to liberation: abolition, true emancipation, for all. In this state, sovereignty is precisely what you refuse since its racist logic is always formulated on the basis of the slave—the anti-sovereign, the antihuman, the radically and racially improper. Becoming object is to collectively refuse, as Fred Moten put it, "what has been refused" to you and your comrades in struggle. As James Baldwin cleverly asked more than a half-century ago, "Do I really *want* to be integrated into a burning house?"[12] The world is on fire: from the destructive effects of climate change to the genocide in Gaza. We—Palestinians, Blacks, the wretched, the less well-off, and the would-be race/class traitors—must decline the liberal state's bad faith invitation to integrate, to join, or rather phantasmatically emulate, the liberal and conservative elites, the privileged of the world.

Anti-Blackness and coloniality remain our disavowed horizons. We have to ask ourselves, What world do we want? Crucially, is living well in an anti-Black world really living well? Is living well during a genocide really living well? Palestinians will not be free unless Blacks are free. Having said that, we must immediately evacuate any humanist or liberal sentimentalism that might be attached to this assertion. I make it in the spirit of the Black Panther Party: "The struggle of the Palestinian people for their freedom and liberation from US imperialism and its lackeys is also our struggle. We recognize that if the Palestinian people cannot get their freedom and liberation, neither can we."[13] The call for joint liberation cannot be simply aspirational, relying on the discredited politics of recognition or empathy, devoid of praxis, class struggle, and (self-)violence. Dismantling the master/settler's house takes a village of anti-racist insurrectionists.

Becoming object breaks with the technologies of the master/settler. The unsovereign is the object par excellence. If becoming object is willing the loss of sovereignty, isn't abolition its politics? The fight for abolition might be another name for the becoming object of the world. Afropessimist Jared Sexton lends support to this claim, since he defines "the struggle for abolition" as "already and of necessity the struggle for the promise of communism, decolonization, and settler decolonization, among other things. Slavery is the threshold of the political world, abolition the interminable radicalization of every radical movement."[14] Commenting on W. E. B Du Bois's biography of John Brown, Nahum Chandler describes the abolitionist's transformation as "a movement of becoming other."[15] As a radical political project, becoming other/object registers that whites can trouble their whiteness; they can become white *otherwise*, or "white without whiteness," akin to what Jacques Derrida expresses as "*sovereign without sovereignty*,"[16] that is, white without the colonial and imperial metaphysics of whiteness that underpins its ideological meaning, where being white is indistinguishable from being human (and thus being *not* Black). The ex-white—or the white at war with his whiteness—is potentially another figure of the "unsovereign." By becoming Black/object/other, John Brown, Marilyn Buck, and fellow race defectors knew that their commitment to the Black cause would entail no reprieve from the white order of things. "I have been treated as an enemy of the state—a traitor to the white race. So I am not holding my breath for any calls," states Marilyn Buck.[17] These ex-white insurrectionists illustrated and enacted what it meant/means to be committed to a just cause.

The stakes of commitment are high; being committed involves and seeks out trouble. Baldwin lucidly articulates its demands: "To act is to be committed, and to be committed is to be in danger. In this case, the danger, in the minds of most white Americans, is the loss of their identity."[18] True commitment or solidarity with the wretched wreaks havoc on your given identity. When what you *think* and *do* no longer coincide with your "species," then you are on your way to becoming an object.[19] We must not underestimate the situation. Becoming object puts you at great risk. In committing to the Black cause during a "very dangerous time," when "the most brutal, and the most determined resistance" awaits teachers who want to educate *otherwise*, these teachers, writes Baldwin, must be willing to risk everything, must be ready "to go for broke."[20]

The message is clear and unnerving. We cannot compromise with supremacists of any shade. In today's context, this means we must still counter the fascist desire to control the teaching of racism in K-12 public schools through spurious anti-CRT legislation.[21] CRT hystericizes white America insofar as it calls for a reckoning with its history, with its murderous whiteness. Baldwin makes such a plea for the active unlearning of a sedimented history that effortlessly overdetermines our thoughts and actions:

> White man, hear me! History, as nearly no one seems to know, is not merely something to be read. And it does not refer merely, or even principally, to the past. On the contrary, the great force of history comes from the fact that we carry it within us, are unconsciously controlled by it in many ways, and history is literally *present* in all that we do. It could scarcely be otherwise, since it is to history that we owe our frames of reference, our identities, and our aspirations. And it is with great pain and terror that one begins to realize this.[22]

CRT's anti-fascist pedagogy lies in its recasting of our identities in history. It strikes at America's myths and racial core, its phantasmatic claims of innocence and Manifest Destiny.[23]

Palestinians and their supporters are confronting a similar problem with the neocolonial guardians of history. A new McCarthyism wants to put an end to any troubling of history. There shall be no "pedagogy of the oppressed," no decolonization of the mind. This Zionist McCarthyism is hell-bent on silencing and criminalizing Palestinian voices in academia (and here the fascists include Democrats as well). We commit to a just cause—we don't "obey in advance"[24]— even as we know that doubling down on the struggle against racial injustice exposes us to harm and violence. (Self-)destitution is the price of commitment, of decolonizing your mind. Likewise, agitating for Palestine deroutinizes your life and social existence. Taking up the Palestinian cause is often experienced as a compulsion and disorientation. This is how I experience it in my own teaching, activism, and scholarship—and I'm not alone. Palestine—the daily massacres in Gaza; settler terrorism in the West Bank—becomes all that you can think about, *as if* you didn't have a choice. You are politicized, interpellated by an injustice that unsettles your very core and resets your priorities.

In an explicitly Marxist vein, Saroj Giri writes about the "comrade as object" in similar terms. By becoming object, the individual rebels against a fetishized account of bourgeois white individuality. She is at war with the capitalist symbolic order, declining to occupy her assigned subject-position. Rather than praising her uniqueness, the comrade as object undergoes a process of "revolutionary *self*-destitution, self-objectification."[25] But what kind of objectification are we talking about here? Let's linger on this question with Fanon. Is the phenomenon of "comrade as object" akin to Fanon's unsettling observations?

> I am an object among other objects.
> A feeling of inferiority? No, a feeling of not existing.[26]

As a being-in-the-midst-of-the-world, Fanon is positioned in the world as an object, ontologically dispossessed of his for-itself by an inescapable white gaze. Fanon experiences the dissolution of the social ego as the site of radical unfreedom.[27] Here Fanon dislocates the Sartrean subtext. The trauma of losing one's ego is not existentially compensated by the possibility of a radical new start. True, the zone of nonbeing is not an "inert" state insofar as it paradoxically creates the possibility of "flight," the birth of a new self, and a life-affirming transformation in being.[28] But if one stops here, what is missed in this "life-affirming" reading is Fanon's key qualification of this moment of transcendence. It holds for human beings insofar as the zone of nonbeing painfully reminds you of your radical freedom, that you're irreducible to your social ego. But if you're Black, the liberatory potential of the hellish zone quickly diminishes. Now whereas Moten grasps this emancipatory possibility in remaining in, and not in exiting, the zone of nonbeing, Afropessimists follow Fanon in his "postmortem reconstruction" and "forensic phenomenology."[29] If you're Black, the zone of nonbeing not only indexes the dissolution of your social ego; it also points to the frailty of being Black. Banned to the zone of nonbeing, a disproportionate of Blacks experience their situation as a state of absolute abandonment. What is disclosed after the destruction of the social ego is not a nausea-inducing nothingness that erupts as radical freedom (as for Roquentin the white antihero of Sartre's novel *Nausea*). Nothingness as freedom is unavailable to *most* Black people. Again, exiting the zone of nonbeing proves extremely challenging. Blacks remain constricted by the racial and differentiating matrix structuring civil society. Only decolonization—pursuing an agenda of complete disorder—holds the promise alchemically transforming the colonized as object into a new man, or, better yet, a revolutionary object.[30] "Through self-consciousness and self-destitution [*dépouillement*]," Black people come to embrace their non-bourgeois freedom.[31]

Ex-whites, conversely, can experience an existential undoing akin to Black experience, but *not* identical to it, for they cannot fully divest themselves of their positioning as humans within this matrix. What ex-whites can do, must do, is to disidentify with and divest from the white symbolic order and decline their reinscription into the normative order of things and to actively sustain their own existential "un-suturing" as the grounds for solidarity. To borrow Glissant's and Moten's language, they consent *not* to be a single race (white). The comrade as object refuses the pull of phantasmatic identity and seek instead a revolutionary being-with with her Black comrades whose experience of this hellish zone of nonbeing is mostly that of unfreedom; together, both work toward a collective upheaval that would not only point to the exit from the zone of nonbeing but would also dismantle the world that engenders this zone as a quasi-permanent condition for the wretched of the world.

To the chagrin of liberals, the comrade as object refuses—by consenting not to be a single being—the limited rewards of identity politics. She expresses her rage otherwise; the depersonalized comrade doesn't make narrow particularist or identity-based demands—the preferred liberal way for racialized nonbeings to "exit" this excruciating zone into the curated multiculturalist world of liberals. I take my inspiration here from a passage by Stefano Harney and Fred Moten from *The Undercommons*. While championing the abolition of prisons, Harney and Moten keep their eyes on the carceral logic of racial capitalism that makes enslavement and the prison-industrial complex possible. What is at play is "not so much the abolition of prisons but the abolition of a society that could have prisons, that could have slavery."[32] Revolutionary insurrections are interventions that not only address a specific problem (anti-Black police brutality; disproportionate incarceration rates; the starvation, humiliation, and massacres of Palestinians), but interventions in the racial matrix of the human, interrogating how the Western image of the human could give birth to a proliferation of inhuman(e) treatment of racialized communities and non-European others.

John Brown and Marilyn Buck plunged into the nonworld of Blacks; in choosing to inhabit this hellish zone, they both willed self-violence and embraced a kind of symbolic suicide, or what Huey P. Newton of the Black Panter Party called "revolutionary suicide," entailing, in Giri's words, "the courage to die, death."[33] The subject/object of the cause can appear mad, will appear mad, or, at the very least, to be suffering from some form of pathology. But as Derek Hook keenly observes, matters are more complicated: "If the subject's commitment is to something greater than his or her own well-being—a social, political, moral cause—then the ethical nature of the commitment can be said to outweigh its contingent 'psychopathological' costs."[34] Insurrectionists are mad objects. Brown and Buck committed to something greater than their well-being and world-making; by unlocking and distancing themselves from the gratification, ferocity, and tyranny of whiteness, they identified with ~~beings~~ who didn't belong, becoming outsiders and pariahs in their former worlds. And by choosing *not* to live in the zone of being/interest, they made themselves vulnerable to state sanctioned violence and white terror in the name of a revolutionary cause: Black liberation.

If your identity comes first—as in transactional solidarities (I help you if you help me) or in identitarian solidarities, based on a shared experience of domination alone (we are all victims of white-supremacy, my struggle is your struggle)— solidarity will eventually fizzle out once your commitment to the cause falters, once your agenda no longer aligns with the other's cause (this is a recurrent Afropessimist complaint about allies). My sense is that a solidarity worthy of its name takes the form of an anti-identitarian insurrectionist project. You "tak[e] up a political cause that is foreign to [yourself]";[35] you commit to a Black agenda, to a project that is bigger than you, beyond the pleasure principle, that alters your (human) identity rather than cements it. In this light, we ask, Does becoming object—becoming a rebellious object or insurrectionist—cast coalition-building in a new light? Is such an ontological upheaval sufficient for Blacks to create solidarity with non-Black comrades, a solidarity that meets or reckons with the concerns of Afropessimists?

Subjective Destitution: Solidarity Beyond the Self

Whiteness is not anybody's destiny. Or as Houria Bouteldja puts it, "if your history made you white, nothing is forcing you to stay that way."[36] John Brown and Marilyn Buck didn't stay that way. They unmade themselves and exemplified how whites do not have to be sutured to their whiteness. "Being un-sutured" is experienced as a rupture in quotidian existence, "a site of openness, loss and great discomfort."[37] Indeed, insurrecting against whiteness is to will disturbance, discomfort, and suffering. This type of insurrection contrasts significantly with the far-Right insurgency at the US Capitol on January 6, 2021, which was fueled by a MAGA desire to *make America white again*. Yes, this was a collective desire but the solidarity that it elicited was driven by a hunger for identity (true patriots against the threats from within and without, from the deep state, the unrest of BLM activists, and the illegal and dangerous migrants) and nostalgia for lost communion and white times (an ontological and temporal reset for, that would return us to, a pure white America).[38]

An insurrectionist intervention against an unjust anti-Black world must follow another path. To return to Wilderson's observation that subjects (non-Blacks, masters, humans) and objects (Blacks, slaves, nonhumans) cannot forge a relation, we can note that an ally remains a subject; academics (Black and non-Black) who ignore the singularity of anti-Blackness contribute to the production, reproduction, and circulation of a Black imago, an ugly Blackness imagined "out of a thousand details, anecdotes, and stories," writes Fanon, lodged deeply in society's cultural imaginary.[39] Wilderson exceptionalizes Brown and Buck, and ironically evokes them only to foreclose the potentiality of non-Black involvement in Black liberation. Here we should remember that for Lacan the logic of the exception aligns with the masculine side of the formulas of sexuation, where it is the sovereign exception that proves the universal rule of castration. Lacan juxtaposes the sovereign exception with the "non-all" or "not-whole" (*pas-tout*) which he identifies with the feminine side. And to be clear, "masculine" and "feminine," for Lacan, do not refer to anatomical differences, but name a subject/object's relation to the phallus.[40] Simply put, "masculine" and "feminine" denote contesting logics and arrangements of enjoyment.

I want to linger on the implication of Lacan's logics for thinking "becoming object." Briefly, Lacan lays out four formulas of sexuation. On the masculine side, there are two: (1) there is at least one X that says no to the phallic function, and (2) all Xs are subject to the phallic function. And on the feminine side, there are two more: (1) there is no X that says no to the phallic function, and (2) not all Xs are subject to the phallic function. The masculine logic is first and foremost a logic of the exception: the exception that proves the rule, that closes the set. While all men are symbolically castrated due to their entry into the symbolic order, a masculine logic hangs on to the notion that there is always one "Man" who does not sacrifice his enjoyment, one Man who must remain immune to the law of castration. For Lacan, the mythical primal father of Freud's *Totem and Taboo* incarnates such a figure. While the primal father—who enjoyed all women at will, "achieving complete satisfaction"[41]—had to be killed for the symbolic order to be erected, his exceptional subject position lives on in the cultural imaginary. The masculine logic does not give up on perfection (from the Latin *perfectio*, meaning completion). Such a logic always holds on to the phantasmatic promise or hope of returning to the prior, full plenitude of a pre-symbolic enjoyment.

On the feminine side, there is no claim of universality rooted in exception. So if there is no exception that stands outside the system, then the system as such is never whole or complete. The feminine logic discloses the lack in the order of things. Woman (unlike the mythical Man) does not constitute a totality. Rather the non-all indexes the failure of totalization. And because there is nothing of woman outside the Law (no constitutive exception), woman is an open set, is non-all, and inside of the social system.[42] Whereas the masculine logic of exception posits a sovereign subject, a subject who has unlimited enjoyment, who stands outside the law of castration that governs social symbolic existence and whose self-presence is transparent, the feminine logic allows no exception to the law of castration. It declines the illusion of an uncastrated Man (and with it the possibility of absolute enjoyment), but, at the same time, takes castration to be non-all, never complete or whole. This is why Žižek says, "*subjectivity as such … is feminine.*"[43] The question, of course, is whether or not individuals accept or avow this ontological reality, the unnerving reality of "the void of the 'barred subject,'"[44] whether or not they decline their interpellation as a phantasmatic, undivided, sovereign subject.

Wilderson's reading of Brown and Buck treats these radicals as constitutive exceptions, as instantiations of the masculine logic (they are the exceptions that prove the rule of nonrelations, that close the set of white humans). Anti-Blackness, as master-signifier, totalizes the field of politics through its constitutive exception, the ex-whites who act otherwise. I argue instead that the feminine logic of the non-all better informs the dynamics of becoming object, which puts it at odds with the totality of anti-Blackness. The field of politics is itself non-all: "Can we say, then, that politics is All, a series of totalizations, of imposing Master-Signifiers which totalize a field through exceptions? But what about the Non-All as politics? 'Everything is political' is misleading, the true formula is 'there is nothing which is not political.'"[45] There are no exceptions to the racist symbolic order. Anti-Blackness marks the Symbolic, baked into social reality. But the anti-Black world is non-all; there is no exception, nothing outside this racist world, but this world is in itself non-all. What does that mean? Brown and Buck are not to be posited as heroic and fetishized figures of resistance, who resisted being subsumed to an anti-Black world, beyond or untouched by the system of Black domination while the rest of us are completely subsumed by the ideological order of anti-Blackness or the Human, capable only of ineffective performative activism. Against the masculine logic undermining the Afropessimist position, the ex-white insurrectionists are redefining politics, and giving the lie to the phantasm of humanism (European humanism, the "'white' egalitarian-emancipatory tradition,"[46] masquerading as universality), pointing to the fact of ontological incompleteness, underscoring that the set of the Human or humanity is never complete, never all. Subsumption in this anti-Black world is unavoidable but untotalizable (for the Afropessimists, that world is both unavoidable and totalizable). While the universal rule of anti-Blackness necessarily implies an exception (the ex-whites of the world), the non-all of the anti-Black world communicates the fallibility of the ideological order. Insurrectionist praxis, the art of becoming object, exposes the incompleteness of this world, unsettles the "balance of the Whole,"[47] and embraces humanity's ontological malleability. In short, humanity is *not* a closed set.

This plasticity of humanity underpins Fanon repeated calls for a "New Humanism" (from the first page of *Black Skin, White Masks*) and a "new human" (the last words from *The Wretched of the Earth*). There is no "new humanism" without a reckoning with the coloniality of being and its self-serving partition of the world. For Wilderson, however, no reckoning is sufficient enough. The problem is not so much with the "Human" as with what the Human is not: "We cannot take the word 'Human' at face value. Like any other word or concept, 'Human' does not come with its meaning neatly tied in a bow. The Human is a construct. To know the Human is to know, first and foremost, what it is not."[48] To be Human is *not* to be Black. Still, from a Fanonian perspective, Wilderson overstates the opposition, removes it from colonial history, the site of interpretive struggle. While beginning his own inquiry by acknowledging that he has no neutral ontology to draw from that would allow him to resist the white/colonial gaze determining his being as nonbeing, ~~being~~, Fanon does not stop here. An "ontological explanation"[49] of being Black might be wanting; the white racist gaze distorts the being of Blacks, but so does the gaze of the subjugated Black man insofar as the grammar of ontology is white, not his own. Ontology may well be anti-Black, but *Black Skin, White Masks* constitutes Fanon's gift to European ontology (translated by Moten as paraontological), a gift that exposes the racism of Western ontology, understood as a field of domination, part of the master's tools, while simultaneously dislocating ontology in his writings, historicizing and decompleting it, and forging, in turn, a new ontology of this racist world and his/

our place within it. And Fanon makes clear that there is no "new man" without a ruthless insurrection against the cherished paradigm of the European human itself, without the colonized seizing ontology and reclaiming it in the name of the improper and for the wretched of the world.

The notion of "becoming object" is a sublimely improper use of ontology since you're imperfecting your being by becoming/siding with the wretched, society's excluded and racialized others. To become other is to refuse answering what Stefano Harney and Fred Moten name "the call to order."[50] As we've seen, Brown and Buck refused their assigned position in an anti-Black world. By frustrating the call to order (for whites and Blacks alike), becoming object holds some promise for coalition-building. Now, I want to inquire further into the viability of cross-racial solidarity and the explicit Afropessimist resistance to it. An axiomatic principle of Afropessimism is that it rejects calls for solidarity with Blacks based on the model of a common enemy: white supremacy. For Afropessimists, the true antagonism is always between Black and non-Black. Whites might be on the top of the racial hierarchical ladder, but all the other non-Blacks earn the disparaging title of "junior partners of civil society,"[51] that is, junior partners of anti-Blackness Inc. As Wilderson claims, "Blacks give even the most degraded position a sense of human possibility because we are the locus of human impossibility. Whatever grace others may fall from, they will never be Black."[52] The position of the nonhuman—the anti-Human—is ontologized and can only be occupied by Blacks—because to be Human is not to be a slave/ Black. In the Afropessimist calculus, nonhumanity trumps degraded humanity.[53] If you're lacking in being, stuck in a state of degradation, you "naturally" want (it is in your interest) to assimilate to whiteness—the most secured way to regain your humanness, and thus recover from your ontological fall from grace.[54] This desire, in turn, makes you by definition anti-Black. Fellow Afropessimist Jared Sexton echoes Wilderson's point, stressing the inadequacies of the "people-of-color" paradigm for its failure to account for the incommensurable struggles between Blacks and non-Blacks;[55] analogies always run the danger of "rendering equivalent slavery and other forms of oppression."[56]

Strictly speaking, non-Black "people-of-color" fall within the paradigm of humanity, while Black people remain excluded from it. The murder of George Floyd was at the hands a white police officer, Derek Chauvin, the incarnation of the "white state," but, as Wilderson argues, he "was also murdered by people of color who are oppressed by white supremacy and who, simultaneously, secure their status as humans (however much degraded) by anti-Blackness."[57] For the Afropessimist, "analogy mystifies, rather than clarifies, Black suffering."[58] The enemy of Black people is not white supremacy alone, but non-Blacks—anyone vying for a piece of humanity, vying to be included in its family and protection. And yet in a 2015 "Roundtable on Anti-Blackness and Black-Palestinian Solidarity" moderated by Noura Erakat, Sexton's intervention opens another possibility for solidarity. Erakat frames the roundtable as an opportunity to critically assess the "similarities" between the two struggles for "survival." Declining the rhetoric of "sameness"—and pushing through any claims about "the 'natural' solidarity between Palestinians and Blacks"—the participants were asked "to highlight those conversations [by Black and Palestinians activists] and synergies in an attempt to better understand what a commitment to anti-blackness should look like in the Palestinian solidarity movement and among Black-Palestinian solidarity efforts."[59] In his contribution, Sexton exerts hermeneutic pressure on what we mean by "solidarity" and "struggle":

> How to tell the difference between solidarity, slight, and seizure? More precisely, the challenge is to understand a solidarity that seems to persist, in principle and in practice, despite problems of asymmetry or even antagonism; a solidarity that does not simply join the struggle, but exceeds it from within; a force of solidarity that is in the struggle *more* than the struggle itself?[60]

Solidarity here takes the form of a politics that breaks with "the pleasure principle," what Freud considered the guiding principle of psychic life, that which regulates all mental processes, compelling human beings to seek pleasure and avoid pain (or unpleasure), to control levels of excitation, maintaining homeostasis.[61] The pleasure principle underwrites the still dominant paradigm of identity politics. Indeed, losing nothing is axiomatic to identity politics.

Sexton's intervention points to a "beyond the pleasure principle." His suggestive formulation, *what is in the struggle more than the struggle itself*, is evocative of the "death drive," *what is in me that is more than myself*. To commit to an ethico-political cause is to be willing to put your well-being aside, to sacrifice or go against your immediate self-interest and particular agenda. The death drive activates "the utmost radical dimensions of human beings."[62] The Symbolic is non-all; the extant taxonomic ordering of the world is not our destiny. Sectarian lines need not be drawn.

I think this is the way we should understand "becoming object." The death drive points to an immanent political agency, grounded in radical negativity. Black-Palestinian solidarity brings two struggles together in the name of liberation, but the agendas of these struggles may not align, will not align perfectly; reciprocity is not and cannot be guaranteed in advance. Group cohesion is a myth, asymmetry and antagonism are baked into any solidarity movement—whence Afropessimist despair, the certainty that the non-Black ally will betray the cause once again, that it's just a question of time. From the Afropessimist standpoint, non-Blacks harness and instrumentalize Black rage in order to achieve their separate identitarian goals. This is a projection of a future that is not unjustified. Anti-Blackness can endlessly reproduce itself—and has done so—insofar as it is supported by basically all political corners: every non-Black consciousness wants to become human. And many if not all would be willing to sacrifice their Black brethren. The ex-whites are the constitutive exception that proves the law of anti-Blackness. But Afropessimism's vision is politically ungenerative; it blunts solidarity by converting risks into predictions, tensions and frictions into failures and betrayals.

There is no room for the world-altering death drive in Afropessimist futurology. There is a totalizing anti-Black world *and nothing more*. It is hard to imagine any "invention"—of the sort Fanon called for when he stated, "I must constantly remind myself that the real *leap* consists of introducing invention into life"[63]—emerging from the Afropessimists's hermeneutic arsenal. Critical pessimism repeats the revolutionary call to abolish the current world, to start over, but it simultaneously insists in its repetition that this anti-Black reality/capitalist world is non-all.[64] The struggle cannot stop with its Fanonian assessment of the problem. Wilderson is fond of calling for the destruction of the world, quoting Fanon's quotation of Césaire's *Notebook of a Return to the Native Land*. Wilderson celebrates Fanon's repetition of Césaire's apocalyptic charge to begin "the end of the world," which, for Césaire/Fanon, is the "only thing ... worth the effort of starting."[65] The Afropessimists' revolutionary call, however, is rooted in the masculine logic of exception, dreaming of a heroic action of destruction, going beyond Fanon, or attempting to be more Fanonian than Fanon—since, Wilderson tells us, "Fanon finds his own flames too incendiary."[66] As with his critical engagement with ontology, Fanon's injunction to destroy the world is better understood as passing through the logic of the non-all. Destruction is precipitated by the decompletion and "desedimentation"[67] of the white/anti-Black world. There is no destruction of the world without a politics of the death drive, invention (what can *still* be added to the world), and cross-racial solidarity—the collective voice of the wretched. Together they promise to destabilize the world at its core, reveal its unnerving but emancipatory groundlessness, and weaken its economic and libidinal control over identities.

Solidarity movements across national and identitarian boundaries are crucial to spurring and sustaining reinvention (of the world and the human). We—the wretched, the permanently racialized and unemployed, the proletariat and lumpenproletariat, the race traitors of the world, the insurrectionists, and so on—can dismantle the master/settler's house, decline to use his tools, refuse his racial identifications, disobey his "call to order," shake his hold of us, and purge his venom or colonial grammar *à la* Caliban, as Césaire imagines him: "I'd vomit you up, all your pomp and designs! Your white poison!"[68] Under the hegemony of global colonial capitalism, this white poison infects us all. Though the impact of this venomous whiteness is differentially experienced by those who inhabit the "zone of subhumanity,"[69] Césaire, like Fanon after him, never lost sight of the fact that colonialization is bad for everyone; it decivilizes and brutalizes the colonizer as well—thingifying the colonized impoverishes the being of the colonizer, shrinking their relational reach.[70] Insurrectionist solidarity cannot afford to rule out in advance the defection and treason of settlers/masters. As Fanon keenly observed, "species" come undone, commitments radically shift, and those in the camp of the oppressors join the camp of the freedom fighters; they "become Blacks or Arabs [se font nègres ou arabes]"[71] and fully assume the consequences, "suffering, torture, and death."[72] Insurrectionists invite those who would dare to commit class suicide or wake up from their colonial slumber, including "sly, shrewd intellectuals,"[73] the professional-managerial class seduced by the rewards of capitalism, and the European Leftists who conveniently treat race/racism as an epiphenomenal problem. They implore those who would dare to de-Zionize, to de-whiten—in short, to become problematic—to actively divest from the existing oppressive system and effectively break from a vicious Manichean dualism that seals the colonized and colonizer in a boundless and fruitless struggle.[74]

Becoming Black, Becoming Palestinian

When Palestinians truly join the struggle for Black liberation, their identities undergo ontological upheaval; they become objects, blackened and criminalized wretched creatures, problems in/of an anti-Black world, and thus subjected to a ubiquitous white terror. Likewise, when many Blacks fully commit to the Palestinian struggle, they too become objects anew, become Palestinians—blackened according to a different set of disciplinary and necropolitical operations—exposed to vicious and spurious charges of anti-Semitism wielded by Zionists and supporters of Israel. The weaponized world-canceling accusation of anti-Semitism is always available to squash any principled critique of Israel's policies and practices. The paternalistic and moralizing message of the white liberal elite to Black activists—particularly for those who were marked by the horizon of BLM—takes the form a "call to order": stay in your lane, translate your demands into the familiar language of identity politics, follow the right protocols of behavior and re-instantiate the law of who counts and doesn't, and, most importantly, forget about the global anti-racist Left, Third Worldism, or transnationalist solidarity with Palestinians.[75] We're dealing with a "colonization"[76] of the mind. *Stop supporting Palestinians. You don't want to be the friends of terrorists. Don't you know, Palestine is not good for you. Care only for your own people.*

In her poem "Moving Towards Home," Black feminist and activist June Jordan refuses to be controlled by the interpellative gaze at home, to play along and submit to the American lopsided Palestine/Israel status quo—to accept a Zionist logic that casts Palestinians fighting for their freedom as terrorists, that casts ethnic cleansing as self-defense. She declines the liberal blackmail: either you support Israel's murderous actions or you're anti-Semitic. Doubling down on her commitment to Palestinians, Jordan moves from being object1 (Black) to becoming object2 (Palestinian). Unlike John Brown and Marilyn Buck, who had to break first with their whiteness in order to act in solidarity, June Jordan's Blackness, her improperness, her commitment to Black liberation, is only intensified in "becoming Palestinian." Though in a precarious position herself, a Black woman in racist patriarchal America, Jordan does not restrict her imaginings exclusively to her own kin, or rather, she opens kinship to a different poetic logic, and, in doing so, invents an "Afro-Palestinian kinship."[77] Jordan's "becoming Palestinian" wasn't a "call to order" (conformity to a new normative mode of conduct) but a "call for and from disorder"[78]—a call that signals her own resistance to the given and a desire to bring more refusals to the colonizers of thoughts and bodies. Palestinian pain and desire reverberate throughout her poem. "Moving Towards Home" begins as a series of negations conveying the poet's reluctance to discuss the inexhaustible details regarding the massacre of hundreds of Palestinians between September 16 and September 18, 1982, at the Sabra and Shatila refugee camps in West Beirut, Lebanon, at the hands of Lebanese Christian Phalangist militia in Israeli-occupied Lebanon:

> I do not wish to speak about the bulldozer and the
> red dirt
> not quite covering all of the arms and legs
> Nor do I wish to speak about the nightlong screams
> that reached
> the observation posts where soldiers lounged about
> Nor do I wish to speak about the woman who shoved her baby
> into the stranger's hands before she was led away[79]

Why this *refusal non refusal* to describe the massacre?[80] Jordan's lines first attest to the ways the atrocities demand a response, call her to speak, despite her reluctance. The poem goes on to attest to the violence such atrocities do to language itself, while at the same time reorienting our gaze to abiding Palestinian *sumud*, sociality and life:

> those are the ones from whom we must redeem
> the words of our beginning
> because I need to speak about home
> I need to speak about living room
> where the land is not bullied and beaten into
> a tombstone
> I need to speak about living room
> where the talk will take place in my language
> I need to speak about living room
> where my children will grow without horror

Jordan defends the dead, defends the living. She manages to index that the zone of nonbeing entails the biological and social deaths of Palestinians, and yet feels compelled "to speak about home," about a Palestinian consciousness and a world that might sustain it, where death is not a permanent guest, where people, no longer cast as problems to eliminate (Zionist necropolitical reason) or save (Western humanitarian reason), can enjoy their sociality, living room, and the presence of loved ones. Jordan ends the poem by registering the transformation of her own voice/consciousness/being:

> I was born a Black woman
> and now
> I am become a Palestinian
> against the relentless laughter of evil
> there is less and less living room
> and where are my loved ones?
> It is time to make our way home.

For Jordan, being/becoming Palestinian entails a self-invention, a revolutionary transformation in consciousness, a speaking truth to power: "Poetry is a political act because it involves telling the truth."[81] Palestinianness here doesn't align with national rootedness, nor is it an exclusive property or marker of the Palestinian people. Palestinianness is contagious; Jordan is irremediably touched by it. She is Black *and* Palestinian, "many beings at the same time," embodying many commitments at the same time. She consents not be a single being, a position that she translates poetically in "the grammatically strange construction 'I am become,'" performing "an open-ended becoming that nonetheless makes itself accountable to the subject position 'Palestinian.'"[82]

By making common cause with Palestinians, Jordan takes a combative stance against an increasingly necropolitical and sadistic world ("the relentless laughter of evil"). "I am become a Palestinian"—object1 to object2 without the latter suppressing the former but rather living with it—is not a willy-nilly assimilation of Palestinian being. As Keith Feldman perceptively notes, "the pivot between Black woman and Palestinian is a recognition not of interchangeable reified identity categories, juxtaposed through a logic of equivalence or comparison. Rather, they are recognized as a set of positional congruencies in relation to the lacerating force of imperial violence."[83] This is why, as Jodi Melamed correctly argues, "Moving Towards Home" is an "anti-identitarian"[84] poem. After Kaja Silverman, we might say that becoming Palestinian involves a "heteropathic identification" rather than "idiopathic identification."[85] If the latter would cannibalize Palestinian difference, immobilizing the Palestinian other and digesting her pain in conformity with the narrator's identificatory logic and imaginary field, the former foregrounds Palestinian alterity, expanding Jordan's sensibility to a concrete Palestinian

Lebenswelt, which gestures, at the same time, to *our* violently shrinking world, a world where "there is less and less living room." This Palestinian *Lebenswelt* stands in sharp contrast to the imperialist/settler's word of choice, *Lebensraum*, "living space," a key ideological concept in the world vision that underpinned Nazi military expansionism and supremacist policies.

The problem for Palestinians, generated by a voracious US imperialism, is a problem for humanity. Elsewhere, Jordan ponders the consequences of the 1982 Israeli invasion: "Wondering about life after Lebanon: What would that be like?"[86] The present and the future of Palestine intertwine. What Palestine is and what it could be. In 2025, we are again concerned about Palestinian lives, *wondering about life after Gaza: What would that be like?* What new directions might lie ahead if Palestine and the world ever freed themselves of Zionist ideology and colonization?

Becoming object today means becoming Palestinian or it means nothing at all. Jordan's trenchant invention "I am become a Palestinian" must be interpreted not as a fetishized difference (exceptionalized and elevated above a calcified Jewish difference, for instance) nor as a humanist abstraction of their shared positive humanity (we are humans under the banner of a static and discredited humanism),[87] but as a concrete universality: being Palestinian, becoming object, crystalizes the reality of bio- and necropolitical violence—from Sabra and Shatila to Gaza.[88] In our global colonial situation, the violence to which Palestinians are subjected is not just an arbitrary case of callous violence of maximalist Israeli Ziofascists but incarnates violence in its essence, an explicit racial segregation of the world's population into zones of interest and disinterest, a vertical and inhumane partition of who matters and who doesn't, who is superior and who is inferior—who is not a problem (the saved) and who is (the damned). There are frankly no limits to the obscenity of the IOF's segregationist logic, whose excesses are perhaps best captured by the holiday village *à la* Club Med that it has built in the northern Gaza Strip. Gideon Levy reports of this paradise in hell, "The village is surrounded by lawns of synthetic grass, cushions for sprawling in every corner. One soldier is enjoying a cappuccino, while another has a glass of XL with ice cubes. There are pampering breakfasts just 'like in a hotel,' and in the evening there's a barbecue."[89] While Israeli soldiers are taking a break from genociding, Palestinians, a few hundred yards away, are starving while navigating the flesh of the dead; reduced to naked existence, they are trying to survive, to withstand the harsh elements of Winter, the stench of death and sewage, the deafening and eerie sounds of drones, and, yes, the indiscriminate bombings happening in Orwellian "safe zones" (read as kill zones).[90]

If the Palestinian cause prompts its supporters to adopt the logic of becoming object, as June Jordan did in her act of solidarity, the IOF fosters an ethos of masculinist omnipotence—you "become God," the ultimate sovereign. The soldiers decide who lives and dies; they decide the exception. Yoel Elizur recounts the testimony of some of the Israeli genocidaires: "The power they received in the army was intoxicating: 'It's like a drug ... you feel like you are the law, you make the rules. As if from the moment you leave the place called Israel and enter the Gaza Strip, you are God.' They viewed brutality as an expression of strength and masculinity."[91] Other soldiers witnessed the wanton behavior of the IOF differently: "I felt like, like, like a Nazi ... it looked exactly like we were actually the Nazis and they were the Jews."[92] What comes across in these reports of atrocities is that Palestinian lives don't matter. Palestinians are there to be eliminated. Becoming Gods—enjoying masculinist invulnerability—is an apt self-description given the fact that the Israeli government believes itself to be beyond international law, immunized and untouchable by all the "anti-Semites" of the world—you know, the usual suspects: International Criminal Court, the International Court of Justice, the United Nations, Amnesty International, Human Rights Watch, Jewish Voice for Peace, IfNotNow, and Israel's own B'Tselem. Despite the global outrage over Israel's genocide, the IOF still declares itself "the most moral army"—sure, it has a few bad apples, *but don't throw the baby out with the bathwater*. Black activists in the United States are too familiar with this narrative that shields the culprit—the US police, whose training in Israel is not an unimportant detail—from an investigation into its systematic anti-Blackness.

The inclusion of Palestinians in the United States' sanctioned ontology can only take the form of an insurrection. As Judith Butler formulates it, "It is not a matter of a simple entry of the excluded into an established ontology, but an insurrection at the level of ontology, a critical opening up of the questions, What is real? Whose lives are real? How might reality be remade?"[93] In the post-BLM world, a June Jordan would have been the first to utter "Palestinian Lives Matter" as an anti-imperialist commitment and call for insurrection (to join Palestinians in their fight for freedom and dignity) against this abominable division of the world and its murderous, racist logic, which dictates that for one group to count, the other must not. In becoming Palestinian, Jordan defies her interpellation by the US symbolic order; she refuses to (only) care about the nation's real, sanctioned victim in this part of the world: the Israeli Jew. Her Black radical internationalist politics railed against both the US feminist movement in its reflexive Zionism and anti-Arab racism,[94] and establishment Black liberalism, whose obligations and attitude toward a Zionist Israel closely mimicked the US State Department's. With her unsanctioned, politicized self-designation, Jordan disorganizes our filiative relations; she strikes at Israel's influence and fortress, its supremacist or whitened immune system[95] that protects its nationals (from the Palestinian intruder/nonself) and projects to them and the West a muscular image of absolute invulnerability while, at the same time, rhetorically continuing to assert its status as forever victimized, which, in turn, authorizes the limitless supply of arms, funded by our taxes, to safeguard Israel. *Why? Because a belligerent nuclear state apparently needs protection from an Indigenous population that refuses to disappear.* June Jordan, like so many pro-Palestinian activists, looks for what lies outside Zionism's walls (literally and figuratively) and aims at short-circuiting Israel's ideological machinery, which ceaselessly turns Palestinians into problems to be relegated to deathly "sterile zones" (zones eradicated of Palestinians around illegal settlements) and zones of nonbeing and disinterest.[96]

The force of Jordan's provocation, of the notion that one can become Palestinian and agitate for the unmaking and remaking of reality is perhaps best gauged by the intensity of the new McCarthyism arising in response to the idea of becoming object/Palestinian, with liberal and centrist Democrats joining an unhinged Right in their pursuit to censor public dissent, performing a sycophantic spectacle for a tantalized pro-Zionist audience (including the anti-Semitic Christian Zionists contingent). There is a general prohibition against political invention, against the formation of any attachment to Palestinians and the Palestinian cause (what would it do to our existing categories?). *There will be no "becoming Palestinian" here* is clearly the message of those in power.

The United States is criminalizing the figure of the pro-Palestinian insurrectionist. The stakes of an insurrectionist uprising are high. Rising in revolt against Israeli butchery and for the Palestinian cause can get you doxed, reprimanded, fired, expelled, deported, jailed, or even murdered. All of this is rationalized by designating such resistance terrorism. Edward Said is a case in point. He was spuriously labeled a "professor of terror" and "ideologue of terrorism" in an article by Edward Alexander in the August 1989 issue of *Commentary*.[97] We also know that employers and university administrators/boards have canceled talks and rescinded job offers, creating an atmosphere of intimidation to chill any sympathies that people might have or develop for Palestine.

But conscientious insurrectionists do not give up on their desire for Palestine. Insurrectionary mobilizations will continue. They persist in agitating for the Palestinian cause. They question, as June Jordan boldly did, the arrogance of an imperial, colonial, and oppressive West who refuses to treat Palestinians with dignity, as equals and humans. Incensed she writes:

> The problem was ... that the Palestinian people, in particular, are not whitemen: They never have been whitemen. Hence they were and they are only Arabs, or terrorists, or animals. Certainly they were not men and women and children; certainly they were not human beings with rights remotely comparable to the rights of whitemen, the rights of a nation of whitemen.[98]

Becoming Palestinian is not a pose but a commitment and imperative. It comes with exposure and backlashes, not only from a generally misinformed public, who has been fed a ubiquitous Zionist narrative ever since Israel's creation in 1948, but also more painfully by some from her feminist communities. Jordan wrote an open letter criticizing well-known American feminist and poet Adrienne Rich's two open letters, titled "...What Does Zionism Mean?" and "Di Vilde Chayes: Zionists Deplore Killings in Lebanon and Criticize Nature of Anti-Israel Protests," along with six other Zionist feminists, which carelessly equated anti-Zionism with anti-Semitism in responding to the critical assessment of Israel's invasion of Lebanon by anti-imperialist feminists. In response, a number of renowned Black feminists, including Audre Lorde and Barbara Smith, as well as Jewish feminists, wrote to the editors of *WomanNews* seeking to prevent its publication on the grounds that it would create (more) discord between Jewish and Black feminists when the movement was aiming to put forward a united front.[99] Jordan judged that they acted in a "wrong and cowardly fashion."[100] Appearances won over substance.

Jordan, as an American citizen and taxpayer, accepted her responsibility for not doing enough to halt the US government funding the Zionist entity's carnage in Lebanon. Jordan's agonistic interlocutors focused on her tone and indifference to the Jewish people rather than addressing the massive carnage happening to Palestinians. Ironically, Lorde, who defends her anger as a justified affective response to anti-Black racism, failed to extend this critical sensibility to Jordan, whose *ressentimental* anger is her/our response to Palestinian suffering, to an unfettered racist Zionism. Jordan hints at the same unrecognized colonial fascism discussed by Césaire, calling out Rich's monopolization of the words "holocaust" and "genocide" to describe Jewish victims normatively and exclusively, and thus neglecting the non-European/non-whites lives of Palestinians:

> Neither the word holocaust nor the word genocide was invented to describe the loss of Jewish or European life. Both of these words mean what they mean whether the victim is Jewish or not. As the majority of the peoples of the world is neither Jewish nor European, it should amaze no one that we, Black and Third World people everywhere, attach fundamental importance to the question of Palestine.[101]

In "On Israel and Lebanon: A Response to Adrienne Rich from One Black Woman," Jordan faults Rich for arguing for Israel's right to exist while avoiding making any comments a month earlier about the Sabra and Shatila massacre. It must be noted that although Rich's cosigned letter was published in October, the letter was written before the Sabra and Shatila massacre in September. Still, Jordan's main point holds. What does it mean to defend Zionism at a time when Palestinian and Lebanese civilians are being slaughtered by Israel? By lending her voice to a Zionist colonial regime, Rich implicitly consented to being a single being and set the tone for other feminists to follow: feminists should stand for Jewish safety (whiteness must be protected), for a Zionist Israel (that posits the Palestinian body as a bloodthirsty terrorist who must be eliminated). As Jordan points out, Rich did not, for instance, "join the Israeli Peace Now dissidents who ... bravely put their white bodies on the line against this massacre committed in their name."[102] These dissident Jews, like today's courageous activists in Jewish Voice for Peace and IfNotNow, consented *not* to be a single being as dictated by Zionism. They consented not to be aligned with Zionism's proper, sanctioned Jewishness; they consented not to embody a narcissistic Jewish identity in a "world of likes"; they weren't crudely and cruelly interested in only the well-being of their people. Palestine spoke to them as it did for Jordan.

Jordan was lucidly aware of the violence of the Zionist playbook, with the "antisemitic industrial complex,"[103] and had already felt its sting. "Jordan's vocal anti-Zionism," Marina Magloire writes, "hamstrung her career for nearly a decade, resulting in death threats, a loss of writing opportunities, and social ostracization within multiracial feminist circles."[104] She was well poised to respond to Rich and other Zionist feminists, prepared to call them out on their bogus charge of anti-Semitism, cynically used to obfuscate the ugly side of Zionism, and cover over its racist and colonial origins. Weaponizing the charge of anti-Semitism displays the ways "oppressive language does more than represent violence; it is violence; does more than represent the limits of knowledge; it limits knowledge."[105] Zionist language is one of "the policing languages of mastery,"[106] the new Zionist category "new anti-Semitism" its crown jewel. The bitter irony is that the new label was never meant to protect Jews; its very purpose was to silence anti-racist, pro-Palestinian scholars and activists, and to limit their knowledge production with/about Palestinians.

If there is a becoming object logic in Jordan's commitment to the Palestinian cause, we might say that there is a "becoming subject" in Rich's Zionist position, leveraging the powers of the "antisemitism industrial complex" to fortify her identity and delegitimize the position of someone like Jordan. In 1982 Rich wanted her feminism and Zionism to coexist. Her position corresponded to that of the liberal Zionist. In contrast to the hard-liners in Israel, the liberal Zionist did condemn Palestinian suffering at the hands of Israeli forces and call for a lasting peace in the form a two-state solution. In the letters cosigned by Rich, you find the following claims:

Like many Israelis, we are critical of the racist, classist, and militaristic policies of the current Israeli government.[107]

We are ... outraged at Israel's attack on Beirut.

We do not accept any ideological or historical justifications for the killing of civilians in Lebanon over the past few weeks.

[We condemn] the military actions of Begin and Sharon.

We ... confirm our commitment to the survival of the Palestinian Arab people.

> They [anti-Israel protestors] ignore groups of Israelis and Palestinians who have for years been trying to work out a policy which would allow for two states, each recognizing and respecting the other.[108]

The authors counterbalance these claims of Palestinian suffering each time by insisting on Israel's right to exist. They claim to be "aware of the complexities surrounding Israel's creation and the displacement of the Palestinian people,"[109] but fail to elaborate. What caused the displacement is a Zionist invasion and theft of Palestinian land. How do Palestinians get justice without an Israeli reckoning with its settler-colonial mentality and practices? For Zionists, Israel's right to existence is unconditional. A genocidal Israel has a right to exist.

The liberal Zionist's move is to redirect: yes, there is a problem, but the problem is not with Israel or Zionism, it is with the nation's political upper echelon. The excess of Israeli violence lies in its warmonger leaders (Begin and Sharon). Israel is the only place of refuge for Jews in the world, and this is why Zionism must be defended. If you single out Israel, blaming it for all the problems of the Middle East, you are anti-Semitic. If you're an anti-Zionist, it means you want the destruction of Israel, that you're against Jewish safety, which makes you anti-Semitic. In other words, the problem is never Zionism as such, Zionism as a colonial ideology. We can recognize the operations of fetishist disavowal in Rich and her cosignatories: *We know very well about the awful suffering of Palestinians that we have caused, but all the same we believe in a Zionist Israel as the guarantor of Jewish safety. Israel can be redeemed; Begin and Sharon are the "bad apples" of Israeli politics* (this logic applies perfectly today: simply replace Begin and Sharon with Netanyahu and Ben-Gvir, for instance). For the committed liberal Zionist, Zionism is a pristine and untouchable idea, but Israeli leaders are corruptible like any other political leaders in the world—*why are you singling out Israel?* So, how can a commitment to a belief system that foregrounds Jewish safety be wrong? The actual guilty parties are the new anti-Semites, now donning anti-imperialist clothing. Israel has a right to exist because Jews have a right to exist. Any challenges to these observations put Jews at risk.

Zionism here can only be imagined as a movement of liberation for Jews; its coloniality is *ab initio* ruled out. Jordan cuts through Rich's argument, insisting that Zionism is a murderous ideology. She ends her open letter with an empathic rejection of Rich's call to order: "Where you raise the accusation of anti-Semitism I accuse you: I accuse you of being anti-Palestinian. More, I accuse you of being anti-life. I refuse to assume responsibility for your actions and your inertia. I do not accept you as my people."[110] Rich's *J'accuse* rings hollow; it decouples Zionism from its excess, offering a Zionism with a feminist face. For Rich, Israel's right to exist nullifies any objections about the state's coloniality; Jordan's *J'accuse* rings true. Jordan begins with self-critique, by accusing herself for not having done enough to prevent the carnage:

> I claim responsibility for the Israeli crimes against humanity, because I am an American and American monies made these atrocities possible. I claim responsibility for Sabra and Shatila, because, clearly, I have not done enough to halt heinous episodes of holocaust and genocide around the globe. I accept this responsibility, and I work for the day when I may help to save any one other life, in fact.[111]

Jordan's claim of responsibility pushes her to do more for the wretched of the world. Rich's responsibility pushes her to reinforce and solidify her commitment to a Zionist feminist identity, that she can be feminist (and thus care for the oppressed) and pro-Israel (and thus care for the Jews around the world):

> In the past we have been pushed to choose one part of our identity at the expense of an other as if they are, of necessity, mutually exclusive. We have been told that we could not be both lesbian and Jew, Jew and anti-racist, anti-racist and Zionist. We are now being asked, yet again, to make false and, for us, impossible choices.[112]

Rich presents herself as a "complex" identity, accusing anti-Zionist feminists of limiting her being. I see it the other way around. By stressing the incompatibility of being Zionist and feminist, Jordan exposes an internal limitation to Rich's white vision of justice, which assumes the oppression of Palestinians might be necessary if it means the protection and survival of Jews in Israel. A true commitment to the oppressed would subject Zionism (as it should any system of belief) to a ruthless critique. A Zionist feminist basically gets to have her cake and eat it too. Rich can feel sorry about Palestinians (Israel is wrong for killing civilians at such a high rate) and commit to the idea of Israel (Zionism's ontological pitch that only Israel can protect Jews). Liberal Zionists want peace, but peace without talks of coloniality and decolonization, without anything that questions the validity of Zionism. And we should keep in mind that peace is by no means anathema to the Occupying forces, since "peace as a rule serves occupiers: after they finish their conquest, they of course want peace."[113] The so-called Israeli peace camp, the political home of liberal Zionists, is really about the normalization of the Occupation. *There will be no de-Zionizing here.*

Jordan's charge of anti-Palestinianism does more than neutralize Rich's anti-Semitism. It describes Zionism as a racist ideology underpinning Israel's murderous settler colonialism, its erasure of Palestinians. "Anti-Palestinian" as a charge is not being used silence Rich on Israel. Quite the contrary, being anti-Palestinian, Zionist, or pro-Israel was and is the norm; it aligned Rich with power and the political status quo, as it does now, though commitments to Zionism have weakened in feminist circles (in no small part due to work of activists such as June Jordan). I read "anti-life" as Jordan's critique of Rich's disprivileging of non-European lives. If terms such as "genocide" and "holocaust" are only applicable to whites and Jews (those who count in the eyes of the racist Western world), then Rich must not consider the lives of Palestinians grievable. It is in this sense that Rich is anti-life; she embraces the lives of those like her, but not the lives of Palestinians who are struggling for their survival and liberation. Jewish survival is a necessity; Palestinian survival is aspirational.

Jordan praised the Israeli Peace Now dissidents for breaking with Zionist authority; "Never again" for them means "Never Again for Everyone"; it means "every life is a universe."[114] In this respect, we should see Jordan's "people" as first and foremost a political category, invested in laying out the fault lines, in talking about divisions and antagonisms, and their overcoming in the name a just future *for all*. "People" doesn't stand for an empty pluralist ideal that corresponds to the white (neo)liberal account of diversity (each cultural other is singular, decontextualized, and depoliticized to be understood/consumed at the individual level). What Jordan is asking of her people, as she puts it elsewhere, is an Intifada: "I say we need a rising up, an Intifada, USA."[115] By agitating for the Palestinian cause, you become other, part of a malleable and dynamic people raging for justice. You sustain the "force of solidarity" underpinning Black and Palestinian struggles; you resist identity politics (and the pleasure principle that sustains it). You side with Palestinians even as you know the blowback is coming—that you'll be targeted as anti-Semitic and risk your standing as a public intellectual and activist for justice.

What Zionist fear: Jordan is an agent of change and unlearning. In her works, Jordan tirelessly tries to weaken Zionism's libidinal hold on the American cultural imaginary and create a space for Palestinian being. Like Edward Said, Jordan wanted to challenge the authority of Zionist discourse in order to attend to its victims. Her response to these victims was not only her commitment to end to their habitual suffering. She offered solidarity, a politics that calls on us to reckon with the coloniality of the Israeli necropolitical regime *and* its American supplier and supporter.

Palestine/Israel from the standpoint of those who are "becoming object" looks quite different from the Zionist framing of Israel as a democratic liberal state. For Jordan, this narrative lies and deceives. Unless you are Jewish and consent to be a single being, dubiously collapsing Judaism and Zionism, a Zionist Israel is a horizon of occupation and dispossession—where Palestinians appear as murderable, disposable, and ungrievable. In contrast, Palestine is a horizon for universal justice—an eventual site for becoming object. And, let's be clear, nothing prevented Rich in 1982 from being included in Jordan's people other than her affective attachment to a murderous colonial Israel: "I believe that you cannot claim a people and not assume responsibility for what that people do or don't do. You cannot claim to be human and not assume responsibility for the value of all human life."[116] You cannot claim a people (again, as imagined by Zionism, which irrevocably ties Jews and only Jews to the land of historic Palestine) and disavow the horrific actions of your people. Your people are genocidaires; they are not my people. Your people discard lives; they are not my people. My people dream of equality, freedom, and justice (from the river to the sea); your people dream of mastery, invulnerability, and conquest (a Greater Israel). Jordan's universalist or transnationalist ethos clashed with Rich's identitarian dispositions and deep sympathies for Zionism, for a Jewish ethnonationalist state. A clash that has repeated itself more than once in American feminist circles.

Though Lorde and others blocked the publication of Jordan's letter, unfairly dismissing it as a "personal attack," "character assassination," insensitive to Jewish sensibilities, and basically too angry (she didn't "express her anger … in a reasonable way"—making Rich the true victim of the affair, and not the Palestinians—the letter was discovered in the Audre Lorde archives and liberated/published in 2024.[117] Jordan, a problem for/in white patriarchal America, became a different kind of problem by becoming Palestinian, touching a nerve in the belly of the beast. Jordan existed, we might say, as a multiple problem for Empire, boldly reminding her feminist communities that oppression abroad concerns us all and, more importantly, the master's house is also an imperial house.[118] Rich's white feminism was ill-equipped to deal with the colonial situation. Why? How effective can your tools ever be if you willfully ignore the racist and colonial system of power at work in Palestine/Israel, if you do not confront the fact that the settler/master's house is built on stolen land and that the fascist Zionism you defend, by your attachment to the idea of Israel, is in the business of racism and genocide—of exterminating the brutes?

What does it mean to side with Israel in the 1980s and now? It means living unproblematically with an Israel that allowed the endless carpet bombing of Lebanon and the Sabra and Shatila massacre to happen.[119] It means living unproblematically with a genocidal Israel, working diligently to meet its daily cruelty quota, exercising every day a minimum level of barbarity in Gaza—including:

- starvation (the UN describes Gaza as "the hungriest place on Earth"),[120]
- child amputations (the highest number of child amputees per capita than anywhere in the world),[121]
- murdering journalists,[122]
- using Palestinian civilians as human shields,[123]
- using food as "bait" for "execution-style" murders of Palestinians waiting in line to feed their families (a new reality created by the aid distribution site run by the militarized Israeli- and US-backed "Gaza Humanitarian

Foundation" (or more correctly described as the "Gaza Holocaust Forces")[124]—the Zionist solution to the UNRWA problem, the linguistic and fleshly erasure of the Palestinian refugee),[125]

- torture,[126]
- bombing aid depots,[127]
- bombing schools,[128]
- bombing hospitals,[129]
- the slaughtering and burning of Palestinians alive in tents.[130]

Living unproblematically in times of genocide means living with all these atrocities. Israel's appetite for cruelty exceeds our wildest imagination. Maybe, Palestinians will get a ceasefire only when there is nothing left to bomb, no one to butcher …

In light of this grim reality, we might respond: *Fuck Golda Meir! Fuck Menachem Begin! Fuck Ariel Sharon! And fuck Benjamin Netanyahu! Basically, fuck all Israeli prime ministers.*[131] At the same time, our rage cannot be consumed by Israel's illustrious list of war criminals. We must redirect our *ressentiment* away from these obscene figures of power and not mythologize them in any way. Why? Because the Palestinian problem doesn't lie primarily with Israel's infamous prime ministers but with a structure, with a Zionist Israel, a supremacist state that has been subjugating Palestinians for over seventy-five years. Sorry liberals, but the problem is never this or that prime minister;[132] Israel's genocidal proclivities are constitutive of the state's muscular Zionism.

With Jordan, we witness, to our horror, the colossal damage that a Zionist, white, and masculinist settler-colonial regime can do to non-Europeans, to the infrastructure of life, and to the rest of the planet: "To Adrienne, I make this public reply: Your evident definition of feminism leaves you indistinguishable from the white men threatening the planet with extinction."[133] From the Sabra and Shatila massacre to the Gaza genocide, the IOF is in the business of destruction. Phantasmatically speaking, the Israeli military forces incarnate a god-phallus. A Zionist masculinist Israel produces Palestinian flesh—a self reduced to bare life; it projects an invulnerable military body hell-bent on Palestinocide and ecocide.[134]

Colonial necropolitics is not a feminism; Ziofascism is not a feminism. Black feminism is an anti-fascist commitment to end all forms of oppression within and beyond America's national borders. It emerges at the sight/site of injustice. As Jordan notes, "the issue of the Palestinian people is the issue of the value of human life, per se, and, more specifically, the issue of the value of human life that is neither Jewish nor European." June Jordan, a feminist killjoy *avant la lettre*, announced that "Palestine is a moral litmus test for the world," a message that Angela Davis has repeated, and that we need to continuously repeat.[135] Black feminists have acted as good problem-makers; their interventions—generative and inventive—touch us all.

Only an Insurrectionist Solidarity Can Save Us

An insurrectionary struggle begins by upending a status quo that narrows the field of possibilities, cruelly manifested in the political class's ironclad support for Israel's killing machine. There is a tragic continuity in the West's callous mistreatment of Palestinians. Born translated, immediately subjected to pathologizing discourses, to a ready-made Orientalist framework and a colonial imaginary schema,[136] the figure of the Palestinian is effortlessly understood and classified as "the natural terrorist,"[137] who, as we've come to know now, is genocidable with complete impunity.[138] Zionism's worldly success lies in its successful honing of Western Orientalist discourse, its collusion with the West in perceiving and constructing Palestinians as fundamentally and irredeemably other. Phenomenologically speaking, a Zionist hermeneutic inaugurates a "natural attitude," installing and securing a number of presuppositions about the "Israeli-Palestinian conflict"—Palestinians are de-Indigenized (they are Arabs and strangers on their own land), irrational and violent (violent *because* irrational), nefarious in their deliberations, always the aggressors, never the victims. They incarnate/symbolize the evils of anti-Semitism by refusing Jews their right to live in peace on their God-given ancestral land. This distorted and distorting representation of Palestinians is uncritically consumed and circulated by a willfully ignorant mainstream Western media. What Palestinians can legitimately do is simply disappear. As Yanis Varoufakis puts it, "Palestinians can be allowed to wither, to die slowly away and perish in silence."[139] Doing anything else would be considered anti-Semitic, a threat to Israel's right to exist (to exist as a supremacist state, that is).

Israeli human rights group B'Tselem not only accuses the IOF of "ethnic cleansing" in northern Gaza, it also underscores the destruction of Palestinian worldhood as a military strategy and objective:

> The magnitude of the crimes Israel is currently committing in the northern Gaza Strip in its campaign to empty it of however many residents are left is impossible to describe, not just because hundreds of thousands of people enduring starvation, disease without access to medical care and incessant bombardments and gunfire defies comprehension, but because Israel has cut them off from the world.[140]

Israel's business is the business of de-worlding Palestinians; or to be more precise, de-worlding Palestinians is the flip side of Zionist world-making. Zionist belonging can never admit Palestinian belonging. What a Zionist Israel wants above all else is the ontological disappearance of Palestinians.

The colonized Palestinian does not comply and thus refuses Zionist temporality; the wretched "is dominated but not domesticated. He is made to feel inferior, but by no means convinced of his inferiority."[141] Palestinian survival is an affront to Zionist reason. Nakba survivors are a reminder and remainder of Israel's past and ongoing crimes. Their struggle is our struggle for justice. Insurrection for the Palestinian cause is not about returning or retreating to one's cultural past (the decolonial temptation). The Palestinian cause at once attests to the land of historic Palestine and exceeds its geographical coordinates. We are not dealing with a mere conflict between two peoples over land (a conflict is, in principle, resolvable and assumes a certain level of symmetry between the parties involved—which is not the case here). Palestine brings to the surface the ills of European modernity. Palestine continues to be a problem for the West; we, who support the Palestinian cause, are a problem. The optics of/for Western leaders are bad. They unconscionably stood with Israel on the side of genocide.

How we talk about Palestine and continue to deal with and think from Palestine will tell us a great deal about our future, about the ways we understand and implement belonging, justice, and equality on a global scale. What is at stake is not merely the cessation of Israel's genocidal war on Gaza (another agreement on a truce to be subsequently violated by Israel either immediately or in months to come), but more importantly the dismantling of a world in which a genocide can happen in plain sight with no global intervention.[142] What kind of world are we witnessing? Will there be a Gazafication of the planet, an oasis for the few surrounded by endless deathscapes? Will the threat of 100,000 tons of explosives function as a negotiation tactic when dealing with "unruly" states? How do we de-normalize genocide? How do we prevent the ongoing Gazafication of Gaza and its potential export and application to the rest of the world? What world do we want? Asking such questions is already the beginning of thinking universally and critically about the Palestinian problem.

An insurrectionist solidarity radicalizes any struggle by reordering, revitalizing, and expanding its orientation and reshaping its desires and values: *Hysterically speaking, why do you treat my neighbor/comrade with such depravity? There is something lacking or missing in your reasoning, in your totalizing account. What makes you such an authority on humanity? Don't you know that the order of the human is non-all? Your neglect and targeting of minority groups—migrants, trans people, Blacks, and Palestinians—is fascist. Palestine is a queer issue. Palestine is a feminist issue. No! We don't accept that Israel or the United States are above international law. No! We don't accept that might makes right.* Palestine at its most universalist figuration is a catalyst for invention and social change.

As a drive for justice and freedom, insurrectionist solidarity cannot be contained or captured in any one particular struggle; its interdependent ties may compel us to question if not set aside our own immediate interests and principles of self-preservation. The "force of solidarity" is not amenable to transactional logics; it is unruly and transformative, always hungering for more, pushing against the limits of our ego or group identity. Afropessimists entertain but rule out their own version of the (im)possible. Reifying the "structural antagonism" between Black and non-Black ironically serves the interests of the system and its reproduction. Afropessimism's ~~identity~~ politics, or its ontologizing of racism and structural Blackness, represents, alas, a false overcoming of identity politics, posing no real political threat to the dominant regime.[143]

In this respect, solidarity is a rejection of a depoliticized pessimism, a pessimism engulfed by one's suffering, too easily seduced by its own apocalyptic visions. And for this reason alone, solidarity and pessimism are not to be opposed but thought together. *Never solidarity before pessimism*, to adapt Edward Said's poignant and memorable saying.[144] Pessimistic solidary—or militant pessimism, the pessimism of the insurrectionist—urges activists and scholars to interrogate their own agenda *and* that of the other(s), to resist the lure of a politics of recognition (which traffics in the language of identity and interests) *and* to universalize their anti-racist struggles (to block the impulse to particularize your agenda while vying for recognition in a relentless and power-serving Oppression Olympics discourse). This dialecticized pessimism is not an obstacle to "trying the impossible,"[145] as Étienne Balibar says in his attempt to push through his own pessimism about the catastrophic Palestinian situation, but, as I argue, its precondition: without critical pessimism I fear that all that we would try is the possible, the permissible, which falls far short of invention.

As a critical Palestinian pessimist I reject with all my heart the coercive rhetoric urging us to accept and endorse—through our vote, through our activism, through our speech—the "lesser of two evils." It clearly has not advanced justice, and chances are that it will not do so in the future, especially when the system of oppression *is* the status quo.[146] The liberal gatekeepers of the status quo are most obsessed with neutralizing conscientious voters, those who are tired of empty promises and are committed to social justice—and potentially to becoming other. Janine Jones admirably cuts through the double-talk of the liberal establishment and names their actual blackmail as *destruction or compliance*. The message, as she puts it, has been: "Continue to fight against structural oppression, and we will destroy you through the conditions those structures produce to dismantle your lives. Alternatively, you can abandon your struggle against systems of oppression, and we will reform (perhaps incrementally) certain aspects of your living conditions and that of your loved ones, who may be incarcerated."[147] The anti-racist Left rejects this forced choice and mobilizes for actual change. It is unflinching in its dissent and critique. It holds both liberal and conservative parties responsible for the state of affairs. Commenting on the US context, Franko Berardi puts it clearly: "Racism is the core of the American unconscious. This is why Trump is the soul of America."[148] The here and now is intolerable. Reversing this reality will be difficult and will require committed Democrats and activists to reckon with the ranking members of their Democratic Party and the liberal center. Two initial moves should be taken immediately by the Democratic leadership. The liberal center must face its failures and stop blaming the far Left for its losses.[149] As Dave Zirin notes, "a centrist liberal" should not worry about "being called anti-Israel more than being called anti-genocide."[150] In a move toward growing a moral spine, liberal elite, stop complaining about the anti-racist Left and start addressing your naturalized, less-toxic colonial racism, crystalized in anti-Blackness (too often conveniently blamed on the populist alt-Right) and anti-Palestinianness (which is not merely the problem of Israel's Ziofascists and settler militias). Insurrections—disruptions in the American quotidian—are not, and shouldn't be, the privilege of the new populist Right. The global Left must insist: *Another transformation of America is possible.*

Unlike the insurrections of fascist nationalists and white supremacists, which are counterrevolutionary, the insurrection of the anti-racist Left doesn't scapegoat the least protected; it doesn't target society's surplus population (including the poor, unhoused, trans, refugees, migrants, the permanently unemployable, and the irremediably blackened). A clear line delineates the two positions. And what makes a leftist insurrection infinitely more appealing is that it welcomes others, and firmly remains *open to all*. Its investment in universality is axiomatic. Everyone can, in principle, become object. The wretched of the world already are! Whites can become ex-whites; Zionists can become anti-Zionists, Gods can become humans, and so on. But how do we do it? We must abandon the libidinal and limited material rewards of identity politics, of rooted identities—particularly those born of "blood and soil" racist fantasies—for an insurrectionist and transnationalist solidarity that exceeds if not overwhelms the specific contours of any given struggle and agenda. The force of solidarity, its indefatigable negativity, lies in its expansive inventiveness, in its capacity to sharpen and invigorate political visions. Becoming object is the zero-level of solidarity in the insurrectionist struggle against ontological walls and partitions at home and across the globe.

Conclusion: Pessimism and Repetition

The world gives us plenty to be pessimistic about. For racialized communities, believing that the moral arc of history bends toward justice, that the state or government is looking out for your interests, that the global community will promote justice and peace, that the police serves and protects all of us, can easily get you killed. These collective illusions or fantasies traffic in hope for the future while at the same time locking us in an unbearable present. Against this unsettling and infuriating backdrop, our pessimism is fully justified and needed; for some of us, it's even a survival strategy. Pessimism compels us to question, resist, and refuse, to reorient the discussion away from the mind-numbing hegemony of pragmatism and common sense. A pessimistic approach jams narratives of racial progress, clearing the ground for a reckoning with the afterlives of slavery and colonialism. Subjugation and domination persist, haunting and tormenting many of us. In the current context, optimism, or having faith in the existing social order, often means compromising on your desire for liberation. Blacks, Palestinians, and their supporters are implicitly or explicitly told: Forget about defunding the police, halting the school-to-prison pipeline, and abolishing the prison-industrial complex, along with the cruel and racist white world that birthed such anti-Black realities; forget about desegregation and dismantling the new incarnations of Jim Crow, and be grateful things are not worse. Forget about your anti-colonial struggle to denaturalize Israel's founding violence. Let Israel "move past the past" and deem Palestinian resistance a minor chapter of an anti-colonial bygone era.[1] Forget about Palestinian unity, dignity, and self-determination, and let the Zionist state fully enjoy the spoils of war and realize its biblically sanctioned dream of a Greater Israel.

The title of Omar El Akkad's book, *One Day, Everyone Will Have Always Been Against This*, gestures to the liberal world's formidable capacity to rework the past to make it comfortable to live with:

One of the hallmarks of Western liberalism is an assumption, in hindsight, of virtuous resistance as the only polite expectation of people on the receiving end of colonialism. While the terrible thing is happening—while the land is still being stolen and the natives still being killed—any form of opposition is terroristic and must be crushed for the sake of civilization. But decades, centuries later, when enough of the land has been stolen and enough of the natives killed, it is safe enough to venerate resistance in hindsight.[2]

Our pessimism tirelessly works against this "malicious fiction,"[3] this retroactive complacency by refusing to give the liberal world a pass, to let it move past the Gaza genocide. No, Western liberals were never *against this*. What Western liberals were/are against is Palestinian resistance, liberation, and revolution. A global Intifada—decolonization by another name—terrifies the ruling class. What the hegemonic West consents to is the Zionist solution to the Palestinian problem: an unabated Palestinocide and land grab.

We will not forgive and forget this betrayal of Western liberalism. You forged a new rule-based international order to prevent the atrocities of the Second World War from ever happening again, but cynically exempted Israel, immunizing it from legal and moral judgment, shielding Israel from any accountability for its lustful war on the Palestinian people. The Israeli exception has revealed the extent to which the Western global order is a sham, thematized its irremediable coloniality and "rotten foundations."[4] The "antisemitism industrial complex"[5] is working overtime, transmogrifying Palestinians and their principled supporters into phobic beings, that is, anti-Semitic terrorists, with the full support of corporate media outlets. Israel is getting away with genocide. And the political class of the Western world is to blame. America stands out in its unconscionable support of the Israeli killing machine. America, however, is not simply complicit with the genocide; we must see the utter destruction of Palestinian lives and landscape as a joint Israeli-US military effort. We have indeed plenty to be angry and pessimistic about.

Pessimism can, of course, also overwhelm resistance, draining its vitality. *The system is rigged; resistance is futile; gratuitous violence is my destiny; you are not me so you're my enemy*. Pessimism is susceptible to the "conceptual trappings"[6] of a discourse of bare life, devoid of resistance and refusals. This is the unqualified and brutal pessimism in its tempting Afropessimist mode. Humanism will not save us; a politics of recognition will not save us; empathy will not save us. I know; I agree. Still, I don't believe that pessimism forces us to rule out emancipatory resistance: pessimism and (collective) resistance can and must coexist. It takes courage to be hopeless, to see the world's possibilities as empty of revolutionary causes, full of "lost causes."[7] My wager is that the opposite of pessimism is not optimism, but a critical pessimism, a dialecticized pessimism that not only jams the identitarian pull, but that also opens, for instance, to a beautiful insurrectionist Black-Palestinian solidarity. As Edward Said stressed, "*any* lost cause can ever really be lost."[8] A Black-Palestinian solidarity revives the lost cause of the anti-colonial Left. In a world ensnared by ideology, the lures of nationalisms and pitfalls of identity politics, a cross-racial Black-Palestinian solidarity adopts a boldly universalist and internationalist orientation, shifting from "I" to "We," from "I am suspicious of you and the world" to "I am skeptical of this world and what it wants for/from us." This skeptical pessimism loves the company of others. *Problem-makers recognize problem-makers*. Let's rage against this unjust world together.

In the modality of being-with, pessimism's force multiplies; its hermeneutic sharpens; its agonistic energy is harnessed. Akin to the generative negativity of the feminist killjoy, pessimism's negativity can be rechanneled for *a world-making project*. This pessimism is open to all and opens to all. It is a pessimism that universalizes the plight of the wretched, that interrogates the paradigm of the human, and that contests the disappearance and denigration of certain beings "decreed by racist, imperial power even before their deaths."[9] It is an unrelenting pessimism that demands justice for the dead and the living, and that expresses a collective *No!* to the exploitation and commodification of lives, *No!* to vertical ontologies of all kinds, *No!* to walls that segregate and suffocate our social existence—"From Palestine to Mexico, All the Walls Have Got to Go."[10]

Critical pessimism fosters and cultivates an eye for problems; it helps us define the contours of a political struggle, making us attentive to the types of violence that often go unnoticed. Pessimistically speaking, we should insist that there can be no return to a pre-George Floyd sensibility, to a time prior to BLM, to colorblind normalcy and implicit in "All Lives Matter" rhetoric,[11] that there can be no return to the daily violence of the siege of Gaza—invisibilized on October 6—when the Palestinian struggle for liberation was a not an immediate concern for Western audiences.

Problems are of course double-edged. As Sara Ahmed avers "to expose a problem is to pose a problem."[12] Palestine fits this adage to a tee. Palestine is radioactive; talking about Palestine makes (some) people uneasy. Under a racist horizon, the source of the unease is not the material reality of an unfolding genocide, the feeling of complicity in the "crime of crimes"; no, it is the language about Palestinian genocide, settler colonialism, apartheid that troubles and offends. Christina Sharpe draws an insightful parallel in observing the ways people react to the use of anti-Blackness and anti-Palestinian racism to render visible a wrong, a violation of being, a denial of lived experience, the becoming ~~being~~. Sharpe observes: "To name a person, institution, state, or a set of acts as racist or anti-Palestinian or antiblack is to cause injury. It is not the racism that injures, it is not the bullets and bombs that injure, it is the words that seek to name the injury—that name a murderous structure like apartheid or settler colonialism—that cause injury."[13] In this twisted logic, naming an injury caused by racist systems of oppression and exploitation causes an injury.[14] Killjoy Francesca Albanese, the UN special rapporteur on the occupied Palestinian territory, is a textbook example of the ways formulating a problem (international companies, like big US tech businesses, shouldn't be profiting from a genocidal occupation) turns you into a problem (you're anti-American, anti-Israeli, i.e., anti-Semitic). After the release of her damning report "From Economy of Occupation to Economy of Genocide," Marco Rubio imposed sanctions on Albanese, dishonestly accusing her of waging "political and economic warfare" against America, Israel, and their genocidaire allies.[15] Rubio and his ilk believe and act as if international law is a luxury of the few. They get to wield the law willy-nilly, weaponize it against their foes, but are never subject to its verdicts. Albanese doesn't comply; she refuses to back down in the face of what she calls "mafia-style intimidation techniques."[16] Naming a problem turns one into a problem.[17]

To exist as a problem is always to appear angry and "unreasonable"—the latter used rhetorically to racialize, delegitimize, and silence the former. As Audre Lorde's anger is for her, my anger is a response to the racism, to a racism is that is constantly denied or relativized, so as to make my claim to it irrelevant or contentious. My anger can, then, only appear unreasonable and regressive to the standards of white normativity. But here we should not forget about reasonableness's colonial overtones. "During the period of decolonization," Frantz Fanon writes, "the colonized are called upon to be reasonable. They are offered rock-solid values, they are told in great detail that decolonization should not mean regression, and that they must rely on values which have proved to be reliable and worthwhile. Now it so happens that when the colonized hear a speech on Western culture they draw their machetes or at least check to see they are close to hand."[18] The colonizers' claim to progress and universality is a sham, "a hallmark of the Western imperialist *episteme*";[19] their "rock-solid values" are lies used to humiliate and alienate the colonized. And what about the virtue of colonial reason? The colonized do not need it; their resistance or revolt is not bereft of rationality.[20] Quite the contrary, anti-colonial reason discloses and exposes the "true locus of trouble,"[21] the naturalized structural violence that subtends a colonial framework; it brings to light "the contours of the background"[22] that colonizers/white liberals willfully deny and refuse to see. Wielding anti-colonial reason, the problem-maker labors incessantly to upend the necrocapitalist structures that make it near impossible for Blacks and Palestinians (among other wretched) to breathe.[23]

To exist as a problem means that you're not intended to survive let alone flourish. The feminist killjoy in me likes to remind white liberals that BLM emerged under a Black president, a Black attorney general, and a Black secretary of homeland security.[24] Obama's election never ushered in a post-racial America. Yes, the liberal center is objectively better than Trump Right (at the very least, it is less misogynistic, less xenophobic, less transphobic, and less anti-Black) but it still operates in a shared anti-Black horizon that spans partisan lines.

For American liberals, the racial problem is always on the side of the Right, with the Trump incarnating its worst possibilities. And yet liberals of shades relate to race in not an unambiguous way. In their dealings with anti-Blackness, they are especially prone to fetishist disavowal: *I know very well that Blacks are mistreated and surveilled, but all the same I believe in the American dream, the nation's ethical core, and that Trump is an anomaly, racist police officers are "bad apples,"* and so on. A liberal subject can have, with no friction or contradiction, BLM yard signs (he knows about anti-Blackness) and a large American flag on the front porch (he believes in America's manifest destiny, its exceptionalism or special role in the world), occasionally pairing it with a Ukrainian flag, which amounts to virtue signaling what I would call "tribal cosmopolitanism" (this is the description of an actual house in Walla Walla!).

White bourgeois liberals support BLM the way they support the legacy of Martin Luther King, Jr., by which I mean poorly. It tends to be abstract, feel-good images of nonviolence and toleration, a kind of decaffeinated politics, devoid of its true anti-capitalism and anti-militarism jolts, devoid of King's commitment to labor unions and anti-Vietnam war protests. It is hard to imagine the liberal elite standing behind that problematic King and his unwavering struggle against "the giant triplets of racism, extreme materialism and militarism."[25] The rabble-rouser King has been effaced in his sanitized biography, or hagiography, as well as his notorious designation by the FBI and the US government as "the most dangerous man in America."[26] Rediscovering King's political force is to reinvent him as a radical problem, a would-be-danger to a depoliticized liberal Left unable to think race and class together as sites for social change and ontological upheavals.

Liberals don't have to stay liberals. If there are potential defectors from the class of liberal elites (and, for the record, we welcome all race and class traitors), white liberals who honestly see that the current system is both unjust and unsustainable, then maybe they could take their cue from the pro-Palestine student encampments and dare to become a problem, or become an object, by flying the Palestinian flag. This provocative gesture (simply imagine what your neighbors would say!) would be a repetition of the BLM protests of 2020; it could reactivate and repoliticize the BLM yard signs—signifying now/again a revolutionary Black liberation rather woke virtue signaling; the struggle against racial capitalism, and the beginning of an actual solidarity movement—let's buck easy alliances (the enemy of my enemy is my friend) and align Palestine and Ukraine in a common fight against belligerent nuclear nations: Israel with America and Russia.[27]

I take repetition seriously. Repetition holds an emancipatory political potential; it does not just reproduce the state of affairs—it can be socially transformative as well, an endless resource for disalienation and human liberation. As Nadia Bou Ali insightfully notes about Lacan's understanding of repetition, there is within its logic a yearning for ontological upheaval in the Symbolic; there is in "repetition— of traumas, historical events, symptoms and so on—an unconscious plea to change the existing order of things."[28] On the one hand, the BLM protests of

2020 could be/have been contextualized away. COVID-19 indirectly intensified the public outrage of police brutality. Undistracted by sports or other leisurely activities, thrown into mass unemployment, and cognizant of their own precarity and vulnerability to death through disease and government inefficiencies, people in America, and around the world, were interpellated as witnesses to this obscene example of anti-Blackness. It was a perfect storm for the expression of a general dissatisfaction with the reality of the world, with the existing world order. For the benefactors of the status quo, we might say that it was an instance of "bad luck," an accident to be corrected through police reform, talks of reform, or, better yet, what Olúfémi O. Táíwò names "elite capture"—the ideological ways in which "elites fight for their own narrow interests using the banner of group solidarity."[29] In any case, Black rage wasn't meant to come back; it was understood as a one-time event. But the Palestine solidarity movement disclosed *again* the political rottenness of the liberal global order. We are witnessing here what Žižek calls a "structural necessity":

> When Napoleon lost for the first time in 1813, it looked like just bad luck; when he lost the second time at Waterloo, it was clear that his time was over. And does the same not hold for the ongoing financial crisis? When it first hit the markets in September 2008, it looked like an accident to be corrected through better regulation, and so on; now that signs of a repeated financial meltdown are gathering, it is clear that we are dealing with a structural necessity.[30]

As with capitalism's financial crises, racial violence/colonial fascism is not an aberration to the liberal international order, but a manifestation of its actual operations. The solidarity movement for Palestine repeats the eruption of the movement for Black lives. "Palestinian Lives Matter" marks a repetition of "Black Lives Matter." Both cries are precisely what the Democratic Party refused to hear let alone embrace.[31] Repetition, as Lacan put it, "demands the new."[32] But for the party's upper echelon, there was no appetite then and there is no appetite now for the new, for a move to alter the racist and exploitive order of beings. The Gaza genocide unsparingly casts the American liberal commitment to social and racial justice as insincere and fake. Palestine compels us to unlearn, to critically reexamine liberal white America's commitment to anti-anti-Blackness. The liberal support for CRT is more self-serving than principled, more performative than actual. Liberals faithfully follow the rules of woke society; they can't say what comes to their minds as Trump and the bigoted ideologues on the far Right do; they defer to people of color for what can and cannot be said. Liberals express their guilt about slavery, but they are not invested in fighting anti-Blackness, in working to undo its structural presence in American life and to shut down the machinery underpinning civil society by opening it to Black folks. Rather than embracing an anti-fascist and anti-racist Left, what liberals typically prefer is what we might call woke *jouissance*, "every renunciation of enjoyment generates an enjoyment in renunciation," writes Žižek .[33] If liberals willingly censure themselves, they gain a surplus-enjoyment in policing the language of non-Black others. And whatever feeling of impotent guilt they may suffer is converted into moral righteousness (my guilt is a sign that I care). There is an economy of *jouissance*, a whole liberal art in "feeling good about feeling bad,"[34] in hating the haters, the traditional or generic fascists who clumsily disturb the hegemonic liberal order (from your racist grandfather to Trump): crudely bigoted, misogynistic, homophobic, transphobic, anti-Semitic, Islamophobic, and so on. Anti-Black violence is ideologically individualized. Consider the 2015 Charleston massacre. Dylann Roof, a white supremacist, killed nine black churchgoers. White liberal Americans immediately condemned him but treated the tragedy as nothing more than a racist, anti-Black, lone shooter.[35] That white liberals fall short, that they are not there yet in their race-conscious awareness, is an understatement![36]

There is a deep resistance to engaging anti-Blackness as a structural problem, as a feature and not a bug of the American system. So when Trump comes into power (again) he is not creating a racist matrix from scratch, he is intensifying what already exists; he is taking full advantage of the afterlives of slavery and colonialism. Liberals are shocked by Trump's policies; for them, Trump is the problem, but Blacks have always been aware of America's racist core, its abusive powers. As Christina Greer avers, "Until we reckon with our fellow citizens' capacity—even hunger—for injustice, we will fail to meet, understand and survive this political moment."[37] Anti-Blackness as a problem runs much deeper. White liberals lack the interpretive tools and the courage to speak truth to power and to speak truth "*about* power."[38] But they are also affectively and materially attached to the status quo. They can openly celebrate and honor Black History Month, but don't ask them to defund the police, to combat systematic anti-Blackness, or consider reparations.

With Palestine, white liberals are forced to shift interpretive gears. You might win over some who are appalled by Israel's genocidal campaign, but when you start talking about ending the Occupation, BDS, the right of armed struggle against colonial domination, apartheid, or settler colonialism, when you shift from Palestinian abjection to Palestinian liberation, when you shift the discussion from one governed by humanitarian reason to one informed by anti-colonial reason, this is when liberal commitment to Palestinians starts to waver, for it points to the need to be open to revolutionary change, to go beyond lip service.[39]

In this respect, we must see and remember that the liberal elite constitutes the first counterinsurgency to both BLM and Palestinian solidarity movements. It has become clear that liberal democracy does not keep fascism at bay. As Alberto Toscano argues, liberalism's entanglement with colonial fascism is more profound: "The ascendance of fascism might initially appear as a break or an exception, but it is deeply rooted in and enabled by a colonial liberalism that will never countenance true liberation."[40] The student protests and encampments for Palestine exposed this internal division within the Left and its implication in a fascist formation. The liberal Left's fruitless and damming war against the radical Left, in which it positions itself, self-servingly, as the "liberal center," reflects a delusional "golden mean" mentality, convincing itself that it is avoiding the extremes on both sides (the radical Left and the radical Right). Let's not forget that Biden's position on the encampments basically included all the talking points of the authoritarian Right: "People have the right to get an education, the right to get a degree, the right to walk across campus safely without fear of being attacked."[41] Shamelessly, Biden associated pro-Palestinian speech with disorder and anti-Semitism, with the creation of a hostile environment, that made *some* Jewish students unsafe (invisibilizing all the Jewish students who stood unflinchingly in support of Palestine). Biden's solution to the anti-war protests is the *re*sedimentation of anti-Palestinianness, an authoritarian call to order: "Order must prevail."[42] Pro-Palestinian protests are not welcomed in America's civil society. Your lived experiences of injustice don't matter. Order must be reestablished, meaning Palestinians and their supporters must be silenced by whatever means necessary, including instrumentalizing the disarming charge of anti-Semitism and calling in the militarized police to brutishly break up the encampments. Though the Trump administration has amplified this fascist logic of order, aggressively policing the thoughts and beliefs of would-be anti-American, anti-Israeli offenders, it is qualitatively the same: that Palestinian voices don't belong in American colleges and universities is a fact that transcends Republican and Democratic states.

But if Republican states have been at work whitewashing American history in both K-12 education and state-funded universities, eradicating the teaching of CRT, redefined to mean anything pertaining to race and racism, Democratic states adopt a loosely pro-CRT and BLM stance, publicly decrying anti-CRT legislation. But on Palestine, Democratic elected officials disclose their racist attitudes insofar as they are often quite willing to endorse the same guardians of white nationalism in supporting spurious anti-BDS bills, deceptively couched as a noble fight against the spread of anti-Semitism on college campuses. Both parties blame BDS for Israel's degraded global reputation. The basically "bipartisan consensus" on anti-BDS legislation should give us pause.[43] Liberals would clearly prefer to decouple the two struggles. I will never tire of pointing out the hypocrisy of the liberal center and its willful failure to cultivate the *repetition* of BLM in the Palestinian solidarity movement.

A penetrating post on X from the progressive Jewish organization IfNotNow makes visible the shared animosity of Democratic and Republican leadership toward Palestinians and the plight for justice. IfNotNow delineates the true stakes: "The fanatical anti-CRT and anti-BDS movements are one and the same: a desperate attempt to hide historical and current reality, to police free speech when it threatens nationalism."[44] While IfNotNow finds the connections between BDS and CRT generative for social justice, as I do, Zionist and right-wing groups note the affinity between the two movements only to lazily condemn them as anti-Israeli and anti-American, meaning anti-Semitic and anti-patriotic.[45] What should not be missed in IfNotNow's intervention is its perspicacious observation that effectively ties Black and Palestinian struggles together, arguing that CRT and BDS share a common enemy: the gatekeepers of an unadulterated nationalism.[46] Nationalism begets fascism. CRT and BDS are problem-makers whereas fascists are in the business of transforming others into problems.

Now I'm of course not saying that anyone who objects to CRT and BDS is a card-carrying fascist (well, maybe "fascist curious"). My point is that until white liberals face their nation's racial logic, they will all too conveniently only see Trump as an exception or aberration to the status quo. As I see it, white liberals are by no means hostile to the racialized "Law and Order" narrative[47] and like other white Americans they aren't willing to sacrifice their ways of knowing and seeing, to let go their privileges and give up their priority in the hierarchical order of citizenry.[48] Talking "tough" about economic and social justice is fine, but don't ask white liberals to forgo their "global gated community."[49] *Exterminate the brutes* is by no means a foreign idea to them. For the white liberal center, America, not unlike Israel, is *not* a racist state or project, nor is it a "failed state" ("a state that cannot sustain itself within its own legal or ideological framework").[50] Liberals are not ready to see America as the New Jim Crow nor as partners with a genocidal Israel. A racialized caste system can exist under a liberal democracy. Their easily tapped white anxiety about the intrusion of "thugs," of raced and criminalized Black and Brown bodies (internal and external "rapists"), into the order of their lives makes them candidates for fascist capture.

The liberal center, Žižek notes, "is at the root of our crises."[51] I agree. Palestinian genocide, the fissures of the healthcare system, the permanent unemployment of a segment of society, and anti-Black police brutality (this list is far from exhaustive) all index the failures of the liberal Left to take a meaningful and principled stand. Reformism is not a politics but a capitulation. The liberal center with its proliferation of identitarian causes is the contemporary manifestation of "the nationalist political parties," that Frantz Fanon warned about, since they "never insist on the need for confrontation precisely because their aim is not the radical overthrow of the system."[52] An insurgent politics is the last thing on the mind of Democratic leaders. The opposition party is toothless.[53] To adapt Walter Benjamin, *every rise of fascism bears witness to a failure to overcome the liberal Left.*[54]

In the Harris–Trump presidential race, the liberal Left "stood for non-politics,"[55] indulging in empty promises. They spoke in platitudes without an agenda for a better America *for all*. The Democratic agenda was at its core counterrevolutionary. As Tatiana Cozzarelli observes, "the Democrats have set the stage for a more repressive domestic environment."[56] In contrast, it was Trump that "stood for politics," announcing changes to the system, albeit an impossible return to phantasmic and harmonious heteronormative white times, times absent of gender ideology and wokeism of all sorts, where (unearned) male and white privileges would be fully restored. Consider it an ideological reset to "the natural order of things."[57] Trump used pseudo-revolutionary language, harnessing and weaponizing the energies of the disappointed, abandoned, and resentful whites who felt that the liberal system has failed them. White folks are not getting their return on their libidinal investment in whiteness (wasn't racial capitalism supposed to spare them?). Trump points to a real suffering, but his fascist remedy—declaring an emergency, as if America is under invasion, fetishizing the border, and scapegoating racialized migrants—will only compound the social problems affecting the world. Following Democratic duplicity with the status quo, Trump enacted a right-wing backlash, affirmed a pro-police stance, and insisted that any talk of racial injustice is Marxist and anti-American.[58] Forget about combatting the New Jim Crow (what the liberal center miserably failed to do), Trump aspires for a return to a Jim Crow era, to pre-civil rights America, that is, to white times. America is in decline—whence the MAGA movement.[59]

In America's white supremacist rebirth, Trump calls for a new set of ideals—Merit, Excellence, and Intelligence—to restore the nation's greatness and save us from DEI, which he blames for the decline of the American way of life, for anything bad happening, including the collision between a passenger jet and an Army helicopter over DC in January 2025.[60] While I obviously condemn Trump's trafficking in racist tropes (namely, that Black inferiority is the cause for the nation's decline), the current framework of DEI is not without its political limitations either. Operating according to the current model of DEI, white liberals eagerly endorse change without change. As Ilan Kapoor pointedly discerns, corporate capitalism appears unaffected by DEI, as wealth and income disparities in the United States have only increased over the period of its rise. Kapoor adds: "DEI is ... a way of putting a human face on corporate inequality. The often tokenistic inclusion of minorities under the guise of 'equity' provides the illusion of creating greater equality. But it doesn't and hasn't."[61] *Minority faces in high places* has not succeeded in pacifying a predatory and voracious capitalism simply because DEI cannot, its tools remain the master/capitalist's tools. Its reformist ideology—which is in the business of managing the anger of people of color—strengthens the existing order and distracts from the urgent need to reckon with New Jim Crow and is its procedures are ill-equipped to dismantle the deep structural imbalances plaguing our socioeconomic system. As George Yancy importantly reminds us, "We mustn't forget that DEI can also function insidiously as a form of appeasement and deception. In other words, hegemonic whiteness, well before Trump, has never ceased to exist within this country. As such, whiteness accommodates differences but maintains its normative power."[62] Corporate DEI is good for liberal capitalism—it offers exploitation with a multicultural face—but bad for racial and economic justice.

And if universities were truly serious about DEI initiatives and not concerned exclusively with window-dressing diversity, they could have embraced rather than suppressed the students protesting against the Gaza genocide, who have boldly identified with the excluded in order to reconfigure their society's skewed distribution of care and dignity. A leftist critique of DEI clearly diverges from the racist rightist version. A DEI with teeth could have mounted a far better defense of the protest movement by relating to the students' anger at their universities and government's joined enterprise in genocide, and by standing with the protesters against scholasticide.[63] DEI officers could have stood with the problem-makers rather than simply complying or collaborating with the government in its witch hunt for a maliciously fabricated anti-Semitic problem. Indeed, a principled DEI could have pushed back against repression creep (sacrificing the freedom of students and faculty to placate those in governmental power).[64] A DEI with emancipatory desires could have linked America's imperial violence and dominance to the injustice taking place at home. The local is global and vice versa. The pernicious logic of un-mattering that turns Palestinian lives into disposable and ungrievable bodies in the Middle East is equally at work in the far Right's demonization of Blacks, trans people, and migrants here in the United States. A committed DEI could have joined students and faculty in becoming a problem for both the Biden and Trump administrations. Imagine a university space invested in the formation and cultivation of problem-makers. Call it liberal arts.

Unlike the alt-Right, who also share a deep discontent with today's global and social arrangements, we have no truck with nostalgia, with distorted and distorting stories about harmonious times, about ancestral land and "the good old days" of the past. Our *parti pris* is with the oppressed, the disenfranchised, the stranger, the proletariat, the wretched, the nothing and the less than nothing or permanently unemployed, the constitutively excluded or society's symptoms, with those who don't count, who are deemed a problem, the scapegoatable and killable, who bear the psychic and material marks of violence and injustice. Gaza displays in a condensed form the deep inadequacies of the world order. Israel's gift to the imperialist West lies in the clarity of its political message, in the renewal of its colonial vows and normalization of genocide. A Zionist Israel has brought to the rest of the world the stark reminder that equality and freedom never meant to apply to the wretched of the world, to the likes of Palestinians and Blacks. To exist as a problem-maker means to be at war with this supremacist mentality. *For you to live, we must die.*

"Defend the dead" is our anti-anti-Black and anti-Zionist *cri de guerre*. We anticipate more backlashes, but our resolve will not waver. We refuse to allow Israel and the United States to get away with their vicious crimes. Liberal and fascist reasons are more alike than different; the former creates the sociopolitical conditions for the latter. While the white liberal order remains hegemonic, its protection of minorities has been abysmal. The United States and Israel are two peas in a pod. White justice, (neo)colonial justice, has only ever meant justice for some, never for all.[65] In the carceral logic that defines the American/Zionist mindset, blackened bodies are a problem to be neutralized by lethal force or locked behind bars: the pipeline from school/refugee camps to the zone of nonbeing. We must turn the tables on our oppressors and the ideological shepherds of the social order. We must reckon with the global color line. *We charge genocide.* The colonized and colonizing world system does not need fine-tuning; it needs a revolutionary overhaul, starting with a dismantling of its racial matrix of the human. *We exist as problems* transforms in meaning and spurs new action, taking the form of a life-affirmation. The chant "Palestinian Lives Matter" defies the "laughter of evil"; it rebukes colonial fascism. It signals, repeats, and harnesses the universalist and disruptive cry of "Black Lives Matter." What the global protests highlight is that Blacks or Palestinians are not the "problem"—*you are*, liberals and fascists alike; white and Zionist gazes be gone. We strike at the West's racist core, its murderous ontology, unjust distributive logic, insatiable privilege, and asphyxiating worlding-making, premised on our erasure and de-worlding. Being Black, being Palestinian point to a repetition—a defiance, an urgency—that will not be ignored.

Notes

Introduction: A Problem of Being

1   W. E. B. Du Bois, *The Souls of Black Folk* (New Haven: Yale University Press, 2015), 3.
2   George Yancy, *Black Bodies, White Gazes: The Continuing Significance of Race in America*, third edition (New York: Bloomsbury, 2025), 105.
3   Frantz Fanon, *Black Skin White Masks*, trans. Richard Philcox (New York: Grove Press, 2008), xii.
4   Fanon, *Black Skin*, 90.
5   As Richard Wright avers, "There is no black problem in the United States, there is only a white problem" (Richard Wright, *Conversation with Richard Wright*, ed. Keneth Kinnamon and Michel Fabre (Jackson: University of Mississippi Press, 1993), 88. There is no "Black problem" as such. Being a Black problem is irremediably the by-product of white obsessions and anxieties.
6   Fanon, *Black Skin*, 91.
7   Fanon, *Black Skin*, 90.
8   Fanon, *Black Skin*, 94.
9   Saidiya V. Hartman, *Lose Your Mother: A Journey Along the Atlantic Slave Route* (New York: Farrar, Straus and Giroux, 2007), 6.
10 See Christina Sharpe, *In the Wake: On Blackness and Being* (Durham: Duke University Press, 2016).
11 Keeanga-Yamahtta Taylor, "Foreword" to Saidiya Hartman's 2022 edition of *Scenes of Subjection* (New York: W.W. Norton & Co, 2022), xxi.
12 Claudia Rankine, *Citizen: An American Lyric* (Minneapolis: Graywolf, 2014), 18. From CITIZEN: AN AMERICAN LYRIC by Claudia Rankine published by Penguin Press. Copyright © Claudia Rankine, 2014. Reprinted by permission of Penguin Books Limited. Citizen: An American Lyric. Copyright © 2014 by Claudia Rankine. Reprinted with the permission of The Permissions Company LLC, on behalf of Graywolf Press, graywolfpress.org.
13 Yancy, *Black Bodies, White Gazes*, 8.
14 Fanon, *Black Masks*, 92, 132.
15 Fanon, *Black Masks*, 92.
16 Qtd. in Patrick Wolfe, "Settler Colonialism and the Elimination of the Native," *Journal of Genocide Research* 8, no. 4 (2006): 388.
17 A self-determined and self-determining sovereignty stays true to David Ben-Gurion's vision of Israel: "Our future depends not on what the gentiles will say, but on what the Jews will do!" (David Ben-Gurion, "David Ben-Gurion: Select Quotations," *Jewish Virtual Library*. https://www.jewishvirtuallibrary.org/select-quotations-of-david-ben-gurion).

18 Shay Hazkani and Tamir Sorek, "Yes to Transfer: 82% of Jewish Israelis Back Expelling Gazans," *Haaretz*, May 28, 2025. https://www.haaretz.com/isr ael-news/2025-05-28/ty-article-magazine/.premium/yes-to-transfer-82-of-jewish-israelis-back-expelling-gazans/00000197-12a4-df22-a9d7-9ef6af930000.

19 Steve Salaita, "Your Crisis of Faith Is Not My Concern (There's a Genocide Going On)," *No Flags, No Slogans*, September 25, 2024. https://stevesalaita.com/your-cri sis-of-faith-is-not-my-concern-theres-a-genocide-going-on/.

20 Andreas Malm, *The Destruction of Palestine Is the Destruction of the Earth* (New York: Verso, 2024), 99.

21 Sharon Zhang, "UN Chief Says Israel Has Made Gaza into 'a Killing Field,'" *Truthout*, April 9, 2025. https://truthout.org/articles/un-chief-says-isr ael-has-made-gaza-into-a-killing-field/.

22 Tayseer Abu Odeh and Shahd Dibas, "Zionist Settler-Colonialism and the Logic of Genocide in Gaza: A Conversation with Professor Avi Shlaim," *Journal of Holy Land and Palestine Studies* 24, no. 1 (2025): 19.

23 Though Hamas's military wing the Qassam Brigades spearheaded the attack on southern Israel, it is important to note that Islamic Jihad, the Popular Front for the Liberation of Palestine, and the Democratic Front for the Liberation of Palestine also participated in the anti-colonial strike, which points to the collective effort of the resistance (Malm, *The Destruction of Palestine*, 76–80); see also Jodi Dean, "Palestine Speaks for Everyone," *Verso Books*, April 9, 2024. https://www.versobo oks.com/blogs/news/palestine-speaks-for-everyone.

24 Mohammed El-Kurd, *Perfect Victims: And the Politics of Appeal* (Chicago: Haymarket Books, 2025), 25.

25 Martin Belam and Lili Bayer, "Middle East Crisis: Famine 'Imminent' in Northern Gaza, UN Report Says, as EU Foreign Policy Chief Calls Area 'Open Air Graveyard'—as It Happened," *The Guardian*, March 18, 2024. https://www.theg uardian.com/world/live/2024/mar/18/middle-east-crisis-live-israel-gaza-palest ine-al-shifa-live-updates.

26 See A. Dirk Moses, *The Problems of Genocide: Permanent Security and the Language of Transgression* (New York: Cambridge University Press, 2021).

27 Haim Bresheeth-Zabner, *An Army Like No Other* (New York: Verso, 2020), 132.

28 Bresheeth-Zabner, *An Army Like No Other*, 132.

29 See Stuart Hall, "'In but Not of Europe': Europe and Its Myths," in *Selected Writings on Race and Difference*, ed. Paul Gilroy and Ruth Wilson Gilmore (Durham: Duke University Press, 2021), 305–45.

30 Victoria Valenzuela, "'Deadly Exchange': US Sends Hundreds of Law Enforcement to Israel to Learn 'Worst Practices' from IDF," *The Real News Network*, January 7, 2025. https://therealnews.com/deadly-exchange-us-sends-hundreds-of-law-enfo rcement-to-israel-to-learn-worst-practices-from-idf.

31 George Yancy, "What Can the Black Freedom Struggle and Palestinian Liberation Teach Each Other?" *Truthout*, September 8, 2024. https://truthout.org/articles/ what-can-the-black-freedom-struggle-and-palestinian-liberation-teach-each-other/.

32 Michel Foucault, "Polemics, Politics, and Problematizations: An Interview with Michel Foucault," in *The Foucault Reader*, ed. Paul Rabinow (New York: Pantheon Books, 1984), 389.

33 Edward Said, *Representations of the Intellectual: The 1993 Reith Lectures* (New York: Vintage Books, 1996), 32.

34 Omer Bartov, "I'm a Genocide Scholar. I Know It When I See It," *The New York Times*, July 15, 2025. https://www.nytimes.com/2025/07/15/opinion/israel-gaza-holocaust-genocide-palestinians.html.

35 John Harfouch and C. Heike Schotten, "Sayegh's Critique of Zionism and the IHRA Definition: Notes Toward a Theory of the Antisemitism Industrial Complex," *Institute for the Critical Study of Zionism* 1, no. 1 (2024). https://criticalzionismstudies.org/sayeghs-critique-of-zionism-and-the-ihra-definition-notes-toward-a-theory-of-the-antisemitism-industrial-complex/.

36 Shaul Magid, "Judeopessimism: Antisemitism, History, and Critical Race Theory," *Harvard Theological Review* 117, no. 2 (2024): 368.

37 Alana Lentin, "Antisemitism and the Proxificaton of Antiracism," in *Race and the Question of Palestine*, ed. Lana Tatour and Ronit Lentin (Stanford: Stanford University Press, 2025), 201.

38 Raz Segal et al., "New Jersey Statement on Antisemitism and Islamophobia." https://docs.google.com/forms/d/e/1FAIpQLSdbHaU_hpCuVB1K9bcx4dG2nHd 9ckGIKRdU_qqiq36AAFDXrA/viewform.

39 "When you hear someone insulting the Jews, pay attention; he is talking about you" (Fanon, *Black Skin*, 101).

40 Slavoj Žižek, "Year of distraction," July 5, 2011. https://www.youtube.com/watch?v=ChWXYNxUFdc.

41 The jury on Israeli apartheid is out, see Amnesty International, "Israel's Apartheid Against Palestinians: Cruel System of Domination and Crime Against Humanity," February 1, 2022. https://www.amnesty.org/en/wp-content/uploads/2022/02/MDE1551412022ENGLISH.pdf; Human Rights Watch, "A Threshold Crossed Israeli Authorities and the Crimes of Apartheid and Persecution," *Human Rights Watch*, April 27, 2021. https://www.hrw.org/report/2021/04/27/threshold-crossed/israeli-authorities-and-crimes-apartheid-and-persecution#; B'Tselem, "A Regime of Jewish Supremacy from the Jordan River to the Mediterranean Sea: This Is Apartheid," January 12, 2021. https://www.btselem.org/publications/fulltext/202101_this_is_ap artheid.

42 For an important supplement to any discussion of Israel and an apartheid framework, see John Reynolds, "Apartheid Without Race," in *Race and the Question of Palestine*, ed. Lana Tatour and Ronit Lentin (Stanford: Stanford University Press, 2025), 59–76; Lana Tatour, "Why Calling Israel an Apartheid State Is Not Enough," *Middle East Eye*, January 18, 2021. https://www.middleeasteye.net/opinion/why-calling-israel-apartheid-state-not-enough; Noura Erakat and John Reynolds, "Understanding Apartheid," *Jewish Currents*, November 1, 2022. https://jewishcurrents.org/understanding-apartheid; Al-Haq, "Israeli Apartheid: Tool of Zionist Settler Colonialism," *Al-Haq*, November 29, 2022. https://www.alhaq.org/publications/20940.html.

43 Fanon, *The Wretched of the Earth*, trans. Richard Philcox (New York: Grove Press, 2004), 2.

44 Du Bois, *The Souls of Black Folk*, 5.

45 Marco Carnelos, "Does the West Really Need to Be Great Again?" *Middle East Eye*, April 25, 2025. https://www.middleeasteye.net/opinion/does-west-rea lly-need-be-great-again.

46 Cathrin Schaer, "Why Are Some in Germany Suggesting Anti-Semitism Is 'Imported'?" *Al Jazeera*, May 28, 2021. https://www.aljazeera.com/news/2021/5/28/in-germany-growing-suggestions-that-antisemitism-is-imported.

47 Mark Davis, "Violence as Method: The 'White Replacement,' 'White Genocide,' and 'Eurabia' Conspiracy Theories and the Biopolitics of Networked Violence," *Ethnic and Racial Studies* 48, no. 3 (2025): 426–46.

48 https://www.congress.gov/bill/119th-congress/house-bill/5722/text

49 Joining Palestinians and Blacks on the list of threats to the American nation are trans folks. M. Gessen situates Trump's attack on trans people within what they call a "denationalization project." By declaring that only two sexes exist: male and female, Trump stripped the being of trans individuals; they don't conform to this ontological binary; consequently, "trans people … do not exist." Trans people are denied a passport that claim the public identity with which they identify: the "X" gender marker is no longer an option. (M. Gessen, "The Hidden Motive Behind Trump's Attacks on Trans People," *The New York Times*, March 17, 2025. https://www.nytimes.com/2025/03/17/opinion/trump-trans-denationalizing.html?smid=nytcore-android-share). Being trans under Trump means that you are, or have been rendered, a lesser citizen and a bigger problem.

50 Debbie Nathan, "The Insidious Doctrine Fueling the Case Against Mahmoud Khalil," *Boston Review*, March 21, 2025. https://www.bostonreview.net/articles/the-insidious-doctrine-fueling-the-case-against-mahmoud-khalil/.

51 Juan Cole, "The Vile Racism of Calling Biden a 'Weak Palestinian,'" *Common Dreams*, June 28, 2024. https://www.commondreams.org/opinion/trump-biden-weak-palestinian.

52 Jenny Gross, "Rights Groups Condemn Trump for Using 'Palestinian' as a Slur Against Schumer," *The New York Times*, March 13, 2025. https://www.nytimes.com/2025/03/13/us/politics/trump-schumer-palestinian.html.

53 Mallory Shelbourne, "Schumer Applauds Trump on Moving US Embassy to Jerusalem," *The Hill*, May 14, 2018. https://thehill.com/homenews/senate/387566-schumer-applauds-trump-on-moving-us-embassy-to-jerusalem/.

54 Nicholas Fandos, "Elise Stefanik Has Gained Widespread Attention in Antisemitism Hearings," *The New York Times*, May 23, 2024. https://www.nytimes.com/2024/05/23/us/elise-stefanik-republican-antisemitism-hearings.html; Shadi Hamid, Brett Max Kaufman, Yousef Munayyer, and Natasha Roth-Rowland, "Is a New McCarthyism Punishing Pro-Palestine Speech at US Universities? Our Panel Reacts," *The Guardian*, December 13, 2023. https://www.theguardian.com/commentisfree/2023/dec/13/israel-gaza-us-universities-free-speech; Gregory Krieg, "College Campus Protests Highlight Tensions in Biden's Coalition," *CNN*, April 30, 2024. https://www.cnn.com/2024/04/30/politics/democrats-biden-college-protests.

55 Joseph Gedeon, "Rubio Boasts of Canceling More than 300 Visas over Pro-Palestine Protests," *The Guardian*, March 27, 2025. https://www.theguardian.com/us-news/2025/mar/27/state-department-visas-pro-palestine-protesters.

56 The White House, "Restoring Truth and Sanity to American," March 27, 2025. https://www.whitehouse.gov/presidential-actions/2025/03/restoring-truth-and-sanity-to-american-history/.

57 Safia Samee Ali, "'Not by Accident': False 'Thug' Narratives Have Long Been Used to Discredit Civil Rights Movements," *NBC News*, September 27, 2020. https://www.nbcnews.com/news/us-news/not-accident-false-thug-narratives-have-long-been-used-discredit-n1240509.

58 Jonathan Greenblatt, who heads the Anti-Defamation League, also sees BLM activists and pro-Palestine activists as cut from the same cloth: "There is a throughline from Occupy Wall Street to BLM to 'defund the police' to 'River to the Sea'" (Arno Rosenfeld and Jacob Kornbluh, "ADL Chief Compares Student Protesters to ISIS and al-Qaida in Address to Republican Officials," *Forward*, June 6, 2025. https://forward.com/news/726133/greenblatt-adl-protesters-terrorists/). Whereas Greenblatt cynically proclaims that what ties these activists together are their "nihilistic" motivations ("They are the same people, these are the same kind of nihilists"), I argue that what unites them is an unflinching commitment to racial and economic justice.

59 For a delusional narrative that conceptualizes Israel as abandoned by the world, and not as a racist and belligerent ethnostate unconditionally backed by the most powerful imperialist nations in the West, see Bernard-Henri Lévy, *Israel Alone*, trans. Steven B. Kennedy (New York: Wicked Son, 2024).

60 Achille Mbembe, *Critique of Black Reason*, trans. Laurent Dubois (Durham: Duke University Press, 2017), 6.

61 Mbembe, *Critique of Black Reason*, 6.

62 Mbembe, *Critique of Black Reason*, 6.

63 Saidiya V. Hartman, *Scenes of Subjection: Terror, Slavery, and Self-Making in Nineteenth-Century America* (Oxford: Oxford University Press, 1997), 12.

64 Achille Mbembe, *Necropolitics*, trans. Steven Corcoran (Durham: Duke University Press, 2019), 75.

65 William Patterson, *We Charge Genocide: The Historic Petition to the United Nations for Relief from the Crime of the United States Government Against the Negro People* (New York: The Civil Rights Congress, 1951), 4. See Bill V. Mullen, *We Charge Genocide: American Fascism and the Rule of Law* (New York: Fordham University Press, 2024); Stephen Leonard Jacobs, "'We Charge Genocide': A Historical Petition All but Forgotten and Unknown," in *Understanding Atrocities: Remembering, Representing and Teaching Genocide*, ed. Scott W. Murray (Calgary: University of Calgary Press, 2017), 125–43.

66 Hartman, *Scenes of Subjection*, 116.

67 Kieron Turner, "Racial Capitalism and Militarized Accumulation," in *Race and the Question of Palestine*, ed. Lana Tatour and Ronit Lentin (Stanford: Stanford University Press, 2025), 172.

68 A Zionist Israel wants both the erasure of racialized Palestinians and their persistence (as the perpetual external and existential threat that legitimizes existing and future genocidal campaigns) to keep Israel's military-industrial complex satiated. Genocide is both good for business and good for (the realizing of) a Greater Israel.

69 Mbembe, *Necropolitics*, 80.

70 Frank B. Wilderson III, *Red, White & Black: Cinema and the Structure of U.S. Antagonisms* (Durham: Duke University Press, 2010), ix.

71 Calvin L. Warren, *Ontological Terror: Blackness, Nihilism, and Emancipation* (Durham: Duke University Press, 2018), 27.

72 Edward Said, *The Question of Palestine* (New York: Vintage Books, 1992), xliv.

73 Alex Frew McMillan, "Sharon: 'We Can Defeat Forces of Evil,'" *CNN*, September 12, 2001. https://www.cnn.com/2001/WORLD/asiapcf/east/09/11/terror.reax/index.html.

74 Edward Said, *Orientalism*, 12.

75 Said, *Orientalism*, 95.

76 Said, *Orientalism*, xvii.

77 Amy Goodman and Juan González, "'Trying to Repeat the Nakba': Israel Launches

Largest Military Raids in West Bank in Two Decades," *Democracy Now!* August 28, 2024. https://www.democracynow.org/2024/8/28/west_bank_raids_mustafa_ba rghouti.

78   Goodman, "Trying to Repeat the Nakba."

79   Balazs Berkovits, "The October 7th Pogrom as a Non-Event on the Western Left," *K.*, January 25, 2024. https://k-larevue.com/en/the-october-7th-pog rom-as-a-non-event-on-the-western-left/.

80   The Wire Staff, " 'No Innocent Civilians in Gaza,' Israel President Says as Northern Gaza Struggles to Flee Israeli Bombs," *The Wire*, October 14, 2023. https://thewire.in/world/northern-gaza-israel-palestine-conflict

81   Dave Reed, "There Is No Proof Palestinian Fighters 'Beheaded' Babies. The Only Source Is a Radical Settler," *Mondoweiss*, October 11, 2023. https://mondoweiss. net/2023/10/there-is-no-proof-palestinian-fighters-beheaded-babies-the-only-sou rce-is-a-radical-settler/; "Letter from the Journalism Academy to *The New York Times*," https://docs.google.com/forms/d/e/1FAIpQLSf9tbDVqvi8-0a2eED4j4cYHK JAJ-blPSRZRrDEalQCWEH8jA/viewform.

82   El-Kurd, *Perfect Victims*, 206. See also Anwar Mhajne, "Understanding Sexual Violence Debates Since 7 October: Weaponization and Denial," *Journal of Genocide Research*, May 30, 2024. https://www.tandfonline.com/doi/ pdf/10.1080/14623528.2024.2359851?casa_token=numIgHN9YgIAAAAA:OuS fMCx4gQhcyV-0D5aX8vbnA-wsOmaGxBhLzpuidOLN4ZnBAQGY6vuLmUq kwG-5DAr-PiSkQmcD.

83   Fayez Sayegh, *Zionist Colonization in Palestine* (Beirut: Research Center, Palestine Liberation Organization, 1965), 27.

84   Michael Sfard, "In Gaza, Israel Is Racing to the Moral Abyss," *Haaretz*, October 23, 2023. https://www.haaretz.com/israel-news/2023-10-23/ty-article-opinion/.prem ium/in-gaza-israel-is-racing-to-the-moral-abyss/0000018b-57d1-d8e2-a1eb-f7d7d c100000.

85   Sylvia Wynter and David Scott, "The Re-Enchantment of Humanism: An Interview with Sylvia Wynter," *Small Axe* 8 (2000): 177.

86   W. E. B. Du Bois, *Black Reconstruction in America* (New York: The Free Press, 1998), 700–1, emphasis added.

87   Sylvia Wynter, "No Humans Involved: An Open Letter to My Colleagues," *Forum N.H.I. Knowledge for the 21st Century* 1, no. 1 (1994): 42.

88   Wynter, "No Humans Involved," 42.

89   Sylvia Wynter, "A Black Studies Manifesto," *Forum N.H.I. Knowledge for the 21st Century* 1, no. 1 (1994): 6.

90   Wynter, "A Black Studies Manifesto," 6.

91   Wynter, "No Humans Involved," 42.

92   *No Other Land*, directed by Basel Adra, Hamdan Ballal, Yuval Abraham, and Rachel Szor (2024).

93   Adam Johnson and Othman Ali, "Coverage of Gaza War in the New York Times and Other Major Newspapers Heavily Favored Israel, Analysis Shows," *The Intercept*, January 9, 2024. https://theintercept.com/2024/01/09/newspapers-israel-palestin e-bias-new-york-times/.

94   Kareem Khadder, Richard Allen Greene, and Ivana Kottasova, "About 1 in 100 People in Gaza Has Been Killed Since October 7, Palestinian Statistics Show," *CNN*, January 8, 2024. https://www.cnn.com/middleeast/live-news/israel-hama s-war-gaza-news-01-08-24#h_1e962a4fad64c2814a917a672e963a28.

95 Slavoj Žižek, "Assange Is Free, but Are We?" *Project Syndicate*, June 27, 2024. https://www.project-syndicate.org/commentary/julian-assa nge-freed-but-media-still-carrying-water-for-the-powerful-by-slavoj-zizek-2024-06.

96 Omar El Akkad, *One Day, Everyone Will Have Always Been Against This* (New York: Alfred A. Knopf, 2025), 70.

97 Gideon Levy, "No Victory Awaits Israel in Rafah. Only More Death and Destruction," *Haaretz*, April 10, 2024. https://www.haaretz.com/opinion/2024-04-10/ty-article-opinion/.premium/no-victory-awaits-israel-in-rafah-only-more-death-and-destruct ion/0000018e-c92f-dd23-a3cf-efaf6ada0000.

98 See Fawas Turki, *The Disinherited: Journal of a Palestinian Exile, With an Epilogue 1974* (New York: Monthly Review Press, 1974), 160.

99 Fanon, *Black Skin*, xii. Philcox's translation leaves out a crucial comma after "an incline stripped bare of every essential." See Geo Maher, *Anticolonial Eruptions: Racial Hubris and the Cunning of Resistance* (Berkeley: University of California Press, 2022), 20.

100 Paget Henry, *Caliban's Reason: Introducing Afro-Caribbean Philosophy* (New York: Routledge, 2000), 79.

101 Du Bois, *The Souls of Black Folk*, 1.

102 Alexander G. Weheliye, *Habeas Viscus: Racializing Assemblages, Biopolitics, and Black Feminist Theories of the Human* (Durham: Duke University Press, 2014), 8.

103 Wilderson, *Afropessimism* (New York: Liveright, 2020), 228–9.

104 Wilderson, " 'We're Trying to Destroy the World': Anti-Blackness and Police Violence After Ferguson," in *Shifting Corporealities in Contemporary Performance Danger, Im/mobility and Politics*, ed. Marina Gržinić and Aneta Stojnić (New York: Palgrave, 2018), 52, emphasis added.

105 Wilderson, "The Inside-Outside," 5.

106 Wilderson, *Red, White & Black*, 35–53.

107 Wilderson returns a number of times to the ways non-Blacks are possessively interested in Afropessimism; appropriating the material of Afropessimists for their own project without seriously taking into consideration the radical demands of Afropessimism. He recounts an exchange with Patrice Douglass—at the time a graduate student—who asked him during a seminar, "So how do we keep Afropessimism Black?" (Siddhant Issar and James Padilioni, Jr., " 'To Address Black Suffering Is to Destroy the World.' An Interview with Frank B. Wilderson, III on *Afropessimism*," *Interfere* 1 [2020]: 94). Elsewhere, Wilderson gives a slightly modified version: "Patrice Douglass asked me, how do we keep Afropessimism for Blacks?" (Wilderson and King, "Staying Ready for Black Study," 56). I don't think that this is a distinction without a difference: how do we keep Afropessimism *Black or for Blacks*? I read the second formulation as a desire by Afropessimists not to have their work diluted by more familiar frameworks (postcolonial, Marxist, etc.) that always risk co-opting and defanging the radicality of some of the Afropessimists' questions. Scholars in Critical Black Studies, who are predominantly but not exclusively Black, are best suited to think with Afropessimism. The first formulation strikes me as much more essentializing, restrictive, and profoundly un-Fanonian. I don't believe destroying the coordinates of the world can be a separatist endeavor. Black pessimism can and must be open to the pessimism of others—that of the Palestinian is where I and others have intervened. A reignited Black-Palestinian solidarity movement points to the vibrancy of an anti-racist, anti-colonial Left capable of mounting a resistance to the paradigm of the human along with the various fascist faces emerging in our contemporary times.

108 Angela Davis, *Freedom Is a Constant Struggle: Ferguson, Palestine, and the Foundations of a Movement* (Chicago: Haymarket Books, 2016).

109 Wilderson, *Red, White & Black*, 28.

110 Wilderson, "The Inside-Outside," 14.

111 "What Afro-pessimism says is 'death to Humanity'" (Wilderson, "'The Inside-Outside of Civil Society': An Interview with Frank B. Wilderson, III," Interview by Samira Spatzek and Paula von Gleich, *Black Studies Papers* 2, no. 1 [2016]: 21).

112 Frank Wilderson and Tiffany Lethabo King, "Staying Ready for Black Study: A Conversation," in *Otherwise Worlds: Against Settler Colonialism and Anti-Blackness*, ed. Tiffany Lethabo King, Jenell Navarro, and Andrea Smith (Durham: Duke University Press, 2020), 69.

113 Keeanga-Yamahtta Taylor, "Black Faces in High Places," *Jacobin*, May 4, 2015. https://jacobin.com/2015/05/baltimore-uprising-protests-freddie-gray-black-politicians/.

114 Eric L. Goldstein, *The Price of Whiteness: Jews, Race, and American Identity* (Princeton: Princeton University Press, 2006).

115 Azad Essa, "Cornel West on US Protests: The Chickens Have Come Home to Roost," *Middle East Eye*, June 16, 2020. https://www.middleeasteye.net/news/cornel-west-america-george-floyd-protests-chickens-have-come-home-roost.

116 José Sanchez, "Against Afro-Pessimism," *Jacobin*, June 13, 2022. https://jacobin.com/2022/06/afro-pessimism-frank-wilderson-socialism-flattening-racism.

117 Wynter, "No Humans Involved," 44.

118 Doreen St. Félix, "The Embarrassment of Democrats Wearing Kente-Cloth Stoles," *The New Yorker*, June 9, 2020. https://www.newyorker.com/culture/on-and-off-the-avenue/the-embarrassment-of-democrats-wearing-kente-cloth-stoles.

119 See Marc Lamont Hill and Mitchell Plitnick, *Except for Palestine: The Limits of Progressive Politics* (New Press, 2021); the 2025 documentary *The Palestine Exception*, directed by Jan Haaken and Jennifer Ruth.

120 Roberto De Vogli, *Selective Empathy: The West Through the Gaze of Gaza* (New York: Brill, 2025).

121 Gastón Gordillo, "The Fascist Disposition," *Verso*, July 18, 2024. https://www.versobooks.com/blogs/news/the-fascist-disposition?srsltid=AfmBOoojDqlDRJ50-SolGAsK-Yqx7RqEh3-c4Gmib04olnaFo4_8Fd.

122 Said, "Zionism from the Standpoint of Its Victims," *Social Text*, no. 1 (1979): 7–58; Ella Shohat, "Sephardim in Israel: Zionism from the Standpoint of Its Jewish Victims," *Social Text*, no. 19–20 (1988): 1–35.

123 Human Rights Watch, "Israel: New Laws Marginalize Palestinian Arab Citizens," *Human Rights Watch*, March 30, 2011. https://www.hrw.org/news/2011/03/30/israel-new-laws-marginalize-palestinian-arab-citizens.

124 See Jamil Khader, "Ziofascist Violence and the Nakba 2.0: Jouissance and Necrocapitalism in the Consolidation of Extremist Messianic Zionist Far-Right Ideology," *Crisis and Critique* 11, no. 1 (2024): 26–54.

125 Joseph Massad, "'Palestinians Don't Exist': Smotrich Only Repeats What Zionists Have Always Said," *Middle East Eye*, March 24, 2023. https://www.middleeasteye.net/opinion/palestinians-dont-exist-smotrich-only-repeats-zionists-always-said.

126 Zahi Zalloua, *Solidarity and the Palestinian Cause: Indigeneity, Blackness, and the Promise of Universality* (New York: Bloomsbury, 2023), 3.

127 Gilles Deleuze and Elias Sanbar, "The Indians of Palestine," in *Two Regimes of*

Madness: Texts and Interviews 1975–1995, ed. David Lapoujade (New York, Semiotext(e), 2006), 199.

128 Knesset, "Knesset Basic Law: Israel as the Nation State of the Jewish People," *Israel Studies* 25, no. 3 (2020): 135–6.

129 Mallory Moench, "Nearly 70% of Gaza War Dead Verified by UN Are Women and Children," *BBC*, November 8, 2024. https://www.bbc.com/news/articles/cn5we l11pgdo.

130 According to Forensic Architecture, "the destruction of agricultural land and infrastructure in Gaza is a deliberate act of ecocide and a critical dimension of Israel's genocidal campaign. The targeted farms and greenhouses are fundamental to local food production for a population already under a decades-long siege" (Forensic Architecture, " 'No Traces of Life': Israel's Ecocide in Gaza 2023–2024." https://forensic-architecture.org/investigation/ecocide-in-gaza).

131 Shree Paradkar, "How Israel's 'Scholasticide' Denies Palestinians Their Past, Present and Future," *Toronto Star*, January 21, 2024. https://www.thestar.com/ news/world/how-israels-scholasticide-denies-palestinians-their-past-present-and-future/article_8f52d77a-b648-11ee-863d-f3411121907b.html; Meron Rapoport and Oren Ziv, " 'Render It Unusable': Israel's Mission of Total Urban Destruction," *+972 Magazine*, May 15, 2025. https://www.972mag.com/israel-gaza-total-urban-destruction/.

132 Fanon, *The Wretched of the Earth*, 149.

133 Christian Noakes, "The Sacred-Secular Dialectic: Zionist Superstructure in Palestine," *Peace, Land, and Bread*, no. 1 (2020): 84.

134 Soledad Santana, "Scholasticide as Cultural Genocide," *Spectre*, November 21, 2024. https://spectrejournal.com/scholasticide-as-cultural-genocide/.

135 Mark O'Connell, "Israel's Revenge: An Interview with Rashid Khalidi," *The New York Review*, December 19, 2024. https://www.nybooks.com/articles/2024/12/19/isra els-revenge-an-interview-with-rashid-khalidi-mark-oconnell/.

136 Alice Speri, "Israel Responds to Hamas Crimes by Ordering Mass War Crimes in Gaza," *The Intercept*, October 9, 2023. https://theintercept.com/2023/10/09/isr ael-hamas-war-crimes-palestinians/.

137 Abbas Alawieh, "An Uncommitted Cofounder Explains the Movement's Strategy," *Jacobin*, September 9, 2024. https://jacobin.com/2024/09/uncommitted-democr ats-alawieh-gaza-israel?mc_cid=b42407cd6e&mc_eid=0317ccf9ee.

138 Amy Goodman and Juan González, "Watch: Palestinian American Lawmaker Gives Speech the DNC Wouldn't Allow on Stage," *Democracy Now!* August 23, 2024. https://www.democracynow.org/2024/8/23/ruwa_romman.

139 See Sarah Aziza, "Can Palestinian Lives Matter?" *The Intercept*, May 13, 2021. https://theintercept.com/2021/05/13/israel-palestinian-lives-matter-blm/.

140 Wynter, "No Humans Involved," 70.

141 We should keep in mind President Ronald Reagan's response to Israeli Prime Minister Menachem Begin's indiscriminate bombings of civilians in the 1982 Israeli invasion of Lebanon, in its military campaign to eliminate or expel the Palestinian Liberation Organization from Lebanon. Witnesses to Reagan's phone call to Begin recount the tense exchange: " 'Menachem, this is a holocaust,' Reagan said. 'Mr. President, I think I know what a holocaust is,' Begin replied, in a voice that [National Security Council staffer Geoffrey] Kemp would recall as 'dripping with sarcasm.' According to [Deputy Chief-of-Staff Michael] Deaver, Reagan continued 'in the plainest of language' to tell Begin what he thought about the bombing of

Beirut, concluding by saying, 'It has gone too far. You must stop it' " (Lou Cannon, *President Reagan: The Role of a Lifetime* [New York: Public Affairs, 2000], 350). And Begin did stop the bombings. A similar logic is playing out in Operation Iron Swords, except that President Biden and then candidate Harris were unwilling to take any significant measures to pressure Israel to halt its carnage in Gaza and now Lebanon, which underwent its own Gazafication. With Trump's crass transactional mentality, there appears to be no concern with America's global image (America is not at war with an Evil Empire as in Reagan's cold war ethos, which shaped, in turn, his response to Begin's human carnage in Lebanon). Trump's imperialist mindset was already present in 2016 when he said that the United States needed to seize Iraq's oil: that the United States was guilty of making a bad economic transaction was the lesson Trump took from the Bush administration's disastrous Iraq war (Julian Borger, "Trump's Plan to Seize Iraq's Oil: 'It's Not Stealing, We're Reimbursing Ourselves,'" *The Guardian*, September 21, 2016. https://www.theg uardian.com/us-news/2016/sep/21/donald-trump-iraq-war-oil-strategy-seizure-isis). Ben Burgis makes a similar observation: "If we were to look at George W. Bush's invasion of Iraq through this lens [foreign wars should benefit American self-interest], the problem wouldn't be that it was an unjustifiable war of aggression—it would be that it was a misguided attempt to help foreigners at the expense of American interests" (Ben Burgis, "Is Donald Trump Just Another Hawk? Manifest Destiny Is a Betrayal of Populism," *UnHeard*, January 23, 2025. https://unherd.com/2025/01/ is-donald-trump-just-another-hawk/). For Trump, there is no pretense of spreading democracy to the Middle East; it is all about maintaining imperial control. There is no affective attachment to being the world's defender of freedom. In Trump's masculinist vision, "soft power" is a weakness and a waste of American money. Consequently, the ideological narrative that America is fighting the good fight, upholding the international liberal order, is relegated to the dustbin of history. This is good for a Zionist Israel, and bad for the rest of us.

142 Ta-Nehisi Coates, "A Palestinian American's Place Under the Democrats' Big Tent?" *Vanity Fair*, August 21, 2024. https://www.vanityfair.com/news/story/dnc-2024- palestine-israel.

143 https://x.com/SecBlinken/status/1823122800095457535.

144 Amnesty International, "Amnesty International Sounds Alarm on a Watershed Moment for International Law amid Flagrant Rule-Breaking by Governments and Corporate Actors," *Amnesty International*, April 24, 2024. https://www.amnesty.org/ en/latest/news/2024/04/amnesty-international-sounds-alarm-international-law-flagr ant-rule-breaking-governments-corporate-actors/.

145 Craig Mokhiber, "Will Western Mainstream Media Be Held Accountable for Their Role in Genocide?" *Truthout*, August 30, 2024. https://truthout.org/articles/will-west ern-mainstream-media-be-held-accountable-for-their-role-in-genocide/.

146 Noura Erakat, "The Boomerang Comes Back," *Boston Review*, February 5, 2025. https://www.bostonreview.net/articles/the-boomerang-comes-back/.

147 Miles Kampf-Lassin, "Out of the Ashes," *In These Times*, November 21, 2024. https://inthesetimes.com/article/trump-harris-democrats-2024-election-uaw.

148 Kampf-Lassin, "Out of the Ashes."

149 Étienne Balibar, "The Genocide in Gaza and Its Consequences for the Israeli- Palestinian Conflict," *e-flux Notes*, September 25, 2024. https://www.e-flux.com/

notes/630154/the-genocide-in-gaza-and-its-consequences-for-the-israeli-palestin
ian-conflict.

150 Slavoj Žižek, *In Defense of Lost Causes* (New York: Verso, 2008), 166.

151 Sylvia Wynter and Katherine McKittrick, "Unparalleled Catastrophe for Our Species?
Or, to Give Humanness a Different Future: Conversations," in *Sylvia Wynter: On
Being Human as Praxis*, ed. Katherine McKittrick (Durham: Duke University Press,
2015), 18.

152 As with DEI, there is a critique of empathy from the far Right and one from the anti-
colonial Left. The former sees empathy as bad for Western civilization; when you
put the interests of (non-Western) others first, you commit a kind of "civilizational
suicide." Against the far Right's paranoid fantasy about the ways the West has been
too empathetic, the anti-colonial Left is skeptical of empathy's "political" effects,
what investing in empathy forecloses once the category becomes the apolitical
solution for existing strife. Moreover, empathy in its dominant manifestation and
practice fosters an identitarian disposition, which is detrimental to a universal
politics, as Roberto De Vogli insightfully notes, "It is the result of a self-serving,
tribal, and parochial form of emotional response that reserves compassion for some
while denying it to others" (De Vogli, *Selective Empathy*, xi). See Julia Carrie Wong,
"Loathe Thy Neighbor: Elon Musk and the Christian Right Are Waging War on
Empathy," *The Guardian*, April 8, 2025. https://www.theguardian.com/us-news/ng-
interactive/2025/apr/08/empathy-sin-christian-right-musk-trump.

153 Césaire, *Discourse on Colonialism*, trans. Joan Pinkham (New York: Monthly Review
Press, 2000), 35.

154 El-Kurd, *Perfect Victims*, 38.

155 El-kurd, *Perfect Victims,* 38.

156 Wynter, "Unsettling the Coloniality of Being/Power/Truth/Freedom: Towards the
Human, After Man, Its Overrepresentation—an Argument," *CR: The New Centennial
Review* 3, no. 3 (2003): 281.

157 Žižek, *In Defense of Lost Causes*, 166.

158 I'm borrowing from Jared Sexton's account of anti-Blackness, which functions as
an "unconscious cultural structure, a grammar, a *weltanschauung*, a metaphysics"
(Jared Sexton, "Affirmation in the Dark: Racial Slavery and Philosophical
Pessimism," *The Comparatist* 43 [2019]: 102).

159 The American Israel Public Affairs Committee, "Anti-Israel Action at the U.N. Since
October 7," *AIPAC*, February 15, 2024. https://aipacorg.app.box.com/s/s3o0s9pr4
ymepmatx00xdjakjsxtf97j.

160 Lazar Berman, "After Walling Itself in, Israel Learns to Hazard the Jungle Beyond,"
The Times of Israel, March 8, 2021. https://www.timesofisrael.com/after-walling-its
elf-in-israel-learns-to-hazard-the-jungle-beyond/.

161 Fredric Jameson, "Cognitive Mapping," in *Marxism and the Interpretation of Culture*,
ed. Cary Nelson and Lawrence Grossberg (Urbana: University of Illinois Press,
1988), 356.

162 Jameson, "Cognitive Mapping," 356.

163 In the United States, the moral stock of Israel has radically dropped, especially with
the younger generation of Americans. See Laura Silver, "How Americans View Israel
and the Israel-Hamas War at the Start of Trump's Second Term," *Pew Research
Center*, April 8, 2025. https://www.pewresearch.org/short-reads/2025/04/08/
how-americans-view-israel-and-the-israel-hamas-war-at-the-start-of-trumps-sec
ond-term/.

164 See Jacqueline Rose, *The Question of Zion* (Princeton: Princeton University Press, 2005).

165 https://x.com/davidsheen/status/1927051596669595655.

166 Mat Nashed and Maram Humaid, "Israel Threatens a Second Nakba, Yet Denies the First Ever Happened," *Al Jazeera*, February 28, 2025. https://www.aljazeera.com/features/2025/2/28/israel-threatens-a-second-nakba-yet-denies-the-first-ever-happened.

167 Diana Buttu, "The Gazafication of the West Bank: 'Is This Really Happening Again?'" *Zeteo*, March 2, 2025. https://zeteo.com/p/the-gaza-ification-of-the-west-bank

168 Audre Lorde, "The Uses of Anger," *Women's Studies Quarterly* 25, no. 1/2 (1997): 282.

169 Alberto Toscano, *Late Fascism: Race, Capitalism and the Politics of Crisis* (New York: Verso, 2023), 148.

170 Toscano, *Late Fascism*, 13.

171 James Baldwin, "A Report from Occupied Territory," *The Nation*. July 11, 1966. https://www.thenation.com/article/culture/report-occupied-territory/.

172 Baldwin, "A Report from Occupied Territory."

173 Albert Memmi, *The Colonizer and the Colonized* (London: Earthscan, 2003), 106–7.

174 Žižek, *In Defense of Lost Causes*, 166.

175 Franco "Bifo" Berardi, "Letter to the Hypocrites of Europe," *Institute of Network Cultures*, January 18, 2024. https://networkcultures.org/tactical-media-room/2024/01/18/letter-to-the-hypocrites-of-europe/.

176 Bashaer Muammar, "Not Just Genocide but Deliberate Ecological Disaster," *The Electronic Intifada*, March 30, 2024. https://electronicintifada.net/content/not-just-genocide-deliberate-ecological-disaster/45506.

177 Yanis Varoufakis, "Yanis Varoufakis on Why Fixating on Palestine Is a Moral Imperative," *DiEM25*, February 4, 2025. https://diem25.org/yanis-varoufakis-on-why-fixating-on-palestine-is-a-moral-imperative/.

178 Varoufakis, "Yanis Varoufakis on Why Fixating on Palestine."

179 Césaire, *Discourse on Colonialism*, 36.

180 Césaire, *Discourse on Colonialism*, 36.

181 Césaire, *Discourse on Colonialism*, 36.

182 Sharpe, *In the Wake*, 11.

183 Nelson Maldonado-Torres, "The U.S. at 250, Coloniality, and Political Zionism in Perspective," *Political Theology*, April 29, 2025. https://politicaltheology.com/the-u-s-at-250-coloniality-and-political-zionism-in-perspective/.

184 Andrew I. Killgore, "25 Years After His Death, Dr. Fayez Sayegh's Towering Legacy Lives On," *Washington Report on Middle East Affairs*, December 2005. https://www.wrmea.org/2005-december/in-memoriam-25-years-after-his-death-dr.-fayez-sayeghs-towering-legacy-lives-on.html.

185 Palestine Royal Commission Report (1937). https://ecf.org.il/media_items/290.

186 Césaire, *Discourse on Colonialism*, 36.

187 Fanon, *The Wretched of the Earth*, 236.

188 Benjamin, "On the Concept of History," 392.

189 Staff, "Journalist Quits Role After Comparing French Actions in Algeria to Nazi Massacre," *The Guardian*, March 9, 2025. https://www.theguardian.com/world/2025/mar/09/jean-michel-aphatie-quits-after-comparing-french-algeria-to-nazi-massacre.

190 Fanon, *Black Skin*, 70. See Zalloua, *Fanon, Žižek, and the Violence of Resistance* (New York: Bloomsbury, 2025), 138–9.

191 Wilderson, "The Inside-Outside of Civil Society," 11.

192 "What is the status of Algeria? A systematic dehumanization" (Fanon, "Letter to the Resident Minister," in *Alienation and Freedom*, ed. Jean Khalfa and Robert J. C. Young [New York: Bloomsbury, 2021], 434).

193 Mullen, *We Charge Genocide*, 120.

194 For Wilderson, the Black grammar of suffering exceeds and is qualitatively different from that of the Indigenous other: "Let's say we look up in the perfect world where Native peoples engage Afro-pessimism. Blackness is the absence of subjectivity and that's so powerful. That's why people want Black peoples in their movement. Why don't Native people, instead of articulating sovereignty as the key thing, why don't they see that their grammar of suffering, as horrifying as it is, is not as bad as the Black grammar of suffering. Why do we have to be, in the face of the evidence, the number one subject of suffering? I don't want to be the number one subject of suffering, I would much rather be a disposed colonial subject than a slave for whom there is no story of dispossession" (Wilderson and King, "Staying Ready for Black Study," 66).

195 See Ilan Kapoor and Zahi Zalloua, *Universal Politics* (Oxford: Oxford University Press, 2021).

196 A. Dirk Moses, "The German Catechism," *Geschichte der Gegenwart*, May 23, 2021. https://geschichtedergegenwart.ch/the-german-catechism/.

197 See Michael Rothberg, *Multidirectional Memory: Remembering the Holocaust in the Age of Decolonization*, (Stanford: Stanford University Press, 2009).

198 Rothberg, *Multidirectional Memory*, 9.

199 Santiago Zabala, "Why Don't We Listen to Warnings? The Horizonless Society," *The Philosophical Salon*, June 16, 2025. https://www.thephilosophicalsalon.com/why-dont-we-listen-to-warnings-the-horizonless-society/.

200 See Jason Stanley, *Erasing History: How Fascists Rewrite the Past to Control the Future* (New York: Atria/One Signal Publishers 2024).

201 Tyson E. Lewis, Silas C. Krabbe, and Alberto Toscano, "Late Fascism and Education: An Interview with Alberto Toscano," *Review of Education, Pedagogy, and Cultural Studies* 46, no. 3 (2024): 534.

202 Lewis, Krabbe, and Toscano, "Late Fascism," 535.

203 Neve Gordon and Penny Green, "Israel's Universities: The Crackdown," *The New York*, Review, June 5, 2024. https://www.nybooks.com/online/2024/06/05/israel-universities-the-crackdown/; Shira Kadari-Ovadia, 'Draconian and McCarthyist': Knesset Advances Bill to Fire Academics for Views Seen as 'Supporting Terror' by Gov't," *Haaretz*, July 10, 2024. https://www.haaretz.com/israel-news/2024-07-10/ty-article/.premium/knesset-advances-bill-to-fire-academics-for-views-seen-as-supporting-terror-by-govt/00000190-9e04-d03e-a5fd-9fb6744f0000; Emma Graham-Harrison, "Draft Israeli Law to Limit Academic Speech Labelled 'McCarthyite,'" *The Guardian*, July 21, 2024. https://www.theguardian.com/world/article/2024/jul/21/draft-israeli-law-to-limit-academic-speech-labelled-mccarthyite.

204 Iker Seisdedos, "Judith Butler, Philosopher: 'If You Sacrifice a Minority Like Trans People, You Are Operating Within a Fascist Logic,'" *El País*, December 14, 2024. https://english.elpais.com/culture/2024-12-15/judith-butler-philosopher-if-you-sacrifice-a-minority-like-trans-people-you-are-operating-within-a-fascist-logic.

html; Robin D. G. Kelley, "Between Fires in Los Angeles and Fascism in America," *Hammer & Hope*, no. 6 (2025). https://hammerandhope.org/article/los-angeles-altadena-fires.

205 Alice Speri and Joseph Gedeon, "Trial to Consider Trump's 'Ideological-Deportation Policy' Targeting Pro-Palestinian Students," *The Guardian*, July 7, 2025. https://www.theguardian.com/us-news/2025/jul/07/trial-trump-ideological-deportation-pol icy-pro-palestinian-students; Jonah Valdez, "The Far-Right Group Building a List of Pro-Palestine Activists to Deport," *The Intercept*, February 6, 2025. https://theinterc ept.com/2025/02/06/betar-palestine-school-activists-target-deport-trump/.

206 Ben Burgis, "Free Speech Means Free Mahmoud Khalil," *Jacobin*, March 13, 2025. https://jacobin.com/2025/03/mahmoud-khalil-arrest-free-speech; Schuyler Mitchell, "The Attack on Mahmoud Khalil Is Straight Out of the 'War on Terror' Playbook," *Truthout*, March 12, 2025. https://truthout.org/articles/the-attack-on-mahmoud-kha lil-is-straight-out-of-the-war-on-terror-playbook/.

207 Natalia Marques, "Trump Intensifies Threats Against Pro-Palestine Student Movement," *Peoples Dispatch*, March 6, 2025. https://peoplesdispatch.org/2025/03/06/trump-intensifies-threats-against-pro-palestine-student-movement/.

208 Mahmoud Khalil, "My Name Is Mahmoud Khalil and I Am a Political Prisoner," *In These Times*, March 18, 2025. https://inthesetimes.com/article/mahmoud-khalil-let ter-from-a-palestinian-political-prisoner-in-louisiana; Jonah E. Bromwich, " 'It Felt Like Kidnapping,' Khalil Says in First Interview Since Release," *The New York Times*, June 22, 2025. https://www.nytimes.com/2025/06/22/nyregion/mahmoud-kha lil-interview-trump.html; Shawn Musgrave, "Mahmoud Khalil Won His Freedom Despite the Best Efforts of ICE's Intelligence Unit," *The Intercept*, June 20, 2025. https://theintercept.com/2025/06/20/mahmoud-khalil-homeland-security-investigati ons-ice-surveillance/?utm_medium=email&utm_source=The%20Intercept%20New sletter.

209 Hannah Arendt, *The Origins of Totalitarianism* (San Diego: Harcourt Brace, 1973), 296.

210 Slavoj Žižek, *Trouble in Paradise: From the End of History to the End of Capitalism* (Brooklyn: Melville House, 2014), 126.

211 Étienne Balibar, *Politics and the Other Scene* (New York: Verso, 2002), 6.

212 Stephanie DeGooyer, Alastair Hunt, Linda Maxwell, and Samuel Moyn, *The Right to Have Rights* (New York: Verso Press, 2020), 6.

213 Mark O'Connell, "Israel's Revenge."

214 Jennifer Ruth, "Boards and Administrators Won't Defend Higher Ed from Trump. It's Up to Us," *Truthout*, April 7, 2025. https://truthout.org/articles/boards-and-adminis trators-wont-defend-higher-ed-from-trump-its-up-to-us/.

215 Tatiana Cozzarelli, "Trump's War Against the Palestine Movement and Universities Is an Attack on Us All," *Left Voice*, March 9, 2025. https://www.leftvoice.org/trumps-attacks-on-the-palestine-movement-and-the-universities-are-the-same-fight/.

216 Marina Dunbar, "New York Governor Orders Removal of Palestinian Studies Job Posting at Cuny," *The Guardian*, February 26, 2025. https://www.theguardian.com/us-news/2025/feb/26/kathy-hochul-palestinian-studies-cuny-job.

217 Dunbar, "New York Governor Orders." Against the backdrop of a hegemonic Zionist horizon, "miracles" can still happen as with the candidature of Zohran Mamdani, the Muslim democratic socialist who defeated the Party-favored former governor Andrew M. Cuomo in the Democratic primary for mayor of New York

City. Mamdani's principled positions on Palestine decompleted NYC's pro-Israel horizon—the anti-Palestinian symbolic order is not-all. You can condemn the Gaza genocide, pledge to abide by the ICC arrest warrant for Netanyahu if elected, be a BDS supporter, insist on the connection between racial justice and economic justice, and win an election (not despite but because of your position on Gaza). Nothing scares establishment Democrats more than leftist candidates who want to enact radical change, that is, who want *change with actual change*. For Mamdani's position on Palestine, Israel, anti-Semitism, and the Democratic Party, see Hannah Feuer, "What Zohran Mamdani Has Actually Said About Jews, Israel and Antisemitism," *Forward*, July 2, 2025. https://forward.com/news/733 657/zohran-mamdani-gaza-israel-jews-antisemitism/; M. Gessen, "The Attacks on Zohran Mamdani Show That We Need a New Understanding of Antisemitism," *The New York Times*, June 24, 2025. https://www.nytimes.com/2025/06/24/opin ion/antisemitism-new-york-city-mayor.html; Peter Beinart, "Democrats Need to Understand That Opinions on Israel Are Changing Fast," *The New York Times*, July 6, 2025. https://www.nytimes.com/2025/07/06/opinion/zohran-mamdani-democr ats-israel.html.

218 Stephanie Saul, "Trump Pulled $400 Million from Columbia. Other Schools Could Be Next," *The New York Times*, March 8, 2025. https://www.nytimes. com/2025/03/08/us/columbia-trump-colleges-antisemitism.html. Nine other universities are in the crosshairs of the Trump administration: Harvard University; George Washington University; Johns Hopkins University; New York University; Northwestern University; the University of California, Los Angeles; the University of California, Berkeley; the University of Minnesota; and the University of Southern California.

219 Josh Moody, "McMahon: Columbia Is on 'Right Track' to Restore Funding," *Inside Higher Ed*, March 25, 2025. https://www.insidehighered.com/news/ quick-takes/2025/03/25/mcmahon-columbia-right-track-restore-funding.

220 Columbia's AAUP chapter captures well the Trump administration's true desire. The threat of cuts "arguably aim less to address antisemitism than to destroy the university as a center of critical thought, professional expertise, democratic self-governance, and scientific inquiry" (Jennifer Ruth, "Wrong Way, Columbia! Solidarity with Columbia AAUP!," *Academe Blog*, March 21, 2025. https://academeblog. org/2025/03/21/wrong-way-columbia-solidarity-with-columbia-aaup/).

221 Slavoj Žižek, *Zero Point* (New York: Bloomsbury, 2025), 65.

222 https://x.com/AlanDersh/status/1732860934954025442.

223 Yancy, "'Striking Hard at Civilians': A Supremacist Ideology Underlies Israeli Policy," *Truthout*, March 24, 2025. https://truthout.org/articles/striking-hard-at-civilians-a-supremacist-ideology-underlies-israeli-policy/.

224 Said, *Representations of the Intellectual: The 1993 Reith Lectures* (New York: Vintage Books, 1996), 100–1.

225 Arundhati Roy, "Stop This Slaughter in Palestine," *Hammer & Hope*, no. 3 (2024) https://hammerandhope.org/article/arundhati-roy-palestine-gaza. I want to thank Ilan Kapoor for this reference. See also Sisonke Msimang, "How to Write About Palestine," *The Intercept*, May 25, 2025. https://theintercept.com/2025/05/25/ how-to-write-about-palestine/?utm_medium=email&utm_source=The%20Interc ept%20Newsletter.

226 Toscano, "Land of the Unfree?" *In These Times*, April 2, 2025. https://inthesetimes. com/article/mahmoud-khalil-repression-detention-democracy-gaza-encampments.

227 Slavoj Žižek, *The Plague of Fantasies* (New York: Verso, 1997), 138n25.

228 Nashwa Bawab, "The Student Movement for Palestine Continues, Despite Crackdowns," *In These Times*, July 14, 2025. https://inthesetimes.com/article/palestine-student-movement-repression-roundtable-momodou-taal-columbia-encampments?link_id=30&can_id=839242f129045dcf95563791cad9b53c&source=email-alberto-toscano-on-defending-the-indefensible-2&email_referrer=email_2818523&email_subject=pentagon-budget-tops-1-trillion-now-what&&.

229 Didier Fassin, *Moral Abdication: How the World Failed to Stop the Destruction of Gaza*, trans. Gregory Elliott (New York: Verso, 2024), 1.

230 Wynter, "Unsettling the Coloniality," 266.

231 Wynter, "Unsettling the Coloniality," 268.

Chapter 1

1 White subjects exercise this policing function in varied ways, whether through direct use of force or through persuasive appeals to authority figures. For example, the phenomenon described as the "Karen" represents a female accuser who deploys her whiteness and gender to harm Black folks through mendacious testimonies to the police or other figures of authority. The word "Karen" came into common use around 2020, but "the behavior which gave birth it has been documented since at least 1955, when Carolyn Bryant, a white woman, falsely accused Emmet Till of whistling at her and caused the 14-year-old Black child to be lynched by a mob" (Ishena Robinson, "Opposition to the Term Karen Continues Because an Unwillingness to Tackle Racism Continues, Despite the Brief Reckoning in 2020," *The Root*, January 2, 2021. https://www.theroot.com/opposition-to-the-term-karen-continues-because-an-unwil-1845978820). Policing happens whenever a member of society activates or reproduces the structures of anti-Blackness; see Tryon P. Woods, *Blackhood Against the Police Power: Punishment and Disavowal in the "Post-Racial" Era* (East Lansing: Michigan State University Press, 2019).

2 Said, *Culture and Imperialism* (New York: Vintage, 1994), 277.

3 We can consider Aimé Césaire's controversial canonization, or co-optation, as a "great humanist" (worthy of burial in the Pantheon) by then–French President Nicolas Sarkozy and others after the writer's death in 2008. What is at stake here are competing visions of the universal: a universalism deeply embedded in European imperialism, a cultural framework that continues to condemn people who look like Césaire to the zone of nonbeing, and a universality that reckons with the racial matrix of the human by politicizing the plight of the historically excluded—the subaltern voices of colonial history. For the politics of appropriating Césaire's legacy, see A. James Arnold, "Césaire Is Dead: Long Live Césaire! Recuperations and Reparations," *French Politics, Culture & Society* 27, no. 3 (2009): 9–18.

4 Wilderson, *Red, White & Black*, 38.

5 It "does not mean a process of coming back or flashing back, feeding back, but of *ana*-lysing, *ana*-mnesing, of reflecting" (Jean-François Lyotard, "Defining the Postmodern," in *The Cultural Studies Reader*, ed. Simon During [London: Routledge, 1993], 173).

6 Slavoj Žižek, *Surplus-Enjoyment: A Guide for the Non-Perplexed* (New York: Bloomsbury, 2022), 227.

7 Lauren Berlant, *Cruel Optimism* (Durham: Duke University Press, 2011).

8 The Pro-Human Camp, "Resist the Dehumanization of Palestinians and Israelis," December 13. https://www.amnesty.org.il/2023/12/13/%D7%9E%D7%9B%D7%AA%D7%91-%D7%A4%D7%AA%D7%95%D7%97-%D7%94%D7%9E%D7%97%D7%A0%D7%94-%D7%94%D7%A4%D7%A8%D7%95-%D7%90%D7%A0%D7%95%D7%A9%D7%99/

9 Fanon, *Black Skin*, xii–xiii.

10 Slavoj Žižek, "Human Rights and Its Discontents," Lecture at Bard College, November 15, 1999. http://www.lacan.com/zizek-human.htm.

11 Fanon, *The Wretched of the Earth*, 239, translation modified.

12 Fanon, *Black Skin*, 204.

13 Abigail B. Bakan, "Race, Class, and Colonialism: Reconsidering the 'Jewish Question,'" in *Theorizing Anti-Racism: Linkages in Marxism and Critical Race Theories*, ed. Abigail Bakan and Enakshi Dua (Toronto: University of Toronto Press, 2014), 252.

14 Aluf Benn, "The Jewish Majority in Israel Still See Their Country as 'a Villa in the Jungle,'" *The Guardian*, August 20, 2013. https://www.theguardian.com/commentisfree/2013/aug/20/jewish-majority-israel-villa-in-the-jungle.

15 Baldwin, "Conversation," 86.

16 Charles Hirschkind, "Exterminate the Brutes," *Mondoweiss*, November 8, 2023. https://mondoweiss.net/2023/11/exterminate-the-brutes/.

17 Joseph Massad, "Palestinians and Jewish History: Recognition or Submission?" *Journal of Palestine Studies* 30, no. 1 (2000): 62. As Rashid Khalidi observes, "the modern history of Palestine can best be understood in these terms: as a colonial war waged against the indigenous population, by a variety of parties [namely British imperialists and Zionists], to force them to relinquish their homeland to another people against their will" (Rashid Khalidi, *The Hundred Years' War on Palestine: A History of Settler Colonialism and Resistance, 1917–2017* [New York: Metropolitan Books, 2020], 13).

18 David Theo Goldberg, "Why 'Black Lives Matter' Because All Lives Don't Matter in America," *The Huffington Post*, September 25, 2015. https://www.huffingtonpost.com/david-theo-goldberg/why-black-lives-matter_b_8191424.html.

19 Adi Callai, "The Gaza Ghetto Uprising," *The Brooklyn Rail*, May 2024 https://brooklynrail.org/2024/05/field-notes/The-Gaza-Ghetto-Uprising/.

20 Western media outlets do not dare to point out the inconvenient truth that an occupying force does not have the international right to self-defense. Who has an unquestionable legal right to self-defense are the Palestinian people, though this right is not without conditions; civilians, for instance, cannot be targeted in your resistance to the occupying military force.

21 Jonathan Cook, "Biden and Starmer Are Destroying International Law to Protect Israel's Genocide," *Middle East Eye*, December 4, 2024. https://www.middleeasteye.net/opinion/biden-starmer-destroying-international-protect-israel-genocide. Despite the influence of Israel's Western backers, the International Criminal Court (ICC) did issue arrest warrants to Netanyahu and former Israeli Defense Minister Yoav Gallant, and Mohammed Deif, Hamas' military chief, for war crimes and crimes against humanity, and thus de-exceptionalizing Israeli leaders, applying the same standard for both Israel and Hamas. The ICC refused to be "just a mask of Western domination" (Žižek, *Zero Point*, 16) but in doing so became a problem for the United States, a global problem no longer exempting the abuses of West (to which Israel clearly belong) from legal scrutiny and accountability.

22 Toni Morrison, "Nobel Lecture," *The Nobel Prize*, December 7, 1993. https://www.nobelprize.org/prizes/literature/1993/morrison/lecture/.

23 Susan Neiman, "Historical Reckoning Gone Haywire," *The New York Review*, October 19, 2023. https://www.nybooks.com/articles/2023/10/19/historical-reckoning-gone-haywire-germany-susan-neiman/.

24 Parth Sharma, " 'We Are Fighting Human Animals': Dehumanization of Palestinians," *The Palestine Chronicle*, May 21, 2024. https://www.palestinechronicle.com/we-are-fighting-human-animals-dehumanization-of-palestinians/.

25 Jeremy Scahill, "The Devil in the Details of Trump's 'Final Proposal' for Gaza Ceasefire," *Drop Site*, July 3, 2025. https://www.dropsitenews.com/p/trump-netanyahu-hamas-united-states-israel-ceasefire.

26 Khader, "Ziofascist Violence and the Nakba 2.0."

27 Emir, "Gaza Babies Dying from the Cold as Winter Temperatures Drop," December 30, 2024. https://www.bbc.com/news/articles/cd0ep0j83p7o.

28 Noura Erakat, *Justice for Some: Law and the Question of Palestine* (Stanford: Stanford University Press, 2019), 73.

29 Gilles Deleuze, "The Indians of Palestine," in *Two Regimes of Madness: Texts and Interviews 1975–1995*, ed. David Lapoujade (New York: Semiotext(e), 2007), 194–5.

30 Deleuze, "The Indians of Palestine," 194–5.

31 Nuraan Davids, Ronald Barnett, Thaddeus Metz, Zahi Zalloua, Suriamurthee Maistry, George Yancy, Janet Orchard, Marianna Papastephanou, Nelson Maldonado-Torres, Steven Robins, James Conroy, Daniella J. Forster, and Lesley le Grange, "Gaza: We Need to Talk!" *Educational Philosophy and Theory* (2025): 8.

32 Pranay Somayajula, "On Condemnation: Terrorism, Violence, and the Question of Palestine," *Culture Shock*, November 26, 2023. https://socialtextjournal.org/periscope_article/on-condemnation-terrorism-violence-and-the-question-of-palestine/.

33 "Palestinians must denounce certain affiliations, determined by the West, to be considered worthy of living. Or, I should correct myself, worthy of *condolences*, as we are doomed regardless" (El-Kurd, *The Perfect Victims*, 68).

34 Deleuze, "The Indians of Palestine," 199.

35 Emmanuel Levinas, *Difficult Freedom: Essays on Judaism*, trans. Seán Hand (Baltimore: Johns Hopkins University Press, 1990).

36 Levinas, *Otherwise than Being, or, Beyond Essence*, trans. Alphonso Lingis (The Hague: Martinus Nijhoff, 1981).

37 Slavoj Žižek, "Afterword: With Defenders Like These, Who Needs Attackers?" in *The Truth of Žižek*, ed. Paul Bowman and Richard Stamp (New York: Continuum, 2007), 234.

38 Wilderson, *Afropessimism*, xi.

39 Zalloua, *Being Posthuman: Ontologies of the Future* (New York: Bloomsbury, 2021), 143–85.

40 Reuters, "All Options on the Table If Israel Does Not Deliver on Gaza Pledges, EU's Kallas Says," *Reuters*, July 22, 2025. https://www.reuters.com/world/middle-east/all-options-table-if-israel-does-not-deliver-gaza-pledges-eus-kallas-says-2025-07-22/.

41 Fanon, *The Wretched of the Earth*, 5.

42 Nicole Simek, "Race and Sex Redux," *symplokē* 32, no. 1–2 (2024): 410.

43 Gabriel Winant, "On Mourning and Statehood: A Response to Joshua Leifer," *Dissent*, October 13, 2023. https://www.dissentmagazine.org/online_articles/a-response-to-joshua-leifer/.

44 Balazs Berkovits, "The October 7th Pogrom as a Non-Event on the Western Left," *K*, January 25, 2024. https://k-larevue.com/en/the-october-7th-pog rom-as-a-non-event-on-the-western-left/.

45 Fanon, *Black Skin*, 95.

46 Warren, *Ontological Terror*, 43.

47 Fanon, "Why We Use Violence," in *Alienation and Freedom*, ed. Jean Khalfa and Robert J. C. Young (New York: Bloomsbury, 2021), 657, 668.

48 Wilderson, *Red, White & Black*, 28.

49 Fanon, *Black Skin*, 89.

50 Fanon, *Black Skin*, 89.

51 Slavoj Žižek, *Less than Nothing: Hegel and the Shadow of Dialectical Materialism* (New York: Verso, 2012), 166.

52 Al Jazeera, "Israeli Soldiers Are Filming Themselves Mocking Palestinians," *Al Jazeera*, January 18, 2024. https://www.aljazeera.com/program/newsf eed/2024/1/18/israeli-soldiers-are-filming-themselves-mocking-palestinians.

53 Fanon, *Black Skin*, 166. The Black imago resides in the collective unconscious where "black = ugliness, sin, darkness, and immorality. In other words, he who is immoral is black. If I behave like a man with morals, I am not black" (Fanon, *Black Skin*, 200). The Black imago affects not only the white perception of Blacks but also that of Black folks who have internalized this dreadful image of themselves. Attentive to the reality of Black agents of anti-Blackness, James Baldwin aptly observed, "We feared black cops even more than white cops, because the black cop had to work so much harder—on your *head*—to prove to himself and his colleagues that he was not like all the other niggers" (James Baldwin, "Negroes Are Anti-Semitic Because They're Anti-White," in *Baldwin: Collected Essays*, ed. Toni Morrison [New York: Library of America, 1998], 740). We see this clearly in the cases where a Black police officer unjustly murders a Black individual. Selective empathy overdetermines the Black-Police encounter. I submit the killing of Tyre Nichols on January 7, 2023. After a traffic stop by officers of the notorious Scorpion unit in the City of Memphis, Nichols, a 29-year-old Black man, was brutalized by five Black officers and died three days later. In an anti-Black world, law and order (no matter who embodies that position) too often means the reproduction of a racialized and murderous status quo (Rick Rojas et al., "What We Know About Tyre Nichols's Lethal Encounter with Memphis Police," *The New York Times*, February 12, 2023. https://www.nytimes.com/article/tyre-nichols-memphis-pol ice-dead.html). White civil society ontologically bribes the Black officer; seduced and mystified by the Black imago, the Black cop implicitly introduces a distinction between "good" Black vs. "thuggish" Black. The former yearns to whiten himself via state power (becoming a problem detector) while the latter is deemed without redemption, a permanent problem, a carcerable or killable problem. The alienation of the Black officer is counterbalanced by the *jouissance* of an anti-Blackness that pretends to exempt him—no need for disalienation. Of course, the fantasy that the Black cop believes he now belongs to the world of those who matter can be shattered by white cops. Consider the story from June 2017: "A 'friendly fire' incident in which an off-duty St. Louis policeman was shot while coming to the aid of fellow officers has taken on racial overtones after an incendiary claim by the injured officer's attorney: The officer was viewed as a threat because he was black" (Cleve R. Wootson, Jr., "A Black Off-Duty Cop Tried to Help Stop a Crime. Another Officer Shot Him," *The Washington Post*, June 25, 2017. https://www.washingtonpost.com/news/post-nation/wp/2017/06/25/a-black-off-dut y-cop-tried-to-help-stop-a-crime-another-officer-shot-him/). The Black imago makes the incident precisely an *un*friendly fire.

54 Benjamin Netanyahu, "Netanyahu's 2024 Address to Congress," *Haaretz*, July 25, 2024. https://www.haaretz.com/israel-news/2024-07-25/ty-article/full-text-netanya hus-2024-address-to-congress/00000190-e6c0-d469-a39d-e6d7117d0000.

55 Daniel Finn, "Israel's Western Backers Are Still Running Interference for Netanyahu's War Crimes," *Jacobin*, October 18, 2023. https://jacobin.com/2023/10/al-ahli-hospital-bombing-gaza-war-israel-war-crimes-western-support-biden.

56 "One is black as a result of being wicked, spineless, evil, and instinctual. Everything that is the opposite of this black behavior is white" (Fanon, *Black Skin*, 168).

57 Fanon, *Black Skin*, 206.

58 Jared Sexton, "African American Studies," in *A Concise Companion to American Studies*, ed. John Carlos Rowe (Malden: Wiley-Blackwell, 2010), 221.

59 Sexton, "African American Studies," 222.

60 Sharpe, "Black Studies: In the Wake," *The Black Scholar* 44, no. 2 (2014): 59.

61 Sharpe, "Black Studies," 59.

62 Hartman, *Lose Your Mother*, 31.

63 Sharpe, *In the Wake*, 10.

64 Jean Améry, *At the Mind's Limits: Contemplations by a Survivor on Auschwitz and Its Realities*, trans. Sidney Rosenfeld and Stella P. Rosenfeld (Bloomington: Indiana University Press, 1980).

65 W. G. Sebald, "Against the Irreversible. On Jean Améry," in *On the Natural History of Destruction* (Toronto: Alfred A. Knopf, 2003), 156, translation modified.

66 Zalloua, *The Politics of the Wretched: Race, Reason, and Ressentiment* (New York: Bloomsbury, 2024).

67 Francesca Albanese, "From Economy of Occupation to Economy of Genocide: Report of the Special Rapporteur on the Situation of Human Rights in the Palestinian Territories Occupied Since 1967," *United Nations*, June 16, 2025. https://www.ohchr.org/en/documents/country-reports/ahrc5923-economy-occupat ion-economy-genocide-report-special-rapporteur.

68 Said, *Orientalism*, xxii.

69 Zionist cognitive mapping appears notably weaker outside of Israel. The global protests in support of Palestine intimate that the fact of Palestinian genocide is compelling many to shed their reflexive support for Israel. The enjoyment that the fetishist disavowal yields must be matched or rather overwhelmed by our collective *ressentiment*, centering the injunction "defend the dead," insisting on not forgiving and forgetting the genocide, on blocking the manufactured nostalgia for the two-state solution.

70 El-Kurd, *Perfect Victims*, 2.

71 Žižek, *Less than Nothing*, 995–6.

72 Walter Benjamin, "On the Concept of History," in *Selected Writings, Volume 4, 1938–1940*, ed. Howard Eiland and Michael W. Jennings (Cambridge: Harvard University Press, 2003), 395.

73 Dikla Taylor-Sheinman, "A Lyd Without the Nakba," *+972 Magazine*, October 25, 2024. https://www.972mag.com/lyd-nakba-film/.

74 Mira Fox, "So What Does 'Intifada' Actually Mean?" *Forward*, December 15, 2023. https://forward.com/culture/573654/intifada-arabic-israeli-hamas-war-meaning-linguistics/.

75 Noura Erakat, "Zionism as a Form of Racism," in *Race and the Question of Palestine*, ed. Lana Tatour and Ronit Lentin (Stanford: Stanford University Press, 2025), 78.

76 Lauren Collee, "Imaginative Resistance: An Interview with 'Lyd' Directors Rami Younis and Sarah Friedland," *Rough Cut Film*, April 10, 2024. https://roughcutfilm.com/2024/04/10/imaginative-resistance-an-interview-with-lyd-directors-rami-younis-and-sarah-friedland/.

77 Said, "The One-State Solution," *The New York Times Magazine*, January 10, 1999.

78 Alexander Shapiro, "Lod: Shared Society in Israel's 'Murder City,'" *The Times of Israel*, October 24, 2018. https://blogs.timesofisrael.com/lod-shared-society-in-israels-murder-city/.

79 MEE staff, "Israel Is Ethnically Cleansing North Gaza, Says B'Tselem," *Middle East Eye*, October 23, 2024. https://www.middleeasteye.net/news/israel-committing-gravest-crimes-laws-war-northern-gaza-btselem.

80 Mira Fox, "A 'Sci-Fi Documentary' Dreaming of Peace Got Banned in Israel. Why?" *Forward*, November 11, 2024. https://forward.com/culture/673651/lyd-israel-palestine-lod-documentary-ban/.

81 Indlieb Farazi Saber, "A Tale of Two Lyds: What if the Nakba Never Happened?" *TRT World*, May 16, 2024. https://www.trtworld.com/magazine/a-tale-of-two-lyds-what-if-the-nakba-never-happened-18163413.

82 Wilderson, *Red, White & Black*, 58.

83 Slavoj Žižek, *Violence: Six Sideways Reflections* (New York: Picador, 2008), 87.

84 Dealing with Palestinian privilege must pass through a critical analysis of capitalist social relations and the affective arrangement that sustains their reproduction. The fight against privilege, if it is to be more than lip service, demands that we think political economy with libidinal economy, and vice versa. In this not-so-other Lyd, we're asked to imagine that capital exploits Eritreans and Sudanese differently, naturalizing their oppression and marginalization, so that bourgeois Palestinians can (continue to) enjoy their privilege or priority over non-Palestinians both economically and libidinally.

85 Ari Shavit, *My Promised Land: The Triumph and Tragedy of Israel* (New York: Spiegel and Grau, 2013), 108.

86 Shavit, *My Promised Land*, 109.

87 Shavit, *My Promised Land*, 131.

88 Shavit, *My Promised Land*, 131.

89 Shavit, *My Promised Land*, 331, 332.

90 Shavit, *My Promised Land*, 131.

91 Omri Boehm, "Tragedy or Political Correctness? Ari Shavit and the Confusion of the Zionist Liberal Left," *Los Angeles Review of Books*, March 27, 2014. https://lareviewofbooks.org/article/tragedy-political-correctness-ari-shavit-confusion-zionist-liberal-left/.

92 Eve Tuck and K. Wayne Yang, "Decolonization Is Not a Metaphor," *Decolonization: Indigeneity, Education, and Society* 1, no. 1 (2012): 10.

93 Nadia Abu El-Haj, "'We Know Well, but All the Same …' Factual Truths, Historical Narratives, and the Work of Disavowal," *History of the Present* 13, no. 2 (2023): 257.

94 Abu El-Haj, "We Know Well," 259.

95 Collee, "Imaginative Resistance."

96 "Politics exists when the natural order of domination is interrupted by the institution of a part of those who have no part" (Jacques Rancière, *Disagreement: Politics and Philosophy*, trans. Julie Rose [Minneapolis: University of Minnesota Press, 1999], 11).

97 Žižek, *In Defense of Lost Causes* (New York: Verso, 2008), 165.

98 Žižek, *In Defense of Lost Causes*, 166.

99 Žižek, *In Defense of Lost Causes*, 166.

100 Žižek, *Surplus-Enjoyment*, 228.

101 Žižek, "Neighbors and Other Monsters," in *The Neighbor: Three Inquiries in Political Theology*. With a New Preface, ed. Slavoj Žižek, Eric L. Santner, and Kenneth Reinhard (Chicago: University of Chicago Press, 2013), 160.

102 Jacques Derrida, *Rogues: Two Essays on Reason*, trans. Pascale-Anne Brault and Michael Naas (Stanford: Stanford University Press, 2005), 213.

103 "Autoimmunity is not an absolute ill or evil. It enables an exposure to the other, to *what* and to *who* comes—which means that it must remain incalculable. Without autoimmunity, with absolute immunity, nothing would ever happen or arrive; we would no longer wait, await, or expect, no longer expect one another, or expect any event" (Derrida, *Rogues*, 152).

104 Yancy, "Introduction: Un-Sutured," in *White Self-Criticality Beyond Anti-Racism: How Does It Feel to Be a White Problem?* ed. George Yancy (Lanham: Lexington Books, 2015), xvii.

105 Butler, *Giving an Account of Oneself* (New York: Fordham University Press, 2005), 103; Yancy, *Black Bodies, White Gazes*, 337–8.

106 Žižek, *Surplus-Enjoyment*, 227.

107 Serving as a soldier in the 1982 Israeli invasion of Lebanon, Folman suffers from amnesia, unable to recollect his behavior during Sabra and Shatila massacres before concluding that his participation in the tragic event was marginal—he only sent up flares so that the Phalangists—the Christian militia enraged by the death of their President Bashir Gemayel—could commit their slaughter. Folman accepts that he wasn't responsible and then ends up forgiving himself. This realization is somewhat prefigured earlier in the film when his psychologist friend Uri Sivan observes that Folman's psychic problems are anterior to the massacres, residing, as it were, in the collective unconscious of the Shoah: "You were engaged with the massacre a long time before it happened, through your parents' Auschwitz memory." Without denying the reality of transgenerational trauma, we can track its ideological deployment in the film. The actual Palestinian victims are deprived of their political relevance and provocation—the turn at the end of the film to the actual footage of Palestinian misery is Folman's appeal to pathos (as if to indicate the Real of the Palestinians, a presence ungentrified by the imaginary-symbolic animation of the film). This dubious gesture of empowerment works instead to further reify Palestinians in their bare life, cementing their otherness and inaccessibility. By displacing the victimization of the Palestinians (how did they become refugees in the first place? Why didn't he interview any of the survivors?), Folman's film attests not only to his trauma, but to his victimization by the war, securing acclaim from the director's liberal audience who enjoyed feasting on this "anti-war" film (political

Zionists were not fans of it). See Gideon Levy, "Gideon Levy 'Antiwar' Film Waltz with Bashir Is Nothing but Charade," *Haaretz*, February 19, 2009. https://www.haar etz.com/2009-02-19/ty-article/gideon-levy-antiwar-film-waltz-with-bashir-is-noth ing-but-charade/0000017f-da81-d42c-afff-dff34b480000.

108 Naomi Klein, "How Israel Has Made Trauma a Weapon of War," *The Guardian*, October 5, 2024. https://www.theguardian.com/us-news/ng-interactive/2024/ oct/05/israel-gaza-october-7-memorials.

109 Klein, "How Israel Has Made Trauma."

110 Shannon Sullivan, "The White Habit of Untrauma," in *The Routledge International Handbook of New Critical Race and Whiteness Studies*, ed. Rikke Andreassen, Catrin Lundström, Suvi Keskinen, and Shirley Anne Tate (New York: Routledge, 2023), 285.

111 Maybe it is time to turn around the observation that Israel does not have a peace partner, that there is no Palestinian Gandhi or Mandela. We're told the Palestinian commitment to violence must be abandoned if coexistence is to be secured. Israel's objection is not to armed struggle but to resistance as such. Moreover, while Gandhi and Mandela renounced armed struggle, they were by no means "not violent"—they helped to dismantle imperialist and apartheid regimes, respectively. Their nonviolence was experienced as a violent unsettling of the structures of domination that existed in India and South Africa. We should look for such a change in Israel itself. We need a Jewish-Israeli Gandhi/Mandela, a figure capable of making the impossible possible: an anti-Zionist Israel.

112 Neve Gordon and Yinon Cohen, "Race and Space in Israel/Palestine," in *Race and the Question of Palestine*, ed. Lana Tatour and Ronit Lentin (Stanford: Stanford University Press, 2025), 37–8.

113 Gideon Levy, "The Anti-Netanyahu Camp Is Longing for a Country That Never Was," *Haaretz*, September 8, 2019. https://www.haaretz.com/opin ion/2019-09-08/ty-article/.premium/the-anti-netanyahu-camp-is-longing-for-a-coun try-that-never-was/0000017f-e998-d62c-a1ff-fdfb85360000.

114 With the Second Intifada and Hamas' attack in southern Israel, many Zionists who were in the "peace camp" have allegedly "sobered up" and are now reconsidering their attachment to a peace with Palestinians. See Hanin Majadli, "Over 30,000 Killed in Gaza, but Even Israel's 'Liberal Left' Says: That's War," *Haaretz*, March 7, 2024. https://www.haaretz.com/opinion/2024-03-07/ty-article-opinion/.prem ium/over-30-000-killed-in-gaza-but-even-israels-liberal-left-says-thats-war/00000 18e-1a3a-d8fb-abff-5f3ad8860000.

115 Bryn Haworth, "Israel's War on Children Is a Stain on Humanity," *Al Majalla*, April 22, 2024. https://en.majalla.com/node/315326/culture-social-affairs/israels-war-child ren-stain-humanity.

116 Lana Tatour, "Preface," in *Race and the Question of Palestine*, ed. Lana Tatour and Ronit Lentin (Stanford: Stanford University Press, 2025), viii.

117 Klein, "How Israel has Made Trauma."

118 There is a straight line of Palestinian un-mattering running through from the Balfour Declaration of 1917 to Israel's Operation Iron Swords. If British Foreign Secretary Arthur Balfour backed the Jewish people's aspiration for statehood in Palestine without consulting its Indigenous Arab population, Prime Minister Netanyahu proudly redraws the map of the Middle East absent of Palestine/Palestinians. In both instances, the aspirations of Palestinians were never meant to matter to the land's Western colonizers and settlers.

119 Slavoj Žižek, "The Middle East War: A Boring Recapitulation," *Substack: Žižek Goads and Prods*, October 19, 2024. https://slavoj.substack.com/p/the-middle-east-war-a-boring-recapitulation.

120 Yara M. Asi, "The Trauma Experienced in Gaza Is Beyond PTSD," *The New York Times*, February 22, 2024. https://www.nytimes.com/2024/02/22/opinion/gaza-palestinians-mental-health.html.

121 Sullivan, "The White Habit of Untrauma," 287.

122 Nadeen Ebrahim and Mike Schwartz, " 'He Got Out of Gaza, but Gaza Did Not Get Out of Him': Israeli Soldiers Returning from War Struggle with Trauma and Suicide," *CNN*, October 21, 2024. https://www.cnn.com/2024/10/21/middleeast/gaza-war-israeli-soldiers-ptsd-suicide-intl/index.html.

123 Slavoj Žižek, "On Shame and Dignity In and Around Gaza," *Substack: Žižek Goads and Prods*, October 26, 2024. https://substack.com/home/post/p-150707949?source=queue.

124 Michel de Montaigne, *The Complete Essays of Montaigne*, trans. Donald Frame (Stanford: Stanford University Press, 1957), 156.

125 Montaigne, *The Complete Essays of Montaigne*, 155, emphasis added.

126 Montaigne, *The Complete Essays of Montaigne*, 155.

127 Montaigne, *The Complete Essays of Montaigne*, 314.

128 Enrique Dussel, "Anti-Cartesian Meditations: On the Origin of the Philosophical Anti-Discourse of Modernity," trans. Geo Maher, *Journal for Culture and Religious Theory* 13, no. 1 (2014): 21–53.

129 Montaigne, *The Complete Essays of Montaigne*, 313, emphasis added.

130 Judith Shklar, *Ordinary Vices* (Cambridge: Harvard University Press, 1984), 8.

131 Montaigne, *The Complete Essays of Montaigne*, 787, emphasis added.

132 Montaigne, *The Complete Essays of Montaigne*, 787.

133 Nelson Maldonado-Torres, "On the Coloniality of Being: Contributions to the Development of a Concept," *Cultural Studies* 21, no. 2–3 (2007), 245.

134 Maldonado-Torres, "On the Coloniality of Being," 245.

135 Mary Turfah, "The Most Moral Army," *Los Angeles Review of Books*, October 1, 2024. https://lareviewofbooks.org/article/the-most-moral-army/.

136 "We will perhaps in time be able to forgive the Arabs for killing our sons, but it will be harder for us to forgive them for having forced us to kill their sons" (qtd. in Oded Na'aman, "Choosing Violence: War Is Almost Always a Choice, a Madness We Go Along With," *Boston Review*, August 15, 2016. https://www.bostonreview.net/articles/oded-naaman-choosing-violence/).

137 Qtd. in Na'aman, "Choosing Violence."

138 "Sin Is Black as Virtue Is White" (Fanon, *Black Skin*, 118).

139 Jacqueline Rose, " 'You Made Me Do It,' " *London Review of Books*, November 30, 2023. https://www.lrb.co.uk/the-paper/v45/n23/jacqueline-rose/you-made-me-do-it.

140 "Both Spanish officials then and Israeli spokesmen now have openly declared their intention to 'conquer' their enemies by forcing their removal from their homes and concentrating them in more controllable areas" (Greg Grandin, "From the Americas to Gaza, the Conquest Never Ends," *The Nation*, May 28, 2025. https://www.thenation.com/article/world/israel-gaza-conquistadors-aztec/).

141 Nathan Lopes Cardozo, "Hanukkah: Jews Should Be Proud of What They Are Hated For," *The Jerusalem Post*, December 28, 2024. https://www.jpost.com/opinion/article-834843.

142 Gavin Lewis, "Corporate News: Racists Obscuring Genocide and Its Historical Continuities," *Arena*, March 28, 2025. https://arena.org.au/corporate-news-racists-obscuring-genocide/.

143 Na'aman, "Choosing Violence."

144 Gideon Levy, "Israel's Military Leaders Are Not 'Only Obeying Orders.' They Could Have Stopped the Gaza Massacre," *Haaretz*, May 22, 2025. https://www.haaretz.com/opinion/2025-05-22/ty-article-opinion/.premium/idf-brass-is-not-only-obeying-orders-it-could-have-stopped-the-gaza-massacre/00000196-f420-d06d-a5df-f5f1b63f0000.

145 The logic of self-defense also applies to the illegal settlements—"victory through settlement" posits settlers not as invaders on Palestinian land but as protectors of Israel. See Ben Reiff, "Smotrich Wants One Million West Bank Settlers. That's Not So Far-Fetched," *+972 Magazine*, July 12, 2023. https://www.972mag.com/settlements-roads-infrastructure-smotrich/.

146 Finn, "Israel's Western Backers."

147 Ali Abunimah, "Israeli Lawmaker's Call for Genocide of Palestinians Gets Thousands of Facebook Likes," *Electronic Intifada*, July 7, 2014. https://electronicintifada.net/blogs/ali-abunimah/israeli-lawmakers-call-genocide-palestinians-gets-thousands-facebook-likes.

148 In a post on X, French President Emmanuel Macron immediately expressed his nation's support of Israel's illegal bombing of Iran's nuclear sites: "France reaffirms Israel's right to defend itself and ensure its security" (https://x.com/EmmanuelMacron/status/1933491906144526764). Cathrin Schaer, "Israel's Iran Attack Sparks Legal Debate," *Deutsche Welle*, June 18, 2025. https://www.dw.com/en/israel-iran-attack-legality-international-law/a-72952324.

149 Dina Porat, "Should We Compare the Hamas Assault to the Holocaust?" *Haaretz*, October 23, 2023. https://www.haaretz.com/opinion/2023-10-23/ty-article-opinion/.premium/should-we-compare-the-hamas-assault-to-the-holocaust/0000018b-5cbb-d307-adbb-7dbb40b50000.

150 Yancy, *Black Bodies, White Gazes*, 338.

151 "Whoever Is Not Willing to Talk About Capitalism Should Also Keep Quiet About Fascism" (Max Horkheimer, "The Jews and Europe," in *Critical Theory and Society: A Reader*, ed. Stephen Bronner and Douglas Kellner [New York: Routledge, 1989], 78).

152 Fanon, *Black Skin*, xii, xiii.

153 David Marriott, "Blackness: N'est Pas?" *Propter Nos* 4 (2020): 27–51.

154 Warren, *Ontological Terror*, 183n33.

155 Wilderson, *Red, White & Black*, 38.

156 Fanon, *Black Skin*, xiii.

157 This is akin to Spivak's formulation of the double bind as "a persistent critique of what we cannot not want" (Gayatri Chakravorty Spivak, *Critique of Postcolonial Reason: Toward a History of the Vanishing Present* [Cambridge: Harvard University Press, 1999], 110).

Chapter 2

1 Fanon, *Black Skin*, xii.

2 Fanon, *The Wretched of the Earth*, 2.

3 George Shulman, "Fred Moten's Refusals and Consents: The Politics of Fugitivity," *Political Theory* 49, no. 2 (2021): 280.

4 Orlando Patterson, *Slavery and Social Death: A Comparative Study* (Cambridge: Harvard University Press, 1982), 38.

5 Fanon, *Black Skin*, 80, translation modified.

6 See Hillel Cohen, *Good Arabs: The Israeli Security Agencies and the Israeli Arabs, 1948–1967* (Berkeley: University of California Press, 2010).

7 Manthia Diawara, "One World in Relation: Édouard Glissant in Conversation with Manthia Diawara," *Journal of Contemporary African Art* 28, trans. Christopher Winks (Spring, 2011): 19.

8 Diawara, "One World," 5.

9 Fred Moten, "Notes on *Narrating Humanity*," *Critical Ethnic Studies* 9, no. 1 (2024). https://manifold.umn.edu/read/ces0901-15/section/e8602e00-1c3d-4bcc-a378-f1fd98fe870a

10 Moten, "Notes on *Narrating Humanity*."

11 Diawara, "One World," 19.

12 Diawara, "One World," 5.

13 James R. Martel, *The Misinterpellated Subject* (Durham: Duke University Press, 2017), 236.

14 Moten, "Notes on *Narrating Humanity*."

15 Moten, *Stolen Life* (Durham: Duke University Press, 2018), 131.

16 Moten, *The Universal Machine* (Durham: Duke University Press, 2018), 230.

17 See Martel, *The Misinterpellated Subject*, 236.

18 Moten, *The Universal Machine*, 142.

19 Julius Gavroche, "Fred Moten: Thinking with Palestine," *Autonomies*, October 32, 2023. https://autonomies.org/2023/10/fred-moten-thinking-with-palestine/.

20 Descartes, *Discourse on Method and Meditations on First Philosophy*, trans. Donald A. Cress (Indianapolis: Hackett, 1998), 35.

21 Houria Bouteldja, *Whites, Jews, and Us: Toward a Politics of Revolutionary Love* (South Pasadena: Semiotext(e), 2017), 34.

22 Moten, "Notes on *Narrating Humanity*."

23 Jack Halberstam, "The Wild Beyond: With and for the Undercommons," in *The Undercommons: Fugitive Planning & Black Study*, ed. Fred Moten and Stefano Harney (New York: Minor Compositions, 2013), 8.

24 Moten, "Notes on *Narrating Humanity*."

25 Moten, "Notes on *Narrating Humanity*."

26 Moten, "Notes on *Narrating Humanity*."

27 Steve Paulson, "Critical Intimacy: An Interview with Gayatri Chakravorty Spivak," *Los Angeles Review of Books*, July 29, 2016. https://lareviewofbooks.org/article/critical-intimacy-interview-gayatri-chakravorty-spivak/.

28 Nelson Maldonado-Torres, "Outline of Ten Theses on Coloniality and Decoloniality". Foundation Frantz Fanon. https://caribbeanstudiesassociation.org/docs/Maldonado-Torres_Outline_Ten_Theses-10.23.16.pdf.

29 Maldonado-Torres, "Outline of Ten Theses."

30 Stefano Harney and Fred Moten, *The Undercommons: Fugitive Planning and Black Study* (New York: Autonomedia, 2013), 28.

31 Marquis Bey, "Anarcho-Blackness: A Conversation with Marquis Bey," *Ill Will*, October 14, 2021. https://illwill.com/anarcho-blackness.

32 Baldwin, "The Dangerous Road Before Martin Luther King," in *Baldwin: Collected Essays*, ed. Toni Morrison (New York: Library of America, 1998), 657.

33 Diawara, "One World," 6.

34 Moten, "Black Op," *PMLA* 123, no. 5 (2008): 1745.

35 Moten, *The Universal Machine* (Durham: Duke University Press, 2018), 151.

36 Moten, *The Universal Machine*, 262n6.

37 Moten, *The Universal Machine*, 140.

38 Moten, *In the Break*, 1.

39 Moten, *The Universal Machine*, 148.

40 Nahum Chandler, "Of Exorbitance: The Problem of the Negro as a Problem for Thought," *Criticism* 50, no. 3 (2008): 351.

41 Moten, "Black Optimism/Black Operation," unpublished paper on file with the author, (2007). https://doubleoperative.com/wp-content/uploads/2009/12/moten-black-optimism_black-operation.pdf.

42 Moten, *The Universal Machine*, 150.

43 Wilderson, *Red, White & Black: Cinema and the Structure of U.S. Antagonisms* (Durham: Duke University Press, 2010), 38.

44 Moten, *The Universal Machine*, 150–1.

45 Fanon 2008, 89.

46 Fanon, *Black Skin*, 89, emphasis added.

47 Fanon, *Black Skin*, 90.

48 Moten, *The Universal Machine*, 150.

49 Fanon, *Black Skin*, 94.

50 Fanon, *Black Skin*, 94.

51 Fanon, *Black Skin*, 94.

52 Du Bois, *The Souls of Black Folk*, xxiii.

53 Du Bois, *The Souls of Black Folk*, xxiii.

54 Fanon, *Black Skin*, 117.

55 Moten, *In the Break: The Aesthetics of the Black Radical Tradition* (Minneapolis: University of Minnesota Press, 2003), 1.

56 Fanon, *Black Skin*, 201.

57 William David Hart, *The Blackness of Black: Key Concepts in Critical Discourse* (Lanham: Lexington Books, 2020), 165. Calvin Warren elucidates further: "Black people are 'touched by Blackness' (Blackness is presented to them much like being is presented to *Dasein* for Heidegger), but Blackness is not the property of black people" (Warren, "Black Mysticism: Fred Moten's Phenomenology of (Black) Spirit," *Zeitschrift für Anglistik und Amerikanistik* 65, no. 2 [2017]: 226).

58 Moten, *Stolen Life*, 215.

59 Moten, *The Universal Machine*, 142.

60 Moten, *Stolen Life*, 243.

61 Moten, *The Universal Machine*, 194.

62 Bouteldja, *Whites, Jews, and Us*, 43.

63 Moten, "Blackness and Nothingness (Mysticism in the Flesh)," *South Atlantic Quarterly* 112, no. 4 (2013): 739.

64 Warren, "Black Mysticism," 226.

65 Moten, *Stolen Life*, 131.

66 Warren, "Black Mysticism," 228.

67 Warren, "Black Mysticism," 227.

68 Warren also mistakenly Kantianizes Blackness, undermining its critical force by designating it as a "noumenon" (Warren, "Black Mysticism," 224).

69 Žižek, *In Defense of Lost Causes*, 327.

70 Žižek, *In Defense of Lost Causes*, 328.

71 Žižek, *In Defense of Lost Causes*, 328.

72 Sara Ahmed, "Killjoy Truths," *feministkilljoys*, October 16, 2023. https://feministkillj oys.com/2023/10/16/killjoy-truths/.

73 Harney and Moten, *The Undercommons*, 125.

74 Brendan Rascius, "Why Did Harris Lose Some Biden 2020 Voters? Poll Finds Gaza War Was the Top Issue," *Miami Herald*, January 15, 2025. https://www.miamiher ald.com/news/nation-world/national/article298600563.html.

75 Paola Nagovitch, "Young Voters on the Left Reject Kamala Harris: 'She Has Made It Clear That She Doesn't Value My Vote,'" *El País*, October 29, 2024. https://english. elpais.com/usa/elections/2024-10-29/young-voters-on-the-left-reject-kamala-harri s-she-has-made-it-clear-that-she-doesnt-value-my-vote.html.

76 Ahmed, *Willful Subjects* (Durham: Duke University Press, 2014), 152.

77 Ahmed, *The Feminist Killjoy Handbook* (New York: Penguin Books, 2024), 262.

78 Chandra Talpade Mohanty, *Feminism Without Borders: Decolonizing Theory, Practicing Solidarity* (Durham: Duke University Press, 2003), 231.

79 El Akkad, *One Day, Everyone Will Have Always Been Against This*, 59.

80 Paul Street, "The Resistance Remains Hollow: The Weimar Ways of the Dismal Democrats," *CounterPunch*, July 2, 2021. https://www.counterpunch.org/2021/07/02/ the-resistance-remains-hollow-the-weimar-ways-of-the-dismal-democrats/.

81 Ahmed, *The Feminist Killjoy Handbook*, 86.

82 Juan Cole, "Ta-Nehisi Coates: If Democrats Can't Draw the Line at Genocide, They Can't Draw the Line at Democracy," *Informed Comment*, February 20, 2025. https://www.juancole.com/2025/02/democrats-genocide-democracy.html.

83 Wilderson, *Red, White & Black*, 37–8.

84 Montaigne, *The Complete Essays of Montaigne*, 383; Fanon, *Black Skin*, 206.

85 Diawara, "One World," 5.

86 Wilderson, *Red, White & Black*, 58.

87 As Wilderson points out in his "auto-theory" *Afropessimism*, he has changed the names or depicted some as composites, so Sameer may be doing theoretical work for Afropessimist Wilderson.

88 Wilderson, *Afropessimism*, 10.

89 Wilderson, *Afropessimism*, 11–12.

90 "I, as a Black person (if person, subject, being are appropriate, since Human is not), am both barred from the denouement of social and historical redemption and needed if redemption is to attain any form of coherence" (Wilderson, *Afropessimism*, 12).

91 Baldwin, "A Report from Occupied Territory."

92 Bayan Abusneineh, "(Re)Producing the Israeli (European) Body: Zionism, Anti-Black Racism and the Depo-Provera Affair," *Feminist Review*, no. 128 (2021): 96–113; Moran Nakar, "Black Lives Matter: Ethiopian Israelis Compare and Contrast Struggle with US," *Middle East Eye*, June 11, 2020. https://www.middleeast eye.net/news/black-lives-matter-israel-ethiopian-police-brutality; Jemima Pierre, "Zionism, Anti-Blackness, and the Struggle for Palestine: Jemima Pierre on the Boycott," *Black Agenda Report*, November 18, 2015. https://www.blackagendarep ort.com/zionism_antiblackness_palestine_boycott.

93 Mumia Abu-Jamal, "Black in Gaza," *Change Links*, April 2024. https://change-links. org/black-in-gaza-by-mumia-abu-jamal/; Marc Lamont Hill, "From Ferguson to Palestine," *Biography* 41, no. 4 (2018): 942–57.

94 J. Kēhaulani Kauanui, "Tracing Historical Specificity: Race and the Colonial Politics of (In)Capacity," *American Quarterly* 69, no. 2 (2017): 259.

95 Kauanui, "Tracing Historical Specificity," 257.

96 Nandita Sharma and Cynthia Wright, "Decolonizing Resistance, Challenging Colonial States," *Social Justice* 35, no. 3 (2009): 121.

97 Yossi Mekelberg, "The Plight of Ethiopian Jews in Israel," *BBC*, May 25, 2015. https://www.bbc.com/news/world-middle-east-32813056.

98 Wilderson, *Afropessimism*, 217.

99 Though Wilderson often stresses that anti-Blackness is not a question of identity but structure, the two are inseparable; a similar point is made by settler colonial scholars who argue after Patrick Wolfe that the settler invasion is a "structure not an event" (Patrick Wolfe, "Settler Colonialism and the Elimination of the Native," *Journal of Genocide Research* 8, no. 4 [2006]: 388); not unlike that of slavery, the afterlife of settler colonialism persists.

100 W. E. B. Du Bois, *Black Reconstruction in America* (New York: The Free Press, 1998), 700.

101 Edward W. Said, *The Question of Palestine* (New York: Vintage Books, 1992), xxviii.

102 Diawara, "One World," 5. Yes to multiplicity, but it shouldn't be simply opposed to unity. I believe in Palestinian unity, captured by the chant, "From the river to the sea, Palestine will be free."

103 Wilderson, *Afropessimism*, 217.

Chapter 3

1 "I ... fundamentally don't believe Black peoples have any coalition partners" (Frank Willderson and Tiffany Lethabo King, "Staying Ready for Black Study: A Conversation," in *Otherwise Worlds: Against Settler Colonialism and Anti-Blackness*, ed. Tiffany Lethabo King, Jenell Navarro, and Andrea Smith [Durham: Duke University Press, 2020], 65).

2 Hartman and Wilderson, "The Position of the Unthought," 190.

3 Hartman and Wilderson, "The Position of the Unthought," 190, emphasis added.

4 NPR, "Transcript: Barack Obama's Speech on Race," *NPR*, March 18, 2008. https://www.npr.org/2008/03/18/88478467/transcript-barack-obamas-spe ech-on-race.

5 See Martin Heidegger, *The Fundamental Concepts of Metaphysics*, trans. William Mcneill and Nicholas Walker (Bloomington: Indiana University Press, 1995), 197–226.

6 "The fact that more than half of the young black men in any large American city are currently under the control of the criminal justice system (or saddled with criminal records) is not—as many argue—just a symptom of poverty or poor choices, but rather evidence of a new racial caste system at work" (Michelle Alexander, *The New Jim Crow: Mass Incarceration in the Age of Colorblindness* [New York: The New Press, 2010], 16).

7 Wilderson, *Red, White & Black*, 231–2.

8 As George Yancy pointedly notes, "No matter how white people feel alienated from the normativity of their whiteness, no matter how 'pro-Black,' no matter how white

abolitionist (race traitorous) they are in their ideological emphasis, they will not be mistaken for a 'nigger' " (Yancy, *Black Bodies, White Gazes*, 12).

9 Fanon describes the obverse version of gnawing when it comes to the colonized: "All this gnawing at the existence of the colonized tends to make of life something resembling an incomplete death" (Frantz Fanon, *A Dying Colonialism*, trans. Haakon Chevalier [New York: Grove Press, 1965], 128).

10 Mbembe, *Critique of Black Reason*, 6.

11 Mbembe, *Critique of Black Reason*, 6.

12 James Baldwin, "The Fire Next Time," in *Baldwin: Collected Essays*, ed. Toni Morrison (New York: Library of America, 1998), 340.

13 Qtd. in Michael R. Fischbach, *Black Power and Palestine: Transnational Countries of Color* (Stanford: Stanford University Press, 2018), 117.

14 Jared Sexton, "The *Vel* of Slavery: Tracking the Figure of the Unsovereign," in *Otherwise Worlds: Against Settler Colonialism and Anti-Blackness*, ed. Tiffany Lethabo King, Jenell Navarro, and Andrea Smith (Durham: Duke University Press, 2020), 108–9.

15 Nahum Dimitri Chandler, *X: The Problem of the Negro as a Problem for Thought* (New York: Fordham University Press, 2013), 117.

16 Jacques Derrida, "Autoimmunity: Real and Symbolic Suicides—A Dialogue with Jacques Derrida," in *Philosophy in a Time of Terror: Dialogues with Jürgen Habermas and Jacques Derrida*, ed. Giovanna Borradori (Chicago: University of Chicago Press, 2004), 191n14.

17 David Gilbert, Laura Whitehorn, and Marilyn Buck, *Enemies of the State: An Interview with Anti-Imperialist Political Prisoners* (Montreal: Abraham Guillen & Arm the Spirit, 2002), 54.

18 Baldwin, "The Fire Next Time," 294.

19 James Yaki Sayles, *Meditations on Frantz Fanon's Wretched of the Earth* (Montreal: Kersplebedeb, 2010), 181.

20 Baldwin, "A Talk to Teachers," in *Baldwin: Collected Essays*, ed. Toni Morrison (New York: Library of America, 1998), 678.

21 There is a similar push to limit the teaching of Palestine in public schools. Here white supremacists hide behind a defense of Jews against anti-Semitism. See Shaanth Nanguneri, "In California Schools, Palestinian History Is Off-Limits," *The Nation*, November 20, 2023. https://www.thenation.com/article/society/califor nia-ethnic-studies-palestine/; Marianne Dhenin, "CA Educators Are Resisting Anti-Palestine Bills Pushing 'Academic Police State,'" *Truthout*, August 20, 2024. https://truthout.org/articles/ca-educators-are-resisting-anti-palestine-bills-pushing-academic-police-state/.

22 Baldwin, "White Man's Guilt," in *Baldwin: Collected Essays*, ed. Toni Morrison (New York: Library of America, 1998), 722–3.

23 "The real meaning and history of Manifest Destiny, for example, is nothing less than calculated and deliberate genocide. But American folklore, which has seduced American history into a radiant stupor, transforms this slaughter into an heroic legend" (Baldwin, *The Evidence of Things Not Seen* [New York: Holt, Rinehart and Winston, 1985], 42).

24 Gessen, "The Chilling Consequences."

25 Saroj Giri, "From the October Revolution to the Naxalbari Movement: Understanding Political Subjectivity," in *Of Concepts and Methods: "On Postisms" and Other Essays*, ed. K. Murali (Ajith) (Paris: Foreign Languages Press, 2020), 11; see also

Slavoj Žižek, "Subjective Destitution in Art and Politics: From Being-Towards-Death to Undeadness," *Enrahonar* 70 (2023): 75–6.

26 Fanon, *Black Skin*, 89, 118.

27 As discussed in Chapter 1, the *Muselmann* captures this sense of radical unfreedom. Devastated by starvation, the *Muselmann*'s objecthood is legible only as pure abjection and facelessness. This terrific and horrific image now circulates in Gaza, constituting a devastating reality engineered every step of the way by the Israeli killing machine.

28 Neil Roberts, *Freedom as Marronage* (Chicago: The University of Chicago Press, 2015), 118.

29 Moten, "Blackness and Nothingness (Mysticism in the Flesh)," *South Atlantic Quarterly* 112, no. 4 (2013): 772.

30 "Decolonization is truly the creation of new men … The 'thing' colonized becomes a man through the very process of liberation" (Fanon, *The Wretched of the Earth*, 2).

31 Fanon, *Black Skin*, 206, translation modified.

32 Stefano Harney and Fred Moten, *The Undercommons: Fugitive Planning & Black Study* (New York: Minor Compositions, 2013), 42.

33 Giri, "From the October Revolution," 11.

34 Derek Hook, "Death-Bound Subjectivity: Fanon's Zone of Nonbeing and the Lacanian Death Drive," *Subjectivity* 13 (2020): 367.

35 Todd McGowan, *Universality and Political Identity* (Columbia: Columbia University Press, 2020), 149.

36 Bouteldja, *Whites, Jews, and Us,* 44. James Baldwin shifts the register of whiteness, making it not a question of color but decision and ethical orientation: "White is a moral choice. It's up to you to be as white as you want to be and pay the price of that ticket" (James Baldwin, "Black English: A Dishonest Argument," in *The Cross of Redemption: Uncollected Writings*, ed. Randall Keenan [New York: Pantheon, 2010], 128).

37 Yancy, *Black Bodies, White Gazes*, 34.

38 Judith Butler makes a similar observation about Trumpism: "I see a kind of restoration fantasy at play in many right-wing movements in the U.S. People want to go back to the idea of being a white country or the idea of the patriarchal family, the principle that marriages are for heterosexuals. I call it a nostalgic fury for an impossible past" (Judith Butler, "Judith Butler, Philosopher: 'If You Sacrifice a Minority Like Trans People, You Are Operating Within a Fascist Logic,'" *El País*, December 15, 2024. https://english.elpais.com/culture/2024-12-15/judith-butler-philosopher-if-you-sacrifice-a-minority-like-trans-people-you-are-operating-within-a-fascist-logic.html). Fascist nostalgia yearns for a better world, a utopian past that serves simultaneously as a critique of the present and a blueprint for the future. White days are back on the agenda, liberated from the governmental clutches of DEI and the teachings of CRT. What Svetlana Boym calls "restorative nostalgia" characterizes the MAGA movement. It dreams of "a transhistorical reconstruction of the lost home"—in this case, a "pristine" America (Svetlana Boym, *The Future of Nostalgia* [New York: Basic Books, 2001], xviii). See Michael Grasso, "Donald Trump and the '80s Aesthetic," *Jacobin*, August 9, 2024. https://jacobin.com/2024/08/donald-trump-nostalgia-80s-aesthetic.

39 Fanon, *Black Skin*, 91. See also: "European culture has an imago of the black man that makes him responsible for every possible conflictual situation" (Fanon, *Black Skin*, 146).

40 As Lacan makes clear the "relation between the subject and the phallus … forms without regard to the anatomical distinction between the sexes" (Lacan, "The Signification of the Phallus," in *Écrits: The First Complete Edition in English*, trans. Bruce Fink [New York: Norton, 2006], 576).

41 Slavoj Žižek, *For They Know Not What They Do: Enjoyment as a Political Factor* (New York: Verso, 2008), 123.

42 Jacques Lacan, *On Feminine Sexuality, The Limits of Love and Knowledge, 1972–1973: Encore, The Seminar of Jacques Lacan, Book XX*, trans. Bruce Fink (New York: Norton, 1998), 78.

43 Žižek, *For They Know Not What They Do*, xxii.

44 Žižek, *For They Know Not What They Do*, xxii.

45 Žižek, *In Defense of Lost Causes*, 480n30.

46 Slavoj Žižek, *First as Tragedy, Then as Farce* (New York: Verso, 2009), 120.

47 Slavoj Žižek, *The Parallax View* (Cambridge: MIT Press, 2006), 103.

48 Wilderson, "Afropessimism," 40–1.

49 Fanon, *Black Skin*, 90.

50 Harney and Moten, *The Undercommons*, 125–6.

51 Wilderson, *Red, White & Black*, 28.

52 Wilderson, *Afropessimism*, 222.

53 Wilderson, "Afro-Pessimism and the End of Redemption," *Humanities Futures. Franklin Humanities Institute: Duke University*, October 20, 2015. https://humanities futures.org/papers/afro-pessimism-end-redemption/.

54 For non-Black people of color, an ontological remedy is, in principle, always available to them. Their current impoverished condition is the result of their dehumanization or animalization and not of their being as such: "Above all, Afropessimists believe Blackness is inextricably bound up with dehumanization. As opposed to other groups, Black people do not exist outside their own dehumanization" (Norman Ajari, *Darkening Blackness: Race, Gender, Class, and Pessimism in 21st Century Black Thought*, trans. Matthew B. Smith [Cambridge: Polity Press, 2023], 61).

55 See Jared Sexton, "People-of-Color-Blindness: Notes on the Afterlife of Slavery," *Social Text* 28, no. 2 (103) (2010): 31–56.

56 Sexton, *Amalgamation Schemes: Antiblackness and the Critique of Multiracialism* (Minneapolis: University of Minnesota Press, 2008), 293n9.

57 George Yancy, "Afropessimism Forces Us to Rethink Our Most Basic Assumptions About Society," *Truthhout*, September 14, 2022. https://truthout.org/articles/afrope ssimism-forces-us-to-rethink-our-most-basic-assumptions-about-society/.

58 Wilderson, *Afropessimism*, 41.

59 Noura Erakat, "Roundtable on Anti-Blackness and Black-Palestinian Solidarity," *Jadaliyya*, June 3, 2015. https://www.jadaliyya.com/Details/32145/Roundta ble-on-Anti-Blackness-and-Black-Palestinian-Solidarity.

60 Erakat, "Roundtable on Anti-Blackness."

61 Sigmund Freud, *Beyond the Pleasure Principle*, trans. James Strachey (New York: Norton, 1961), 3.

62 Slavoj Žižek, "On Lacan as Philosopher," *The Dark Fantastic*, May 4, 2013. https://socialecologies.wordpress.com/2013/05/04/slavoj-zizek-on-lacan-as-philosop her/#:~:text=For%20Lacan%2C%20the%20discourse%20of,are%20constitut ive%20of%20our%20lives.

63 Fanon, *Black Skin*, 204.

64 Fanon, *The Wretched of the World*, 239.

65 Wilderson, *Red, White & Black*, 337.

66 Wilderson, *Red, White & Black*, 338.

67 Chandler, *X: The Problem of the Negro*, 137.

68 Aimé Césaire, *A Tempest*, trans. Richard Miller (New York: TCG Translations, 2002), 57. Fanon also notes the decolonizing purge of the enemy's venom: "In the colonial context the colonist only quits undermining the colonized once the latter have proclaimed loud and clear that white values reign supreme. In the period of decolonization the colonized masses thumb their noses at these very values, shower them with insults and vomit them up" (Fanon, *The Wretched of the World*, 8).

69 Maldonado-Torres, "Outline of Ten Theses."

70 "We must study how colonization works to *decivilize* the colonizer, to *brutalize* him in the true sense of the word, to degrade him, to awaken him to buried instincts, to covetousness, violence, race hatred, and moral relativism" (Césaire, *Discourse on Colonialism*, 35).

71 Fanon, *The Wretched of the Earth*, 94, translation modified.

72 Fanon, *The Wretched of the Earth*, 94.

73 Fanon, *The Wretched of the Earth*, 12.

74 "This colossal task, which consists of reintroducing man into the world, man in his totality, will be achieved with the crucial help of the European masses who would do well to confess that they have often rallied behind the position of our common masters on colonial issues. In order to do this, the European masses must first of all decide to wake up, put on their thinking caps and stop playing the irresponsible game of Sleeping Beauty" (Fanon, *The Wretched of the Earth*, 62).

75 See Too Black and Rasul A. Mowatt, *Laundering Black Rage: The Washing of Black Death, People, Property, and Profits* (New York: Routledge, 2014).

76 Harney and Moten, *The Undercommons*, 128.

77 Russell Rickford. "'To Build a New World': Black American Internationalism and Palestine Solidarity," *Journal of Palestine Studies* 48, no. 4 (2019): 53.

78 Harney and Moten, *The Undercommons*, 133.

79 "Moving Towards Home" from *Directed by Desire: The Complete Poems of June Jordan*, Copper Canyon Press © Christopher D. Meyer, 2007. Reprinted by permission of the Frances Goldin Literary Agency.

80 The negated list obviously still conveys the horror visited on the Palestinian refugees.

81 Julie Quiroz-Martinez, "Poetry Is a Political Act," *Color Lines*, December 15, 1998. https://colorlines.com/article/poetry-political-act/.

82 Nasser Abourahme and Iyko Day, "Palestine After Analogy," *Critical Ethnic Studies* 9, no. 1 (2024). https://manifold.umn.edu/read/ces0901-01/section/6832dc1e-d3fe-4c59-839d-71007c7261c3

83 Keith P. Feldman, *A Shadow over Palestine: The Imperial Life of Race in America* (Minneapolis: University of Minnesota Press, 2015), 216.

84 Jodi Melamed, "Making Racialized and Gendered Difference Work for Neoliberal Multiculturalism," in *Strange Affinities: The Gender and Sexual Politics of Comparative Racialization*, ed. Grace Kyungwon Hong and Roderick A. Ferguson (Durham: Duke University Press, 2011), 79. Marina Magloire also casts Jordan's intervention as a destabilization of "a marketable notion of identity—as static, extractable, something that can be bought and sold" (Marina Magloire, "Who Might We Become for Each Other?" *Jewish Currents*, June 17, 2025, https://jewishcurre

nts.org/who-might-we-become-for-each-other).

85 Kaja Silverman, *The Threshold of the Visible World* (London: Routledge, 2013), 23.

86 Jordan, "Life After Lebanon," in *Some of Us Did Not Die: New and Selected Essays* (New York: Civitas Books, 2002), 193.

87 June Jordan avoids the pitfalls of empathy as formulated by Saidiya Hartman: "It's as though in order to come to any recognition of common humanity, the other must be assimilated, ... utterly displaced and effaced" (Wilderson and Hartman, "The Position of the Unthought," 189).

88 Slavoj Žižek, "Foreword: The Importance of Theory," in *Žižek on Race: Toward an Anti-Racist Future*, by Zahi Zalloua (New York: Bloomsbury, 2020), xii.

89 Gideon Levy, "The IDF's Own Sickening 'Zone of Interest' in the Heart of Gaza," *Haaretz*, December 26, 2024. https://www.haaretz.com/opin ion/2024-12-26/ty-article-opinion/.premium/the-idfs-own-sickening-zone-of-inter est-in-the-heart-of-gaza/00000193-ff80-df5b-a9b3-ff857a4a0000.

90 Mohammed al-Hajjar, "In Gaza, You Don't Only See Death. You Smell It. You Breathe It," *Middle East Eye*, January 14, 2024. https://www.middleeasteye.net/ opinion/gaza-dont-only-see-death-smell-breathe-it.

91 Yoel Elizur, "'When You Leave Israel and Enter Gaza, You Are God': Inside the Minds of IDF Soldiers Who Commit War Crimes," *Haaretz*, December 23, 2024. https://www.haaretz.com/opinion/2024-12-23/ty-article-opinion/.premium/ when-you-enter-gaza-you-are-god-inside-the-minds-of-idf-soldiers-who-com mit-war-crimes/00000193-f2a4-dc18-a3db-fee62b540000.

92 Elizur, "When You Leave Israel."

93 Butler, *Precarious Life: The Powers of Mourning and Violence* (New York: Verso, 2004), 33.

94 Feldman, *A Shadow over Palestine*, 185–219.

95 Bouteldja, *Whites, Jews, and Us*, 43.

96 MEE staff, "Israel-Palestine War: Far-Right Minister Smotrich Calls for 'Sterile Zones' Free of Palestinians near Settlements," *Middle East Eye*, November 6, 2023. https:// www.middleeasteye.net/news/israel-palestine-war-far-right-smotrich-calls-ster ile-zones-west-bank.

97 Edward Alexander, "Professor of Terror," *Commentary*, August 1989. https://www. commentary.org/articles/edward-alexander/professor-of-terror/.

98 Jordan, "Life After Lebanon," 191.

99 Commenting on Jordan's letter, Barbara Smith said that it was overtly antagonistic and could risk splintering the "multiracial" Women's Movement, that there was already "a lot of tension between Black and Jewish women in the early 1980s"; Smith also acknowledged her doubts about taking the "same decision today" (Joseph R. Fitzgerald and Jaimee A. Swift, "On the Record: Barbara Smith on Palestine, June Jordan, Audre Lorde, and Adrienne Rich," *Black Women Radicals*. https://squid-fox-bzpx.squarespace.com/blog-feed/on-the-record-barb ara-smith-on-palestine-june-jordan-audre-lorde-and-adrienne-rich).

100 Jordan, "June Jordan on Israel and Lebanon: A Response to Adrienne Rich," *The Massachusetts Review*, September 19, 2024. https://massreview.org/node/12147/.

101 Jordan, "June Jordan on Israel and Lebanon."

102 Jordan, "June Jordan on Israel and Lebanon."

103 Harfouch and Schotten, "Sayegh's Critique of Zionism."

104 Marina Magloire, "Moving Towards Life," *Los Angeles Review of Books*, August 7, 2024. https://lareviewofbooks.org/article/moving-towards-life/. See also

Valerie Kinloch, *June Jordan: Her Life and Letters. Women Writers of Color* (Westport: Praeger, 2006), 162.

105 Morrison, "Nobel Lecture."

106 Morrison, "Nobel Lecture."

107 Evelyn T. Beck, Nancy K. Bereano, Gloria Z. Greenfield, Melanie Kaye, Irena Klepfisz, Bernice Mennis, and Adrienne Rich, "…What does Zionism Mean?" *Off Our Backs* 12, no. 7 (July 1982): 21.

108 Evelyn T. Beck, Nancy K. Bereano, Melanie Kaye, Irena Klepfisz, Bernice Mennis, and Adrienne Rich, "Di Vilde Chayes: Zionists Deplore Killings in Lebanon and Criticize Nature of Anti-Israel Protests," *Off Our Backs* 12, no. 9 (October 1982): 27.

109 Beck, Bereano, Greenfield, Kaye, Klepfisz, Mennis, and Rich, "…What does Zionism Mean?"

110 Jordan, "June Jordan on Israel and Lebanon."

111 Jordan, "June Jordan on Israel and Lebanon."

112 Beck, Bereano, Greenfield, Kaye, Klepfisz, Mennis, and Rich, "Di Vilde Chayes."

113 Slavoj Žižek, "The Gentrification of Gaza," *Substack: Žižek Goads and Prods*, January 11, 2024. https://slavoj.substack.com/p/the-gentrification-of-gaza.

114 With Jewish Voice for Peace, we witness an alternate vision of Judaism, an anti-Zionist Judaism that opens to Palestinians: "We refuse to accept a world in which only some deaths are grieved, in which the humanity of only some people is recognized. We recognize the enormous discrepancy in Palestinian lives lost, compared to Israelis. And we do not waver from our core belief that every life is a universe" (https://www.jewishvoiceforpeace.org/2024/09/03/all-life-is-precious/); Brant Rosen, "Amid Israel's Brutality in Gaza, It's Time to Commit to Anti-Zionism," *Truthout*, December 5, 2023. https://truthout.org/articles/amid-israels-brutal ity-in-gaza-its-time-to-commit-to-anti-zionism/.

115 Can you imagine the reaction of the self-righteous Stefanik if any of the disgraced university presidents—who displayed a shocking level of ignorance about Palestine—during the congressional hearings on campus anti-Semitism, quoted June Jordan back to her, educating her and America writ large that Intifada means uprising for social justice (not genocide), indexing a sense of justice akin to what sparked the civil rights movement and BLM?

116 Adrienne Rich came to break with Zionist ideology, and, in 2009, she even endorsed the US Campaign for the Academic and Cultural Boycott of Israel.

117 Later in her life, Lorde did also moderate her views on Palestine. In her 1989 Oberlin commencement address, three years before her death, Lorde expressed support for Palestinian self-determination, and pushed her audience members to exert pressure on their elected officials to realize this necessary end: "Encouraging your congresspeople to press for a peaceful solution in the Middle East, and for recognition of the rights of the Palestinian people, is not altruism, it is survival" (qtd. in Magloire, "Moving Towards Life").

118 Lorde herself made her critique of imperialism clear, but when it came to Israel, her radicalism typically halted for most of her academic life, falling prey to "the Israel exception": criticize imperialist and colonial powers as much as you want, but simply don't include Israel among this lot of oppressors.

119 Jordan draws a further distinction between the many Israeli Jews who, ashamed of their government, took the streets and Rich's inaction: "Does she now [claim responsibility], after 400,000 Israelis plunged into the streets to demand a tribunal to investigate Israeli function in the massacre of the people of those miserable refugee camps, does she now join that outcry with her own? She does not" (Jordan, "June Jordan on Israel and Lebanon"). It would be an understatement to say the genocidal war on Gaza has not produced the same kind of outrage from Israelis.

120 Alex de Waal, "Starvation in Gaza," *London Review of Books*, May 14, 2025. https://www.lrb.co.uk/blog/2025/may/starvation-in-gaza; Lorenzo Tondo, "Gaza Is 'Hungriest Place on Earth' with All Its People at Risk of Famine, Says UN," *The Guardian*, May 30, 2025. https://www.theguardian.com/world/2025/may/30/gaza-hungriest-place-earth-all-people-risk-famine-un.

121 Ahmed Moor, "There Are More Child Amputees in Gaza than Anywhere Else in the World. What Can the Future Hold for Them?" *The Guardian*, March 27, 2025. https://www.theguardian.com/world/ng-interactive/2025/mar/27/gaza-palestine-children-injuries.

122 See "Joint Letter to End the Forced Starvation and Targeted Killing of Journalists in Gaza," *Al Jazeera*, August 6, 2025. https://network.aljazeera.net/en/press-relea ses/joint-letter-end-forced-starvation-and-targeted-killing-journalists-gaza; Robert Greenwald, *Gaza: Journalists Under Fire* (2025).

123 Illy Pe'ery, "Israeli Soldiers Used an 80-Year-Old Gazan as a Human Shield. Then They Killed Him," *+972*, February 16, 2025. https://www.972mag.com/gaza-human-shield-mosquito/; Sam Mednick and Samy Magdy, "Israeli Use of Human Shields in Gaza Was Systematic, Soldiers and Former Detainees Tell the AP," *Associated Press*, May 24, 2025. https://apnews.com/article/israel-palestini ans-hamas-war-army-human-shields-80f358dd2c87a1123f26ffada159701c.

124 US Campaign For Palestinian Rights Action, "Alert: Israel Wants to Build a Concentration Camp City," July 9, 2025 [email].

125 Yahya Abou-Ghazala, Jeremy Diamond, Abeer Salman, Gianluca Mezzofiore, Mohammad Al-Sawalhi, and Madalena Araújo, "'Death and Hunger': Videos, Expert Analysis and Witnesses Point to Israeli Gunfire in Gaza Aid Site Shooting," *CNN*, June 5, 2025. https://www.cnn.com/2025/06/04/middleeast/israel-milit ary-gaza-aid-shooting-intl-invs; Amy Goodman and Juan González, "'One Mass Casualty After Another': U.S. Doctor in Gaza on Ongoing Israeli Massacres at Aid Sites," *Democracy Now!* June 25, 2025. https://www.democracynow. org/2025/6/25/gaza_healthcare; Amnesty International, "GAZA: Starvation or Gunfire—This Is Not a Humanitarian Response," *Amnesty International*, July 1, 2025. https://www.amnesty.org/en/latest/news/2025/07/gaza-starvation-or-gunf ire-this-is-not-a-humanitarian-response/.

126 Maha Hussaini, "Israeli Torture: Urinating on Palestinian Prisoners, Burying Them Alive and Beating the Sick," *Middle East Eye*, March 9, 2025. https:// www.middleeasteye.net/news/israeli-torture-urinating-palestinian-prisoners-bury ing-them-alive-and-beating-sick; Amnesty International, "Israel Must End Mass Incommunicado Detention and Torture of Palestinians from Gaza," *Amnesty International*, July 18, 2024. https://www.amnesty.org/en/latest/news/2024/07/ israel-must-end-mass-incommunicado-detention-and-torture-of-palestini ans-from-gaza/.

127 Michael F. Brown, "Ben-Gvir Touts Bombing Food Depots While at Mar-a-Lago," *The Electronic Intifada*, April 30, 2025. https://electronicintifada.net/blogs/mich ael-f-brown/ben-gvir-touts-bombing-food-depots-while-mar-lago.

128 Nick Turse, "Israel's Bloody Record of Bombing Schools in Gaza," *Intercept*, October 6, 2024. https://theintercept.com/2024/10/06/israel-bombing-scho

ols-children-gaza-education/.

129 Patrick Kingsley, "Strike on Hospital Highlights Israeli Attacks on Gaza Health System," *The New York Times*, May 14, 2025. https://www.nytimes.com/2025/05/14/world/middleeast/israel-medical-facility-strikes-gaza-hamas.html; Kavitha Chekuru, "Israeli Forces Bombed Two Gaza Hospitals in One Day," *Drop Site*, May 14, 2025. https://www.dropsitenews.com/p/european-hospital-nasser-gaza-israeli-airstrikes; Ghada Ageel, "Israel Is Killing Doctors so Gaza Can Never Heal from Genocide," *Al Jazeera*, July 9, 2025. https://www.aljazeera.com/opinions/2025/7/9/israel-is-killing-doctors-so-gaza-can-never-heal-from-genocide.

130 Ghada Ageel, "Israel Is Burning Gaza's Children. And the World Lets It Happen," *Al Jazeera*, May 29, 2025. https://www.aljazeera.com/opinions/2025/5/29/israel-is-burning-gazas-children-and-the-world-lets-it-happen; Tareq S. Hajjaj, " 'We Smelled the Stench of Burning Human Flesh': Israel Burns 8 Children to Death in Gaza 'Safe Zone,' " *Mondoweiss*, April 18, 2025. https://mondoweiss.net/2025/04/we-smelled-the-stench-of-burning-human-flesh-israel-burns-8-children-to-death-in-gaza-safe-zone/.

131 Some may wonder if "peace-maker" Yitzhak Rabin represents an exception, but we must not forget that the Oslo Accords were overdetermined to fail, that Rabin's framing of the "peace process" always meant the further dispossession of the Palestinian people. And we must recall as well that when he was the Israeli defense minister, during the First Intifada in 1987, he callously instructed his army commanders to break the bones of Palestinian protesters. From bonebreakers to genocidaires, Israel's prime ministers may look and sound different, but they have all been committed to the erasure of Palestinians, by whatever means necessary. See Ali Abunimah, " 'Force, Might and Beatings': Indelible Images of the First Intifada," *The Electronic Intifada*, December 9, 2011. https://electronicintifada.net/blogs/ali-abunimah/force-might-and-beatings-indelible-images-first-intifada.

132 Liberals, for instance, are fond of objecting to Netanyahu's policies in order to shield Israel from critique, intimating "an Israel after Netanyahu."

133 Jordan, "June Jordan on Israel and Lebanon."

134 Malm, *The Destruction of Palestine Is the Destruction of the Earth*.

135 Upfront, "Angela Davis: 'Palestine Is a Moral Litmus Test for the World,'" *Al Jazeera*, October 27, 2023. https://www.aljazeera.com/program/upfront/2023/10/27/angela-davis-palestine-is-a-moral-litmus-test-for-the-world.

136 Frantz Fanon, "The North African Syndrome," in *Toward the African Revolution*, trans. Haakon Chevalier (New York: Grove Press, 1967), 7. Fanon always sought to contextualize the mental illness of the (internally) colonized, tying it to their oppression. Under a "triumphant colonization," the colonized will experience the colonizer's normality as abnormality and will suffer the fate of "psychic institutions" (Fanon, *The Wretched of the World*, 182).

137 Nigel C. Gibson, "Situational Awareness Fanon and Gaza," *Spectre*, November 7, 2024. https://spectrejournal.com/situational-awareness/.

138 While civilizational Zionists view Palestinians as ontologically degraded (they're inferior creatures, human animals, savages, irrational, vicious, etc.), the Israeli government sought to give legal or ontical support to the destruction of Palestinians by loosening its rules covering collateral damage or the killing of civilians. See Yuval Abraham, " 'Lavender': The AI machine Directing Israel's Bombing Spree in Gaza," *+972 Magazine*, April 3, 2024. https://www.972mag.com/lavender-ai-israeli-army-gaza/; Patrick Kingsley, Natan Odenheimer, Bilal Shbair, Ronen Bergman,

John Ismay, Sheera Frenkel, and Adam Sella, "Israel Loosened Its Rules to Bomb Hamas Fighters, Killing Many More Civilians," *The New York Times*, December 26, 2024. https://www.nytimes.com/2024/12/26/world/middleeast/israel-hamas-gaza-bombing.html.

139 Slavoj Žižek and Yanis Varoufakis, "'Israel Needed War': Slavoj Žižek Meets Yanis Varoufakis (Part 3)." https://www.youtube.com/watch?v=zkKFFueepMg.

140 B'Tselem, "The World Must Stop the Ethnic Cleansing of Northern Gaza," *B'Tselem*, October 22, 2024. https://www.btselem.org/press_releases/20241022_the_world_must_stop_the_ethnic_cleansing_of_northern_gaza.

141 Fanon, *The Wretched of the Earth*, 16.

142 The major culprit here is, of course, the United States with its repeated abuse of the veto power, thwarting multiple ceasefire resolutions from being adopted by the UN Security Council. But, as Mjriam Abu Samra and Sara Troian point out, the problem with international law is also baked into the United Nations itself: "The UN Security Council's veto system is the most ostentatious admission of the post-WWII system's renewed commitment to the hegemony of superpowers" (Mjriam Abu Samra and Sara Troian, "Palestine Beyond the Colonial Logic of International Law," *Mondoweiss*, April 2, 2025. https://mondoweiss.net/2025/04/palestine-beyond-the-colonial-logic-of-international-law/.

143 Kevin Ochieng Okoth similarly observes that "at times, it might sound like [the Afropessimists] Fanon is theorising Blackness as an eternal and *essentialist* category. But this isn't the case" (Kevin Ochieng Okoth, *Red Africa: Reclaiming Revolutionary Black Politics* [New York: Verso, 2023], 79–80).

144 "Never solidarity before criticism" (Said, *Representations of the Intellectual: The 1993 Reith Lectures* [New York: Vintage Books, 1996], 32).

145 Balibar, "The Genocide in Gaza."

146 Janine Jones, "Editor's Introduction / Présentation du numéro," *Simone de Beauvoir Studies* 34 (2023): 172–3; Saqib Bhatti, "I Am Done Voting for the Lesser of Two Evils. I Will Not Vote for Joe Biden in 2024," *In These Times*, October 25, 2023. https://inthesetimes.com/article/muslims-palestinians-vote-biden-2024-election-bhatti.

147 Jones, "Editor's Introduction," 172–3.

148 Franco "Bifo" Berardi, "The American Unconscious and the Disintegration of the Western World," *Critical Inquiry*, December 9, 2024. https://critinq.wordpress.com/2024/12/09/the-american-unconscious-and-the-disintegration-of-the-western-world/.

149 Ironically, Donald Trump and the alt-Right repeatedly and deliberately distort the positions of the liberal center, whose political leadership are very friendly to the marketplace, calling them Marxists and far-Left ideologues. See Slavoj Žižek, "From MAGA to MEGA: After Trump's Victory," *Substack: Žižek Goads and Prods*, November 9, 2024. https://slavoj.substack.com/p/from-maga-to-mega-after-trumps-victory.

150 Dave Zirin, "It's Not Antisemitic to Say That Israel Is Responsible for the Unfolding Genocide in Gaza," *The Nation*, July 8, 2025. https://www.thenation.com/article/world/israel-antisemitism-genocide-christian-zionists/.

Conclusion: Pessimism and Repetition

1 Nasser Abourahme, "In Tune with Their Time," *Radical Philosophy* 2, no. 16 (2024): 13.

2 El Akkad, *One Day, Everyone Will Have Always Been Against This*, 17.

3 El Akkad, *One Day, Everyone Will Have Always Been Against This*, 18.

4 Alberto Toscano, "Defending the Indefensible," *In These Times*, July 11, 2025. https://inthesetimes.com/article/palestine-action-gaza-genocide-manufacture-cons ent-trump-zionist?link_id=3&can_id=839242f129045dcf95563791cad9b53c&sou rce=email-america-for-sale-everything-must-go-2&email_referrer=email_2810 645&email_subject=alberto-toscano-on-defending-the-indefensible&&.

5 Harfouch and Schotten, "Sayegh's Critique of Zionism."

6 Yancy, *Black Bodies, White Gazes*, 13.

7 See Slavoj Žižek, *The Courage of Hopelessness: Chronicles of a Year of Acting Dangerously* (New York: Allen Lane, 2017).

8 Said, *Reflections on Exile and Other Essays* (Cambridge: Harvard University Press, 2000), 553. See Žižek, *In Defense of Lost Causes*; Richard Falk, "On 'Lost Causes' and the Future of Palestine," *The Nation*, December 16, 2014. https://www.thenat ion.com/article/archive/lost-causes-and-future-palestine/.

9 Moten, *Stolen Life*, 153.

10 https://uscpr.org/activist-resource/from-palestine-to-mex ico-all-the-walls-have-got-to-go/.

11 Though the racist slogan "All Lives Matter" was a response to chant "Black Lives Matter," we should read it retroactively back into the white status quo. *I know very well that all human beings are alike, but all the same I believe whites are superior and that meritocracy is an ideal worth protecting.*

12 Ahmed, *The Feminist Killjoy Handbook*, 262.

13 Christina Sharpe, "The Shapes of Grief: Witnessing the Unbearable," *The Yale Review* 112, no. 3, (2024): 16.

14 Zadie Smith exemplified this model of reasoning, masquerading as an ethics of reading, an attentiveness to the most vulnerable on campus amid the pro-Palestine encampments. Smith framed and criminalized pro-Palestine protests as "weapons of mass destruction": "In the case of Israel/Palestine, language and rhetoric are and always have been weapons of mass destruction." More specifically, she singled out the Jewish student interpellated as Zionist, the object of uncare by pro-Palestinian students: "For it may well be—within the ethical zone of interest that is a campus, which was not so long ago defined as a safe space, delineated by the boundary of a generation's ethical ideas—*it may well be* that a Jewish student walking past the tents, who finds herself referred to as a Zionist, and then is warned to keep her distance, is, in that moment, the weakest participant in the zone" (Zadie Smith, "Shibboleth," *The New Yorker*, May 5, 2024. https://www.newyorker.com/news/ essay/shibboleth-the-role-of-words-in-the-campus-protests). Speaking of zones, the Jewish student evoked by Smith is likely comfortably dwelling in the zone of being (her position aligns with those in power) whereas the pro-Palestinian students, which include many Jewish students, are risking their (further) banishment to the zone of nonbeing. About a year later, Smith added her signature, along with a number of prominent authors, to a letter condemning Israel's war on Gaza as "genocidal," and called for an immediate ceasefire. I'm not sure this recent intervention will shift the argument in any meaningful way. We've already heard from multiple scholars on the question of genocide. If the cosigners wants to contribute generatively to the Palestinian plight, then I would suggest that they start by dismantling the Zionist narrative that still forms the letter's background, as it diagnoses the problem as "the genocidal policies of the current Israeli government," without questioning the genocidal structure of the Zionist state itself. The letter urges "a ceasefire which guarantees safety and justice for all Palestinians." Yes, but how do you move from stopping the genocide to provide justice for Palestinians? The letter ends with "This genocide implicates us all. We bear witness to the crimes of genocide, and we refuse to approve them by our silence" ("Writers Demand Immediate Gaza Ceasefire," *Medium*, May 27, 2025. https://medium.com/@horatioclare/writers-dem and-immediate-gaza-ceasefire-65ae44bd7241). Yes, the Gaza genocide touches us all, but the letter leaves us stuck in a liberal Zionist horizon—a Greater Israel without an active genocide—which, as I've argued, entails its own settler logic of elimination. See MEE staff, "'Hypocrisy': Zadie Smith Faces Backlash After Signing Letter Calling for Gaza Ceasefire," *Middle East Eye*, May 29, 2025. https://www.middleeasteye. net/trending/hypocrisy-zadie-smith-faces-backlash-after-signing-letter-ceasefire-call ing-gaza-ceasefire?utm_source=substack&utm_medium=email.

15 Ali Harb, "US Sanctions UN Expert Francesca Albanese over Israel Criticism," *Al Jazeera*, July 9, 2025. https://www.aljazeera.com/news/2025/7/9/us-sanctions-un-expert-albanese-over-israel-criticism.

16 Harb, "US Sanctions UN Expert Francesca Albanese."

17 The United States is not alone in its absurdist disposition. The UK has deemed the nonviolent group Palestine Action a terrorist group for its opposition to the Israeli genocidal campaign; the group was deemed beyond the pale when it damaged "property owned by, or connected to, Israeli arms company Elbit Systems" (Hil Aked, "Palestine Action: Peace Activists, Not Terrorists," *In These Times*, July 4, 2025. https://inthesetimes.com/article/palestine-action-terrorism-laws). Elbit Systems matters, peace activists for Palestine don't.

18 Fanon, *The Wretched of the Earth*, 8.

19 Peter Hudis, "Fanon's 'New Humanism': The Struggle for Alternatives to Capitalism," *Spectre*, May 16, 2025. https://spectrejournal.com/fanons-new-humanism/.

20 Nigel C. Gibson, *Fanon and the "Rationality of Revolt"* (Ottawa: Dajara Press, 2020), 3.

21 Žižek, *Violence*, 24.

22 Žižek, *Violence*, 11.

23 Fanon, *Black Skin*, 201.

24 Essa, "Cornel West: Black Lives Matter and the Fight Against US Empire Are One and the Same."

25 William Hartung, "Dr. King's 1967 Anti-War Speech Was Unpopular, but Prophetic," *Truthout*, January 18, 2022. https://www.commondreams.org/views/2022/01/18/ dr-kings-1967-anti-war-speech-was-unpopular-prophetic.

26 Cornel West, "Introduction: The Radical King We Don't Know," in Martin Luther King, Jr., *The Radical King*, ed. Cornel West (Boston: Beacon Press, 2015), x.

27 Hudis, "Fanon's 'New Humanism.'"

28 Nadia Bou Ali, "Measure Against Measure: Why Lacan Contra Foucault?" in *Lacan Contra Foucault: Subjectivity, Sex and Politics*, ed. Nadia Bou Ali (New York: Bloomsbury, 2019), 1.

29 Olúfẹ́mi O. Táíwò, *Elite Capture: How the Powerful Took over Identity Politics (and Everything Else)* (Chicago: Haymarket Books, 2022), 32.

30 Žižek, *Less Than Nothing*, 996.

31 Democratic leadership acknowledges the BLM movement but only to better contain it (namely its "faithful" Black voters)—the party has absolutely no desire to engage the demands of BLM.

32 Jacques Lacan, *The Seminar of Jacques Lacan: The Four Fundamental Concepts of Psychoanalysis*, ed. Jacques-Alain Miller, trans. Alan Sheridan (New York: Norton, 1978), 61.

33 Slavoj Žižek, *Freedom: A Disease Without Cure* (New York: Bloomsbury, 2023), 86.

34 As Ahmed points out in relation to liberal shame: "The subject that is shamed by its racism is ... also a subject that is proud about its shame. The very claim to feel bad (about this or that) also involved a self-perception of 'being good'" (Sara Ahmed, "The Politics of Bad Feelings," *Australian Critical Race and Whiteness Studies Association Journal* 1 [2005]: 81).

35 John Metta, "The Danger of the White American Liberal," *Al Jazeera*, September 1, 2017. https://www.aljazeera.com/features/2017/9/1/the-danger-of-the-white-ameri can-liberal.

36 As Martin Luther King rightly assessed decades ago about the severe political deficiencies of white moderates: "I must confess that over the past few years I have been gravely disappointed with the white moderate. I have almost reached the regrettable conclusion that the Negro's great stumbling block in his stride toward freedom is not the White Citizen's Counciler or the Ku Klux Klanner, but the white moderate, who is more devoted to 'order' than to justice; who prefers a negative peace which is the absence of tension to a positive peace which is the presence of justice; who constantly says, 'I agree with you in the goal you seek, but I cannot agree with your methods of direct action'" (Martin Luther King, Jr., *Why We Can't Wait* [London: Signet, 2001], 96–7).

37 Christina Greer, "Black Americans Are Not Surprised," *The New York Times*, April 7, 2025. https://www.nytimes.com/2025/04/07/opinion/black-americans-trump-polit ics.html.

38 Norman Solomon, "'Speaking Truth to Power' Is No Substitute for Taking Power," *Truthout*, March 13, 2019. https://truthout.org/articles/speak ing-truth-to-power-is-no-substitute-for-taking-power/.

39 This not about a fetishized nonviolence position; violence or armed resistance is not the problem insofar as liberals do not object in mass to arming Ukraine against the Russian invasion.

40 Alberto Toscano, "The War on Gaza and Israel's Fascism Debate," *Verso*, October 19, 2023. https://www.versobooks.com/blogs/news/the-war-on-gaza-and-israel-s-fascism-debate?srsltid=AfmBOooJxfEPWBUyq5TmQDHuqvFlgimz4GeqWEBAt v4ON2UxSyifl88B.

41 Chris Megerian, "Biden Says 'Order Must Prevail' During Campus Protests over the War in Gaza," *Associated Press*, May 2, 2024. https://apnews.com/article/ biden-silence-college-protests-police-gaza-israel-d5f3092671951c3bc2968b875 1c93ba6.

42 Megerian, "Biden Says 'Order Must Prevail.'"

43 Michael Arria, "What Anti-Palestinian Legislation to Look Out for in the New Congress," *Mondoweiss*, February 18, 2025. https://mondoweiss.net/2025/02/ what-anti-palestinian-legislation-to-look-out-for-in-the-new-congress/.

44 https://x.com/IfNotNowOrg/status/1448709689127030789.

45 See, for example, Zionist Organization of America, "The BLM Organization Files," *Zionist Organization of America*. https://zoa.org/the-blm-organization-files/.

46 Writing for *The American Mind*, a publication of the American conservative think tank The Claremont Institute, Samuel Lair ties CRT explicitly to settler-colonial studies, dubbing it CRT 2.0: "[Settler-colonial studies] is an ideology of sedition, which is why it fetishizes indigenous 'resistance and resilience.' Under these terms, the calls heard in far-flung corners of the world to 'kill the Boer' and liberate Palestine 'from the river to the sea' are just as much a threat to America as they are to Israel or South Africa" (Samuel Lair, "CRT 2.0," *The American Mind*, January 23, 2025. https://americanmind.org/salvo/crt-2-0/). Unrecognized white victimhood is the new fetish of the alt-Right. Trump masterfully exploited this white rage and envy for victimhood in his presidential runs. In office, the Trump administration granted refugee status to fifty-nine Afrikaners, white South Africans. The liberal center did express dismay at Trump's unfair and draconian policies on refugees, but its position on BDS and CRT 2.0 (settler-colonial studies) is identical to that of the alt-Right.

47 "I had hoped that the white moderate would understand that law and order exist for the purpose of establishing justice and that when they fail in this purpose they become the dangerously structured dams that block the flow of social progress" (King, *Why We Can't Wait*, 97). White moderates are not only not understanding but profiting affectively and economically from the lack of social progress.

48 Shannon Sullivan, "White Priority," *Critical Philosophy of Race* 5, no. 2 (2017): 171–82.

49 Michael R. Fischbach, "Black-Palestinian Solidarity and the Global Color Line," in *Race and the Question of Palestine*, ed. Lana Tatour and Ronit Lentin (Stanford: Stanford University Press, 2025), 166.

50 Slavoj Žižek, "Žižek on Soft Fascism, AI, and the Collapse of Shame," *Sri Lanka Guardian*, December 7, 2024. https://slguardian.org/zizek-on-soft-fasc ism-ai-and-the-collapse-of-shame/. Lorenzo Veracini describes Israel as "a failed settler society" (Lorenzo Veracini, "Genocide in Gaza and the End of Settler Colonialism," *The Journal of Imperial and Commonwealth History*, May 17, 2025. https://www.tandfonline.com/doi/pdf/10.1080/03086534.2025.2501221?casa_to ken=d5OfnRol_AYAAAAA:FyNut2Iwdh6F6I5LGmJ94Kg073jNEW6zVsQVcRT1I OT9_EMJ46Dj7qJqem_JtCjNmtGOg9Gx2VCM.

51 Slavoj Žižek, *Against Progress* (New York: Bloomsbury, 2025), 53.

52 Fanon, *The Wretched of the Earth*, 22.

53 Jeet Heer, "How to Save the Democratic Party from Itself," *The Nation*, March 7, 2025. https://www.thenation.com/article/politics/save-democratic-party-takeover/.

54 Walter Benjamin, "Theories of German Fascism," in *Selected Writings, Volume 2, 1927–1930*, ed. Michael W. Jennings, Howard Eiland, and Gary Smith, trans. Rodney Livingstone et al. (Cambridge: Harvard University Press, 1999), 321.

55 Žižek, "From MAGA to MEGA."

56 Cozzarelli, "Trump's War."

57 Amy Goodman and Nermeen Shaikh, "'Crack-Up Capitalism': Historian Quinn Slobodian on Trump, Musk & the Movement to 'Shatter' the State," *Democracy Now!* February 20, 2025. https://www.democracynow.org/2025/2/20/quinn_slo bodian_maga_doge_capitalism.

58 Despite the Democratic Party's best effort to signal to America's white middle class that Democrats are also pro-police (recall Joe Biden's 2022 State of the

Union address, in which he aligned squarely with the police, stating with absolute confidence: "We should all agree. The answer is not to defund the police. It's to fund the police. Fund them. Fund them. Fund them with resources and training. Resources and training they need to protect their communities" [Jamelle Bouie, "Biden Says 'Fund the Police.' Well, They Aren't Exactly Hurting for Cash," *The New York Times*, March 4, 2022. https://www.nytimes.com/2022/03/04/opinion/the-police-arent-exactly-running-out-of-cash.html]); the Law and Order narrative is baked into the Right's cultural DNA. And though Biden undeservingly benefited from the insurgency of BLM after the murder of George Floyd in winning the election in 2020, Biden and the Democratic Party at large are seen by the general American public as Law and Order light. In contradistinction, the Right consistently offers a militarized vision of Law and Order, and in a country that systematically refuses to reckon with its anti-Blackness, Trump and his ilk will always find a receptive audience among "moderates."

59 Derek Hook, *Whiteness at the Abyss: A Lacanian Reading of "White Anxiety"* (New York: Palgrave Macmillan, 2025), 28; David Smith, "Wrecking Ball: Trump's War on 'Woke' Marks US Society's Plunge into 'Dark Times,'" *The Guardian*, February 2, 2025. https://www.theguardian.com/us-news/2025/feb/02/trump-woke-dei-culture-wars.

60 Zeke Miller and Chris Megerian, "Trump Blames Diversity Hiring as Probe into Deadly DC Plane Crash Begins," *Associated Press*, January 30, 2025. https://apnews.com/article/trump-crash-reagan-washington-buttigieg-diversity-biden-ef1e07684bbc845e9e7981c1ae060af2.

61 Ilan Kapoor, "The Short Shelf Life of Corporate DEI," *Al Jazeera*, January 13, 2025. https://www.aljazeera.com/opinions/2025/1/13/the-short-shelf-life-of-corporate-dei.

62 George Yancy, "Authoritarian Wave in US Shows Democracy's Fragility, South African Scholar Says," *Truthout*, September 6, 2025. https://truthout.org/articles/authoritarian-wave-in-us-shows-democracys-fragility-south-african-scholar-says/.

63 Students agitating for Palestine make a compelling case that institutions of higher education should actively divest from the military-industrial complex; after Gaza, profiting from Israel's war machine, its destruction of lives and environments, can only appear obscene for our students, as it should for the rest of us.

64 See Abena Ampofoa Asare, "DEI in a Time of Genocide or Re-Calling June Jordan's Years at Stony Brook," *The Radical Teacher*, no. 131 (2025): 68–75.

65 Erakat, *Justice for Some*.

Bibliography

Abou-Ghazala, Yahya, Jeremy Diamond, Abeer Salman, Gianluca Mezzofiore, Mohammad Al-Sawalhi, and Madalena Araújo. "'Death and Hunger': Videos, Expert Analysis and Witnesses Point to Israeli Gunfire in Gaza Aid Site Shooting." *CNN*, June 5, 2025. https://www.cnn.com/2025/06/04/middleeast/israel-military-gaza-aid-shooting-intl-invs.

Abourahme, Nasser. "In Tune with Their Time." *Radical Philosophy* 2, no. 16 (2024): 13–20.

Abourahme, Nasser, and Iyko Day. "Palestine After Analogy." *Critical Ethnic Studies* 9, no. 1 (2024). https://manifold.umn.edu/read/ces0901-01/section/6832dc1e-d3fe-4c59-839d-71007c7261c3

Abraham, Yuval. "'Lavender': The AI Machine Directing Israel's Bombing Spree in Gaza." *+972 Magazine*, April 3, 2024. https://www.972mag.com/lavender-ai-israeli-army-gaza/.

Abu El-Haj, Nadia. "'We Know Well, but All the Same…' Factual Truths, Historical Narratives, and the Work of Disavowal." *History of the Present* 13, no. 2 (2023): 257–64.

Abu-Jamal, Mumia. "Black in Gaza." *Change Links*, April 2024. https://change-links.org/black-in-gaza-by-mumia-abu-jamal/.

Abunimah, Ali. "'Force, Might and Beatings': Indelible Images of the First Intifada." *The Electronic Intifada*, December 9, 2011. https://electronicintifada.net/blogs/ali-abunimah/force-might-and-beatings-indelible-images-first-intifada.

Abunimah, Ali. "Israeli Lawmaker's Call for Genocide of Palestinians Gets Thousands of Facebook Likes." *Electronic Intifada*, July 7, 2014. https://electronicintifada.net/blogs/ali-abunimah/israeli-lawmakers-call-genocide-palestinians-gets-thousands-facebook-likes.

Abusneineh, Bayan. "(Re)Producing the Israeli (European) Body: Zionism, Anti-Black Racism and the Depo-Provera Affair." *Feminist Review*, no. 128 (2021): 96–113.

Adra, Basel, Hamdan Ballal, Yuval Abraham, and Rachel Szor, directors. *No Other Land* [Documentary], 2024.

Ageel, Ghada. "Israel Is Burning Gaza's Children. And the World Lets It Happen." *Al Jazeera*, May 29, 2025. https://www.aljazeera.com/opinions/2025/5/29/israel-is-burning-gazas-children-and-the-world-lets-it-happen.

Ahmed, Sara. *The Feminist Killjoy Handbook*. New York: Penguin Books, 2024.

Ahmed, Sara. "Killjoy Truths." *feministkilljoys*, October 16. 2023. https://feministkilljoys.com/2023/10/16/killjoy-truths/.

Ahmed, Sara. *On Being Included: Racism and Diversity in Institutional Life*. Durham: Duke University Press, 2012.

Ahmed, Sara. "The Politics of Bad Feelings." *Australian Critical Race and Whiteness Studies Association Journal* 1 (2005): 72–85.

Ahmed, Sara. *Willful Subjects*. Durham: Duke University Press, 2014.

Ajari, Norman. *Darkening Blackness: Race, Gender, Class, and Pessimism in 21st Century Black Thought*, translated by Matthew B. Smith. Cambridge: Polity Press, 2023.

Aked, Hil. "Palestine Action: Peace Activists, Not Terrorists." *In These Times*, July 4, 2025. https://inthesetimes.com/article/palestine-action-terrorism-laws).

Alawieh, Abbas. "An Uncommitted Cofounder Explains the Movement's Strategy." *Jacobin*, September 9, 2024. https://jacobin.com/2024/09/uncommitted-democr ats-alawieh-gaza-israel?mc_cid=b42407cd6e&mc_eid=0317ccf9ee.

Albanese, Francesca. "From Economy of Occupation to Economy of Genocide: Report of the Special Rapporteur on the Situation of Human Rights in the Palestinian Territories Occupied Since 1967." *United Nations*, June 16, 2025. https://www.ohchr. org/en/documents/country-reports/ahrc5923-economy-occupation-economy-genoc ide-report-special-rapporteur.

Alexander, Edward. "Professor of Terror." *Commentary*, August 1989. https://www.com mentary.org/articles/edward-alexander/professor-of-terror/.

Alexander, Michelle. *The New Jim Crow: Mass Incarceration in the Age of Colorblindness*. New York: The New Press, 2010.

al-Hajjar, Mohammed. "In Gaza, You Don't Only See Death. You Smell It. You Breathe It." *Middle East Eye*, January 14, 2024. https://www.middleeasteye.net/opinion/ gaza-dont-only-see-death-smell-breathe-it.

Al-Haq. "Israeli Apartheid: Tool of Zionist Settler Colonialism." *Al-Haq*, November 29, 2022. https://www.alhaq.org/publications/20940.html.

Al Jazeera. "Israeli Soldiers Are Filming Themselves Mocking Palestinians." *Al Jazeera*, January 18, 2024. https://www.aljazeera.com/program/newsfeed/2024/1/18/isra eli-soldiers-are-filming-themselves-mocking-palestinians.

American Israel Public Affairs Committee. "Anti-Israel Action at the U.N. Since October 7." *AIPAC*, February 15, 2024. https://aipacorg.app.box.com/s/s3o0s9pr4ymepmatx 00xdjakjsxtf97j.

Améry, Jean. *At the Mind's Limits: Contemplations by a Survivor on Auschwitz and Its Realities*, translated by Sidney Rosenfeld and Stella P. Rosenfeld. Bloomington: Indiana University Press, 1980.

Amnesty International. "Amnesty International Sounds Alarm on a Watershed Moment for International Law amid Flagrant Rule-Breaking by Governments and Corporate Actors." *Amnesty International*, April 24, 2024. https://www.amnesty.org/en/latest/ news/2024/04/amnesty-international-sounds-alarm-on-a-watershed-moment/.

Amnesty International. "GAZA: Starvation or Gunfire—This Is Not a Humanitarian Response." *Amnesty International*, July 1, 2025. https://www.amnesty.org/en/latest/ news/2025/07/gaza-starvation-or-gunfire-this-is-not-a-humanitarian-response/.

Amnesty International. "Israel Must End Mass Incommunicado Detention and Torture of Palestinians from Gaza." *Amnesty International*, July 18, 2024. https://www.amnesty. org/en/latest/news/2024/07/israel-must-end-mass-incommunicado-detention-and- torture-of-palestinians-from-gaza/.

Amnesty International. *Israel's Apartheid Against Palestinians: Cruel System of Domination and Crime Against Humanity*. London: Amnesty International, February 1, 2022. https://www.amnesty.org/en/wp-content/uploads/2022/02/MDE1551412022 ENGLISH.pdf.

Arendt, Hannah. *The Origins of Totalitarianism*. San Diego: Harcourt Brace, 1973.

Arnold, A. James. "Césaire Is Dead: Long Live Césaire! Recuperations and Reparations." *French Politics, Culture & Society* 27, no. 3 (2009): 9–18.

Arria, Michael. "What Anti-Palestinian Legislation to Look Out for in the New Congress." *Mondoweiss*, February 18, 2025. https://mondoweiss.net/2025/02/what-anti-pale stinian-legislation-to-look-out-for-in-the-new-congress/.

Asare, Abena Ampofoa. "DEI in a Time of Genocide or Re-Calling June Jordan's Years at Stony Brook." *The Radical Teacher*, no. 131 (2025): 68–75.

Asi, Yara M. "The Trauma Experienced in Gaza Is Beyond PTSD." *The New York Times*, February 22, 2024. https://www.nytimes.com/2024/02/22/opinion/gaza-palestini ans-mental-health.html.

Azoulay, Ariella. *Potential History: Unlearning Imperialism*. London: Verso, 2019.

Bakan, Abigail B. "Race, Class, and Colonialism: Reconsidering the 'Jewish Question.'" In *Theorizing Anti-Racism: Linkages in Marxism and Critical Race Theories*, edited by Abigail Bakan and Enakshi Dua, 252–73. Toronto: University of Toronto Press, 2014.

Baldwin, James. "Black English: A Dishonest Argument." In *The Cross of Redemption: Uncollected Writings*, edited by Randall Kenan, 126–30. New York: Pantheon, 2010.

Baldwin, James. "Conversation: Ida Lewis and James Baldwin." In *Conversations with James Baldwin*, edited by Fred L. Stanley and Louis H. Pratt, 83–92. Jackson: University Press of Mississippi, 1989.

Baldwin, James. "The Dangerous Road Before Martin Luther King." In *Baldwin: Collected Essays*, edited by Toni Morrison, 638–58. New York: Library of America, 1998.

Baldwin, James. *The Evidence of Things Not Seen*. New York: Holt, Rinehart and Winston, 1985.

Baldwin, James. "The Fire Next Time." In *Baldwin: Collected Essays*, edited by Toni Morrison, 291–348. New York: Library of America, 1998.

Baldwin, James. "Negroes Are Anti-Semitic Because They're Anti-White." In *Baldwin: Collected Essays*, edited by Toni Morrison, 739–48. New York: Library of America, 1998.

Baldwin, James. "A Report from Occupied Territory." *The Nation*, July 11, 1966. https://www.thenation.com/article/culture/report-occupied-territory/.

Baldwin, James. "A Talk to Teachers." In *Baldwin: Collected Essays*, edited by Toni Morrison, 678–86. New York: Library of America, 1998.

Baldwin, James. "White Man's Guilt." In *Baldwin: Collected Essays*, edited by Toni Morrison, 722–7. New York: Library of America, 1998.

Balibar, Étienne. "The Genocide in Gaza and Its Consequences for the Israeli-Palestinian Conflict." *e-flux Notes*, September 25, 2024. https://www.e-flux.com/notes/630154/ the-genocide-in-gaza-and-its-consequences-for-the-israeli-palestinian-conflict.

Balibar, Étienne. *Politics and the Other Scene*. New York: Verso, 2002.

Bari, Suhail. "Criminalizing Palestinians Is Part of the Israeli Strategy to Destroy the Right of Return." *Middle East Monitor*, February 2, 2024. https://www.middleeastmoni tor.com/20240202-criminalizing-palestinians-is-part-of-the-israeli-strategy-to-dest roy-the-right-of-return/.

Barker, Corey. "The Other Genocide: American Indian Genocide in the Era of United States Formation." *American Indian Culture and Research Journal* 29, no. 4 (2005): 115–39.

Beck, Evelyn T., Nancy K. Bereano, Gloria Z. Greenfield, Melanie Kaye, Irena Klepfisz, Bernice Mennis, and Adrienne Rich. "…What Does Zionism Mean?" *Off Our Backs* 12, no. 7 (July 1982): 21.

Beck, Evelyn T., Nancy K. Bereano, Melanie Kaye, Irena Klepfisz, Bernice Mennis, and Adrienne Rich. "Di Vilde Chayes: Zionists Deplore Killings in Lebanon and Criticize Nature of Anti-Israel Protests." *Off Our Backs* 12, no. 9 (October 1982): 27.

Beinart, Peter. "Democrats Need to Understand That Opinions on Israel Are Changing Fast." *The New York Times*, July 6, 2025. https://www.nytimes.com/2025/07/06/opinion/zohran-mamdani-democrats-israel.html.

Belam, Martin, and Lili Bayer. "Middle East Crisis: Famine 'Imminent' in Northern Gaza, UN Report Says, as EU Foreign Policy Chief Calls Area 'Open Air Graveyard'—as It Happened." *The Guardian*, March 18, 2024. https://www.theguardian.com/world/live/2024/mar/18/middle-east-crisis-live-israel-gaza-palestine-al-shifa-live-updates.

Ben-Gurion, David. "David Ben-Gurion: Select Quotations." *Jewish Virtual Library*, 2019. https://www.jewishvirtuallibrary.org/select-quotations-of-david-ben-gurion.

Benjamin, Walter. "On the Concept of History." In *Selected Writings. Volume 4, 1938–1940*, edited by Howard Eiland and Michael W. Jennings, 389–400. Cambridge: Harvard University Press, 2003.

Benjamin, Walter. "Theories of German Fascism." In *Selected Writings, Volume 2, 1927–1930*, edited by Michael W. Jennings, Howard Eiland, and Gary Smith, 321–34, translated by Rodney Livingstone et al. Cambridge, MA: Harvard University Press, 1999.

Benn, Aluf. "The Jewish Majority in Israel Still See Their Country as 'a Villa in the Jungle.'" *The Guardian*, August 20, 2013. https://www.theguardian.com/commentisfree/2013/aug/20/jewish-majority-israel-villa-in-the-jungle.

Berardi, Franco "Bifo." "The American Unconscious and the Disintegration of the Western World." *Critical Inquiry*, December 9, 2024. https://critinq.wordpress.com/2024/12/09/the-american-unconscious-and-the-disintegration-of-the-western-world/.

Berardi, Franco "Bifo." "Letter to the Hypocrites of Europe." *Institute of Network Cultures*, January 18, 2024. https://networkcultures.org/tactical-media-room/2024/01/18/letter-to-the-hypocrites-of-europe/.

Berkovits, Balazs. "The October 7th Pogrom as a Non-Event on the Western Left." *K*, January 25, 2024. https://k-larevue.com/en/the-october-7th-pogrom-as-a-non-event-on-the-western-left/.

Berlant, Lauren. *Cruel Optimism*. Durham: Duke University Press, 2011.

Berman, Lazar. "After Walling Itself in, Israel Learns to Hazard the Jungle Beyond." *The Times of Israel*, March 8, 2021. https://www.timesofisrael.com/after-walling-itself-in-israel-learns-to-hazard-the-jungle-beyond/.

Bernard-Henri, Lévy. *Israel Alone*, translated by Steven B. Kennedy. New York: Wicked Son, 2024.

Bey, Marquis. "Anarcho-Blackness: A Conversation with Marquis Bey." *Ill Will*, October 14, 2021. https://illwill.com/anarcho-blackness.

Bhatti, Saqib. "I Am Done Voting for the Lesser of Two Evils. I Will Not Vote for Joe Biden in 2024." *In These Times*, October 25, 2023. https://inthesetimes.com/article/muslims-palestinians-vote-biden-2024-election-bhatti.

Boehm, Omri. "Tragedy or Political Correctness? Ari Shavit and the Confusion of the Zionist Liberal Left." *Los Angeles Review of Books*, March 27, 2014. https://lareview ofbooks.org/article/tragedy-political-correctness-ari-shavit-confusion-zionist-libe ral-left/.

Borger, Julian. "Netanyahu Says Israel Working Closely with US on Trump's Plan for Gaza." *The Guardian*, February 16, 2025. https://www.theguardian.com/world/2025/ feb/16/israel-netanyahu-trump-plan-gaza.

Borger, Julian. "Trump's Plan to Seize Iraq's Oil: 'It's Not Stealing, We're Reimbursing Ourselves.'" *The Guardian*, September 21, 2016. https://www.theguardian.com/ us-news/2016/sep/21/donald-trump-iraq-war-oil-strategy-seizure-isis.

Bou Ali, Nadia. "Measure Against Measure: Why Lacan Contra Foucault?" In *Lacan Contra Foucault: Subjectivity, Sex and Politics*, edited by Nadia Bou Ali, 1–24. New York: Bloomsbury, 2019.

Bouie, Jamelle. "Biden Says 'Fund the Police.' Well, They Aren't Exactly Hurting for Cash." *The New York Times*, March 4, 2022. https://www.nytimes.com/2022/03/04/ opinion/the-police-arent-exactly-running-out-of-cash.html.

Bouteldja, Houria. *Whites, Jews, and Us: Toward a Politics of Revolutionary Love*. South Pasadena: Semiotext(e), 2017.

Boym, Svetlana. *The Future of Nostalgia*. New York: Basic Books, 2001.

Bresheeth-Zabner, Haim. *An Army Like No Other*. New York: Verso, 2020.

Bromwich, Jonah E. "Mahmoud Khalil Discusses 3-Month Detention in First Interview Since Release." *The New York Times*, June 22, 2025. https://www.nytimes. com/2025/06/22/nyregion/mahmoud-khalil-interview-trump.html.

Brown, Michael F. "Ben-Gvir Touts Bombing Food Depots While at Mar-a-Lago." *The Electronic Intifada*, April 30, 2025. https://electronicintifada.net/blogs/mich ael-f-brown/ben-gvir-touts-bombing-food-depots-while-mar-lago.

B'Tselem. "The World Must Stop the Ethnic Cleansing of Northern Gaza." *B'Tselem*, October 22, 2024. https://www.btselem.org/press_releases/20241022_the_world_ must_stop_the_ethnic_cleansing_of_northern_gaza.

B'Tselem. "A Regime of Jewish Supremacy from the Jordan River to the Mediterranean Sea: This Is Apartheid." *B'Tselem*, January 12, 2021. https://www.btselem.org/publi cations/fulltext/202101_this_is_apartheid.

Burgis, Ben. "Is Donald Trump Just Another Hawk? Manifest Destiny Is a Betrayal of Populism." *UnHerd*, January 23, 2025. https://unherd.com/2025/01/is-don ald-trump-just-another-hawk/.

Burgis, Ben. "Free Speech Means Free Mahmoud Khalil." *Jacobin*, March 13, 2025. https://jacobin.com/2025/03/mahmoud-khalil-arrest-free-speech.

Burgis, Ben. "The Right Has Embraced the Cancel Culture It Claimed to Hate." *Jacobin*, May 19, 2025. https://jacobin.com/2025/05/rozos-nyu-cancel-culture-israel.

Butler, Judith. *Giving an Account of Oneself*. New York: Fordham University Press, 2005.

Butler, Judith. "Judith Butler, Philosopher: 'If You Sacrifice a Minority Like Trans People, You Are Operating Within a Fascist Logic.'" *El País*, December 15, 2024. https:// english.elpais.com/culture/2024-12-15/judith-butler-philosopher-if-you-sacrifice-a- minority-like-trans-people-you-are-operating-within-a-fascist-logic.html.

Butler, Judith. *Precarious Life: The Powers of Mourning and Violence*. New York: Verso, 2004.

Butler, Judith. "Why Is the Idea of 'Gender' Provoking Backlash the World Over?" *The Guardian*, October 23, 2021. https://www.theguardian.com/us-news/commentisf ree/2021/oct/23/judith-butler-gender-ideology-backlash.

Buttu, Diana. "The Gazafication of the West Bank: 'Is This Really Happening Again?'" *Zeteo*, March 2, 2025. https://zeteo.com/p/the-gaza-ification-of-the-west-bank.

Callai, Adi. "The Gaza Ghetto Uprising." *The Brooklyn Rail*, May 2024. https://brooklynrail.org/2024/05/field-notes/The-Gaza-Ghetto-Uprising/.

Cannon, Lou. *President Reagan: The Role of a Lifetime*. New York: Public Affairs, 2000.

Cardozo, Nathan Lopes. "Hanukkah: Jews Should Be Proud of What They Are Hated For." *The Jerusalem Post*, December 28, 2024. https://www.jpost.com/opinion/article-834843.

Carnelos, Marco. "Does the West Really Need to Be Great Again?" *Middle East Eye*, April 25, 2025. https://www.middleeasteye.net/opinion/does-west-really-need-be-great-again.

Césaire, Aimé. *Discourse on Colonialism*, translated by Joan Pinkham. New York: Monthly Review Press, 2000.

Césaire, Aimé. *A Tempest*, translated by Richard Miller. New York: TCG Translations, 2002.

Chandler, Nahum Dimitri. "Of Exorbitance: The Problem of the Negro as a Problem for Thought." *Criticism* 50, no. 3 (2008): 345–410.

Chandler, Nahum Dimitri. *X: The Problem of the Negro as a Problem for Thought*. New York: Fordham University Press, 2013.

Chekuru, Kavitha. "Israeli Forces Bombed Two Gaza Hospitals in One Day." *Drop Site*, May 14, 2025. https://www.dropsitenews.com/p/european-hospital-nasser-gaza-israeli-airstrikes.

Chomsky, Noam. "The Israel Lobby and U.S. Foreign Policy." *The Nation*, September 2006. https://www.thenation.com/article/archive/israel-lobby-and-us-foreign-policy/.

Coates, Ta-Nehisi. "A Palestinian American's Place Under the Democrats' Big Tent?" *Vanity Fair*, August 21, 2024. https://www.vanityfair.com/news/story/dnc-2024-palestine-israel.

Cohen, Hillel. *Good Arabs: The Israeli Security Agencies and the Israeli Arabs, 1948–1967*. Berkeley: University of California Press, 2010.

Cole, Juan. "Ta-Nehisi Coates: If Democrats Can't Draw the Line at Genocide, They Can't Draw the Line at Democracy." *Informed Comment*, February 20, 2025. https://www.juancole.com/2025/02/democrats-genocide-democracy.html.

Cole, Juan. "The Vile Racism of Calling Biden a 'Weak Palestinian.'" *Common Dreams*, June 28, 2024. https://www.commondreams.org/opinion/trump-biden-weak-palestinian.

Collee, Lauren. "Imaginative Resistance: An Interview with 'Lyd' Directors Rami Younis and Sarah Friedland." *Rough Cut Film*, April 10, 2024. https://roughcutfilm.com/2024/04/10/imaginative-resistance-an-interview-with-lyd-directors-rami-younis-and-sarah-friedland/.

Cook, Jonathan. "Biden and Starmer Are Destroying International Law to Protect Israel's Genocide." *Middle East Eye*, December 4, 2024. https://www.middleeasteye.net/opinion/biden-starmer-destroying-international-protect-israel-genocide.

Cozzarelli, Tatiana. "Trump's War Against the Palestine Movement and Universities is an Attack on Us All." *Left Voice*, March 9, 2025. https://www.leftvoice.org/trumps-attacks-on-the-palestine-movement-and-the-universities-are-the-same-fight/.

Davids, Nuraan, Ronald Barnett, Thaddeus Metz, Zahi Zalloua, Suriamurthee Maistry, George Yancy, Janet Orchard, et al. "Gaza: We Need to Talk!" *Educational Philosophy and Theory* (2025): 1–26.

Davis, Angela Y. *Freedom Is a Constant Struggle: Ferguson, Palestine, and the Foundations of a Movement*. Chicago: Haymarket Books, 2016.

Davis, Mark. "Violence as Method: The 'White Replacement,' 'White Genocide,' and 'Eurabia' Conspiracy Theories and the Biopolitics of Networked Violence." *Ethnic and Racial Studies* 48, no. 3 (2025): 426–46.

Dean, Jodi. "Palestine Speaks for Everyone." *Verso Books*, April 9, 2024. https://www.versobooks.com/blogs/news/palestine-speaks-for-everyone.

DeGooyer, Stephanie, Alastair Hunt, Linda Maxwell, and Samuel Moyn. *The Right to Have Rights*. New York: Verso Press, 2020.

Deleuze, Gilles, and Elias Sanbar. "The Indians of Palestine." In *Two Regimes of Madness: Texts and Interviews 1975–1995*, edited by David Lapoujade, 194–200. New York: Semiotext(e), 2006.

Derrida, Jacques. "Autoimmunity: Real and Symbolic Suicides—A Dialogue with Jacques Derrida." In *Philosophy in a Time of Terror: Dialogues with Jürgen Habermas and Jacques Derrida*, edited by Giovanna Borradori, 85–136. Chicago: University of Chicago Press, 2004.

Derrida, Jacques. *Rogues: Two Essays on Reason*, translated by Pascale-Anne Brault and Michael Naas. Stanford: Stanford University Press, 2005.

Descartes, René. *Discourse on Method and Meditations on First Philosophy*, translated by Donald A. Cress. Indianapolis: Hackett, 1998.

De Vogli, Roberto. *Selective Empathy: The West Through the Gaze of Gaza*. New York: Brill, 2025.

De Waal, Alex. "Starvation in Gaza." *London Review of Books*, May 14, 2025. https://www.lrb.co.uk/blog/2025/may/starvation-in-gaza.

Dhenin, Marianne. "CA Educators Are Resisting Anti-Palestine Bills Pushing 'Academic Police State.'" *Truthout*, August 20, 2024. https://truthout.org/articles/ca-educators-are-resisting-anti-palestine-bills-pushing-academic-police-state/.

Diawara, Manthia. "One World in Relation: Édouard Glissant in Conversation with Manthia Diawara," translated by Christopher Winks. *Journal of Contemporary African Art* 28 (2011): 4–19.

Dikla Taylor-Sheinman. "A Lyd Without the Nakba." *+972 Magazine*, October 25, 2024. https://www.972mag.com/lyd-nakba-film/.

Du Bois, W. E. B. *Black Reconstruction in America*. New York: The Free Press, 1998.

Du Bois, W. E. B. *The Souls of Black Folk*. New Haven: Yale University Press, 2015.

Dunbar, Marina. "New York Governor Orders Removal of Palestinian Studies Job Posting at CUNY." *The Guardian*, February 26, 2025. https://www.theguardian.com/us-news/2025/feb/26/kathy-hochul-palestinian-studies-cuny-job.

Dussel, Enrique. "Anti-Cartesian Meditations: On the Origin of the Philosophical Anti-Discourse of Modernity." *Journal for Culture and Religious Theory* 13, no. 1 (2014): 21–53.

Ebrahim, Nadeen, and Mike Schwartz. "'He Got Out of Gaza, but Gaza Did Not Get Out of Him': Israeli Soldiers Returning from War Struggle with Trauma and Suicide." *CNN*, October 21, 2024. https://www.cnn.com/2024/10/21/middleeast/gaza-war-israeli-soldiers-ptsd-suicide-intl/index.html.

El Akkad, Omar. *One Day, Everyone Will Have Always Been Against This*. New York: Alfred A. Knopf, 2025.

Elizur, Yoel. "'When You Leave Israel and Enter Gaza, You Are God': Inside the Minds of IDF Soldiers Who Commit War Crimes." *Haaretz*, December 23, 2024. https://www.haaretz.com/opinion/2024-12-23/ty-article-opinion/.premium/when-you-enter-gaza-you-are-god-inside-the-minds-of-idf-soldiers-who-commit-war-crimes/00000193-f2a4-dc18-a3db-fee62b540000.

El-Kurd, Mohammed. *Perfect Victims: And the Politics of Appeal*. Chicago: Haymarket Books, 2025.

Erakat, Noura. "The Boomerang Comes Back." *Boston Review*, February 5, 2025. https://www.bostonreview.net/articles/the-boomerang-comes-back/.

Erakat, Noura. *Justice for Some: Law and the Question of Palestine*. Redwood City: Stanford University Press, 2019.

Erakat, Noura. "Roundtable on Anti-Blackness and Black-Palestinian Solidarity." *Jadaliyya*, June 3, 2015. https://www.jadaliyya.com/Details/32145/Roundtable-on-Anti-Blackness-and-Black-Palestinian-Solidarity.

Erakat, Noura. "Zionism as a Form of Racism." In *Race and the Question of Palestine*, edited by Lana Tatour and Ronit Lentin, 77–97. Stanford: Stanford University Press, 2025.

Erakat, Noura, and John Reynolds. "Understanding Apartheid." *Jewish Currents*, November 1, 2022. https://jewishcurrents.org/understanding-apartheid.

Essa, Azad. "Cornel West: Black Lives Matter and the Fight Against US Empire Are One and the Same." *Middle East Eye*, June 12, 2020. https://www.middleeasteye.net/news/cornel-west-black-lives-matter-fight-us-empire.

Falk, Richard. "On 'Lost Causes' and the Future of Palestine." *The Nation*, December 16, 2014. https://www.thenation.com/article/archive/lost-causes-and-future-palestine/.

Fandos, Nicholas. "Elise Stefanik Has Gained Widespread Attention in Antisemitism Hearings." *The New York Times*, May 23, 2024. https://www.nytimes.com/2024/05/23/us/elise-stefanik-republican-antisemitism-hearings.html.

Fanon, Frantz. *Black Skin, White Masks*, translated by Richard Philcox. New York: Grove Press, 2008.

Fanon, Frantz. *A Dying Colonialism*, translated by Haakon Chevalier. New York: Grove Press, 1965.

Fanon, Frantz. "Letter to the Resident Minister." In *Alienation and Freedom*, edited by Jean Khalfa and Robert J. C. Young, 433–5. New York: Bloomsbury, 2021.

Fanon, Frantz. "The North African Syndrome." In *Toward the African Revolution*, translated by Haakon Chevalier, 3–16. New York: Grove Press, 1967.

Fanon, Frantz. "Why We Use Violence." In *Alienation and Freedom*, edited by Jean Khalfa and Robert J. C. Young, 653–9. New York: Bloomsbury, 2021.

Fanon, Frantz. *The Wretched of the Earth*, translated by Constance Farrington. New York: Grove Press, 1963.

Farazi Saber, Indlieb. "A Tale of Two Lyds: What if the Nakba Never Happened?" *TRT World*, May 16, 2024. https://www.trtworld.com/magazine/a-tale-of-two-lyds-what-if-the-nakba-never-happened-18163413.

Fassin, Didier. *Moral Abdication: How the World Failed to Stop the Destruction of Gaza*, translated by Gregory Elliott. New York: Verso, 2024.

Featherstone, Liza. "Noam Chomsky on Israel-Palestine and the Lessons of Gaza." *The Intercept*, October 23, 2023. https://theintercept.com/2023/10/23/noam-chomsky-israel-palestine-gaza/.

Feldman, Keith P. *A Shadow over Palestine: The Imperial Life of Race in America*. Minneapolis: University of Minnesota Press, 2015.

Feuer, Hannah. "What Zohran Mamdani Has Actually Said About Jews, Israel and Antisemitism." *Forward*, July 2, 2025. https://forward.com/news/733657/zohran-mamdani-gaza-israel-jews-antisemitism/.

Finn, Daniel. "Israel's Western Backers Are Still Running Interference for Netanyahu's War Crimes." *Jacobin*, October 18, 2023. https://jacobin.com/2023/10/al-ahli-hospital-bombing-gaza-war-israel-war-crimes-western-support-biden.

Fischbach, Michael R. *Black Power and Palestine: Transnational Countries of Color*. Stanford: Stanford University Press, 2018.

Fischbach, Michael R. "Black-Palestinian Solidarity and the Global Color Line." In *Race and the Question of Palestine*, edited by Lana Tatour and Ronit Lentin, 150–67. Stanford: Stanford University Press, 2025.

Fitzgerald, Joseph R., and Jaimee A. Swift. "On the Record: Barbara Smith on Palestine, June Jordan, Audre Lorde, and Adrienne Rich." *Black Women Radicals*. https://squid-fox-bzpx.squarespace.com/blog-feed/on-the-record-barbara-smith-on-palestine-june-jordan-audre-lorde-and-adrienne-rich.

Forensic Architecture. "'No Traces of Life': Israel's Ecocide in Gaza 2023–2024." https://forensic-architecture.org/investigation/ecocide-in-gaza.

Foucault, Michel. "Polemics, Politics, and Problematizations: An Interview with Michel Foucault." In *The Foucault Reader*, edited by Paul Rabinow, 381–90. New York: Pantheon Books, 1984.

Fox, Mira. "A 'Sci-Fi Documentary' Dreaming of Peace Got Banned in Israel. Why?" *Forward*, November 11, 2024. https://forward.com/culture/673651/lyd-israel-palestine-lod-documentary-ban/.

Fox, Mira. "So What Does 'Intifada' Actually Mean?" *Forward*, December 15, 2023. https://forward.com/culture/573654/intifada-arabic-israeli-hamas-war-meaning-linguistics/.

Freud, Sigmund. *Beyond the Pleasure Principle*, translated by James Strachey. New York: W. W. Norton, 1961.

Friedman, Thomas. "Israel's Security Dilemma." *The New York Times*, April 19, 2002. https://www.nytimes.com/2002/04/19/opinion/israel-s-security-dilemma.html.

Gavroche, Julius. "Fred Moten: Thinking with Palestine." *Autonomies*, October 2023. https://autonomies.org/2023/10/fred-moten-thinking-with-palestine/.

Gedeon, Joseph. "Rubio Boasts of Canceling More than 300 Visas over Pro-Palestine Protests." *The Guardian*, March 27, 2025. https://www.theguardian.com/us-news/2025/mar/27/state-department-visas-pro-palestine-protesters.en.wikipedia.org+15theguardian.com+15theguardian.com+15.

Gessen, M. "The Attacks on Zohran Mamdani Show That We Need a New Understanding of Antisemitism." *The New York Times*, June 24, 2025. https://www.nytimes.com/2025/06/24/opinion/antisemitism-new-york-city-mayor.html.

Gessen, M. "The Chilling Consequences of Going Along with Trump." *The New York Times*, February 10, 2025. https://www.nytimes.com/2025/02/08/opinion/trump-power-surrender.html.

Gessen, M. "The Hidden Motive Behind Trump's Attacks on Trans People." *The New York Times*, March 17, 2025. https://www.nytimes.com/2025/03/17/opinion/trump-trans-denationalizing.html?smid=nytcore-android-share.

Gibson, Nigel C. *Fanon and the Rationality of Revolt*. Ottawa: Daraja Press, 2020.

Gibson, Nigel C. "Situational Awareness: Fanon and Gaza." *Spectre*, November 7, 2024. https://spectrejournal.com/situational-awareness/.

Gilbert, David, Laura Whitehorn, and Marilyn Buck. *Enemies of the State: An Interview with Anti-Imperialist Political Prisoners*. Montreal: Abraham Guillen & Arm the Spirit, 2002.

Ginsberg, Jodie. "Trump Called the Press 'the Enemy of the People.' Now It's Time to Defend Ourselves." *The Guardian*, February 14, 2025. https://www.theguardian.com/commentisfree/2025/feb/14/trump-press-journalists-enemy.

Giri, Saroj. "From the October Revolution to the Naxalbari Movement: Understanding Political Subjectivity." In *Of Concepts and Methods: "On Postisms" and Other Essays*, edited by K. Murali (Ajith), 11–38. Paris: Foreign Languages Press, 2020.

Goldberg, David Theo. "Why 'Black Lives Matter' Because All Lives Don't Matter in America." *The Huffington Post*, September 25, 2015. https://www.huffingtonpost.com/david-theo-goldberg/why-black-lives-matter_b_8191424.html.

Goldstein, Eric L. *The Price of Whiteness: Jews, Race, and American Identity*. Princeton: Princeton University Press, 2006.

Goodman, Amy, and Juan González. "'One Mass Casualty After Another': U.S. Doctor in Gaza on Ongoing Israeli Massacres at Aid Sites." *Democracy Now!* June 25, 2025. https://www.democracynow.org/2025/6/25/gaza_healthcare.

Goodman, Amy, and Juan González. "Ta-Nehisi Coates: I Was Told Palestine Was Complicated. Visiting Revealed a Simple, Brutal Truth." *Democracy Now!* October 8, 2024. https://www.democracynow.org/2024/10/8/ta_nehisi_the_message_2.

Goodman, Amy, and Juan González. "'Trying to Repeat the Nakba': Israel Launches Largest Military Raids in West Bank in Two Decades." *Democracy Now!* August 28, 2024. https://www.democracynow.org/2024/8/28/west_bank_raids_mustafa_barghouti.

Goodman, Amy, and Juan González. "Watch: Palestinian American Lawmaker Gives Speech the DNC Wouldn't Allow on Stage." *Democracy Now!* August 23, 2024. https://www.democracynow.org/2024/8/23/ruwa_romman.

Goodman, Amy, and Nermeen Shaikh. "'Crack-Up Capitalism': Historian Quinn Slobodian on Trump, Musk & the Movement to 'Shatter' the State." *Democracy Now!* February 20, 2025. https://www.democracynow.org/2025/2/20/quinn_slobodian_maga_doge_capitalism.

Gordon, Neve, and Penny Green. "Israel's Universities: The Crackdown." *The New York Review*, June 5, 2024. https://www.nybooks.com/online/2024/06/05/israel-universities-the-crackdown/.

Gordon, Neve, and Yinon Cohen. "Race and Space in Israel/Palestine." In *Race and the Question of Palestine*, edited by Lana Tatour and Ronit Lentin, 37–57. Stanford: Stanford University Press, 2025.

Gordillo, Gastón. "The Fascist Disposition." *Verso*, July 18, 2024. https://www.versobooks.com/blogs/news/the-fascist-disposition?srsltid=AfmBOoojDqlDRJ50-SolGAsK-Yqx7RqEh3-c4Gmib04olnaFo4_8Fd.

Graham-Harrison, Emma. "Draft Israeli Law to Limit Academic Speech Labelled 'McCarthyite.'" *The Guardian*, July 21, 2024. https://www.theguardian.com/world/article/2024/jul/21/draft-israeli-law-to-limit-academic-speech-labelled-mccarthyite.

Grandin, Greg. "From the Americas to Gaza, the Conquest Never Ends." *The Nation*, May 28, 2025. https://www.thenation.com/article/world/israel-gaza-conquistadors-aztec/.

Grasso, Michael. "Donald Trump and the '80s Aesthetic." *Jacobin*, August 9, 2024. https://jacobin.com/2024/08/donald-trump-nostalgia-80s-aesthetic.

Greer, Christina. "Black Americans Are Not Surprised." *The New York Times*, April 7, 2025. https://www.nytimes.com/2025/04/07/opinion/black-americans-trump-polit ics.html.

Gross, Jenny. "Rights Groups Condemn Trump for Using 'Palestinian' as a Slur Against Schumer." *The New York Times*, March 13, 2025. https://www.nytimes. com/2025/03/13/us/politics/trump-schumer-palestinian.html.

Hajjaj, Tareq S. "'We Smelled the Stench of Burning Human Flesh': Israel Burns 8 Children to Death in Gaza 'Safe Zone.'" *Mondoweiss*, April 18, 2025. https://mon doweiss.net/2025/04/we-smelled-the-stench-of-burning-human-flesh-israel-burns-8- children-to-death-in-gaza-safe-zone/.

Halberstam, Jack. "The Wild Beyond: With and for the Undercommons." In *The Undercommons: Fugitive Planning & Black Study*, by Fred Moten and Stefano Harney, 5–12. New York: Minor Compositions, 2013.

Hall, Stuart. "'In but Not of Europe': Europe and Its Myths." In *Selected Writings on Race and Difference*, edited by Paul Gilroy and Ruth Wilson Gilmore, 305–45. Durham: Duke University Press, 2021.

Hamid, Shadi, Brett Max Kaufman, Yousef Munayyer, and Natasha Roth-Rowland. "Is a New McCarthyism Punishing Pro-Palestine Speech at US Universities? Our Panel Reacts." *The Guardian*, December 13, 2023. https://www.theguardian.com/commen tisfree/2023/dec/13/israel-gaza-us-universities-free-speech.

Harb, Ali. "US Sanctions UN Expert Francesca Albanese over Israel Criticism." *Al Jazeera*, July 9, 2025. https://www.aljazeera.com/news/2025/7/9/us-sanctions-un- expert-albanese-over-israel-criticism.

Harfouch, John, and C. Heike Schotten. "Sayegh's Critique of Zionism and the IHRA Definition: Notes Toward a Theory of the Antisemitism Industrial Complex." *Institute For the Critical Study of Zionism* 1, no. 1 (2024). https://criticalzionismstudies.org/ sayeghs-critique-of-zionism-and-the-ihra-definition-notes-toward-a-theory-of-the- antisemitism-industrial-complex/.

Harney, Stefano, and Fred Moten. *The Undercommons: Fugitive Planning and Black Study*. New York: Autonomedia, 2013.

Hart, William David. *The Blackness of Black: Key Concepts in Critical Discourse*. Lanham: Lexington Books, 2020.

Hartman, Saidiya V. *Lose Your Mother: A Journey Along the Atlantic Slave Route*. New York: Farrar, Straus and Giroux, 2007.

Hartman, Saidiya. *Scenes of Subjection: Terror, Slavery, and Self-Making in Nineteenth- Century America*. Oxford: Oxford University Press, 1997.

Hartman, Saidiya, and Frank B. Wilderson III. "The Position of the Unthought." *Qui Parle* 13, no. 2 (2003): 183–201.

Hartung, William. "Dr. King's 1967 Anti-War Speech Was Unpopular, but Prophetic." *Truthout*, January 18, 2022. https://www.commondreams.org/views/2022/01/18/ dr-kings-1967-anti-war-speech-was-unpopular-prophetic.

Hasson, Nir, Yaniv Kubovich, and Bar Peleg. "'It's a Killing Field': IDF Soldiers Ordered to Shoot Deliberately at Unarmed Gazans Waiting for Humanitarian Aid." *Haaretz*, June 27, 2025. https://www.haaretz.com/israel-news/2025-06-27/ty-article-magazine/. premium/idf-soldiers-ordered-to-shoot-deliberately-at-unarmed-gazans-waiting-for- humanitarian-aid/00000197-ad8e-de01-a39f-ffbe33780000.

Haworth, Bryn. "Israel's War on Children Is a Stain on Humanity." *Al Majalla*, April 22, 2024. https://en.majalla.com/node/315326/culture-social-affairs/israels-war-child ren-stain-humanity.

Hazkani, Shay, and Tamir Sorek. "Yes to Transfer: 82% of Jewish Israelis Back Expelling Gazans." *Haaretz*, May 28, 2025. https://www.haaretz.com/israel-news/2025-05-28/ty-article-magazine/.premium/yes-to-transfer-82-of-jewish-israelis-back-expelling-gazans/00000197-12a4-df22-a9d7-9ef6af930000.

Heer, Jeet. "How to Save the Democratic Party from Itself." *The Nation*, March 7, 2025. https://www.thenation.com/article/politics/save-democratic-party-takeover/.

Heidegger, Martin. *The Fundamental Concepts of Metaphysics*, translated by William McNeill and Nicholas Walker. Bloomington: Indiana University Press, 1995.

Henry, Paget. *Caliban's Reason: Introducing Afro-Caribbean Philosophy.* New York: Routledge, 2000.

Hirschkind, Charles. "Exterminate the Brutes." *Mondoweiss*, November 8, 2023. https://mondoweiss.net/2023/11/exterminate-the-brutes/.

Hook, Derek. "Death-Bound Subjectivity: Fanon's Zone of Nonbeing and the Lacanian Death Drive." *Subjectivity* 13 (2020): 355–75.

Hook, Derek. *Whiteness at the Abyss: A Lacanian Reading of "White Anxiety."* New York: Palgrave Macmillan, 2025.

Horkheimer, Max. "The Jews and Europe." In *Critical Theory and Society: A Reader*, edited by Stephen Bronner and Douglas Kellner, 77–94. New York: Routledge, 1989.

Hudis, Peter. "Fanon's 'New Humanism': The Struggle for Alternatives to Capitalism." *Spectre*, May 16, 2025. https://spectrejournal.com/fanons-new-humanism/.

Human Rights Watch. "A Threshold Crossed: Israeli Authorities and the Crimes of Apartheid and Persecution." *Human Rights Watch*, April 27, 2021. https://www.hrw.org/report/2021/04/27/threshold-crossed/israeli-authorities-and-crimes-apartheid-and-persecution.

Human Rights Watch. "Israel: New Laws Marginalize Palestinian Arab Citizens." *Human Rights Watch*, March 30, 2011. https://www.hrw.org/news/2011/03/30/israel-new-laws-marginalize-palestinian-arab-citizens.

Hussaini, Maha. "Israeli Torture: Urinating on Palestinian Prisoners, Burying Them Alive and Beating the Sick." *Middle East Eye*, March 9, 2025. https://www.middleeasteye.net/news/israeli-torture-urinating-palestinian-prisoners-burying-them-alive-and-beating-sick.

Issar, Siddhant, and James Padilioni, Jr. " 'To Address Black Suffering Is to Destroy the World.' An Interview with Frank B. Wilderson, III on Afropessimism." *Interfere* 1 (2020): 94–106.

Jacobs, Stephen Leonard. " 'We Charge Genocide': A Historical Petition All but Forgotten and Unknown." In *Understanding Atrocities: Remembering, Representing and Teaching Genocide*, edited by Scott W. Murray, 125–43. Calgary: University of Calgary Press, 2017.

Jameson, Fredric. "Cognitive Mapping." In *Marxism and the Interpretation of Culture*, edited by Cary Nelson and Lawrence Grossberg, 347–60. Urbana: University of Illinois Press, 1988.

Jewish Voice for Peace. "All Life Is Precious." *Jewish Voice for Peace*, September 3, 2024. https://www.jewishvoiceforpeace.org/2024/09/03/all-life-is-precious/.

Johnson, Adam, and Othman Ali. "Coverage of Gaza War in the New York Times and Other Major Newspapers Heavily Favored Israel, Analysis Shows." *The Intercept*, January 9, 2024. https://theintercept.com/2024/01/09/newspapers-israel-palestine-bias-new-york-times/.

Jones, Janine. "Editor's Introduction / Présentation du numéro." *Simone de Beauvoir Studies* 34 (2023): 171–93.

Jordan, June. "June Jordan on Israel and Lebanon: A Response to Adrienne Rich." *The Massachusetts Review*, September 19, 2024. https://massreview.org/node/12147/.

Jordan, June. "Life After Lebanon." In *Some of Us Did Not Die: New and Selected Essays*, 193–8. New York: Civitas Books, 2002.

Jordan, June. "Moving Towards Home." In *Naming Our Destiny: New & Selected Poems*, 142–3. New York: Thunder's Mouth Press, 1989.

Journalism Academy. "Letter from the Journalism Academy to *The New York Times*." https://docs.google.com/forms/d/e/1FAIpQLSf9tbDVqvi8-0a2eED4j4cYHKJAJ-bIPSRZRrDEalQCWEH8jA/viewform.

"Journalist Quits Role After Comparing French Actions in Algeria to Nazi Massacre." *The Guardian*, March 9, 2025. https://www.theguardian.com/world/2025/mar/09/jean-michel-aphatie-quits-after-comparing-french-algeria-to-nazi-massacre.

Kadari-Ovadia, Shira. "'Draconian and McCarthyist': Knesset Advances Bill to Fire Academics for Views Seen as 'Supporting Terror' by Gov't." *Haaretz*, July 10, 2024. https://www.haaretz.com/israel-news/2024-07-10/ty-article/.premium/knesset-advances-bill-to-fire-academics-for-views-seen-as-supporting-terror-by-govt/00000190-9e04-d03e-a5fd-9fb6744f0000.

Kampf-Lassin, Miles. "Out of the Ashes." *In These Times*, November 21, 2024. https://inthesetimes.com/article/trump-harris-democrats-2024-election-uaw.

Kapoor, Ilan, and Zahi Zalloua. *Universal Politics*. Oxford: Oxford University Press, 2021.

Kapoor, Ilan. "The Short Shelf Life of Corporate DEI." *Al Jazeera*, January 13, 2025. https://www.aljazeera.com/opinions/2025/1/13/the-short-shelf-life-of-corporate-dei.

Kauanui, J. Kēhaulani. "Tracing Historical Specificity: Race and the Colonial Politics of (In) Capacity." *American Quarterly* 69, no. 2 (2017): 257–65.

Kelley, Robin D. G. "Between Fires in Los Angeles and Fascism in America." *Hammer & Hope*, no. 6 (2025). https://hammerandhope.org/article/los-angeles-altadena-fires.

King, Martin Luther, Jr. *Why We Can't Wait*. London: Signet, 2001.

Khader, Jamil. "Ziofascist Violence and the Nakba 2.0: Jouissance and Necrocapitalism in the Consolidation of Extremist Messianic Zionist Far-Right Ideology." *Crisis and Critique* 11, no. 1 (2024): 26–54.

Khalidi, Rashid. *The Hundred Years' War on Palestine: A History of Settler Colonialism and Resistance, 1917–2017*. New York: Metropolitan Books, 2020.

Khalil, Mahmoud. "My Name is Mahmoud Khalil and I Am a Political Prisoner." *In These Times*, March 18, 2025. https://inthesetimes.com/article/mahmoud-khalil-letter-from-a-palestinian-political-prisoner-in-louisiana.

Killgore, Andrew I. "25 Years After His Death, Dr. Fayez Sayegh's Towering Legacy Lives On." *Washington Report on Middle East Affairs*, December 2005. https://www.wrmea.org/2005-december/in-memoriam-25-years-after-his-death-dr.-fayez-sayeghs-towering-legacy-lives-on.html.

King, Martin Luther, Jr. *Why We Can't Wait*. London: Signet, 2001.

Kingsley, Patrick. "Strike on Hospital Highlights Israeli Attacks on Gaza Health System." *The New York Times*, May 14, 2025. https://www.nytimes.com/2025/05/14/world/middleeast/israel-medical-facility-strikes-gaza-hamas.html.

Kingsley, Patrick, Natan Odenheimer, Bilal Shbair, Ronen Bergman, John Ismay, Sheera Frenkel, and Adam Sella. "Israel Loosened Its Rules to Bomb Hamas Fighters, Killing Many More Civilians." *The New York Times*, December 26, 2024.

https://www.nytimes.com/2024/12/26/world/middleeast/israel-hamas-gaza-bombing.html.

Kinloch, Valerie. *June Jordan: Her Life and Letters*. Westport, CT: Praeger, 2006.

Klein, Naomi. "How Israel Has Made Trauma a Weapon of War." *The Guardian*, October 5, 2024. https://www.theguardian.com/us-news/ng-interactive/2024/oct/05/israel-gaza-october-7-memorials.

Knesset. "Knesset Basic Law: Israel as the Nation State of the Jewish People." *Israel Studies* 25, no. 3 (2020): 135–6.

Krieg, Gregory. "College Campus Protests Highlight Tensions in Biden's Coalition." *CNN*, April 30, 2024. https://www.cnn.com/2024/04/30/politics/democrats-biden-college-protests.

Lacan, Jacques. *On Feminine Sexuality, The Limits of Love and Knowledge, 1972–1973: Encore, The Seminar of Jacques Lacan, Book XX*, edited by Jacques-Alain Miller, translated by Bruce Fink. New York: W. W. Norton, 1998.

Lacan, Jacques. *The Seminar of Jacques Lacan: The Four Fundamental Concepts of Psychoanalysis*, edited by Jacques-Alain Miller, translated by Alan Sheridan. New York: Norton, 1978.

Lacan, Jacques. "The Signification of the Phallus." In *Écrits: The First Complete Edition in English*, translated by Bruce Fink, 575–84. New York: W. W. Norton, 2006.

Lair, Samuel. "CRT 2.0." *The American Mind*, January 23, 2025. https://americanmind.org/salvo/crt-2-0/.

Lamont Hill, Marc. "From Ferguson to Palestine." *Biography* 41, no. 4. (2018): 942–57.

Lamont Hill, Marc, and Mitchell Plitnick. *Except for Palestine: The Limits of Progressive Politics*. New York: New Press, 2021.

Lentin, Alana. "Antisemitism and the Proxification of Antiracism." In *Race and the Question of Palestine*, edited by Lana Tatour and Ronit Lentin, 200–17. Stanford: Stanford University Press, 2025.

Levinas, Emmanuel. *Difficult Freedom: Essays on Judaism*, translated by Seán Hand. Baltimore: Johns Hopkins University Press, 1990.

Levinas, Emmanuel. *Otherwise than Being, or, Beyond Essence*, translated by Alphonso Lingis. The Hague: Martinus Nijhoff, 1981.

Levy, Gideon. "The Anti-Netanyahu Camp Is Longing for a Country That Never Was." *Haaretz*, September 8, 2019. https://www.haaretz.com/opinion/2019-09-08/ty-article/.premium/the-anti-netanyahu-camp-is-longing-for-a-country-that-never-was/0000017f-e998-d62c-a1ff-fdfb85360000.

Levy, Gideon. "Gideon Levy 'Antiwar' Film Waltz with Bashir Is Nothing but Charade." *Haaretz*, February 19, 2009. https://www.haaretz.com/2009-02-19/ty-article/gideon-levy-antiwar-film-waltz-with-bashir-is-nothing-but-charade/0000017f-da81-d42c-afff-dff34b480000.

Levy, Gideon. "The IDF's Own Sickening 'Zone of Interest' in the Heart of Gaza." *Haaretz*, December 26, 2024. https://www.haaretz.com/opinion/2024-12-26/ty-article-opinion/.premium/the-idfs-own-sickening-zone-of-interest-in-the-heart-of-gaza/00000193-ff80-df5b-a9b3-ff857a4a00.

Levy, Gideon. "Israel's Military Leaders Are Not 'Only Obeying Orders.' They Could Have Stopped the Gaza Massacre." *Haaretz*, May 22, 2025. https://www.haaretz.com/opinion/2025-05-22/ty-article-opinion/.premium/idf-brass-is-not-only-obeying-orders-it-could-have-stopped-the-gaza-massacre/00000196-f420-d06d-a5df-f5f1b63f0000.

Lewis, Gavin. "Corporate News: Racists Obscuring Genocide and its Historical Continuities." *Arena*, March 28, 2025. https://arena.org.au/corporate-news-racists-obscuring-genocide/.

Lewis, Tyson E., Silas C. Krabbe, and Alberto Toscano. "Late Fascism and Education: An Interview with Alberto Toscano." *Review of Education, Pedagogy, and Cultural Studies* 46, no. 3 (2024): 534–56.

Lorde, Audre. "The Uses of Anger." *Women's Studies Quarterly* 25, no. 1–2 (1997): 278–85.

Lyotard, Jean-François. "Defining the Postmodern." In *The Cultural Studies Reader*, edited by Simon During, 173–86. London: Routledge, 1993.

Magid, Shaul. "Judeopessimism: Antisemitism, History, and Critical Race Theory." *Harvard Theological Review* 117, no. 2 (2024): 368–90.

Magloire, Marina. "Moving Towards Life." *Los Angeles Review of Books*, August 7, 2024. https://lareviewofbooks.org/article/moving-towards-life/.

Magloire, Marina. "Who Might We Become for Each Other?" *Jewish Currents*, June 17, 2025. https://jewishcurrents.org/who-might-we-become-for-each-other.

Mahdawi, Arwa. "The Adultification of Children Has Consequences from Palestine to the US." *The Guardian*, May 4, 2024. https://www.theguardian.com/commentisfree/article/2024/may/04/adultification-children-palestine-us.

Maher, Geo. *Anticolonial Eruptions: Racial Hubris and the Cunning of Resistance*. Berkeley: University of California Press, 2022.

Majadli, Hanin. "Over 30,000 Killed in Gaza, but Even Israel's 'Liberal Left' Says: That's War." *Haaretz*, March 7, 2024. https://www.haaretz.com/opinion/2024-03-07/ty-article-opinion/.premium/over-30-000-killed-in-gaza-but-even-israels-liberal-left-says-thats-war/0000018e-1a3a-d8fb-abff-5f3ad8860000.

Maldonado-Torres, Nelson. "On the Coloniality of Being: Contributions to the Development of a Concept." *Cultural Studies* 21, no. 2–3 (2007): 235–65.

Maldonado-Torres, Nelson. "Outline of Ten Theses on Coloniality and Decoloniality." *Frantz Fanon Foundation*, October 23, 2016. https://caribbeanstudiesassociation.org/docs/Maldonado-Torres_Outline_Ten_Theses-10.23.16.pdf.

Maldonado-Torres, Nelson. "The U.S. at 250, Coloniality, and Political Zionism in Perspective." *Political Theology*, April 29, 2025. https://politicaltheology.com/the-u-s-at-250-coloniality-and-political-zionism-in-perspective/.

Malm, Andreas. *The Destruction of Palestine Is the Destruction of the Earth*. New York: Verso, 2024.

Marriott, David. "Blackness: N'est Pas?" *Propter Nos* 4 (2020): 27–51.

Marques, Natalia. "Trump Intensifies Threats Against Pro-Palestine Student Movement." *Peoples Dispatch*, March 6, 2025. https://peoplesdispatch.org/2025/03/06/trump-intensifies-threats-against-pro-palestine-student-movement/.

Martel, James R. *The Misinterpellated Subject*. Durham: Duke University Press, 2017.

Massad, Joseph. "Palestinians and Jewish History: Recognition or Submission?" *Journal of Palestine Studies* 30, no. 1 (2000): 62–78.

Massad, Joseph. "'Palestinians Don't Exist': Smotrich Only Repeats What Zionists Have Always Said." *Middle East Eye*, March 24, 2023. https://www.middleeasteye.net/opinion/palestinians-dont-exist-smotrich-only-repeats-zionists-always-said.

Mbembe, Achille. *Critique of Black Reason*, translated by Laurent Dubois. Durham: Duke University Press, 2017.

Mbembe, Achille. *Necropolitics*, translated by Steven Corcoran. Durham: Duke University Press, 2019.

McGowan, Todd. *Universality and Political Identity*. New York: Columbia University Press, 2020.

McKittrick, Katherine, and Sylvia Wynter. "Unparalleled Catastrophe for Our Species? Or, to Give Humanness a Different Future: Conversations." In *Sylvia Wynter: On Being Human as Praxis*, edited by Katherine McKittrick, 1–40. Durham: Duke University Press, 2015.

McMillan, Alex Frew. "Sharon: 'We Can Defeat Forces of Evil.'" *CNN*, September 12, 2001. https://www.cnn.com/2001/WORLD/asiapcf/east/09/11/terror.reax/index.html.

Mednick, Sam, and Samy Magdy. "Israeli Use of Human Shields in Gaza Was Systematic, Soldiers and Former Detainees Tell the AP." *Associated Press*, May 24, 2025. https://apnews.com/article/israel-palestinians-hamas-war-army-human-shie lds-80f358dd2c87a1123f26ffada159701c.

MEE Staff. "'Hypocrisy': Zadie Smith Faces Backlash After Signing Letter Calling for Gaza Ceasefire." *Middle East Eye*, May 29, 2025. https://www.middleeasteye.net/trending/hypocrisy-zadie-smith-faces-backlash-after-signing-letter-ceasefire-call ing-gaza-ceasefire?utm_source=substack&utm_medium=email.

MEE Staff. "Israel Is Ethnically Cleansing North Gaza, Says B'Tselem." *Middle East Eye*, October 23, 2024. https://www.middleeasteye.net/news/israel-committing-gravest-crimes-laws-war-northern-gaza-btselem.

MEE Staff. "Israel-Palestine War: Far-Right Minister Smotrich Calls for 'Sterile Zones' Free of Palestinians Near Settlements." *Middle East Eye*, November 6, 2023. https://www.middleeasteye.net/news/israel-palestine-war-far-right-smotrich-calls-ster ile-zones-west-bank.

Megerian, Chris. "Biden Says 'Order Must Prevail' During Campus Protests over the War in Gaza." *Associated Press*, May 2, 2024. https://apnews.com/article/biden-silence-college-protests-police-gaza-israel-d5f3092671951c3bc2968b8751c93ba6.

Mekelberg, Yossi. "The Plight of Ethiopian Jews in Israel." *BBC*, May 25, 2015. https://www.bbc.com/news/world-middle-east-32813056.

Melamed, Jodi. "Making Racialized and Gendered Difference Work for Neoliberal Multiculturalism." In *Strange Affinities: The Gender and Sexual Politics of Comparative Racialization*, edited by Grace Kyungwon Hong and Roderick A. Ferguson, 78–109. Durham: Duke University Press, 2011.

Memmi, Albert. *The Colonizer and the Colonized*. London: Earthscan, 2003.

Metta, John. "The Danger of the White American Liberal." *Al Jazeera*, September 1, 2017. https://www.aljazeera.com/features/2017/9/1/the-danger-of-the-white-ameri can-liberal.

Mhajne, Anwar. "Understanding Sexual Violence Debates Since 7 October: Weaponization and Denial." *Journal of Genocide Research*, May 30, 2024. https://www.tandfonline.com/doi/pdf/10.1080/14623528.2024.2359851?casa_to ken=numIgHN9YgIAAAAA:OuSfMCx4gQhcyV-0D5aX8vbnA-wsOmaGxBhLzpuidOL N4ZnBAQGY6vuLmUqkwG-5DAr-PiSkQmcD.

Miller, Zeke, and Chris Megerian. "Trump Blames Diversity Hiring as Probe into Deadly DC Plane Crash Begins." *Associated Press*, January 30, 2025. https://apnews.com/article/trump-crash-reagan-washington-buttigieg-diversity-biden-ef1e07684bbc8 45e9e7981c1ae060af2.

Mitchell, Schuyler. "The Attack on Mahmoud Khalil Is Straight Out of the 'War on Terror' Playbook." *Truthout*, March 12, 2025. https://truthout.org/articles/the-attack-on-mahmoud-khalil-is-straight-out-of-the-war-on-terror-playbook/.

Moench, Mallory. "Nearly 70% of Gaza War Dead Verified by UN Are Women and Children." *BBC*, November 8, 2024. https://www.bbc.com/news/articles/cn5we l11pgdo.

Mohanty, Chandra Talpade. *Feminism Without Borders: Decolonizing Theory, Practicing Solidarity*. Durham: Duke University Press, 2003.

Mokhiber, Craig. "Will Western Mainstream Media Be Held Accountable for Their Role in Genocide?" *Truthout*, August 30, 2024. https://truthout.org/articles/will-western-mai nstream-media-be-held-accountable-for-their-role-in-genocide/.

Montaigne, Michel de. *The Complete Essays of Montaigne*, translated by Donald Frame. Stanford: Stanford University Press, 1957.

Moody, Josh. "McMahon: Columbia Is on 'Right Track' to Restore Funding." *Inside Higher Ed*, March 25, 2025. https://www.insidehighered.com/news/ quick-takes/2025/03/25/mcmahon-columbia-right-track-restore-funding.

Moor, Ahmed. "There Are More Child Amputees in Gaza than Anywhere Else in the World. What Can the Future Hold for Them?" *The Guardian*, March 27, 2025. https://www. theguardian.com/world/ng-interactive/2025/mar/27/gaza-palestine-children-injuries.

Moore, Yancy. "'Striking Hard at Civilians': A Supremacist Ideology Underlies Israeli Policy." *Truthout*, March 24, 2025. https://truthout.org/articles/striking-hard-at-civili ans-a-supremacist-ideology-underlies-israeli-policy/.

Morieson, Nicholas, and Ihsan Yilmaz. "Why Does Populist Netanyahu Seek To Reform Israel's Judiciary?" *European Center for Populism Studies*, July 2, 2023. https://www. populismstudies.org/why-does-populist-netanyahu-seek-to-reform-israels-judiciary/.

Morrison, Toni. "Nobel Lecture." *NobelPrize.org*, 1993. https://www.nobelprize.org/pri zes/literature/1993/morrison/lecture/.

Morrison, Toni. "Nobel Lecture." *The Nobel Prize*, December 7, 1993. https://www.nob elprize.org/prizes/literature/1993/morrison/lecture/.

Moses, A. Dirk. "The German Catechism." *Geschichte der Gegenwart*, May 23, 2021. https://geschichtedergegenwart.ch/the-german-catechism/.

Moses, A. Dirk. *The Problems of Genocide: Permanent Security and the Language of Transgression*. New York: Cambridge University Press, 2021.

Moten, Fred. "Black Op." *PMLA* 123 no. 5 (2008): 1745–7.

Moten, Fred. "Black Optimism/Black Operation" [Unpublished paper]. 2007. https:// doubleoperative.com/wp-content/uploads/2009/12/moten-black-optimism_black-operation.pdf.

Moten, Fred. "Blackness and Nothingness (Mysticism in the Flesh)." *South Atlantic Quarterly* 112, no. 4 (2013): 737–80.

Moten, Fred. *In the Break: The Aesthetics of the Black Radical Tradition*. Minneapolis: University of Minnesota Press, 2003.

Moten, Fred. "Notes on *Narrating Humanity*." *Critical Ethnic Studies* 9, no. 1 (2024). https://manifold.umn.edu/read/ces0901-15/section/e8602e00-1c3d-4bcc-a378-f1fd98fe870a

Moten, Fred. *Stolen Life*. Durham: Duke University Press, 2018.

Moten, Fred. *The Universal Machine*. Durham: Duke University Press, 2018.

Msimang, Sisonke. "How to Write About Palestine." *The Intercept*, May 25, 2025. https://theintercept.com/2025/05/25/how-to-write-about-palestine/?utm_med ium=email&utm_source=The%20Intercept%20Newsletter.

Muammar, Bashaer. "Not Just Genocide but Deliberate Ecological Disaster." *The Electronic Intifada*, March 30, 2024. https://electronicintifada.net/content/not-just-genocide-deliberate-ecological-disaster/45506.

Mullen, Bill V. *We Charge Genocide: American Fascism and the Rule of Law*. New York: Fordham University Press, 2024.

Musgrave, Shawn. "Mahmoud Khalil Won His Freedom Despite the Best Efforts of ICE's Intelligence Unit." *The Intercept*, June 20, 2025. https://theintercept. com/2025/06/20/mahmoud-khalil-homeland-security-investigations-ice-surveilla nce/?utm_medium=email&utm_source=The%20Intercept%20Newsletter.

Na'aman, Oded. "Choosing Violence: War Is Almost Always a Choice, a Madness We Go Along With." *Boston Review*, August 15, 2016. https://www.bostonreview.net/ articles/oded-naaman-choosing-violence/.

Nader, Emir. "Gaza Babies Dying from the Cold as Winter Temperatures Drop." *BBC News*, December 30, 2024. https://www.bbc.com/news/articles/cd0ep0j83p7o.

Nagovitch, Paola. "Young Voters on the Left Reject Kamala Harris: 'She Has Made It Clear That She Doesn't Value My Vote.'" *El País*, October 29, 2024. https://english. elpais.com/usa/elections/2024-10-29/young-voters-on-the-left-reject-kamala-harri s-she-has-made-it-clear-that-she-doesnt-value-my-vote.html.

Nakar, Moran. "Black Lives Matter: Ethiopian Israelis Compare and Contrast Struggle with US." *Middle East Eye*, June 11, 2020. https://www.middleeasteye.net/news/ black-lives-matter-israel-ethiopian-police-brutality.

Nanguneri, Shaanth. "In California Schools, Palestinian History Is Off-Limits." *The Nation*, November 20, 2023. https://www.thenation.com/article/society/california-ethnic-stud ies-palestine/.

Nashed, Mat, and Maram Humaid. "Israel Threatens a Second Nakba, Yet Denies the First Ever Happened." *Al Jazeera*, February 28, 2025. https://www.aljazeera.com/ features/2025/2/28/israel-threatens-a-second-nakba-yet-denies-the-first-ever-happened.

Nathan, Debbie. "The Insidious Doctrine Fueling the Case Against Mahmoud Khalil." *Boston Review*, March 21, 2025. https://www.bostonreview.net/articles/the-insidi ous-doctrine-fueling-the-case-against-mahmoud-khalil/.

Neiman, Susan. "Historical Reckoning Gone Haywire." *The New York Review of Books*, October 19, 2023. https://www.nybooks.com/articles/2023/10/19/historical-reckon ing-gone-haywire-germany-susan-neiman/.

Netanyahu, Benjamin. "Netanyahu's 2024 Address to Congress." *Haaretz*, July 25, 2024. https://www.haaretz.com/israel-news/2024-07-25/ty-article/full-text-netanya hus-2024-address-to-congress/00000190-e6c0-d469-a39d-e6d7117d0000.

Noakes, Christian. "The Sacred-Secular Dialectic: Zionist Superstructure in Palestine." *Peace, Land, and Bread*, no. 1 (2020): 82–95.

NPR. "Transcript: Barack Obama's Speech on Race." *NPR*, March 18, 2008. https:// www.npr.org/2008/03/18/88478467/transcript-barack-obamas-speech-on-race.

O'Connell, Mark. "Israel's Revenge: An Interview with Rashid Khalidi." *The New York Review*, December 19, 2024. https://www.nybooks.com/articles/2024/12/19/isra els-revenge-an-interview-with-rashid-khalidi-mark-oconnell/.

Okoth, Kevin Ochieng. *Red Africa: Reclaiming Revolutionary Black Politics*. New York: Verso, 2023.

Orgad, Yoav. "Before the Majority Becomes a Minority." *Haaretz*, July 21, 2008. https:// www.haaretz.com/2008-07-21/ty-article/before-the-majority-becomes-a-minor ity/0000017f-f3ff-d497-a1ff-f3ff5f510000.

Palestine Royal Commission Report. 1937. https://ecf.org.il/media_items/290.

Paradkar, Shree. "How Israel's 'Scholasticide' Denies Palestinians Their Past, Present and Future." *Toronto Star*, January 21, 2024. https://www.thestar.com/news/world/

how-israels-scholasticide-denies-palestinians-their-past-present-and-future/article_8 f52d77a-b648-11ee-863d-f3411121907b.html.

Patterson, Orlando. *Slavery and Social Death: A Comparative Study*. Cambridge: Harvard University Press, 1982.

Patterson, William. *We Charge Genocide: The Historic Petition to the United Nations for Relief from the Crime of the United States Government Against the Negro People*. New York: The Civil Rights Congress, 1951.

Paulson, Steve. "Critical Intimacy: An Interview with Gayatri Chakravorty Spivak." *Los Angeles Review of Books*, July 29, 2016. https://lareviewofbooks.org/article/critical-intimacy-interview-gayatri-chakravorty-spivak/.

Pe'ery, Illy. "Israeli Soldiers Used an 80-Year-Old Gazan as a Human Shield. Then They Killed Him." *+972 Magazine*, February 16, 2025. https://www.972mag.com/gaza-human-shield-mosquito/.

Pierre, Jemima. "Zionism, Anti-Blackness, and the Struggle for Palestine: Jemima Pierre on the Boycott." *Black Agenda Report*, November 18, 2015. https://www.blackagendareport.com/zionism_antiblackness_palestine_boycott.

Porat, Dina. "Should We Compare the Hamas Assault to the Holocaust?" *Haaretz*, October 23, 2023. https://www.haaretz.com/opinion/2023-10-23/ty-article-opinion/.premium/should-we-compare-the-hamas-assault-to-the-holocaust/00000 18b-5cbb-d307-adbb-7dbb40b50000.

Pro-Human Camp. "Resist the Dehumanization of Palestinians and Israelis." *Amnesty International Israel*, December 13, 2023. https://www.amnesty.org.il/2023/12/13/%D7%9E%D7%9B%D7%AA%D7%91-%D7%A4%D7%AA%D7%95%D7%97-%D7%94%D7%9E%D7%97%D7%A0%D7%94-%D7%94%D7%A4%D7%A8%D7%95-%D7%90%D7%A0%D7%95%D7%A9%D7%99.

Quiroz-Martinez, Julie. "Poetry Is a Political Act." *Color Lines*, December 15, 1998. https://colorlines.com/article/poetry-political-act/.

Rancière, Jacques. *Disagreement: Politics and Philosophy*, translated by Julie Rose. Minneapolis: University of Minnesota Press, 1999.

Rankine, Claudia. *Citizen: An American Lyric*. Minneapolis: Graywolf, 2014.

Rapoport, Meron, and Oren Ziv. "'Render It Unusable': Israel's Mission of Total Urban Destruction." *+972 Magazine*, May 15, 2025. https://www.972mag.com/israel-gaza-total-urban-destruction/.

Rascius, Brendan. "Why Did Harris Lose Some Biden 2020 Voters? Poll Finds Gaza War Was the Top Issue." *Miami Herald*, January 15, 2025. https://www.miamiherald.com/news/nation-world/national/article298600563.html.

Reed, Dave. "There Is No Proof Palestinian Fighters 'Beheaded' Babies. The Only Source Is a Radical Settler." *Mondoweiss*, October 11, 2023. https://mondoweiss.net/2023/10/there-is-no-proof-palestinian-fighters-beheaded-babies-the-only-source-is-a-radical-settler/.

Reiff, Ben. "Smotrich Wants One Million West Bank Settlers. That's Not So Far-Fetched." *+972 Magazine*, July 12, 2023. https://www.972mag.com/settlements-roads-infrastructure-smotrich/.

Reuters. "All Options on the Table if Israel Does Not Deliver on Gaza Pledges, EU's Kallas Says." *Reuters*, July 22, 2025. https://www.reuters.com/world/middle-east/all-options-table-if-israel-does-not-deliver-gaza-pledges-eus-kallas-says-2025-07-22/.

Reynolds, John. "Apartheid Without Race." In *Race and the Question of Palestine*, edited by Lana Tatour and Ronit Lentin, 59–76. Stanford: Stanford University Press, 2025.

Rickford, Russell. "'To Build a New World': Black American Internationalism and Palestine Solidarity." *Journal of Palestine Studies* 48, no. 4 (2019): 52–70.

Roberts, Neil. *Freedom as Marronage*. Chicago: University of Chicago Press, 2015.

Robinson, Ishena. "Opposition to the Term Karen Continues Because an Unwillingness to Tackle Racism Continues, Despite the Brief Reckoning in 2020." *The Root*, January 2, 2021. https://www.theroot.com/opposition-to-the-term-karen-continues-because-an-unwil-1845978820.

Rose, Jacqueline. *The Question of Zion*. Princeton: Princeton University Press, 2005.

Rose, Jacqueline. "'You Made Me Do It.'" *London Review of Books*, November 30, 2023. https://www.lrb.co.uk/the-paper/v45/n23/jacqueline-rose/you-made-me-do-it.

Rosen, Brant. "Amid Israel's Brutality in Gaza, It's Time to Commit to Anti-Zionism." *Truthout*, December 5, 2023. https://truthout.org/articles/amid-israels-brutality-in-gaza-its-time-to-commit-to-anti-zionism/.

Rosenfeld, Arno, and Jacob Kornbluh. "ADL Chief Compares Student Protesters to ISIS and al-Qaida in Address to Republican Officials." *Forward*, June 6, 2025. https://forward.com/news/726133/greenblatt-adl-protesters-terrorists/.

Rothberg, Michael. *Multidirectional Memory: Remembering the Holocaust in the Age of Decolonization*. Stanford: Stanford University Press, 2009.

Roy, Arundhati. "Stop This Slaughter in Palestine." *Hammer & Hope*, no. 3 (2024). https://hammerandhope.org/article/arundhati-roy-palestine-gaza.

Ruth, Jennifer. "Boards and Administrators Won't Defend Higher Ed from Trump. It's Up to Us." *Truthout*, April 7, 2025. https://truthout.org/articles/boards-and-administrators-wont-defend-higher-ed-from-trump-its-up-to-us/.

Ruth, Jennifer. "Wrong Way, Columbia! Solidarity with Columbia AAUP!" *Academe Blog*, March 21, 2025. https://academeblog.org/2025/03/21/wrong-way-columbia-solidarity-with-columbia-aaup/.

Saeed, Tayseer Abu Odeh, and Shahd Dibas. "Zionist Settler-Colonialism and the Logic of Genocide in Gaza: A Conversation with Professor Avi Shlaim." *Journal of Holy Land and Palestine Studies* 24, no. 1 (2025): 17–36.

Said, Edward W. *Culture and Imperialism*. New York: Vintage, 1994.

Said, Edward W. "The One-State Solution." *The New York Times Magazine*, January 10, 1999.

Said, Edward W. *Orientalism*. 25th Anniversary ed. New York: Vintage Books, 2003.

Said, Edward W. *The Question of Palestine*. New York: Vintage Books, 1992.

Said, Edward W. *Reflections on Exile and Other Essays*. Cambridge, MA: Harvard University Press, 2000.

Said, Edward W. *Representations of the Intellectual: The 1993 Reith Lectures*. New York: Vintage Books, 1996.

Said, Edward W. "Zionism from the Standpoint of Its Victims." *Social Text*, no. 1 (1979): 7–58.

Salaita, Steve. "Your Crisis of Faith Is Not My Concern (There's a Genocide Going On)." *No Flags, No Slogans*, September 25, 2024. https://stevesalaita.com/your-crisis-of-faith-is-not-my-concern-theres-a-genocide-going-on/.

Samee Ali, Safia. "'Not by Accident': False 'Thug' Narratives Have Long Been Used to Discredit Civil Rights Movements." *NBC News*, September 27, 2020. https://www.nbcnews.com/news/us-news/not-accident-false-thug-narratives-have-long-been-used-discredit-n1240509.

Samra, Mjriam Abu, and Sara Troian. "Palestine Beyond the Colonial Logic of International Law." *Mondoweiss*, April 2, 2025. https://mondoweiss.net/2025/04/palestine-beyond-the-colonial-logic-of-international-law/.

Samuels, Ben, Chaim Levinson, Liza Rozovsky, and Jack Khoury. "Meeting with Trump, Netanyahu Endorses Mass Population Transfer from Gaza: 'It's Free Choice.'" *Haaretz*. July 8, 2025. https://www.haaretz.com/us-news/2025-07-08/ty-article/.premium/trump-hosts-netanyahu-as-gaza-cease-fire-teams-await-outcome-in-qatar/00000197-e624-d1ad-ab97-e7ed6de40000.

Sanchez, José. "Against Afro-Pessimism." *Jacobin*, June 13, 2022. https://jacobin.com/2022/06/afro-pessimism-frank-wilderson-socialism-flattening-racism.

Santana, Soledad. "Scholasticide as Cultural Genocide." *Spectre*, November 21, 2024. https://spectrejournal.com/scholasticide-as-cultural-genocide/.

Saul, Stephanie. "Trump Pulled $400 Million from Columbia. Other Schools Could Be Next." *The New York Times*, March 8, 2025. https://www.nytimes.com/2025/03/08/us/columbia-trump-colleges-antisemitism.html.

Sayegh, Fayez. *Zionist Colonization in Palestine*. Beirut: Research Center, Palestine Liberation Organization, 1965.

Sayles, James Yaki. *Meditations on Frantz Fanon's Wretched of the Earth*. Montreal: Kersplebedeb, 2010.

Scahill, Jeremy. "The Devil in the Details of Trump's 'Final Proposal' for Gaza Ceasefire." *Drop Site*, July 3, 2025. https://www.dropsitenews.com/p/trump-netanyahu-hamas-united-states-israel-ceasefire.

Schaer, Cathrin. "Israel's Iran Attack Sparks Legal Debate." *Deutsche Welle*, June 18, 2025. https://www.dw.com/en/israel-iran-attack-legality-international-law/a-72952324.

Schaer, Cathrin. "Why Are Some in Germany Suggesting Anti-Semitism Is 'Imported'?" *Al Jazeera*, May 28, 2021. https://www.aljazeera.com/news/2021/5/28/in-germany-growing-suggestions-that-antisemitism-is-imported.

Schotten, C. Heike, and John Harfouch. "Sayegh's Critique of Zionism and the IHRA Definition: Notes Toward a Theory of the Antisemitism Industrial Complex." *Institute For the Critical Study of Zionism* 1, no. 1 (2024). https://criticalzionismstudies.org/2024/10/26/sayeghs-critique-of-zionism-and-the-ihra-definition-notes-toward-a-theory-of-the-antisemitism-industrial-complex/.

Sebald, W. G. "Against the Irreversible. On Jean Améry." In *On the Natural History of Destruction*, 143–67. Toronto: Alfred A. Knopf, 2003.

Segal, Raz, et al. "New Jersey Statement on Antisemitism and Islamophobia." https://docs.google.com/forms/d/e/1FAIpQLSdbHaU_hpCuVB1K9bcx4dG2nHd9ckGIKRdU_qqiq36AAFDXrA/viewform.

Seisdedos, Iker. "Judith Butler, Philosopher: 'If You Sacrifice a Minority like Trans People, You Are Operating Within a Fascist Logic.'" *El País*, December 14, 2024. https://english.elpais.com/culture/2024-12-15/judith-butler-philosopher-if-you-sacrifice-a-minority-like-trans-people-you-are-operating-within-a-fascist-logic.html.

Sexton, Jared. "Affirmation in the Dark: Racial Slavery and Philosophical Pessimism." *The Comparatist* 43 (2019): 99–110.

Sexton, Jared. "African American Studies." In *A Concise Companion to American Studies*, edited by John Carlos Rowe, 221–32. Malden: Wiley-Blackwell, 2010.

Sexton, Jared. *Amalgamation Schemes: Antiblackness and the Critique of Multiracialism*. Minneapolis: University of Minnesota Press, 2008.

Sexton, Jared. "People-of-Color-Blindness: Notes on the Afterlife of Slavery." *Social Text* 28, no. 2 (103) (2010): 31–56.

Sexton, Jared. "The *Vel* of Slavery: Tracking the Figure of the Unsovereign." In *Otherwise Worlds: Against Settler Colonialism and Anti-Blackness*, edited by Tiffany Lethabo King, Jenell Navarro, and Andrea Smith, 102–16. Durham: Duke University Press, 2020.

Sfard, Michael. "In Gaza, Israel Is Racing to the Moral Abyss." *Haaretz*, October 23, 2023. https://www.haaretz.com/israel-news/2023-10-23/ty-article-opinion/.premium/in-gaza-israel-is-racing-to-the-moral-abyss/0000018b-57d1-d8e2-a1eb-f7d7dc100000.

Shadi Hamid, Brett Max Kaufman, Yousef Munayyer, and Natasha Roth-Rowland. "Is a New McCarthyism Punishing Pro-Palestine Speech at US Universities? Our Panel Reacts." *The Guardian*, December 13, 2023. https://www.theguardian.com/commentisfree/2023/dec/13/israel-gaza-us-universities-free-speech.

Shapiro, Alexander. "Lod: Shared Society in Israel's 'Murder City.'" *The Times of Israel*, October 24, 2018. https://blogs.timesofisrael.com/lod-shared-society-in-israels-murder-city/..

Sharma, Nandita, and Cynthia Wright. "Decolonizing Resistance, Challenging Colonial States." *Social Justice* 35, no. 3 (2009): 120–38.

Sharma, Parth. "'We Are Fighting Human Animals': Dehumanization of Palestinians." *The Palestine Chronicle*, May 21, 2024. https://www.palestinechronicle.com/we-are-fighting-human-animals-dehumanization-of-palestinians/.

Sharpe, Christina. "Black Studies: In the Wake." *The Black Scholar* 44, no. 2 (2014): 59–69.

Sharpe, Christina. "The Shapes of Grief: Witnessing the Unbearable." *The Yale Review* 112, no. 3 (2024): 11–22.

Sharpe, Christina. *In the Wake: On Blackness and Being*. Durham: Duke University Press, 2016.

Shavit, Ari. *My Promised Land: The Triumph and Tragedy of Israel*. New York: Spiegel & Grau, 2013.

Shelbourne, Mallory. "Schumer Applauds Trump on Moving US Embassy to Jerusalem." *The Hill*, May 14, 2018. https://thehill.com/homenews/senate/387566-schumer-applauds-trump-on-moving-us-embassy-to-jerusalem/.

Shklar, Judith. *Ordinary Vices*. Cambridge: Harvard University Press, 1984.

Shohat, Ella. "Sephardim in Israel: Zionism from the Standpoint of Its Jewish Victims." *Social Text*, no. 19–20 (1988): 1–35.

Shulman, George. "Fred Moten's Refusals and Consents: The Politics of Fugitivity." *Political Theory* 49, no. 2 (2021): 272–313.

Silver, Laura. "How Americans View Israel and the Israel-Hamas War at the Start of Trump's Second Term." *Pew Research Center*, April 8, 2025. https://www.pewresearch.org/short-reads/2025/04/08/how-americans-view-israel-and-the-israel-hamas-war-at-the-start-of-trumps-second-term/.

Silverman, Kaja. *The Threshold of the Visible World*. London: Routledge, 2013.

Simek, Nicole. "Race and Sex Redux." *symplokē* 32, no. 1–2 (2024): 410–24.

Smith, David. "Wrecking Ball: Trump's War on 'Woke' Marks US Society's Plunge into 'Dark Times.'" *The Guardian*, February 2, 2025. https://www.theguardian.com/us-news/2025/feb/02/trump-woke-dei-culture-wars.

Smith, Zadie. "Shibboleth." *The New Yorker*, May 5, 2024. https://www.newyorker.com/news/essay/shibboleth-the-role-of-words-in-the-campus-protests.

Solomon, Norman. "'Speaking Truth to Power' Is No Substitute for Taking Power." *Truthout*, March 13, 2019. https://truthout.org/articles/speaking-truth-to-power-is-no-substitute-for-taking-power/.

Somayajula, Pranay. "'On Condemnation: Terrorism, Violence, and the Question of Palestine." *Culture Shock*, November 26, 2023. https://socialtextjournal.org/periscope_article/on-condemnation-terrorism-violence-and-the-question-of-palestine/.

Speri, Alice, and Joseph Gedeon. "Trial to Consider Trump's 'Ideological-Deportation Policy' Targeting Pro-Palestinian Students." *The Guardian*, July 7, 2025. https://www.theguardian.com/us-news/2025/jul/07/trial-trump-ideological-deportation-policy-pro-palestinian-students.

Speri, Alice. "Israel Responds to Hamas Crimes by Ordering Mass War Crimes in Gaza." *The Intercept*, October 9, 2023. https://theintercept.com/2023/10/09/isr ael-hamas-war-crimes-palestinians/.

Spivak, Gayatri Chakravorty. *Critique of Postcolonial Reason: Toward a History of the Vanishing Present*. Cambridge: Harvard University Press, 1999.

Stanley, Jason. *Erasing History: How Fascists Rewrite the Past to Control the Future*. New York: Atria/One Signal Publishers, 2024.

St. Félix, Doreen. "The Embarrassment of Democrats Wearing Kente-Cloth Stoles." *The New Yorker*, June 9, 2020. https://www.newyorker.com/culture/on-and-off-the-ave nue/the-embarrassment-of-democrats-wearing-kente-cloth-stoles.

Street, Paul. "The Resistance Remains Hollow: The Weimar Ways of the Dismal Democrats." *CounterPunch*, July 2, 2021. https://www.counterpunch.org/2021/07/02/the-resistance-remains-hollow-the-weimar-ways-of-the-dismal-democrats/.

Sullivan, Shannon. "The White Habit of Untrauma." In *The Routledge International Handbook of New Critical Race and Whiteness Studies*, edited by Rikke Andreassen et al., 285–99. New York: Routledge, 2023.

Sullivan, Shannon. "White Priority." *Critical Philosophy of Race* 5, no. 2 (2017): 171–82.

Táíwò, Olúfẹ́mi O. *Elite Capture: How the Powerful Took over Identity Politics (and Everything Else)*. Chicago: Haymarket Books, 2022.

Tatour, Lana. "Preface." In *Race and the Question of Palestine*, edited by Lana Tatour and Ronit Lentin, viii–xiv. Stanford: Stanford University Press, 2025.

Tatour, Lana. "Why Calling Israel an Apartheid State Is Not Enough." *Middle East Eye*, January 18, 2021. https://www.middleeasteye.net/opinion/why-calling-israel-aparth eid-state-not-enough.

Tatour, Lana, and Ronit Lentin, eds. *Race and the Question of Palestine*. Stanford: Stanford University Press, 2025.

Taylor, Keeanga-Yamahtta. "Black Faces in High Places." *Jacobin*, May 4, 2015. https://jacobin.com/2015/05/baltimore-uprising-protests-freddie-gray-black-politicians/.

Taylor, Keeanga-Yamahtta. "Foreword" to Saidiya Hartman's 2022 edition of *Scenes of Subjection*, xiii–xxviii. New York: W. W. Norton & Co, 2022.

Tondo, Lorenzo. "Gaza Is 'Hungriest Place on Earth' With All Its People at Risk of Famine, Says UN." *The Guardian*, May 30, 2025. https://www.theguardian.com/world/2025/may/30/gaza-hungriest-place-earth-all-people-risk-famine-un.

Too Black and Rasul A. Mowatt. *Laundering Black Rage: The Washing of Black Death, People, Property, and Profits*. New York: Routledge, 2014.

Toscano, Alberto. "Defending the Indefensible." *In These Times*, July 11, 2025. https://inthesetimes.com/article/palestine-action-gaza-genocide-manufacture-cons

ent-trump-zionist?link_id=3&can_id=839242f129045dcf95563791cad9b53c&sou rce=email-america-for-sale-everything-must-go-2&email_referrer=email_2810 645&email_subject=alberto-toscano-on-defending-the-indefensible&&.

Toscano, Alberto. "Land of the Unfree?" *In These Times*, April 2, 2025. https://inthe setimes.com/article/mahmoud-khalil-repression-detention-democracy-gaza-enca mpments.

Toscano, Alberto. *Late Fascism: Race, Capitalism and the Politics of Crisis*. New York: Verso, 2023.

Toscano, Alberto. "The War on Gaza and Israel's Fascism Debate." *Verso*, October 19, 2023. https://www.versobooks.com/blogs/news/the-war-on-gaza-and-israel-s-fasc ism-debate?srsltid=AfmBOooJxfEPWBUyq5TmQDHuqvFlgimz4GeqWEBAtv4ON 2UxSyifl88B.

Tuck, Eve and K. Wayne Yang. "Decolonization Is Not a Metaphor." *Decolonization: Indigeneity, Education, and Society* 1, no. 1 (2012): 1–40.

Turfah, Mary. "The Most Moral Army." *Los Angeles Review of Books*, October 1, 2024. https://lareviewofbooks.org/article/the-most-moral-army/.

Turki, Fawas. *The Disinherited: Journal of a Palestinian Exile, With an Epilogue 1974*. New York: Monthly Review Press, 1974.

Turner, Kieron. "Racial Capitalism and Militarized Accumulation." In *Race and the Question of Palestine*, edited by Lana Tatour and Ronit Lentin, 168–83. Stanford, CA: Stanford University Press, 2025.

Turse, Nick. "Israel's Bloody Record of Bombing Schools in Gaza." *The Intercept*, October 6, 2024. https://theintercept.com/2024/10/06/israel-bombing-schools-child ren-gaza-education/.

United States Campaign for Palestinian Rights (USCPR). "From Palestine to Mexico, All the Walls Have Got to Go." https://uscpr.org/activist-resource/from-palestine-to-mex ico-all-the-walls-have-got-to-go/.

Upfront. "Angela Davis: 'Palestine Is a Moral Litmus Test for the World.'" *Al Jazeera*, October 27, 2023. https://www.aljazeera.com/program/upfront/2023/10/27/ang ela-davis-palestine-is-a-moral-litmus-test-for-the-world.

Valdez, Jonah. "The Far-Right Group Building a List of Pro-Palestine Activists to Deport." *The Intercept*, February 6, 2025. https://theintercept.com/2025/02/06/betar-palest ine-school-activists-target-deport-trump/.

Valenzuela, Victoria. "'Deadly Exchange': US Sends Hundreds of Law Enforcement to Israel to Learn 'Worst Practices' from IDF." *The Real News Network*, January 7, 2025. https://therealnews.com/deadly-exchange-us-sends-hundreds-of-law-enforcem ent-to-israel-to-learn-worst-practices-from-idf.

Varoufakis, Yanis. "Yanis Varoufakis on Why Fixating on Palestine Is a Moral Imperative." *DiEM25*, February 4, 2025. https://diem25.org/yanis-varoufakis-on-why-fixating-on- palestine-is-a-moral-imperative/.

Varoufakis, Yanis, and Slavoj Žižek. "Israel Needed War." *Slavoj Žižek Meets Yanis Varoufakis (Part 3)* [YouTube video]. https://www.youtube.com/watch?v=zkKFFueepMg.

Veracini, Lorenzo. "Genocide in Gaza and the End of Settler Colonialism." *The Journal of Imperial and Commonwealth History*, May 17, 2025. https://www.tandfonline.com/ doi/pdf/10.1080/03086534.2025.2501221.

Warren, Calvin L. "Black Mysticism: Fred Moten's Phenomenology of (Black) Spirit." *Zeitschrift für Anglistik und Amerikanistik* 65, no. 2 (2017): 225–38.

Warren, Calvin L. *Ontological Terror: Blackness, Nihilism, and Emancipation*. Durham: Duke University Press, 2018.

Weheliye, Alexander G. *Habeas Viscus*. Durham: Duke University Press, 2014.

West, Cornel. "Introduction: The Radical King We Don't Know." In *The Radical King*, by Martin Luther King, Jr., edited by Cornel West, ix–xxv. Boston: Beacon Press, 2015.

White House. "Restoring Truth and Sanity to American," March 27, 2025. https://www.whitehouse.gov/presidential-actions/2025/03/restoring-truth-and-sanity-to-ameri can-history/.

Wilderson, Frank B. III. *Afropessimism*. New York: Liveright, 2020.

Wilderson, Frank B. III. "Afro-Pessimism and the End of Redemption." *Humanities Futures*. Franklin Humanities Institute, Duke University, October 20, 2015. https://humanitiesfutures.org/papers/afro-pessimism-end-redemption/.

Wilderson, Frank B. III. "'The Inside-Outside of Civil Society': An Interview with Frank B. Wilderson, III." Interview by Samira Spatzek and Paula von Gleich. *Black Studies Papers* 2, no. 1 (2016): 4–22.

Wilderson, Frank B. III. *Red, White & Black: Cinema and the Structure of U.S. Antagonisms*. Durham: Duke University Press, 2010.

Wilderson, Frank B. III. "'We're Trying to Destroy the World': Anti-Blackness and Police Violence After Ferguson." In *Shifting Corporealities in Contemporary Performance Danger, Im/mobility and Politics*, edited by Marina Gržinić and Aneta Stojnić, 45–59. New York: Palgrave, 2018.

Wilderson, Frank, and Tiffany Lethabo King. "Staying Ready for Black Study: A Conversation." In *Otherwise Worlds: Against Settler Colonialism and Anti-Blackness*, edited by Tiffany Lethabo King, Jenell Navarro, and Andrea Smith, 65–78. Durham, NC: Duke University Press, 2020.

Winant, Gabriel. "On Mourning and Statehood: A Response to Joshua Leifer." *Dissent*, October 13, 2023. https://www.dissentmagazine.org/online_articles/a-response-to-joshua-leifer/.

Wire Staff. "'No Innocent Civilians in Gaza,' Israel President Says as Northern Gaza Struggles to Flee Israeli Bombs." *The Wire*, October 14, 2023. https://thewire.in/world/northern-gaza-israel-palestine-conflict

Wolfe, Patrick. "Settler Colonialism and the Elimination of the Native." *Journal of Genocide Research* 8, no. 4 (2006): 387–409.

Wong, Julia Carrie. "Loathe Thy Neighbor: Elon Musk and the Christian Right Are Waging War on Empathy." *The Guardian*, April 8, 2025. https://www.theguardian.com/us-news/ng-interactive/2025/apr/08/empathy-sin-christian-right-musk-trump.

Woods, Tryon P. *Blackhood Against the Police Power: Punishment and Disavowal in the "Post-Racial" Era*. East Lansing: Michigan State University Press, 2019.

Wright, Richard. *Conversation with Richard Wright*, edited by Kenneth Kinnamon and Michel Fabre. Jackson: University of Mississippi Press, 1993.

Wynter, Sylvia. "A Black Studies Manifesto." *Forum N.H.I. Knowledge for the 21st Century* 1, no. 1 (1994): 3–11.

Wynter, Sylvia. "No Humans Involved: An Open Letter to My Colleagues." *Forum N.H.I. Knowledge for the 21st Century* 1, no. 1 (1994): 42–70.

Wynter, Sylvia. "Unsettling the Coloniality of Being/Power/Truth/Freedom: Towards the Human, After Man, Its Overrepresentation—an Argument." *CR: The New Centennial Review* 3, no. 3 (2003): 257–337.

Wynter, Sylvia, and David Scott. "The Re-Enchantment of Humanism: An Interview with Sylvia Wynter." *Small Axe* 8 (2000): 119–207.

Yancy, George. "Afropessimism Forces Us to Rethink Our Most Basic Assumptions About Society." *Truthout*, September 14, 2022. https://truthout.org/articles/afrope ssimism-forces-us-to-rethink-our-most-basic-assumptions-about-society/.

Yancy, George. "Authoritarian Wave in US Shows Democracy's Fragility, South African Scholar Says." *Truthout*, September 6, 2025. https://truthout.org/articles/authoritar ian-wave-in-us-shows-democracys-fragility-south-african-scholar-says/.

Yancy, George. *Black Bodies, White Gazes: The Continuing Significance of Race in America*. 3rd ed. New York: Bloomsbury Academic, 2025.

Yancy, George. "Introduction: Un-Sutured." In *White Self-Criticality Beyond Anti-Racism: How Does It Feel to Be a White Problem?* edited by George Yancy, xi–xxvii. Lanham, MD: Lexington Books, 2015.

Yancy, George. "'Striking Hard at Civilians': A Supremacist Ideology Underlies Israeli Policy." *Truthout*, March 24, 2025. https://truthout.org/articles/striking-hard-at-civili ans-a-supremacist-ideology-underlies-israeli-policy/.

Yancy, George. "What Can the Black Freedom Struggle and Palestinian Liberation Teach Each Other?" *Truthout*, September 8, 2024. https://truthout.org/articles/ what-can-the-black-freedom-struggle-and-palestinian-liberation-teach-each-other/.

Younis, Rami, and Sarah Friedland, directors. *Lyd*, 2023.

Zabala, Santiago. "Why Don't We Listen to Warnings? The Horizonless Society." *The Philosophical Salon*, June 16, 2025. https://www.thephilosophicalsalon.com/ why-dont-we-listen-to-warnings-the-horizonless-society.

Zalloua, Zahi. *Being Posthuman: Ontologies of the Future*. New York: Bloomsbury, 2021.

Zalloua, Zahi. *Fanon, Žižek, and the Violence of Resistance*. New York: Bloomsbury, 2025.

Zalloua, Zahi. *The Politics of the Wretched: Race, Reason, and Ressentiment*. New York: Bloomsbury, 2024.

Zalloua, Zahi. *Solidarity and the Palestinian Cause: Indigeneity, Blackness, and the Promise of Universality*. New York: Bloomsbury, 2023.

Zalloua, Zahi. *Žižek on Race: Toward an Anti-Racist Future*. New York: Bloomsbury, 2020.

Zhang, Sharon. "UN Chief Says Israel Has Made Gaza into 'a Killing Field.'" *Truthout*, April 9, 2025. https://truthout.org/articles/un-chief-says-israel-has-made-gaza-into-a-killing-field/.

Zionist Organization of America. "The BLM Organization Files." *Zionist Organization of America*. https://zoa.org/the-blm-organization-files/.

Zirin, Dave. "It's Not Antisemitic to Say That Israel Is Responsible for the Unfolding Genocide in Gaza." *The Nation*, July 8, 2025. https://www.thenation.com/article/ world/israel-antisemitism-genocide-christian-zionists/.

Žižek, Slavoj. "Afterword: With Defenders like These, Who Needs Attackers?" In *The Truth of Žižek*, edited by Paul Bowman and Richard Stamp, 197–255. New York: Continuum, 2007.

Žižek, Slavoj. *Against Progress*. New York: Bloomsbury, 2025.

Žižek, Slavoj. "Assange Is Free, but Are We?" *Project Syndicate*, June 27, 2024. https:// www.project-syndicate.org/commentary/julian-assange-freed-but-media-still-carry ing-water-for-the-powerful-by-slavoj-zizek-2024-06.

Žižek, Slavoj. *The Courage of Hopelessness: Chronicles of a Year of Acting Dangerously*. New York: Allen Lane, 2017.

Žižek, Slavoj. *In Defense of Lost Causes*. New York: Verso, 2008.

Žižek, Slavoj. *First as Tragedy, Then as Farce*. New York: Verso, 2009.

Žižek, Slavoj. *For They Know Not What They Do: Enjoyment as a Political Factor*. New York: Verso, 2008.

Žižek, Slavoj. "Foreword: The Importance of Theory." In *Žižek on Race: Toward an Anti-Racist Future*, by Zahi Zalloua, x–xiii. New York: Bloomsbury, 2020.

Žižek, Slavoj. *Freedom: A Disease Without Cure*. New York: Bloomsbury, 2023.

Žižek, Slavoj. "From MAGA to MEGA: After Trump's Victory." *Substack: Žižek Goads and Prods*, November 9, 2024. https://slavoj.substack.com/p/from-maga-to-mega-after-trumps-victory.

Žižek, Slavoj. "The Gentrification of Gaza." *Substack: Žižek Goads and Prods*, January 11, 2024. https://slavoj.substack.com/p/the-gentrification-of-gaza

Žižek, Slavoj. "Human Rights and Its Discontents." Lecture at Bard College, November 15, 1999. http://www.lacan.com/zizek-human.htm.

Žižek Slavoj. " 'Israel Needed War': Slavoj Žižek Meets Yanis Varoufakis (Part 3)" [YouTube video]. https://www.youtube.com/watch?v=zkKFFueepMg.

Žižek, Slavoj. *Less Than Nothing: Hegel and the Shadow of Dialectical Materialism*. New York: Verso, 2012.

Žižek, Slavoj. "The Middle East War: A Boring Recapitulation." *Substack: Žižek Goads and Prods*, October 19, 2024. https://slavoj.substack.com/p/the-middle-east-war-a-boring-recapitulation

Žižek, Slavoj. "Neighbors and Other Monsters." In *The Neighbor: Three Inquiries in Political Theology*, edited by Slavoj Žižek, Eric L. Santner, and Kenneth Reinhard, 134–90. Chicago: University of Chicago Press, 2013.

Žižek, Slavoj. "On Lacan as Philosopher." *The Dark Fantastic* [blog], May 4, 2013. https://socialecologies.wordpress.com/2013/05/04/slavoj-zizek-on-lacan-as-philosopher/.

Žižek, Slavoj. "On Shame and Dignity In and Around Gaza." *Substack: Žižek Goads and Prods*, October 26, 2024. https://substack.com/home/post/p-150707949?source=queue.

Žižek, Slavoj. *The Parallax View*. Cambridge, MA: MIT Press, 2006.

Žižek, Slavoj. *The Plague of Fantasies*. New York: Verso, 1997.

Žižek, Slavoj. "Subjective Destitution in Art and Politics: From Being-Towards-Death to Undeadness." *Enrahonar* 70 (2023): 67–82.

Žižek, Slavoj. *Surplus-Enjoyment: A Guide for the Non-Perplexed*. New York: Bloomsbury, 2022.

Žižek, Slavoj. *Trouble in Paradise: From the End of History to the End of Capitalism*. Brooklyn: Melville House, 2014.

Žižek, Slavoj. *Violence: Six Sideways Reflections*. New York: Picador, 2008.

Žižek, Slavoj. "Year of Distraction" [YouTube video]. July 5, 2011. https://www.youtube.com/watch?v=ChWXYNxUFdc.

Žižek, Slavoj. *Zero Point*. New York: Bloomsbury, 2025.

Žižek, Slavoj. "Žižek on Soft Fascism, AI, and the Collapse of Shame." *Sri Lanka Guardian*, December 7, 2024. https://slguardian.org/zizek-on-soft-fascism-ai-and-the-collapse-of-shame/.

Index